Speak the Culture | Britain

Speak the Culture | Britain

BE FLUENT IN BRITISH LIFE AND CULTURE

HISTORY, SOCIETY AND LIFESTYLE • LITERATURE AND PHILOSOPHY
ART AND ARCHITECTURE • CINEMA, PHOTOGRAPHY AND FASHION
MUSIC AND DRAMA • FOOD AND DRINK • MEDIA AND SPORT

THOROGOOD

www.thorogoodpublishing.co.uk   www.speaktheculture.co.uk

All has been done to trace
the owners of the various
pieces of material used
for this book. If further
information and proof of
ownership should be made
available then attribution
will be given or, if
requested, the said material
removed in subsequent
editions.

A CIP catalogue record for
this book is available from
the British Library.

ISBN: 1 85418 627 2 / 978-
185418627-0

Thorogood Publishing Ltd
10-12 Rivington Street
London EC2A 3DU

Telephone: 020 7749 4748
Fax: 020 7729 6110
info@thorogoodpublishing.co.uk

www.thorogoodpublishing.co.uk
www.speaktheculture.co.uk

© 2009
Thorogood Publishing Ltd

Publisher

Neil Thomas

Editorial Director
Angela Spall

Editor in chief

Andrew Whittaker

*Additional editorial
contributors*
Sam Bloomfield
Alexandra Fedoruk
Amy Wilson Thomas
David Banks
Jess Fitch
Paul Sutton Reeves

Design & images

Johnny Bull
plumpState
www.plumpstate.com

iStockphoto

Nial Harrington
Harrington Moncrieff
www.hmdesignco.com

Printed in the UK by
Henry Ling Ltd
www.henryling.co.uk

Acknowledgements

Special thanks to Lucy Miller,
Kathy Crawford, Ronan Conway,
Dudley Whittaker, Sue Parkin
and Marcus Titley
(www.seckfordwines.co.uk)

**River Thames from the top
of Tower Bridge at Southwark
looking towards the skyscrapers
of Docklands**

Contents

First, a word from the publisher...

This series of books and this book are designed to look at a country's culture – to give readers a real grasp of it and to help them develop and explore that culture.

The world is shrinking – made smaller by commerce, tourism and migration – and yet the importance of national culture, of national identity, seems to grow.

By increasing your cultural knowledge and appreciation of a country, be it your own or a foreign land, you reach a genuine understanding of the people and how they live.

We're talking about culture in all its guises: the creative arts that give a country its spirit as well as the culture of everyday life.

Speak the Culture books sit alongside guidebooks and language courses, serving not only as a companionable good read but also as an invaluable tool for understanding a country's current culture and its heritage.

1 Identity: the foundations of British culture

1.1 Geography

It's the original island nation. Standing aloof on Europe's western fringe, battered by some of the world's roughest seas, Britain has clung to its detachment for centuries. From outside it looks homogenous, defiantly separate from continental Europe in body and soul. However, step ashore and it dissolves into a stew of landscapes, people and cultures.

Table for four please

The British state harbours four nations – <u>Wales</u>, <u>Scotland</u>, <u>England</u> and Northern Ireland – each with its own distinct culture. All four nations can be broken down further, into regions where landscape, language and lifestyle vary markedly. And then there's the dense historical jigsaw, from stone circles to ruined abbeys, each corner of Britain has its story to tell. Surely no other country so modest in scale is so regionally pronounced, so packed with cultural variety, so connected to its past yet steadfastly modern.

So, is it Britain, the United Kingdom or the British Isles?

The term Great Britain, or just Britain (or *Breatainn Mhòr* in Scottish Gaelic and *Prydain Fawr* in Welsh), is usually taken to mean <u>England, Wales and Scotland.</u> The United Kingdom throws <u>Northern Ireland</u> into the mix. The British Isles includes the Republic of Ireland and any island lumps surrounding mainland Britain. Informally – and for most Brits – the term Britain is taken to mean England, Wales, Scotland and Northern Ireland, and is used as such throughout this book.

GB →
U.K. →

Small but beautiful: the lie of the land

Britain squeezes a pleasingly diverse landscape into its modest frame. Emily Brontë's feral moorland with its 'bare masses of stone' might sound a long way from William Blake's 'pleasant pastures', but they coexist closely and comfortably. If we're looking for a vague rule, the further north and west you travel the lumpier Britain gets. <u>Fertile lowlands in south-eastern</u> England are relieved by <u>soft hills before the West Country breaks out</u> into stretches of moorland. In <u>northern England</u> the Pennine <u>hills form a spine running from the Peak District through</u> the Dales up to the <u>border country with Scotland</u>, while <u>the winsome peaks of the Lake District</u> cover England's north-west. <u>Much of Wales, to the west of England,</u> and

6

Scotland, to the north, are mountainous. Scotland harbours the Highlands and Islands, rare in Britain for retaining an element of wilderness. Only these northerly uplands, rugged, boggy and cold, escaped the centuries of farming that tamed Britain's countryside, native deciduous forests included. Across the Irish Sea, west of southern Scotland, lies Northern Ireland, a land of bare, peaty hills encircling Lough Neigh, the largest freshwater lake in the British Isles.

Counting counties

Britain breaks down into a complex map of regions, counties, boroughs, districts, unitary authorities and parishes. Some are historic and familiar but unofficial; others are new and sanctioned by government but rarely used in conversation. Each of the four British nations has been divided into counties (so called because local regions were once controlled by counts (or earls)) for hundreds of years. England has 39 'historic' counties, each with its own cultural identity shaped by customs, accents and sporting teams. However, for the purposes of local government, the old, geographical arrangement of counties has been sliced and diced to accommodate metropolitan counties (urban zones that spread, connected, across the old boundaries) and unitary authorities. Wales, Scotland and Northern Ireland have been similarly affected by modern reshuffling. In Wales the 13 historic counties were reduced to eight in the 1970s and then carved into 22 unitary authorities in 1996. In Northern Ireland the ratio is six old counties – still used in everyday chat by the majority – to 26 new district council areas. Scotland's current set up accommodates 32 council areas although, again, the map of 34 old counties has more day-to-day resonance for most people.

Eng. 39
Wales 13-8-22
Scotland 32-34

Dear old Blighty
Blighty, a kindly term for Britain, was used first by soldiers in the Indian Army. It corrupts an Urdu word for 'foreigner', itself derivative of an Arabic term. Blighty entered common usage in the First World War, popularised in music hall songs like *Take Me Back to Dear Old Blighty*.

The mother of all ditches
The borderlands
between England and
Wales are sometimes
called the Welsh
Marches. The term
more often refers to
the counties on the
English side, namely
Herefordshire,
Shropshire and Cheshire.
Offa's Dyke, the deep
physical groove cut
between England and
Wales by Mercia's king
in the eighth century,
still runs through much
of the Marches.

Iron in the soul
Northern Ireland is
sometimes referred to
as Ulster, one of the four
aged provinces of Ireland
(sharing its island with
Leinster, Munster and
Connacht). Ulster is
actually larger than
Northern Ireland, with
only six of its nine
counties falling within
the state. 'Norn Iron'
is a more informal,
affectionate name for
the province, a phonetic
homeland homage
made with a thick Ulster
brogue. "We're not
Brazil, we're Norn Iron,"
chant the sagacious
football fans at Windsor
Park.

Urban legends: British cities

Britain's cities are the product of organic growth, of building, demolition and rejuvenation over the course of centuries. Each has its personality, rapidly recognised through buildings, accents and vistas London the most multifaceted city and the biggest by impressive proportions (nearest rival Birmingham is a seventh of the size), is among the most multicultural cities on Earth, a flurry of ethnicities, creeds and nationalities. They're here because, most of the time, Europe's second largest city (Moscow is bigger) is a tolerant, rewarding place. Of course, like anywhere else it has its darker side – London's mixed cultural milieu doesn't translate to some social utopia, and deprivation can be high, often in areas where migrant communities reside in greatest number.

Some British cities – notably Bristol, Liverpool, Glasgow, Cardiff and Belfast – are defined by their waterside location. Built on maritime trade (including the profits of slavery), they've endured years of decline to resurface afresh, and now buzz with cultural life.

Only Belfast lags slightly behind. In the former engine room of industrial Britain, Manchester, Leeds, Sheffield and Newcastle reinvent themselves with gentrification and cultural credibility yet retain something of the atmosphere that first made them great. In the West Midlands, Birmingham and Coventry were torn apart by the Luftwaffe in the Second World War before dour architecture compounded their woe in the 1960s. Money is pouring in to make up for lost charm but it's slow going.

Where do the British live?

Over 80 per cent of Britain's inhabitants live in England. Around a third squeeze themselves into the south-eastern corner of England, and a snug 20 per cent or so live in or around London. As a whole, England has a population density of 984 sq/mile (380 sq/km) (three times the EU average); Scotland's is around 168 sq/mile (65 per sq/km) (one of Europe's lowest); Wales' comes in at 361 sq/mile (140 per sq/km); and Northern Ireland's is 315/sq mile (122 sq/km). Slowly, almost imperceptibly, Britain's

London in five songs

Waterloo Sunset
(1967) The Kinks.

I Don't Want to Go to Chelsea
(1978) Elvis Costello and the Attractions.

Down in the Tube Station at Midnight
(1978) The Jam.

Baker Street
(1978) Gerry Rafferty.

A Rainy Night in Soho
(1986) The Pogues.

9

predominantly urban population (four out of five people live in towns and cities) is seeping out to rural areas, reversing the migratory trends of the 19th and early to mid 20th centuries.

Cultural differences between town and country remain and mild sniping still occurs: 'townies' are rude and self-important; rural folk are unsophisticated bumpkins (these are the stereotypes). Occasionally the differences get drawn into wider spats. The debate over a ban on fox hunting with dogs (outlawed in 2005) was used by pro-hunt campaigners to shout about urbanites (and Westminster in particular) killing off the 'rural way of life'. Other episodes have brought a more balanced reflection on the urban/rural relationship: the foot and mouth crisis of 2001 found city, town and country folk alike in sympathy with rural communities, and reminded British people of the old, inescapable bonds between rural and urban life.

The island nation's main islands

Britain works to keep its myriad small islands in the fold, from the southerly Isle of Wight (where genuine natives are called Caulkheads) to the Northern Isles of Orkney and Shetland (closer to the Arctic Circle than London). Two island groups boast significant autonomy, claiming the status of Crown Dependencies, a standing that distinguishes them from overseas territories and colonies, and which allows them to pass their own laws, mint their own coins and to excuse themselves from being in both the UK (but not the British Isles!) and the EU.

The first, the Isle of Man is an ancient Celtic outpost in the Irish Sea. It has its own parliament, the Tynwald (the longest running in the world) and gave the Bee Gees their first breath. The second, the Channel Islands, comprising Jersey, Guernsey and the rest are just off the coast of Normandy, France. Strange to think that Victor Hugo wrote *Les Miserables* in the British Isles whilst exiled on Guernsey.

What's the weather like?

Britain's climate can be a disappointingly tepid affair. It's often cited as unpredictable, and it is – rain and sun come in quick succession – but it's unpredictable within a rather predictable range. As an island lodged in the Gulf Stream's mild westerly flow, Britain is warmer than its northerly latitude would otherwise allow. It never gets painfully cold (winter temps rarely drop below minus ten Celsius), nor does it become truly hot (anything over 30 degrees is a rarity). In general, the west is wetter than the east, and also milder in winter and cooler in summer, although the differences aren't large. The further south you go the more sun you'll see, although if you get the right June day in northern Scotland you can enjoy a whopping 18 hours of sunshine. Upland areas, as you would expect, are colder and wetter: the very tops of the Scottish Highlands may retain snow throughout the year, although this is increasingly unusual. Snow can fall anywhere in winter but rarely stays for more than a couple of days at lower levels where it inevitably evokes media hysteria and transport chaos. But even while the weather isn't biblical, the British talent for talking about it surely is: it's the default icebreaker in conversation with friends or strangers.

Defoe's tour de storm force
Daniel Defoe's first book, *The Storm* (1704), reflected on the most severe storm ever recorded in Britain. With 120mph winds the Great Storm of November 1703 destroyed 13 Royal Navy ships, killed 8,000 people and deposited cows up trees.

Rivers of crud
The unusually hot summer of 1858 created The Great Stink, when the Thames, then recipient of London's untreated sewage (and the source of its drinking water), became a fetid, faeces-clogged hazard. The House of Commons soaked their curtains in chloride of lime to try and quell the stench. The city's modern sewerage system was duly initiated in the same year.

"THERE ARE TWO SEASONS IN SCOTLAND: JUNE AND WINTER."
Billy Connolly

Britain's vital statistics

Area 94,248 square miles (244,101 sq/km) (about half the size of France).

Length 840 miles (1,350km) from Lands End, Cornwall, to John O'Groats in Scotland.

Width just under 300 miles (480km) (and this is the widest point – you're never more than 77 miles (125km) from the sea).

Coastline 7,723 miles (12,429km).

Highest mountain Ben Nevis (Scotland) at 4,406ft (1,343m).

Population approximately 61 million (roughly 52 million in England, five million in Scotland, three million in Wales and 1.7 million in Northern Ireland).

Life expectancy 76 for men and 81 for women.

Hebrides, Bailey, variable becoming south-westerly three or four… The shipping forecast drifts from the radio four times a day. It serves anyone brave enough to navigate the waters around the British Isles, yet has a mystical appeal that reaches well inland. With only 370 words to play with (including intro), the forecast sounds like a coded incantation (read slowly so that mariners may write it down) with its outline of wind speed, sea state, weather and visibility (good, moderate, poor and fog). The region names, from Dogger to Lundy to German Bight (there are 31 in all, read in a set order), are strange but familiar to British ears, absorbed on childhood journeys in the back of the car, radio on. Many claim a haunting poetry for the shipping forecast, and its undulating metre has absorbed the great and the good of modern lyricism, from Seamus Heaney (who wrote a sonnet, *The Shipping Forecast*) to Radiohead (they referenced the forecast on *Kid A*). The day's final reading of the forecast, delivered at 12.48am, is usually preceded by *Sailing By*, a dreamy string piece by Ronald Binge intended as an airwave beacon to sailors in search of the right radio frequency.

Local boys done good: extraordinary folk from ordinary places

Eric Clapton God to some, Slowhand to others and 'Our Eric' to the residents of Ripley, Surrey.

Anthony Minghella The late Oscar-winning director of *The English Patient* grew up above an ice cream shop on the Isle of Wight.

Dudley Moore The comedian, pianist and Hollywood star no doubt found his roots in Dagenham, Essex, useful for the Derek and Clive routines.

Bryan Ferry The Roxy Music frontman is a farmer's son from Washington, Tyne and Wear.

Richard Burton The boy from Pontrhydyfen, South Wales, became Hollywood's highest earner.

Billy Connolly Scotland's biggest comedian was a shipyard welder in his native Glasgow before turning entertainer, initially as a folk singer, in 1965.

Van Morrison The son of a Belfast shipyard worker and a singing tap dancer, George Ivan (van) worked as a window cleaner before climbing fame's ladder.

13

1.2 History

The saga of British history has it all: raging monarchs, epic battles, weeping pustules, shameful bullying, heroic defence, unforgivable haircuts... The story follows modern British life around like a shadow, its every twist and turn contributing to national identity.

1.2.1 Come in, make yourself at home:
Celts, Saxons, Vikings and Normans

Key dates

6,000BC Britain and its hunter-gatherer types are separated from the European mainland as sea levels rise.

500BC The Celts have settled from Europe and Iron Age culture begins to bloom.

43AD Rome finally gets around to invading Britain but meets stiff resistance in the north.

5th to 8th centuries As Roman rule crumbles, Anglo-Saxon tribes carve southern Britain into kingdoms, while Scotland and Wales start to take shape.

9th century Viking raids culminate in the establishment of Danelaw, a Norse province in eastern Britain.

11th century Power switches between Saxon and Danish kings before…

1066 The Normans invade, defeat King Harold and duly set up shop in power.

Sticks and stones

The bones of Cheddar Man, Britain's oldest complete skeleton, went cold around 7,150BC, when Britain still adjoined continental Europe by way of a large marsh. A hunter-gatherer, like his ancestors of 30,000 years, 23-year-old Cheddar Man died from a whack on the head, probably in advance of being chopped up for the cooking pot. Despite such barbarity, cultured civilisation was just around the corner and farming, brought in by continental types, was de rigueur by the fourth century BC. At Skara Brae on Orkney, unearthed from the dunes by a vicious 19th century storm, you can see how Neolithic farmers lived. When the Bronze Age took hold 4,000 years ago, the burial mounds and mysterious stone circles that still mark the British landscape began to appear.

Life with the Celts

As the Bronze Age progressed, the Beaker People of western Europe made the crossing to Britain around 2,000BC, ceramic cups clutched to their lips. But another set of migrants, the Celts of central Europe, left a greater impression. They, like the Iron Age, settled over Britain by 500BC. They were relative sophisticates with their farming methods, defensive hill forts (or drystone brochs in Scotland) and trade with Europe (out went tin, in came wine). Learned Druid priests practised a roughly organised polytheistic religion and artisans made swirling jewellery in gold. Britain's virgin forest came up against the iron axe and the neat pattern of fields still found today began to take shape. Celtic culture was traditionally thought to have arrived from Europe, but these days Iron Age Britain is viewed more as a self-made success, the product of home-grown evolution.

Chip off the (very) old block

DNA sampling carried out in 1997 discovered Adrian Targett, a history teacher living less than a mile from Cheddar Gorge, Somerset, to be a direct descendant of Cheddar Man, dead some 9,000 years. "Maybe this explains why he likes his steaks rare," pondered his wife, Catherine.

Albion and Britannia (…no, it's not a building society)

The Celts gave Britain its first name: Albion, derived from a Celtic word for white, which was apparently uttered in wonder on that first fateful encounter with the white cliffs of Dover. Rome chose the name Britannia, but that too may have Celtic origins. It probably came from *pretani*, a Celtic word for painted, referring to their taste for blue woad-based war paint.

The Romans stuck the female figure of Britannia on their coinage, a tradition reinstated by Charles II in the 17th century on the halfpenny and maintained on the 50 pence piece right through to 2008 when the poor old dear was ditched. Somewhere along the way (probably in the Elizabethan era) she acquired a dangerous looking trident and became the nation personified; a symbol of colonial clout no less.

"IT IS ALL TOO TYPICAL OF A GOVERNMENT WITH AN INADEQUATE SENSE OF BRITISH PRIDE AND AN IGNORANCE OF HISTORY TO WANT TO DO AWAY WITH SUCH A SYMBOL." Ex-Tory leader William Hague got hot under the collar when Britannia was removed from the 50 pence piece

Magic circles

Stone circles first appeared in Britain around 3,300BC. Many were 'henges', a marriage of circular ditch and standing stones or posts. They survive in various windswept spots, from Calanais in the Western Isles and Beaghmore in County Tyrone to the most famous, Stonehenge in Wiltshire. Chin stroking has, as yet, failed to decipher their purpose: most educated guesses talk about rituals and astronomy.

Well this is very
civilised... is it
underfloor heating?
The worldly mod con
perks of life among
Roman nobility – the
plumbing, heating
systems and healthcare
– that dwindled in the
fifth century didn't
reappear in Britain for
well over a thousand
years.

The Romans called the
untamed Scots Picti
'the painted' (they
smeared themselves in
blue battle paint), later
anglicised to Picts.

A tricky away fixture for the Romans

After abortive forays by Julius Caesar in the mid first century BC (in part defeated by the weather), Emperor Claudius annexed much of southern Britain a century later. Albion's Celtic tribes didn't present a united front to the Romans. Indeed, some probably called the Latins in to help quash aggressive rivals. Some tribes were more testy than others: Queen Boudicca of the Iceni took the fight to London before her ragbag army was crushed and she drank poison, while the Welsh tribes were crippled but never really gave up. Northern England took 30 years to rein in. The Romans had a go at Scotland but Emperor Hadrian admitted effective defeat in 122AD by building his boundary wall from Newcastle to Carlisle. A turf barrier built further north 20 years later, the Antonine Wall, proved a short-lived frontier and the Romans resigned themselves to containing rather than conquering Caledonia, as they called the northern lands. There's little archaeological evidence to siggest they attempted taming Ireland.

Good Queen Boudicca inspiring some righteous blood lust or Woad Rage as we now call it...

The Romans stayed for nearly 400 years. Their leaders built classy villas in the country and their garrison towns became thriving settlements. Some towns, St Albans among them, were built on commerce; others, notably Bath, were designed for leisure. Compliant natives were rewarded with local power, becoming Romanised along the way, but indigenous Celtic culture survived, particularly among the peasantry. The Romans gave southern Britain its first sense of collective identity, its first pretensions of 'nationhood'. Inadvertently they did the same for Scotland, uniting its tribes against

1. Identity: the
foundations
of British culture

2. Literature
and philosophy

3. Art, architecture
and design

4. Performing
arts

5. Cinema,
photography
and fashion

6. Media and
communications

7. Food and drink

8. Living culture:
the state of
modern Britain

successive emperors. They also left behind a network of impressively straight roads and the new religion of choice, Christianity.

...and right here we'll have Pizza Express. OK, chaps?

Londinium AD43: Catering Corps making plans for Dean Street

Tribes and tribulations: Anglo-Saxon Britain

Rome's finest had sloped off by the fourth century, and the remaining Romano-British culture slowly shrivelled, its requests for help rejected by emperors who had their own problems elsewhere. Southern Britain was being raided by Teutonic tribes from across the North Sea. The Romano-British and the Celts (many of whom retreated to Wales, Scotland and Cornwall) wasted energy fighting each other while the Germanic plunderers, impressed with the land, began to settle. By the late sixth century the Angles and Saxons had established kingdoms throughout the majority of England. Some Celts took it upon themselves to resist and, who knows, it might have been a mysterious Arthur, a chieftain with a round table, some knights and a magician, that put up the best fight. What we do know is that the kingdom of Northumbria initially lorded it over Anglo-Saxon Britain, followed in the eighth century by Mercia and then, another century on, by Wessex.

Celtic culture remained strong in the upland margins of Anglo-Saxon Britain. In Wales, Celtic settlers found themselves periodically attacked from behind the long dyke dug by Mercian King Offa in the eighth century. By then Wales' tribes were working together, sometimes even referring to themselves as Cymry – 'us' – a word with clear connections to the modern Welsh name for Wales, Cymru. In eastern Scotland the entrenched Picts fought against – and later alongside – the Dalridans from Ireland, whom they dubbed the Scotti. A relatively homogenous region soon formed under Scotland's first king, Kenneth MacAlpin, in the ninth century.

The great conversion

Britain confirmed its faith during the Anglo-Saxon period. Christianity had arrived with the Romans but the Anglo Saxons, with their many gods, had initially shoved it out to the Celtic fringes. Slowly, between the fifth and eighth centuries, Christianity worked its way back in. Columba came from Ireland, based himself on the Western Isle of Iona and converted the Picts and much of northern England with the Celtic brand of Christianity. One of his monks, Aidan, ran a similar op from Lindisfarne in Northumbria. Rome, anxious at the spread of Celtic Christianity with its variances from their own practice, dispatched Augustine in 597 to push its own agenda. He succeeded, working his way up from Kent converting kings as he went. When the two ends of the Church met at the Whitby Synod in 644, the Roman version won out and Britain fell in step with continental Europe.

The not so Dark Ages
England's modern Brits aren't as remote from their Anglo-Saxon forebears as they might think. Language, place names and elements of British law can all be traced back to the Dark Ages, while the very term 'Anglo-Saxon' is still used, sometimes pejoratively, to describe white English speakers.

The word 'Sassenachs', a Scottish term for the English and a bastardised Gaelic version of the Latin 'Saxones', usually carries a similarly derogatory tone. Some of the earliest 'British' works of art were produced in the Anglo-Saxon period. *Beowulf*, the epic man-slays-monster poem, was finally written down, while Northumbrian monk Bede set new literary standards with his *Ecclesiastical History of the English People* (731), . a work later translated by King Alfred, the thinking man's monarch who also commissioned the *Anglo-Saxon Chronicle* (890), a Wessex-friendly history of Britain.

Hair raids: here come the Vikings

The Vikings came in two waves in the ninth century: from Norway and from Denmark, the tales of their bloodlust only moderately exaggerated. Raiding soon became settling and by 891 much of eastern England had fallen under the so-called Danelaw territory. Only King Alfred kept them out of his ascendant kingdom, Wessex. Significantly, in London Alfred was labelled Lord of the English (a title that excluded the Danish territories); his grandson, Athelstan, was crowned first king of England in 927, by which time the Danelaw and most of Scotland and Wales were in his pocket.

However, the Vikings hadn't evaporated. The good work of Alfred (posthumously subtitled 'the Great') was undone in the early 11th century when Ethelred the Unready was replaced by Canute, first Danish king of England. But yet again a dynasty faltered, allowed to deteriorate on this occasion by Canute's son and grandson.

Bayeux Watch:
Like an early Zapruder film clip, this is the moment, caught on tapestry, when King Harold is killed. Harold is the one arrowed.

The Ulster Viking connection
Local Celtic chieftains ensured neither Anglo-Saxons nor Vikings advanced much beyond the coastal fringes of Ireland, and the region retained the Celtic identity that became diluted elsewhere. The Vikings, however, did leave some impression; the province of Ulster (within which modern day Northern Ireland lies) took its name from Uladztír, a Viking term itself derivative of Ulaidh, Irish name for the region's ancient inhabitants.

By 1066 another Saxon, Harold, the Earl of Wessex distinguished by a bloody campaign to subdue the Welsh, was on the throne. He fell off just nine months later when Britain was invaded and conquered for the last time (to date). The date in question, 1066, chimes in the subconscious of every Brit; a reminder that for most of them the Normans (from northern France but, as the name suggests, descended from Norsemen), led by Duke William to victory against Harold at the Battle of Hastings, will feature somewhere in their family tree.

Ends of the beginning: early towns

Roman
-*chester* (Manchester), -*caster* (Doncaster) or -*cester* (Cirencester).

Anglo-Saxon
-*ford* (Stamford), -*ham* (Chippenham), -*ton* (Luton) and -*wich* (Greenwich).

Viking
-*by* (Derby) and -*thorpe* (Scunthorpe)

North Scots' Norse nous
Ties with the Vikings remain stronger in the far north of Scotland than elsewhere in Britain. Shetland, after all, is as close to Bergen as it is to Edinburgh, let alone London. Orkney and the Western Isles were under Norse control for centuries, and Shetland was ruled

from Bergen as recently as the 15th century, four hundred years after the Vikings had left most of Britain. The language up here still has a bouncing Scandinavian rhythm and festivals like Up Helly Aa, the annual longboat burning in Lerwick, recall the connections.

Englisc heritage
By the time Alfred the Great was on the throne in the ninth century, the people of southern Britain were being called the Englisc, a name taken from the 'Angle' folk that settled in the sixth century.

Do as you're told: life with the Normans

Having defeated Harold, albeit narrowly, William the Conqueror (no doubt relieved to lose his previous epithet, William the Bastard) spent much of the subsequent two decades brutalising England on a bender of burning, murder and famine. Only Hereward the Wake, a Saxon guerrilla hiding out in the marshy Fens around Ely, had much success at resistance. Others succumbed quickly, bullied by Norman and French lords in the sturdy stone fortresses that still stand on the British landscape. The Welsh didn't escape; the Marcher castles (from which the Welsh Marches take their name) kept them in line, while in lowland Scotland King Malcolm III was made compliant. On the mainland only the fierce Highlanders in their remote clans remained untamed as the Norman language, culture and way of life were assimilated into Anglo-Saxon Britain. It took a century for the Normans to make an impression on Ireland, and even then the earls that took land in Ulster tended to absorb more than exude, adopting the Celtic culture as their own.

Ooo, that's a big book
It took William I's scribes less than a year to compile the Domesday Book in 1086; not bad for a work that went through every shire and hundred in England, noting who lived where and owned what livestock. Their job was made easier by existing Saxon records. The book was popularly named 'Domesday' with a degree of derision by the English.

Serf 'n' turf: the feudal system
Life in the late Middle Ages was governed by the feudal system. Serfs were beholden to the local knight, from whom they received a small patch of land and notional protection. In return they gave him an agreed amount of labour. The knights gave military service and allegiance to a layer of barons and bishops, above which hovered the king.

Mr Scotland

William Wallace is *the* Scottish hero. Why? Because he thrashed the English at Stirling Bridge against the odds, before taking the fight to England itself with an informal but fearsome army. His legend was shaped by 19th century Romantics and then bolstered by Mel Gibson's painted turn in the film *Braveheart* (1995). He wasn't the unwashed orphan of the Highlands conjured by Hollywood but rather, more likely, the son of a landowner in south-west Scotland. However, his father was killed by the English and his wife may have been slain by a sheriff whom Wallace then personally chopped into small pieces, earning outlaw status. Apparently he also skinned one of Edward I's officers at Stirling, fashioning the hide into a belt. Quite the little craftsman. In 2002 he topped *The Sunday Mail*'s poll of the 100 Greatest Scots.

Murder in the cathedral and the Magna Carta

William's direct heirs withstood two shaky generations on the English throne before the Plantagenet kings took over in 1154. Henry II did a reasonable job – introducing trial by jury, keeping a tight grip on the barons – before finding notoriety with the murder of Thomas Becket, Archbishop of Canterbury, clumsily asserting the power of throne over pulpit. Henry's son, Richard I (the Lionheart) spent his decade of kingship crusading in the Middle East, before his weaselly brother, King John, lost the bits of France brought over by William I, had a big row with the Pope and signed the Magna Carta in 1215, granting his pushy barons more power. Some explanations assert (rather ambitiously) that the document set Britain on the long path to parliamentarianism and civil liberty.

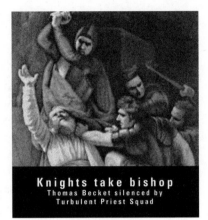

Knights take bishop
Thomas Becket silenced by Turbulent Priest Squad

Trouble up north

Edward I took more of a grip on power. Wales, in particular, got it in the neck. Until the 1270s the Welsh had their own kings but, after ten years of battle, Edward declared the region a principality and made his son the first Prince of Wales. In Scotland a succession crisis allowed Edward to put his man, John de Balliol, on the throne, only for de Balliol to betray his boss and sign Scotland up with France, creating the Auld Alliance. Edward's retaliation earned him the nickname

Hammer of the Scots and de Balliol was removed. The dashing William Wallace took up the fight and crushed English troops at Stirling Bridge in 1297, but was hung drawn and quartered the following year. And so it fell to Robert the Bruce, self-declared king of Scotland, to batter the English. He did so against Edward II at Bannockburn in 1314.

My advice? Live for the moment

Anyone who made it into their 40s in the 14th century was considered lucky. It was a dismal time. The Plague (or the Black Death) arrived in 1348, not long after the country was recovering from famine. Around a third of the population died. Next up was the English Peasants' Revolt of 1381, triggered by new laws to cap wages and the introduction of a poll tax. Alas, the angry, archbishop-murdering mob that marched on London, led by the blacksmith Wat Tyler, was deceived and slyly slain by 14-year-old King Richard II. All this happened in the century when the Hundred Years' War with France kicked off. For a long time the sporadic bouts of fighting went England's way, most famously at Agincourt in 1415 when Henry V's men slaughtered thousands of French and took their crown. But in the end the English, outmanoeuvred when peasant girl Joan of Arc set the French up for a comeback, settled for ownership of Calais. Scotland, which suffered similar bouts of disease and civil strife, sent troops to help France.

House breaking: the Wars of the Roses

By the early 15th century the House of Lancaster (Henrys IV to VI) reigned in England, but was challenged all the way by the House of York. The ensuing blood-soaked round of battles, in which the English crown switched heads six times in 25 years, were later dubbed the Wars of the Roses, a reference to the flowers of

Auld friends
The Auld Alliance between France and Scotland lasted nearly 300 years from 1295. It was a military marriage of convenience aimed at countering English power.

Did he or didn't he? Richard III and the Princes in the Tower
Edward IV died young amid the Wars of the Roses, leaving the throne to his 12-year-old son, Edward V. Richard, the boy king's uncle, sent young Eddie and his brother, another Richard, to the Tower of London for safekeeping. But somehow safekeeping turned into death. Uncle Richard stepped manfully into the breach and became Richard III. Even today historians disagree on whether Richard was responsible for killing the Princes in the Tower. Current thought seems to say he was. Even so, it appears he wasn't quite the hunchbacked bastard portrayed by Shakespeare; he was actually reasonably popular during his brief reign.

York (white) and Lancaster (red). The Yorks appeared to have come out on top until a distant relative, Henry Tudor, of Welsh (Tewdwr) stock, killed Richard III at the Battle of Bosworth in 1485. And so Henry VII, the first of the Tudor monarchs, forced his way onto the English throne. Under Henry, relations with the Scots improved, particularly with the marriage of his daughter to James IV of Scotland, thereby linking the Tudor and Stewart (later Gallicised to Stuart) houses.

Anyone for marriage?

In 1509 the Tudors placed their second monarch on the English throne, Henry VIII. Educated, sporty and handsome (a long way from the fat, gout-riddled man that he became), in the end Henry was defined by his attempts to produce a strong male heir. He got through six wives in the effort, but could only manage the sickly Edward VI who died in his teens after six years as king. Henry's divorce from his first wife, Catherine of Aragon, created the almighty rift with Rome that bore the Church of England, Henry at its head. For good measure, in the 1530s he dissolved (and plundered) the monasteries of England, Wales and Ireland. Under Henry, the Acts of Union in 1536 and 1543 finally bound England and Wales by the same parliament and law; a boon for the Welsh gentry, as trade prospered, but for the poor majority an attack on their language (Welsh was outlawed) and customs. Scotland, meanwhile, continued to resist English advances. Its sequence of weak child Stewart monarchs was forgotten during the impressive reign of James IV, although he died in battle with the English at Flodden Field in 1513. Under Mary, Queen of Scots the Scottish lowlands were repeatedly battered by Henry VIII as he tried to push English influence northwards. Catholic in an increasingly Protestant land, she was eventually forced into exile in England by rebellion.

"HENRY VIII, OR KING SYPHILIS
GUT BUCKET WIFE MURDERER VIII
AS I PREFER TO CALL HIM,
WAS BORN IN 1491."
Jo Brand

1. Identity: the   2 Literature   3. Art, architecture   4. Performing   5. Cinema,   6. Media and   7. Food and drink   8. Living culture:
foundations   and philosophy   and design   arts   photography   communications   the state of
of British culture   and fashion   modern Britain

The Virgin Queen

The brief, Protestant-bashing reign of Queen Mary (not the Scottish one, but Henry VIII's daughter by Catherine of Aragon), who lost England's last French possession, Calais, was followed by the 45-year tenure of Elizabeth I. She balanced the religious tensions of the era as a Protestant with no great enthusiasm for persecuting Catholics (if you overlook imprisoning Mary, Queen of Scots for nearly 20 years prior to killing her). In an age when a woman, queen or no, was still considered intellectually deficient, she made England a global power, crushing Spain's Armada in 1588, dispatching Walter Raleigh, Francis Drake et al to claim the spoils of the New World and reigning over a golden literary age in which Shakespeare, Bacon and Marlow were all at work. For all that, historians usually view her as grimly dogged (although undeniably charismatic) rather than heroic. She died, the Virgin Queen, with no strong heir.

Ireland, controlled for so long by Gaelic lords, finally began toeing the English line under the Tudor monarchs. Ulster chieftain Hugh O'Neill put up a stirring final show of resistance in the reign of Elizabeth I but eventually lost in 1607. His defeat changed Ulster from the point of greatest Irish resistance – of strongest Gaelic culture – to the region with closest ties to England. English and Scottish 'planters' arrived and took up land seized from the Catholic earls, establishing the northern region's Protestant bias and setting the scene for long-term divisions.

The global Virgin brand: actually established in 1588 by Elizabeth I

Bones of contention

In 2008, a mere 421 years after Mary, Queen of Scots was put to death for treason by Elizabeth I, Scottish MP Christine Grahame demanded the Queen's remains, interred at Westminster Abbey, be exhumed and repatriated. "She was an iconic historical Scots figure and ultimately the victim of English plotting," explained Ms Grahame of the French-speaking Mary.

Colonies close to home

When Ireland fell under English control in the early 17th century, plantations were established on which English and Scottish settlers could take root. County Coleraine in Ulster was given to the City of London for colonisation and its main town went from being Derry to Londonderry.

"SHE IS ONLY A WOMAN, ONLY MISTRESS OF HALF AN ISLAND, AND YET SHE MAKES HERSELF FEARED BY SPAIN, BY FRANCE, BY THE EMPIRE, BY ALL."
Pope Sixtus V ponders the talents of Elizabeth I

The Gunpowder Plot,
or Powder Treason as it
was called at the time,
was led by Robert
Catesby, an aristocrat
convinced that England
should be Catholic.
He and a small band of
conspirators hoped to
blow up Parliament,
King James I with it,
and install the malleable
Princess Elizabeth on
the throne as a Catholic
monarch. Explosives
maestro Guy Fawkes
was discovered in the
cellars of Parliament,
looking shifty beside 36
barrels of gunpowder.
Fawkes and the other
plotters were hung,
drawn and quartered or
shot in the process of
being caught. Over the
centuries, murderous
violence has turned to
perky tradition, and the
celebration of failure (or
perhaps anarchy) that is
Guy Fawkes Night every
5th November unleashes
an evening of fireworks
and bonfires with
effigies of Fawkes
placed on top. A less
publicised tradition finds
the Yeoman of the Guard
(the Queen's official
bodyguard) searching
the vaults of Parliament,
sword and lanterns in
hand, before the State
Opening each November.

Anglicans, Puritans and Presbyterians: Britain does the Reformation

Although Henry VIII launched the Church of England
with a loosely Catholic doctrine, it became increasingly
Protestant after he died, caught up in the European
Reformation that rejected the supremacy of bishops
and focussed on a more direct connection with God,
nurtured through scripture. Under Elizabeth I, the
English variation on the theme, Anglicanism, took root,
although the Puritans felt she didn't go nearly far
enough in simplifying the processes of worship. The
Reformation went down particularly well in lowland
Scotland where the traditional wealth of the Catholic
Church was stripped: land, property and cash were
appropriated from the bishops and monasteries, and
civil war broke out when Mary, Queen of Scots, reared
on the Catholic faith as the wife of a French king, took
to the throne. The Church (or Kirk) of Scotland that
formally broke with Rome in 1560 was Presbyterian,
named for 'presbyter', a New Testament word for
priest; the Scottish Protestants elected their own.
As ever, the Catholic Highlands did their own thing.

Explosive times: Guy Fawkes, Civil War and the Commonwealth

With Elizabeth shunning motherhood, the English
throne fell to the nearest in line, king of Scotland,
James, the Stuart son of murdered Mary, Queen of
Scots. In Scotland he was James VI, in England
James I, the first monarch to unite the Scots and
English thrones if not the kingdoms themselves – each
retained its own parliament. Unlike his mother, James
was a Protestant, yet tried to smooth relations with
Catholics. His conciliatory efforts foundered when
the Catholic Guy Fawkes and co tried to blow up
parliament in 1605. The next Stuart, Charles I, was

absolutist and arrogant. When, in 1640, he recalled the parliament he'd dissolved 11 years earlier, hoping they'd support him against the recalcitrant Scottish Kirk, they refused to help. And so the king and his Cavaliers took up arms against Oliver Cromwell's parliamentarian Roundheads in the English Civil War. Charles lost and was executed in 1649. Cromwell joylessly ruled the new 'Commonwealth of England' as Lord Protector (while brutally suppressing Scotland and Ireland), but England's dalliance with republicanism didn't last and in 1660, two years after Cromwell died, Parliament reintroduced the monarchy in the shape of Charles II, a move commonly referred to as the Restoration.

A glorious revolution

Charles II, no doubt mindful of what happened to his father, played it cool. He pursued something like religious tolerance and established a balance between Crown and Parliament, recognising that neither could govern without the other. Science and the arts flourished while growing chunks of America and India fell under British rule. On a more personal level, his record of at least 17 illegitimate children by eight or more different mistresses (even while he failed to produce a genuine heir for the throne) suggested he was something of a free spirit. His reign, however, wasn't without crises, notably the Great Plague of 1665 and the Great Fire of London a year later.

James II, Charles' brother, was less shrewd. Openly Catholic, he put prominent Protestants to the sword, tried to sideline Parliament and cosied up to the French. But by now Parliament was too powerful; the Protestant lords ganged up and asked Dutch prince William of Orange to step in. He did so with his queen, Mary (actually James II's daughter) in 1688. The Glorious

Hero or villain: judging Cromwell
Oliver Cromwell's reputation has always been debated. When he died of malaria in 1658, a vast sum, around £60,000, was spent on the hero's funeral. Yet, three years later, his treasonous body was dug up and his head stuck on a pole at Tyburn. Such swings in posthumous popularity have continued for 350 years. His reputation was resurrected in the 19th century, with his image shaped as that of a great leader. A Cromwell statue was placed aside the Houses of Parliament in 1899. Today the jury remains out; historians argue over the merits and flaws of his character and rule. In England, he's most often seen as dynamic but dictatorial.

Of the 190,000 or so deaths brought about by the English Civil War, more than half were caused by disease.

There may be
Troubles ahead
When the forces of William of Orange sailed to Ireland to repel James II, they made landfall at Derry, in Ulster. The city was glad to see them, having been under siege from James' army for 105 days. The efforts of those who stood firm, led by a group of 13 young apprentices, are celebrated in the Loyalist Orange Order's Apprentice Boys march each August. The Orange Order marching season also includes a 12th July commemoration of victory in the Battle of the Boyne, rankling the Catholic population that deem the parades triumphalist. The Apprentice Boys march through the Catholic Bogside district of Derry in 1969 sparked riots that ultimately led to the mobilisation of British troops in Northern Ireland, seen by many as the start of what became known as the Troubles in which 3,500 people would die.

Revolution, as it became known, delivered England a new royal house without the usual puddles of blood. In Scotland the transition was less smooth; here the Campbells, egged on by the English, famously massacred the Jacobite (Stuart supporters – Jacobus being Latin for 'James') MacDonalds in Glencoe in 1692. Meanwhile, having fled to France, James and his Jacobite friends tried to get back in via Ireland, where they were repelled at the Battle of the Boyne in 1690. While Britain was now established as a Protestant nation, for Ireland the faith divide was far from sorted.

United in name at least

Queen Anne came after William and Mary in a rule most notable for the 1707 Act of Union gathering Scotland, England and Wales under one parliament (the one in London). The Scots didn't join up with any great enthusiasm, and Highlanders in particular weren't happy. When Queen Anne died, the throne passed to the House of Hanover, George I atop, in accordance with the 1701 Act of Settlement that forbade Catholics from the succession. Two Jacobite rebellions in Scotland pushed the issue, attempting to reinstall the Catholic Stuart line. The first, in 1715, quickly faltered. The second, in 1745, got further – as far as Derby in fact – before the Jacobite pretender, Bonnie Prince Charlie (Charles Stuart) and his Highland supporters retreated and were mercilessly thumped at Culloden, near Inverness, in 1746. This, the last battle fought on mainland Britain, remains etched in the Scottish psyche. Finally, the Highlands were subdued; tartan and bagpipes were outlawed in the 1747 Act of Proscription and the clan system was effectively deconstructed. Meanwhile, in London, power was gradually drifting from Crown to Parliament; and with the Whig MP Robert Walpole Britain got its first Prime Minister in the 1720s.

1. Identity: the
foundations
of British culture

2. Literature
and philosophy

3. Art, architecture
and design

4. Performing
arts

5. Cinema,
photography
and fashion

6. Media and
communications

7. Food and drink

8. Living culture:
the state of
modern Britain

1.2.3 The modern age:
empire, slavery and sacrifice

Ruling the waves

By the mid 18th century Britannia was ruling the waves (James Thomson's poem *Rule Britannia!* was set to music by Thomas Arne in 1740 and was an overnight hit), Georges II and III at the helm. With a refreshing period of peace on home turf, she took the fight to other parts of the globe, building a vast empire. France was usually on the opposing side, notably in the Seven Years War that netted colonies in India and Canada. In 1769 Captain James Cook made it to the Antipodes, bagging further territory. The blip came with defeat in the American War of Independence between 1775 and 1783, but further success wasn't long in coming. Having tiptoed nervously round the French Revolution of 1789, imperial Britain charged on under Messrs Horatio Nelson and Arthur Wellesley (Duke of Wellington) in battles against Napoleon at Trafalgar (1805) and Waterloo (1815). At home, George III was unaware of the triumph: his famed madness gripped hard and he died blind, demented and alone in Windsor Castle in 1820, six decades after being crowned.

The Irish Question

After decades of repression, in 1800 the Catholics in Ireland (always threatening to rebel) were offered 'emancipation' by British Prime Minister William Pitt, but only once they'd agreed to the Act of Union that brought Ireland under British parliamentary rule in a new United Kingdom (previously Ireland was under the British crown but had its own parliament). However, promises weren't met: once the Irish signed up, George III vetoed Catholic freedom. Decades of

c.1765 Scotsman James Watt cracks steam power, key to the Industrial Revolution.

Late 18th century The Highland Clearances force peasants off Scottish land.

1801 Act of Union creates the United Kingdom, with Ireland ruled from Westminster.

1805 and 1815 Decisive British wins at Trafalgar and Waterloo end the Napoleonic Wars.

1853 Britain gets involved in the Crimean War.

1914-18 The First World War against Germany costs nearly a million British lives.

1921 Anglo-Irish Treaty separates Northern Ireland from a new Irish state to the south.

1926 Tough times for your average Brit bring on the General Strike.

1928 Women get the vote after years of Suffragette lobbying.

1939-45 The Second World War pushes Britain into its 'finest hour'.

1982 Britain fights Argentina for the Falkland Islands.

1999 Wales gets an assembly and Scotland a parliament amid devolution.

2005 Islamist extremists kill 52 London commuters.

Kilt coup for King
No British monarch visited Scotland between 1641 (Charles I) and 1822 when George IV turned up on a PR jolly organised by the writer Walter Scott. The King's outfit apparently inspired a revival in tartan kilts.

Hunger pangs that still ache
Ireland's Great Famine, in which the damage done by potato blight was greatly worsened by political and social circumstances, lasted six years from 1845. It affected Ulster less than it did the regions further south, but nevertheless the population fell by an estimated 15 per cent. Overall, Ireland lost as many as two million people, a reduction brought about by starvation, disease and large-scale migration. The British Government's apparent failure to save Ireland from the famine remains a thorny issue 150 years on. Some suggest they wilfully tried to crush Irish culture. Murals painted in the Catholic areas of modern day Belfast still refer to 'Britain's genocide by starvation'.

discord followed. A failed nationalist uprising in 1916 inspired support for independence, launching a guerrilla war against British troops. It ended in 1921 with the Anglo-Irish Treaty and partition. Six counties in the Protestant north remained within the UK as Northern Ireland; the remaining 26 became the Irish Free State, and soon after, the Republic of Ireland.

Put up your hands and give us your country: building an empire

For three centuries Britain stuck its flag in any patch of foreign dirt it could find, even if its empire did grow as much by accident as design. It began with Walter Raleigh's exploration of the North American and Caribbean coast in the late 16th century, where chunks of land were bitten off for England. Initially it was all about trade (tobacco, cotton and fur), but the idea of escaping to North America soon found religious separatists making the move. Elsewhere, the East India Trading Company established a strong British presence in Asia. A second wave of empire building began after the loss of America to independence in 1776. Victory against Napoleon soon opened up the world to Britain; it controlled trade and conquered vast areas of territory, building a congregation of more than 400 million souls by the early 20th century. India, Burma, Australia, New Zealand, Canada, the Caribbean, a line of dependencies running through Africa from Egypt down to the Cape: the Empire covered a quarter of the globe. In the second half of the 20th century the Empire ebbed away, cutting the apron strings from Britain whilst the motherland recovered from world war. Among the last to fly the nest was Hong Kong, returned to China in 1997.

Britain was one of the worst offenders in the slave trade that grew with colonial expansion. West Africans were snatched on a grand scale, transported to North America and the Caribbean and forced to work on tobacco, sugar and cotton plantations. The abolition of the slave trade eventually came in 1807 and slavery itself was made illegal in 1833.

Final Straw for colonies
In 2002 the then Home Secretary Jack Straw blamed contemporary troubles in Israel, Kashmir, Afghanistan and Iraq on Britain's messy withdrawal from its Empire in the 20th century.

Britain goes industrial

In the century after 1750, the British population trebled to more than 16 million. By 1901 it had doubled again. An agricultural revolution stopped them all going hungry, although improved technology actually reduced the agrarian workforce (by 1850 Britain had fewer workers on the land (less than a quarter of the workforce) than any other country in the world), and freed up labour for a much more celebrated transformation.

The Industrial Revolution began with cloth and the mechanised textile mills in Lancashire and Derbyshire, before the arrival of steam power in the late 19th century quickened the pace of change dramatically. Factories producing metalwork and textiles mushroomed, built close to coal supplies in South Wales, the North and the Midlands. People migrated en masse to the new industrial cities: Manchester and Sheffield quadrupled in size in the first 50 years of the 19th century. In Glasgow and Belfast, where the shipyards began to boom, the growth was even greater. By the 1840s the railways were being laid, upping the pace of change again, and a few years later the telegraph revolutionised communications. Political reform took a while to catch up. Riots and discontent, led by the Chartist movement, rumbled for a decade

Before the Industrial Revolution, Britain operated on various time zones. In Bristol, for example, with the sun rising later than London, the clocks ran ten minutes behind the capital. This brought various timetabling problems in the age of the train, so most of the rail companies adopted Greenwich Mean Time by 1848. GMT was legally set throughout Britain in 1880. Five years later some bright spark invented the clocking-on machine.

In 1812 Spencer Perceval distinguished himself by becoming the only British Prime Minister to be assassinated (so far), when he was shot through the heart at close range by a madman.

before the Reform Act of 1832 initiated the sedate journey to popular representation. Social reform was even slower. Industrialisation often brought wretched living conditions, only partially relieved by measures like the amended Poor Law of 1834 that passed 'care' for the destitute over to workhouses.

Get off my land: the Highland Clearances

The migration of people from countryside to city occurred ahead of schedule in northern Scotland. Landlords kicked peasants out of their homes in the Highland Clearances in the late 18th century, replacing them with more profitable tenants, sheep. Thousands of Highlanders fled to North America and Australia, others moved to new industrial cities. Those that remained, pushed into a subsistence life of weaving or fishing on whatever wild margin of land they could get, were known as crofters. It only took 50 years for the Highlands to become one of the most sparsely peopled regions of Europe.

**Arthur Wellesley
1st Duke of Wellington (1769-1852)**
Called the 'The Iron Duke' after fitting shutters to his house to protect his windows from the stone-flinging public

"IT WILL ONLY ENCOURAGE THE LOWER CLASSES TO MOVE ABOUT."
The Duke of Wellington on the coming of the railways (and they still named a railway station after his success at Waterloo).

Victorian values

When the gluttonous fop that was George IV waddled into the grave he was succeeded first by his brother William IV and then by his niece, Victoria. She came to the throne in 1837, aged just 18. Under Victoria, Britain enjoyed naval supremacy and duly dominated trade, while the manufacturing bonanza of the Industrial Revolution revved up and engineers like Isambard Kingdom Brunel dazzled with railways, bridges and behemoth steam ships.

1872: The new table miniskirt makes an appearance at Frobisher Mansions

Slut

A newly moneyed middle class enthusiastically spent its cash on seaside holidays, material goods and opium. Most people, however, were more concerned with simple survival, often living in the squalid, overcrowded cities that grew with the industrial age. Parliament began to work intermittently on their behalf, notably in the late 19th century under two distinctive Prime Ministers, Benjamin Disraeli (Conservative) and William Gladstone (Liberal). Despite Britain's dominance overseas, the wars continued. The Crimean War (shambolic work of slaughter in which pushy Florence Nightingale, pioneer of modern nursing, starred), Indian Mutiny and Boer War all kicked off during Victoria's reign.

Phwoar, look at the legs on that table
Contrary to popular myth the Victorians didn't dissolve at the sight of an uncovered table leg, flustered by such an overt display of sexuality. In fact, in 19th century Britain, pornography found its first mass market in the shape of Lady Pokingham literature and explicit daguerreotype photographs.

The big shoot up
in Flanders
In 1916 you could
stroll into Harrods in
Knightsbridge and buy
'A Welcome Present for
Friends at the Front'.
The pack contained
cocaine, morphine and
syringes. Alternatively,
you could treat your
Tommy of choice to a
gel pack of heroin. Anti-
drug laws were rapidly
passed following reports
of drug-crazed soldiers
at the front.

War in the industrial age

Edward VII's ten-year reign at the start of the 21st century turned out to be a genteel lull before the brusque arrival of the modern era. When Germany invaded Belgium on its way to France in 1914, Britain honoured its new Entente Cordiale with the old enemy and declared war on the Germans. Britain's new working class signed up to fight in their millions, and this, the first big conflict of the mechanised era, the first big war in the age of national identity, killed 700,000 of them, most mown down by machine gun fire in northern France where trench fighting yielded a four-year stalemate. Virtually every village in Britain counted its casualties; some lost a whole generation of young men. The First World War ended with Germany's surrender in November 1918.

How Britain remembers

In 1919 George V set 11th November aside as Remembrance Day. Today, Britain (and much of the Commonwealth) still stops – in offices, schools and supermarkets – for two minutes' silence at the 11th hour on the 11th day of the 11th month, the moment the guns stopped firing on the Western Front. At the Cenotaph in Whitehall, London, a solemn ceremony marks the occasion, with royals and political leaders laying wreaths. *Nimrod* from Elgar's *Enigma Variations* (see section 4.1.2. for more on Elgar) brings the marching veterans to a reflective halt. Brits buy and wear paper poppies in the run up to Remembrance Day, sold by the Royal British Legion to raise funds for ex-servicemen and their families. Poppies bloomed in the churned fields of Flanders when the fighting stopped. When Channel Four newsreader Jon Snow was criticised for not wearing a poppy on air in 2006 he talked about a "rather unpleasant breed of poppy fascism."

1. Identity: the
foundations
of British culture

2. Literature
and philosophy

3. Art, architecture
and design

4. Performing
arts

5. Cinema,
photography
and fashion

6. Media and
communications

7. Food and drink

8. Living culture:
the state of
modern Britain

Going to the polls between the wars

The divisions in British society had always been obvious, but prior to the First World War most people simply accepted their place in the pecking order. However, the gulf between the elite, often behind the lines giving orders, and the largely disenfranchised multitude, doing the dying up at the front, became glaring during the conflict. No doubt mindful of what was happening in Russia with its revolution, the Government acted in 1918 and gave all men over 21 and women over 30 the vote. The Suffragette movement had been demanding universal voting rights since the turn of the century and finally won all adult women the vote in 1928. Victoria was the last monarch to really meddle in state affairs and Parliament was now running the country, its lower chamber composed largely of Tories, Liberals and new boys Labour, born of the unions' thirst for representation in 1900 and first in power under Ramsay MacDonald in 1924. The gaiety of the Roaring Twenties roared right past most of the country; they were too busy coping with economic hardship. Spiralling unemployment caused the General Strike of 1926 and the Great Depression of 1929 made things worse: a significant number of Brits gave up and moved to the New World.

Shrewd move George
In 1917, amid fervent anti-German feeling in Britain, George V changed the family name from Saxe-Coburg und Gotha to Windsor.

The Dunkirk Spirit

The Second World War did much to mould the British psyche. Churchill's bulldog spirit wasn't quickly forgotten (even if he was voted out of office two months after Germany surrendered) and certain episodes of British resistance became engrained in the mind of every citizen: the escape from Dunkirk in 1940, when every available boat sailed to evacuate 330,000 troops (Brits still talk of a belligerent 'Dunkirk Spirit' when faced with adversity), the airborne Battle of Britain that punctured Hitler's invasion plans in 1940, and the Blitz that hammered Coventry, the East End of London, Glasgow and other areas, and in which Britons clung to their resolve. Such events are still readily trumpeted when Britain talks about its character in positive terms.

England vs. Germany: the second leg

Preoccupied with putting food on the table, Britain paid little attention when Germany began rearming under Adolf Hitler in the 1930s. Even when he teamed up with Mussolini and began sabre rattling, British MP Neville Chamberlain infamously pursued appeasement with the Munich Agreement in 1938. A year later, Britain was at war. Winston Churchill replaced Chamberlain in 1940 when Poland, France, Holland, Belgium and Norway had already fallen to the Nazis, and manoeuvred Britain through the Second World War, mobilising the country mentally and physically, helping it deal with large civilian losses as the major towns and cities were bombed in the Blitz, and pushing it on, in alliance with the USA and Russia, to victory in 1945. A quarter of a million Brits died in the fighting and over 40,000 in the bombing raids. London, in particular, suffered: the Blitz of 1940 to 1941 killed more than 30,000 civilians in the capital.

"I'M GLAD... IT MAKES ME FEEL I CAN LOOK THE EAST END IN THE FACE."
The Queen Mother's comment after Buckingham Palace was hit during the Blitz.

From austerity to flares

The Second World War exhausted Britain. As the country slowly rebuilt, austerity reigned with food and basic goods rationed. The Empire slipped away, most of it opting for self-governance. India went in 1947, Malaya in 1957 and Kenya in 1963. The empire was replaced by the Commonwealth of Nations, under which ties with the old territories were maintained. Back home, Britain began looking after its own like never before. The 'Welfare State' of 1948 brought a free National Health Service and dole payments while the nationalisation of railways, coalmines and steelworks helped millions into a job. In the 1950s the colonial legacy came good in the shape of people, as West Indian migrants made Britain their home. The wave continued in subsequent decades – migrants from the Indian subcontinent began arriving in the 1960s and 70s – establishing Britain as the multicultural state it remains today. By the late 1950s Britain was prospering again; by the 1960s it was swinging. Bands like The Beatles and The Rolling Stones gave a familiar face to the cultural and social revolution that loosened attitudes to sex, fashion and class. Legislation followed, notably relaxing the laws on homosexuality and abortion.

Meltdown, Maggie and the miners

Come and have a go: three modern riots

Poll Tax
On 31st March 1990, the biggest riot in London for a century began as a fairly peaceful protest against the Poll Tax. By the time the violence in Trafalgar Square had calmed, buildings and cars were smouldering, 113 people had been injured and 340 arrested.

May Day
In 2000, anti-globalisation demonstrations in Parliament Square turned ugly. It kicked off with the destruction of a McDonalds in Whitehall and ended with pitched battles against riot police.

Race riots
Riots in Oldham, Bradford and Burnley in Summer 2001 saw white and Asian youths attacking each other and anything nearby. The subsequent inquiry mentioned ethnically divided communities, where race issues were exacerbated by 'grinding poverty' and exploited by white racists.

The 1970s were a struggle. Membership of the European Economic Community and decimalisation early in the decade couldn't assuage soaring inflation later on. In 1979 the Winter of Discontent brought everyone from nurses to bin men and gravediggers out on strike. The discovery of oil and gas off the coast of Scotland gave fresh voice to those seeking Scottish independence, but also resentment when English firms walked off with a significant share of the proceeds. Ultimately, the 1970s strife served Britain with its first handbag-wielding Prime Minister, Margaret Thatcher. Some loved her – she served three terms and the middle classes never had it better; but many hated her – the coal pit closures that led to a bitter miners' strike in the early 1980s ruined communities in South Wales and northern England. War with Argentina over the Falkland Islands in 1982 got a similarly mixed response, despite the jingoistic flag waving of the time. Meanwhile, an IRA bombing campaign, aimed at kicking the British out of Northern Ireland, was getting bloodier by the year, both in Northern Ireland and Britain. The introduction of a wildly unpopular poll tax finally did for Thatcher in 1990.

"I THINK, HISTORICALLY, THE TERM 'THATCHERISM' WILL BE SEEN AS A COMPLIMENT."
Margaret Thatcher considers her legacy.

Tony keeps smiling

The 1990s were less turbulent, with Britain experiencing a period of economic growth (some said reaping the benefit of Thatcher's tenure). Finally, in 1997, the electorate deemed Labour – or New Labour as they were calling themselves – worthy of power and 18 years of Tory government came to an end. Tony Blair strode, grinning, into Downing Street and stayed for the next decade. Devolution in the late 1990s brought change for Scotland with its parliament and Wales with its assembly, if not vast constitutional powers. Finally, after several false dawns, Northern Ireland appeared to be on the road to lasting peace when a National Assembly, first conceived in the 1998 Belfast Agreement (or the Good Friday Agreement as it's more commonly known), reconvened in 2007 led by a power sharing executive that featured both Nationalists and Unionists. The British army, on the streets of Northern Ireland for 38 years, left soon after.

When Gordon Brown replaced Blair as Labour PM in 2007, Britain was still soul searching about the merits or otherwise of following the USA into war in the Middle East: the London bombings of July 2005, linked to Islamic militants, had brought the 'War against Terror' closer to home with the death of 52 commuters. Only the biting economic downturn of 2008 drew the front pages away from the debate on national security and foreign policy. The monarchy clung, perhaps unexpectedly, to a degree of popularity, having coped with various modern crises, most notably the death of Diana, Princess of Wales.

Tony Blair. Good sketch material, as you can see

1. **Identity: the foundations of British culture**

2. Literature and philosophy

3. Art, architecture and design

4. Performing arts

5. Cinema, photography and fashion

6. Media and communications

7. Food and drink

8. Living culture: the state of modern Britain

1.3 Language and belonging

GB wrestles with its psyche, determined to define 'Britishness' with a perky little statement. It fails, of course – there are 60 million different theories to contend with. And yet certain common characteristics – not least the thriving, evolving language – do generate some fuzzy sense of national character and identity.

Text matches

Old English
Beowulf

Middle English
Chaucer's
Canterbury Tales

Early Modern English
King James Bible
Shakespeare

Word counts
As many as 4,300 words
of modern English derive
from Old English, 1,000
are from Old Norse and
10,000 are from Norman
French.

Where does English come from?
Like most strands of British culture, the national tongue has twisted this way and that across the centuries. The Romans didn't establish the English language. For that we look to the Angles and Saxons of north-west Germany. From the fifth century they deposited Old English, which, while largely unrecognisable compared to the modern version, established the fundamental bits of the language: *moon, woman, think* – that kind of stuff. Not many Old English words survive but those that do are the most used in the modern language. Subsequent centuries saw the tongue added to and adapted with Old Norse (thank you Vikings), Latin (good work missionary folk) and, in greatest measure, Old French (Normans take a bow). By the 12th century, this mangle of words had become Middle English. Three hundred years later the language changed again, this time moved by the 'Great Vowel Shift'. It began in the south east of England, where vowel sounds evolved and standardised, spread north and created the sounds of modern English. The shift may have been caused by a mass migration of people trying to flee the plague, modifying their accents as they went in order to be understood. It's worth remembering that while much of this was going on, Scotland, Wales, Ireland and Cornwall stuck to their ancient Celtic languages.

The four Celtic tongues of Britain

As English dug its claws into the lump of land that would become Britain, so the region's elderly Celtic languages were pushed to the margins. Four variants have just about survived to modern times, although the speakers of each are also fluent in English.

Welsh (Cymraeg)

Once spoken across the whole of southern Britain, today it claims about half a million speakers, two thirds of whom speak Welsh on a daily basis: admirable stats considering how rapidly the language declined in the 20th century. The farther north or west you go in Wales, the more Welsh speakers you find. Dialects change with location, with a rough divide between north and south. Welsh occupies a mandatory slot on the national curriculum and bilingual road signs are proudly erected nationwide; measures pushed forward by the Welsh Language Act of 1993 that gave Welsh home-turf parity with English for the first time in 450 years.

Scottish Gaelic (Gàdhlig)

Largely confined to the Highlands and Islands (particularly the Western Isles), where it's spoken by around 60,000 people, Scottish Gaelic is the remnant voice of a language that blanketed Scotland until the 12th century. Despite the Scottish Parliament's official recognition of the language in the Gaelic Language Act of 2005 and the use of bilingual road signs, Scottish Gaelic's long decline is starting to look terminal.

A nod to the Mod
Scottish Gaelic speakers let their hair down each October at the Royal National Mod (or Am Mòd Nàiseanta Rìoghail), a competitive festival of native music, dance, art and literature.

Saying goodbye to good day
In 2007 Vale of Glamorgan Council barred its telephone operators from answering the blower with a chirpy *bore da* (good morning). Union officials decided that making the largely English speaking telephonists use Welsh was straining their vocal chords and thus contravening health and safety regs.

Patagonian patter
Around 1,500 people in the Chubut Province of Patagonia in southern Argentina speak Welsh; They are the descendants of 153 migrants who made the crossing west in 1865 to establish a Welsh state with the Argentine Government's consent.

Cornish (Kernewek)

The plucky 3,000 or so West Country folk who bang the drum for Cornish have artificially resurrected the language – it hasn't been a working 'native' language since the 18th century. Only around 400 of the revivalists are fluent. In 2002 the British Government formally recognised Cornish as a minority language.

Irish (Gaeilge)

The Republic of Ireland has clung more successfully to the Gaelic Irish language than Northern Ireland, although survival in the north has been ensured by its symbolism, by its connection to a unified Ireland (Sinn Féin leader Gerry Adams apparently learned Irish whilst in prison). The Good Friday Agreement gave the language official status in Northern Ireland and initiated measures to promote it. Around ten per cent of the population now have some knowledge of Irish, specifically its strong Ulster dialect.

The great dialect divide

Given Britain's modest scale, and the fluidity with which its people move around, regional accents and dialects remain impressively diverse. Perhaps the biggest variation comes in England's north/south split. Conjure a rough dividing line north of London, reaching up to the Wash and down to the Severn Estuary, and either side of it the vowels diverge. To the north they're kept short; to the south, usually, they're longer. However, variations in local accents can be noticeable within a distance of ten miles.

Ah dinnae unnerstaun ye: Scots dialect

Scots, or Lallans (meaning 'Lowlands'), contains bits of Gaelic but derives largely from English. While Lallans reflects the old vernacular language of the Scottish lowlands, its evolution has been partly synthetic. Poets like Robert Burns, and later Hugh MacDiarmid in the Scottish Renaissance of the early 20th century, attempted to 'clean up' the Scottish tongue, establishing Scots. It's written as it sounds: words like out become 'oot' and work becomes 'wark'. Few people actually speak Lallans; today it's more of a literary form. Confusingly, much of mainland Scotland speaks Scottish Standard English, in theory closer to English than Lallans. However, get up to Aberdeen, where proximity to the Norse ports across the water has given the local accent a dense Scandinavian burr, and you'll do well to understand anything they're saying at all.

Mersey melting pot
The Scouse accent of Merseyside evolved in the late 19th century, born of Liverpool's dockside blur of Irish, Welsh, Scots and Lancastrian visitors. The word Scouse derives from lobscouse, a traditional Merseyside sailors' dish of stewed lamb and hardtack (a dry biscuit-related affair).

Dairy dialect
In 2006, language specialists identified regional differences in the way cows around the UK mooed, in particular noting the distinctive West Country drawl of Devon's bovine beauties. Similar claims have been made about frogs and birds.

Talking Scots in Ulster
Alongside English and Irish, both official languages, Northern Ireland also harbours the Ulster Scots language (also called Ullans, Scots-Irish or simply Scots among the local population). It's an Ulster-twanged variation on the Lowland Scots language, as carried over to Ireland by plantation settlers from Scotland in the 17th century. It has around 30,000 speakers in Northern Ireland, although the recently established (and Government funded) Ulster Scots Agency is working to extend its reach.

Exporting English

300 to 400 million people around the world speak English as a first language (over a billion have basic English).

The biggest chunk of first language English speakers, about 215 million, live in the USA.

English is an official language in more than 50 countries.

Talking in class

Britain's inky linguistic pool is clouded further by class. You can go pretty much anywhere and discover a well-heeled 'local' coughing up Received Pronunciation (RP) ('received' meaning accepted or approved). RP began as a regional accent of the south Midlands, but was in the right place at the right time when its patrons moved south to London in the late medieval period and grew wealthy. By the 19th century, the accent had become the oral hallmark of Britain's upper classes. RP is also sometimes referred to as Queen's English; go back 20 years and it was also called BBC English, a term no longer appropriate at the linguistically egalitarian Beeb. The changes on television reflect a wider shift in accents in the south-east of England, where the growth of Estuary English, in which the twang of Cockney meets the airs of RP, gives the burgeoning middle classes the feel of workaday credibility. Tony Blair, the common man, would occasionally slip into Estuary English (perhaps subconsciously) during his time as PM. Some analysts suggest that even the Queen has shifted toward the Estuary in recent years.

Begged, borrowed and stolen: the evolving language
The English language in Britain evolves constantly.
Foreign words have long been de rigueur (pilfered
most notably from the French), and today they're
absorbed from all over the place. In 2007, for example,
the word wiki found its way into the Oxford English
Dictionary, derived from a Hawaiian word meaning
quick but now applied to a certain type of Internet site.
The words irritainment (annoying TV) and bimbette (an
attractive but intellectually-challenged young woman)
were included among the same batch of new
additions.

Metaphor and simile are equally prone to rapid
evolution. The British love new, glib phrases (it's a
country where pretty much anything can go 'pear-
shaped', particularly when it's 'cheap as chips'),
repeated interminably for a couple of years until some
intangible social code decides they're 'past their sell-by
date'. Slang offers even greater linguistic opportunity.
Informal words come and go, sometimes limited to
certain regions, but some stalwarts of universal slang,
from skint (moneyless) to cakehole (mouth) to blower
(telephone), persist. Urban Britain is particularly
inventive, its multicultural streets generating a new
tongue for the 21st century with the unstoppable rise
of Jafaican. Despite the name, experts claim it's not
actually an affectation but a shift in language born
of multicultural mingling in post-war Britain, most
notably with the mix of Jamaican, West African and
Bangladeshi cultures. Such has been Jafaican's growth
that today you'll find youngsters from Tower Hamlets
to Torquay calling each other 'blud' and discussing
whether those 'skets' is 'butters'. *Daily Mail* readers
are no doubt aquiver.

1. Identity: the   2. Literature   3. Art, architecture   4. Performing   5. Cinema,   6. Media and   7. Food and drink   8. Living culture:
foundations   and philosophy   and design   arts   photography   communications   the state of
of British culture   and fashion   modern Britain

The great British identity crisis
In England the terms 'British' and 'English' are virtually interchangeable. Venture into Wales or Scotland, however, and any notion of British identity is soon shot down. Here they're Welsh or Scots, rarely British. Mistakenly calling someone English will induce a weary sigh, or worse. The old English hegemony over Celtic neighbours has fostered a strong sense of identity in the smaller nations. They happily display the Welsh dragon or the Scottish saltire, and the rest of the world admires their national pride. Doing the same in England with the cross of St George – or even the Union Jack with its whiff of old colonialism and, from the 1980s, its association with right-wing groups – can bring accusations of jingoism. In England, if pushed to consider their collective identity, people are perhaps as likely to think of a region as a nation. Cornwall, Yorkshire, the North East and the North West all have strong personalities, while the wider north/south split cuts a distinct, usually amicable divide. Urban Britain – London especially – can feel like a different country to pastoral areas, and some still define themselves in terms of 'town or country'.

The complexities of national identity deepen across the water in Northern Ireland. Ask a local their nationality and you'll get one of three answers: British, Irish or Northern Irish. The 'British' will almost certainly be Protestant (and therefore Unionist), the 'Irish' will probably be Catholic (Nationalist) and the small but growing minority that answer 'Northern Irish' may be either or neither faith but will, in the context of this part of the UK, be considered moderates and will probably be from younger generations.

There are exceptions. Some Catholics are Unionists, although far fewer than before the Troubles began in the 1960s; the violence and hatred of that period nailed ideas about national identity (of being Unionist or Nationalist) strongly to faith. Today, the violence has subsided, but the divisions haven't simply melted away. The issues of faith – and their strong connection to nationality – still dictate where people live, go to school or socialise, despite 'cross-community' initiatives. It's also worth noting that background and allegiances in Northern Ireland are sensed more than discussed; divined from names, clothing, school attended, football team supported. The question of faith, of which side of the fence you're on, isn't asked directly. (See section 8.2. for more on the sectarian divide in Northern Ireland.)

The grass is greener… Anyone born in Northern Ireland is entitled to take joint Republic of Ireland citizenship if they so desire.

Our song's better than yours
No one is quite sure who wrote *God Save the Queen*, the dirgeful (and still unofficial) British national anthem, although many point to Dr Henry Carey for the words and Thomas Arne for the tune. Scholars even suggest the music has French origins. First performed in 1745, there are six (often varying) verses in all. Few Brits can recite beyond the first, although Scots will happily direct you to the final (optional) couplet containing the "Rebellious Scots to crush" line. The Queen must be sick of it – it plays on royal occasions and when England (and in the Olympics, Britain) takes to the sports field. The Scots and the Welsh have their own anthems for most events: *Flower of Scotland*, by contemporary folk singer Roy Williamson, and *The Land of My Fathers* (*Mae Hen Wlad Fy Nhadau*), written in 1856 by Evan James and his son James James, are usually sung with more gusto than their English equivalent. In Northern Ireland, the choice of anthem is unsurprisingly contentious. State and sporting events use *God Save the Queen*, unless the team is playing one of the other home nations, when *A Londonderry Air* (also known as *Danny Boy*) is called upon. The united national rugby side has its own rousing, specially written song, *Ireland's Call*, but sometimes gets *Amhrán na bhFiann*, the Irish anthem, as well.

Superiority complex

Regional and national differences acknowledged,
where does Britain, as a country, see itself in the
global order? High up, is the short answer. It may lack
the territorial reach of old, and the days of industrial
supremacy are long gone, but Britain still considers
itself a world power. It's in the G8, is one of only five
permanent members of the UN Security Council,
positions itself as the USA's prime ally (some say
lapdog), still spends an awful lot on its armed forces
and retains its nuclear weapons. The average Brit is
aware of this primacy from childhood; they're raised
with a fuzzy, underlying awareness that being born
'British' is a fortunate state of affairs. Today, the mild
British sense of national superiority, of independence
at best and insularity at worst, emerges in a reluctance
to fully join the European party: to give up its currency
or 'give in to Brussels'.

What are the Brits actually like?

Of course there is no archetypal British personality,
no set character to which they all conform. The media
is convinced that there used to be, and discusses the
collapse of British values at length: boozed up, greedy,
oversexed, rude and thuggish – the country's going
to the dogs. Obviously, they exaggerate: the quiet
majority slip under the radar and the loud minority are
mistaken for the norm. While there is no consensus
on character, most Brits share some common ground.
Tolerance remains a key ingredient.

1. Identity: the   2. Literature   3. Art, architecture   4. Performing   5. Cinema,   6. Media and   7. Food and drink   8. Living culture:
foundations   and philosophy   and design   arts   photography   communications   the state of
of British culture   and fashion   modern Britain

The multi-dimensional nature of British society, with its mix of ethnicity, race and religion, speaks of its open-mindedness, as does the proportion (over three quarters) of first generation immigrants and their children who define themselves as 'British'.

In a similar vein, the British won't tolerate queue jumping, argue for hours about why they, not their companion, should pay for a round of drinks and have a weakness for the underdog. This sense of democracy, a quiet dignity (the old stiff upper lip) and the intolerance of corruption are perhaps best summed up by the rather woolly sense of 'fair play'. For all that, it's worth noting that open-mindedness, particularly where race is concerned, may ebb somewhat behind closed doors – public persona and private opinion in Britain (like anywhere else) don't always tally. Most Brits are still embarrassed by self-promotion (although bashfulness seems to subside as you travel north) and overt displays of emotion, hiding instead behind a cynical and self-depreciatory, yet rather smug, brand of humour. However, the stereotype of the uptight, repressed Brit no longer seems that valid; attitudes to sex and sexuality are liberal even while the intimate details are rarely discussed.

Jack and the dragon
The British flag, the Union Flag (or more commonly the Union Jack), its current design dating from 1801, represents the grouping of nations in the United Kingdom. Its 'Jack' name is thought to be nautical, ascribed to its positioning as a 'jack' flag on the bow of a ship. At present it features the crosses of St George (England), St Andrew (Scotland) and St Patrick (Ireland). But where's the Welsh dragon? In 2007, Wrexham MP Ian Lucas launched a campaign to cut Wales a piece of the action. "Let the debate begin," he called. "Let the rest of the world know that the iconic symbol of the United Kingdom may change and that the reason that it will change is that we have a new constitutional settlement that affords Wales its true place in the Union." "We'll think about it", was roughly the response.

An island of two halves

Britain has had a north/south identity split since the Industrial Revolution. It runs from somewhere near the Humber estuary across central England in a rough, disputed line down to the Bristol Channel. Wales, despite its southerly reaches, is 'northern'. On an obvious level the divide is about wealth: the south, with London as its guiding light, has always been richer than the north and its large industrial cities. But there's much more to it than that.

The split is about culture, psychology and language; it's about politics, drinking habits and humour; about southern fairies and northern monkeys. The north beams with pride at its working-class credibility, the south seems embarrassed by its easy ride. They're friendlier up north, more reserved in the south, or so the stereotypes say. These days the differences are usually played out with humour, through the intentionally patronising images of flat caps and whippets (north) or flash convertibles and cappuccinos (south).

Colourful characters: three British eccentrics

William Cavendish-Scott-Bentinck. A reclusive 19th century English aristocrat who did everything he could to stop people looking at him. Eccentricities included keeping a room full of green boxes, each containing a single brown wig, and constructing a 15-mile long maze of tunnels and rooms under his Nottinghamshire estate.

Quentin Crisp. Self-proclaimed Stately Homo of Britain who worked as a nude model, book designer and prostitute before finding late-life fame as an author in the 1970s. He would wander the streets of his adoptive home, New York, in mauve hair and a cravat. Once described England as a "merciless place".

Francis Henry Egerton. The 18th century Earl of Bridgewater, who did much to champion natural theology, was a patron of the arts and a member of the Royal Society, is also remembered as the man who threw dinner parties for his pet dogs. He dressed them up for the role, miniature shoes included.

2 Literature and philosophy

Robert Burns
Scotland's favourite son
(1759 – 1796)

2.1 Literature

If you're looking for the high achievers of British culture, the library shelves are a good place to start. Few nations boast such a rich literary tradition; an inheritance that runs from Chaucer through Dickens and on to McEwan, and which grows, taken as read, every year.

A 2007 Teletext poll concluded that *Vernon God Little* (2003), a blackly comic Booker winner by Australian author DBC Pierre, was the work of fiction that British readers were least likely to finish. One in three gave up on it before the end. *Harry Potter and the Goblet of Fire* (2000) came second; James Joyce's *Ulysses* (1922) was the third.

Best of British

Of all the arts, none has contributed more to Britain's cultural identity than literature. The last 200 years have been particularly bounteous. The novel, still relatively young as a literary device, relentlessly breeds great British writers. Scott, Austen, Dickens, Woolf, Orwell, McEwan: the list is long and rich. Of course, the roots of British literature lie much further back, in a poetic tradition that reaches from Chaucer through Milton and Burns and on to Motion, with language and style shaped by different eras. These days, verse has a limited audience, even while a number of excellent poets continue to publish. Consistently, throughout its journey, British literature has drawn on wide, exotic influences, from the Scandinavian lore of Anglo-Saxon poem *Beowulf* to the Caribbean thread of V.S. Naipaul's 20th century novels.

Geoffrey Chaucer (1343-1400) Father of Thomas Chaucer and some say, English Literature

What do the British read?

Despite the best efforts of TV and the pummelling schedules of modern life, Brits still regularly find time to reach for a good book. Perhaps a certain gulf remains between more 'literary' fiction and the popular novel; the former, while not stigmatised, finds fewer readers, although classic authors like Austen continue to sell well. Above all, the modern British reader is a creature of crime fiction and the homicide detective, from forensic scientist Kay Scarpetta, the creation of American author Patricia Cornwell, to Ian Rankin's hardboiled Scottish DI, John Rebus. Science fiction, fantasy and romance also move many, but nothing seems to rival the clamour for a good murder mystery. However, while the novel remains hugely popular, and the *Harry Potter* series outsold everything else in the first years of the 21st century, non-fiction usually sells in greater quantities. Autobiographies and cookbooks, both driven by celebrity 'authors', claim the biggest market share.

In the club
Bookworms have always gathered in literary circles, eager to pass criticism on any given title. However, the recent growth of book groups has been unprecedented. Hundreds of thousands of Brits now regularly gather in small clubs to dissect and appraise the latest novel. Chat show hosts Richard and Judy have been acknowledged as contributing to the boom, and their TV book club has had an undeniable impact on the bestsellers lists. Bookstore chains and even supermarket giants have tried to mirror the initiative, promoting certain titles in their own 'clubs'. Critics grumble about the homogenisation of literature, about readers being directed, unwitting, by corporations.

Reading habits: some stats

Today, two-thirds of British adults read books; three decades ago only half did.

Around half the population reads a minimum of five books a year. One in five read 20 or more.

Males aged between 16 and 24 are the least likely sector of society to read books.

A BBC RaW (Reading and Writing) survey in 2006 found that 69 percent of respondents considered reading a more important activity than sex.

Half of all Brits have a library card.

2.1.2 Well versed: Brit lit in the medieval era

Bede's Anglo-Saxon audience would have been tiny; clerics were about the only people who could read.

Caedmon follows his dreams

You might have heard how Paul McCartney dreamed *Yesterday*: he just woke up one day and there it was in his head. Something similar happened to Caedmon, the illiterate seventh century Whitby cowherd. He woke reciting the *Hymn of Creation*, an ode to God sung not in Latin but in the Englisc vernacular of the common Anglo-Saxons. It wasn't a one-off either; Caedmon gushed sacred verse until his death in 680. He's the first Old English poet whose work has made it to modern day. Most of the surviving literature from the Anglo-Saxon period was written instead in the missionaries' Latin. And the most famous Latin scribe – indeed, the one who devoted a whole chapter to Caedmon – was Bede, or the 'Venerable Bede' as he's known to generations of British schoolchildren. The most famous of Bede's 60 or so books, *Historia Ecclesiastica Gentis Anglorum* (*Ecclesiastical History of the English People*) (731), was an engaging, humanised – albeit Anglo-Saxon-centric – account of British history up to 730.

"THEY HAVE SEEN MY STRENGTH FOR THEMSELVES, HAVE WATCHED ME RISE FROM THE DARKNESS OF WAR, DRIPPING WITH MY ENEMIES' BLOOD."
Beowulf

Beowulf: an Old English epic

Old English was rarely committed to parchment, but brought to life instead by the great oral tradition, by bards who learned stories by rote. The poems, usually devoid of rhyme but packed with alliteration, were didactic affairs about heroic individuals, biting tragedy, faith and the vagaries of fate. The longest, most rewarding survivor is *Beowulf*. Set on the Baltic coast in the sixth century, it's an epic tale of monsters and dynasties, a violent introduction to the Scandinavian folk that would sail west and take up residence in Britain. Beowulf, the heroic, virtuous king of the Geats kills the monster Grendel and its mother, and later lays down his own life to quell a fire-breathing dragon. Whoever wrote it down in the tenth century had a remarkable talent for plot development, elegiac atmosphere and stirring tone.

1. Identity: the foundations of British culture **2. Literature and philosophy** *3. Art, architecture and design* *4. Performing arts* *5. Cinema, photography and fashion* *6. Media and communications* *7. Food and drink* *8. Living culture: the state of modern Britain*

Stirring stuff from Ulster

Across the Irish Sea, the storytellers of Ulster had their own epic. The *Ulaid Cycle* (or *Ulster Cycle*) told of Irish legends from the time of Christ. Recorded in Old and Middle Irish between the eighth and 11th centuries (and, unlike *Beowulf*, written largely in prose), the sagas swirled mystically around King Conchobar mac Nessa whose court in County Armagh rapidly filled with the body parts of defeated enemies. His nephew, Cú Chulainn, a bit like Achilles but without the heel issues or the suntan, provided the heroics. The *Ulaid Cycle* was greedily mined by Irish writers eager to establish a pre-British folklore for Ireland in the Gaelic Revival of the late 19th century. In particular, W.B. Yeats wrote plays and poems based on the legends, most famously for the cycle's great love tragedy, *Derdriu*.

Early Welsh war correspondents

Y Cynfeirdd, as early Welsh poetry is known, evolved from the seventh century onwards. As per the coverage of the Welsh language in the Anglo-Saxon period, the verse comes from northern England and southern Scotland as well as Wales. The Celts had similar literary preoccupations to the Anglo-Saxons – mysticism, loyalty and battles. Taliesin, a sixth century poet who used his verse to praise various kings, is a name that survives. Another is Aneirin, author of *Y Gododdin*, an epic recount of the Battle of Catraeth, a showdown between Celtic Britons and Anglo-Saxons.

In English please: literature in the Middle Ages

After the Normans arrived in Britain, their thriving literature usurped the Old English variety. As the language of intellect, French was used in poetry and prose, with Latin reserved for law-making, religion and the like. However, English fought back, resurfacing a

Dirge anyone?
Elegies were important to early English poetry. *The Exeter Book*, a manuscript of poetry copied in about 940, contains some of the best, most famously *The Wanderer* and *The Seafarer*, both short, mournful laments on the fleeting nature of life. The elegy would become a trusted friend to British poets in later centuries. W.H. Auden was directly inspired by *The Wanderer*, offering his own version in 1930. American Ezra Pound did the same for *The Seafarer* in 1912.

Old English, the new Latin
King Alfred was important to the emergence of Old English as a literary language. He steered the translation of historic Latin texts into English, notably Bede's *Ecclesiastical History*, even doing some of the translating himself. He also wrote poetry in the heroic tradition and oversaw the start of the *Anglo-Saxon Chronicle*, a record of English history maintained right through to the 12th century.

couple of centuries later as Middle English, tinged with French and Latin. With it came the first literature that modern day Brits can just about read. The so-called *romans*, French medieval love poems, found their Middle English variant, often shaped around Arthurian legend, while the traditions of heroic poetry found new subject matter as the Crusades set forth. Hagiographic literature was also produced in large quantities, as were biblical stories retold. The 14th century saw a revival of the alliterative poetry common to bards of the Old English era. John Gower took things forward in lengthy, moralising poems that played with syllables and couplets (octosyllabic couplets no less) in English, French and Latin; he often used morally corrupt characters to get his message across, as in *Confessio Amantis* (c.1386-93). His good friend Geoffrey Chaucer borrowed the technique for *The Canterbury Tales* (c.1387-1400). It's worth mentioning that the only people able to read all this literature moved in courtly circles; the masses didn't learn to read for another 500 years.

Five big literary works of Middle English

Piers Plowman (1367-70). William Langland's alliterative dreamy poem espoused piety, offering social commentary on the side.

Sir Gawain and the Green Knight (late 14th century). Influenced by the French *romans*, this anonymously penned Arthurian poem sees Gawain manfully battling temptations of the flesh and a virescent knight.

Pearl (c.1370). Pearl is all heavenly visions. The unknown author, distraught at the death of his two-year-old daughter, Pearl, decides to join her in Paradise.

The Canterbury Tales (c.1387-1400). More storytelling, but Chaucer's ragbag of characters broke new ground in characterisation and subtlety. For many, the founding work of modern English literature.

Le Morte d'Arthur (1470). Arthurian legend resurrected once more along French models but written in fine Middle English prose by Sir Thomas Malory.

The first great author of English lit

Geoffrey Chaucer was the first author to show how much the English language could achieve with literature. He wrote of love and its agonies in *Troilus and Criseyde* (c.1385), using the characterisation and scene-setting that later jumped off the pages of *The Canterbury Tales*. By the time he died in 1400, he'd been writing the unfinished *Tales* for 13 years. The stories, interrelated and written in rhyming couplets, drew on the London of Chaucer's era. Characters, backpacking dutifully from Southwark on their way to adulate Becket at Canterbury, were examined not simply for their piety (or lack of it) but also for their place in 14th century society. The tales – of the miller, the prioress, the knight and 21 others – would speak to contemporary readers with their habits, beliefs and earthy pleasures. Some were even painted with irony, even while moral judgements are left to the reader.

Lovely, oh, did I mention we'd cancelled the hogroast?

William Caxton (1415-1492)
Here he is delivering the very first wedding invitations

Chaucer hits the barrel
Edward III clearly liked Chaucer; he granted the poet a gallon of wine per day for life in reward of some unrecorded feat.

Press release
William Caxton introduced the printing press to Britain in 1476. He printed Chaucer's *The Canterbury Tales* and Malory's *Le Morte d'Arthur*, and helped speed the growth of English prose.

Three female authors of Middle English

Marie de France. She was French (it's in the name see) but lived most of her life in England, writing rhyming couplets in Anglo-Norman. Her major work was *Lais* (late 12th century), 12 Breton tales of courtly love.

Julian of Norwich. Julian was dying, aged 30, when a miraculous vision intervened and inspired a profound, perceptive volley on faith and, in particular, sin; *Sixteen Revelations of Divine Love* (c.1393) gathered her near-deathbed visions.

Margery Kempe. The wandering King's Lynn housewife (she travelled to Jerusalem, Rome and Poland) dictated her thoughts on life (she was illiterate), notably childbirth (she went through it 14 times) and wild lust. Read all about it in the *Book of Margery Kempe* (late 1430s). Some have called it the first autobiography in English.

Scottish makars and the Welsh Shakespeare

There's a paucity of surviving medieval text from Scotland. John Barbour's *The Brus* (1375), a long verse about King Robert Bruce, is the first major work. A similar effort on William Wallace (*The Actes and Deidis of the Illustre and Vallyeant Campioun Schir William Wallace*) (c.1460) came from the quill of Harry the Minstrel a century later. A group of professional poets in the royal Scottish court began writing in Scots in the second half of the 15th century, apparently inspired by *Kingis Quair* (c.1424), an allegorical *romans* poem sometimes ascribed to James I. In Scotland the court poets are known as the *makars*, in England as the Scottish Chaucerians. The term *makar* lives on in Scotland, given to the national poet as appointed by the Scottish Parliament.

In Wales the *Beirdd y Tywysogion* or Poets of the Princes wrote in the 12th and 13th centuries, gathered in a guild that performed for (and gushingly praised) the Welsh nobility. When the English Crown absorbed Welsh kingdoms in 1282, bards wrote instead for their lords, praising their military prowess, breeding and all round greatness, but also branching out into love and satire. They became known as the Poets of the Nobility or *Cywyddwyr* poets, named for the *cywydd* meter in their work. Dafydd ap Gwilym was the best. No doubt inspired by the French *romans*, he wrote about love, the natural world and the general stuff of mid 14th century life. He placed himself at the centre of his verse. In *Cywydd y Gal*, for example, he waxed lyrical about the properties of his own penis. The Welsh still regard him as their very own forerunner to Shakespeare.

1. Identity: the
foundations
of British culture

**2. Literature
and philosophy**

3. Art, architecture
and design

4. Performing
arts

5. Cinema,
photography
and fashion

6. Media and
communications

7. Food and drink

8. Living culture:
the state of
modern Britain

Britain chews on the Renaissance

Britain's Renaissance began a century after Italy's, and literature, not the visual arts, was the main beneficiary. The Reformation was key: as man's relationship with God evolved, creativity explored the changes. Writers pondered their own place in the grand scheme of things, weaving in the expressive humanism that was reviving the spirit of Antiquity on the Continent. Thomas More's *Utopia* (1516) explored these ideas in prose but the greatest literary advances came in poetry. Poets took up Chaucer's mantle using the sonnet, a 14-line verse form pioneered by early Italian Renaissance word mogul, Petrarch. English writers mimicked Petrarch's idealised love poetry and, as the 16th century grew old, wrapped classical allusions and contemporary concerns in increasingly innovative language. Sonnet writing in the Elizabethan and Jacobean era wasn't the preserve of 'authors' – writing poetry was evidence of your Renaissance Man/Woman credentials, so the likes of Walter Raleigh and even Queen Elizabeth herself had a go, while Shakespeare saw poems, not plays, as his path to acceptance among the literati.

Sir Thomas Wyatt, suspected lover of Anne Boleyn, introduced the Petrarchan sonnet to England in the early 16th century.

Super sonnet: three masters of the 14-liner

Philip Sydney. The exemplar Renaissance Man (knows his Classics, and loves, fights and dies heroically) wrote the first great home-grown sequence of Petrarchan sonnets, *Astrophel and Stella* (1580s), packed with imagery for the telling of unhappy love.

Edmund Spencer. Spencer's unfinished *The Faerie Queene* (1590-96), the most significant piece of Elizabethan poetry, mixed mysticism and a classical awareness with contemporary issues like religion, sexuality and politics. The title alluded to Elizabeth I.

William Shakespeare. His 154 sonnets exploring power and love used both the Petrarchan mode and a new verse arrangement introduced by Sydney. Shakespeare also wrote longer poems like *The Rape of Lucrece* (1594).

Prose in the Renaissance

While Renaissance prose was overshadowed by poetry, a few notables did emerge. They used the classical spirit of the era. John Lyly wrote *Euphues, The Anatomy of English Wit* (1578) a florid romantic treatise-cum-novel that gave England its first encounter with 'euphemism'. However, Francis Bacon was the major contributor. His thoroughly readable *Essays* (1597) chewed on the day's gristle, from revenge to gardening, forever questioning the established order. (See section 2.2. for more on Bacon.) Other Renaissance prose included 'behaviour' manuals for the aspiring gentleman, satirical pamphlets lampooning the clergy or conjuring low-life colour (so-called coney-catchers) and travel literature about the great explorers. The *King James Bible* (1611) was also significant as a triumph of translation and linguistic dexterity, finally confirming English, not Latin, as the language of British literature. The spread of English and the lack of a Lallans translation of the Bible stunted the spread of Scots as a literary language.

Not the Donne thing
Donne's poetry fell from favour within 30 years of his death in 1631, derided as uncouth. He remained neglected until the early 20th century when T.S. Eliot led a reappraisal of his talents. Some now view him as the most expressive of British pre-Romantic poets.

Name games
The metaphysical poets were labelled so by Samuel Johnson, a good century after most of them were dead. He intended the term as an insult.

"NO MAN IS AN ILAND, INTIRE OF IT SELFE."
John Donne,
Devotions upon Emergent Occasions (1623)

Brilliant conceits: the metaphysical poets

The sonnet was joined by something more challenging in the early 17th century when the metaphysical poets jumped in with a wordy, witty formula of elaborate imagery, using unconventional metaphor (the *conceit*, as it's known) to jolt the reader into some new, vivid realisation on man and his place in the world. The soul could be compared to a drop of dew, while the two legs of a compass are like husband and wife, sometimes separate but always joined. It didn't always make for easy reading, particularly when they messed around with rhythm. John Donne was the main man, employing the *conceit* to great effect in *Songs and Sonnets* (early 17th century), a collection of sensorial love poems that jarred with the conformity of most Elizabethan verse. Donne, who ended his years as dean of St Paul's Cathedral, also wrote emotive religious verse and amassed an influential collection of sermons. George Herbert, whose *The Temple: Sacred Poems and Private Ejaculations* (1633) revealed a talent for clever metaphor if not poem titles, was another metaphysical poet.

The King's men

By the time Charles I was king, poets were reining themselves in, reacting against the luxuriance of the Elizabethan bards and the intricacies of the metaphysical poets. In the royal court a small group of Cavalier Poets emerged, taking a restrained, classical but light approach to love and honour, as pioneered by the Jacobean playwright and poet, Ben Jonson. Robert Herrick, a vicar, was the prime mover among the Cavalier Poets, writing about the political strife of his time (Civil War was raging). "Gather ye rosebuds while ye may", he urged in *To the Virgins, to Make Much of Time* (1648).

The human touch: John Milton

England's Renaissance closed with the greatest poet of them all, John Milton. An unconventional Puritan, he wrote pamphlets slating the high clergy during the Commonwealth years and, most famously, *Areopagitica* (1644), an attack on censorship. He worked for Cromwell for a while, and even wrote about the import of beheading Charles I; choices that saw him briefly imprisoned after the Restoration. His poetry carried the humanist touch of an extensive Classical education. *Paradise Lost* (1667), all 12 books of it, was his masterpiece. As the name suggests, it explores Adam and Eve's transgression in the Garden of Eden and Satan's part (almost heroic under Milton's pen) in the whole sorry affair. Like Milton's subsequent poems, *Paradise Regained* (1671) and *Samson Agonistes* (1671), the work was written in blank verse. Milton's poetry was hugely influential, particularly among early 19th century Romantics; William Wordsworth exalted his talents while Mary Shelley kicked *Frankenstein* off with a quote from *Paradise Lost*.

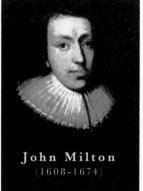

John Milton
(1608-1674)

Milton went blind in 1654. He dictated *Paradise Lost* to his third wife (the previous two died).

Classical restraint: literature in the Augustan Age

Milton was among the last to champion Renaissance values. Other writers in the Restoration period followed the neo-Classical spirit of restraint drifting over from France, replacing the free flamboyance of Donne and Spencer with moderation, rationale and taste along Greek and Latin lines. Observers drew parallels between Charles II and Emperor Augustus, basking in post-Republican calm, and duly dubbed it the start of Britain's Augustan Age, now deemed to stretch, with its appreciation of Ovid, Virgil and other Augustan writers, into the mid 18th century. It wasn't a golden literary age – drama shone brighter.

The three Restoration writers you should know about

John Dryden. Charles II's Poet Laureate was also a playwright and critic. He dived headlong into the satire of the Augustan Age, scything away at politicians or the Catholic Church with a clarity that few contemporaries matched. The allegorical *Absalom and Achitophel* (1681), commenting on Charles II's dealings with an errant son, was his best. The Restoration period has been called the Age of Dryden.

John Bunyan. Preacher man Bunyan wrote most of *The Pilgrim's Progress* (published in two parts, in 1678 and 84) in prison, serving time for bible thumping without a licence. It's a moral allegory about the path to heaven, the dreamy tale of Christian, a pilgrim who leaves his family in the City of Destruction and travels through Vanity Fair, the Valley of the Shadow of Death and other tourist hotspots on his way to the Celestial City. Written in a simple prose at odds with the Augustan Age, it was enormously popular. Its language and characters became part of the English lexicon.

John Wilmot. Wilmot, the Earl of Rochester, was like the Anti-Bunyan. His poetry drew on the metaphysicals, the Cavaliers and the Augustans, cooking them up in sexually liberated satire. He lampooned the social and moral stricture of the post-Renaissance age with impressive wit. Wilmot was sacked as a court poet when he wrote about the King's obsession with sex in *A Satyr on Charles II*. Partisan biographers said Wilmot was drunk for five years solid and discussed his religious conversion on a syphilitic deathbed, aged 33.

On good form: Pope and Johnson

The Augustan spirit reached its height in the first half of the 18th century led by poet Alexander Pope. Like Dryden a generation before, Pope translated the Greek classics, and then pushed the limits of poetry with technical skill. The *Rape of the Lock* (1712-14) fell into the mock-heroic genre, its verse about a chopped lock of hair expertly satirising the bumptious world of the drawing room. His critiques were perhaps more entertaining than his poems: *An Essay on Man* (1732-34) revealed a caustic wit. Literature's conservative, neo-Classical phase continued into the later 18th century under the guidance of Samuel Johnson – that's Dr Johnson to you. He fought the rising tide of Romanticism with Pope-like poetry but is best remembered for his *Dictionary of the English Language* (1755).

Bard boy Wilmot on film
The 2005 film *The Libertine* was based on the life of John Wilmot, Earl of Rochester. Johnny Depp stepped into the breeches. 'He didn't resist temptation. He pursued it', read the poster blurb.

Sam's log
Samuel Pepys, Clerk of the King's Ships, wasn't a literary figure as such but has become known for his *Diary*, kept between 1660 and 1669. The codified content was only deciphered in 1825. In the age of the Great Fire and the Great Plague he recorded the details of London life, from the streets to the royal court.

"There is nothing which has yet been contrived by man, by which so much happiness is produced as by a good tavern..."

Samuel Johnson (1709-1784)
Gentleman and scholar
of specific gravity

Keeping it rural: the Scottish poets

While England enjoyed its Augustan Age, Scottish writers carved a tradition of pastoral poetry that revived vernacular Scots literature in the mid 18th century. Allan Ramsay wrote poems and plays and gathered collections of old Scots verse, and later Robert Fergusson created poetry in the rustic mode, all excited about farming and, later, the street life of Edinburgh in *Auld Reekie* (1773). He committed suicide, aged 24, but Fergusson's pastoral style had done enough to have a profound effect on Robert Burns, usually recognised as Scotland's national poet.

Burns wrote in both Lallans Scots (see section 1.3.1.) and English (often within the same poem), bringing sublime imagery and a rare lyrical touch to his rural verse. He explored the grit of Scottish life in a way that Augustan sensibilities seemed to proscribe south of the border, while still enjoying the neo-Classical taste for satire. *Tam o' Shanter* (1791) told of a drunk Ayrshire farmer's encounter with a witches' coven, while *To a Mountain Daisy* (1786) laments a flower crushed beneath his plough. Burns also reworked old Scottish songs and ballads, most famously rejuvenating *Auld Lang Syne*. In Ulster they had their own Burns, a poet called James Orr. One of the Weaver Poets, a group of textile workers writing in the Ulster Scots language,

Robbie the playboy bard of farming
Scotland's Favourite Son, the Bard of Ayrshire, the Heaven-Taught Ploughman or just plain old Rabbie, was a bad farmer turned good poet. His first anthology of poetry, *Poems, Chiefly in the Scottish Dialect* (1786), would, he hoped, pay for emigration to Jamaica. It made him a star overnight and he stayed put, although his farm went out of business and he took a job instead as a taxman. Burns was a bit of a looker by all accounts (one of which was written by Walter Scott) and had a string of relationships that bore 15 children, only nine of whom were by his wife. His wicked humour and disdain for authority were well documented. He died in 1796, aged 37, from rheumatic heart disease.

JD Salinger's *Catcher in the Rye* took its title from a line by Robert Burns.

"THE BEST LAID SCHEMES O'MICE AN' MEN, GANG AFT AGLEY,"
wrote Burns in *To a Mouse* (1785), fed up about destroying a field mousenest while out ploughing.

72

Orr wrote of rural life in his native Ballycarry but also produced verse on the failed Irish Rebellion of 1798. He fled to America, fearing punishment for his own role in the uprising.

A first tryst with the novel

In the 18th century a growing upper middle class, in particular its female portion, declared its preferred literature to be the novel. Critics sneered. Only the explosion of the Romantic novel a century later brought prose fiction credibility among the literary old guard. The content of those early novels was sometimes exotic, but more often dealt with behavioural stuff, with a polite, urbane society that would have been readily recognised by readers and was befitting of Augustan Age protocol.

The three 18th century novels you should read

Robinson Crusoe (1719) Daniel Defoe. The eponymous traveller survives a shipwreck while transporting slaves and spends 28 years on a tropical island.

Clarissa (1747-48) Samuel Richardson. Richardson's disturbing epistolary novel on the duping of its heroine by a malevolent suitor explored the roles of the sexes.

The History of Tom Jones, a Foundling (1749) Henry Fielding. The picaresque tale of a cheeky, philandering young man in search of his true inheritance has a moral, neo-Classical conclusion.

"All women together, ought to let flowers fall upon the grave of Aphra Behn..."

Virginia Woolf

Early women novelists

Early British novels were enlivened by a raft of very good female authors. Aphra Behn, a former royal spy stationed in the Netherlands, wrote *Oroonoko* (1688), a daring indictment of the slave trade and the Christian colonisers, a good three decades before Defoe allegedly wrote the first English novel. She faced frequent accusations of immorality in relation to her writings for the theatre, charges related more to her sex and political leanings than any actual lewdness. Delarivière Manley faced similar prejudice. She wrote *The New Atlantis* (1709), a racy *roman à clef* that ripped into various high profile figures, most of them Whigs. Manley's bigamous marriage to her cousin probably didn't help limit the backlash, although the book sold very well. Later in the 18th century Fanny Burney scored a huge, initially anonymous hit with *Evelina* (1778), an epistolary novel of manners of the type that Jane Austen later made her own.

Enlightened times in Scotland

Scotland took a more active role in the 18th century Enlightenment than England. Indeed, the Scottish Enlightenment carries its own distinct identity. It was more about philosophy than literature (see section 2.2. for more), but a few notable tomes emerged, the *Encyclopedia Britannica* (1768-71) among them. Novelist Walter Scott caught the tail end of the Scottish Enlightenment but became more associated with the Romantic era (see section 2.1.4). The Enlightenment also bore Scotland's first big name novelist, Tobias Smollett, author of *The Expedition of Humphrey Clinker* (1771), a picaresque satire on the Union with England. Smollett would prove a big influence on Charles Dickens. Henry Mackenzie's *The Man of Feeling* (1771) was another important early Scottish novel.

74

Emotional times: the Romantic Age

If the Augustan Age discussed order, refinement and progress in muted tones, the Romantic Age cried out for disobedience. Literature, poetry especially, turned on the emotion, looking for the inconsistencies of individual expression that were getting lost in Britain's newly mechanised society. Writers saw the human soul represented in the natural world, questioned society and spoke for the common man. The 40 years from 1790 duly turned into a lustrous period for British literature.

"ALL THINGS EXIST IN THE HUMAN IMAGINATION ALONE."
William Blake

Two schools of thought: Romantic poets

The Romantic poets came in two waves. Both were initially inspired by the French Revolution and its implications for personal freedom, but soon became disenchanted with the realities of regime change across the Channel. The first wave cherished the individual, blurred reality, enjoyed the exotic and mystical and lauded the elemental, natural world. Some used the language of everyday life. The second generation were angrier, more cynical about the hierarchies that limited individual expression. And yet they also voiced great hope for the human soul and its capacity for love.

Romantic poets: the first wave

William Blake wrote illuminated poetry, brilliant in its symbolism. A first volume of verse, *Songs of Innocence* (1789), explored the joys of nature; a second, *Songs of Experience* (1794), returned darkly to the same poems (the French Revolution had just gone sour). Longer poems condemned tyranny, instead touting a mystical freedom of the human spirit. Blake, son of a stocking maker, eulogised today, wasn't appreciated in his own time, and scraped a living as an engraver.

William Wordsworth was more interested in the simple beauty of life. He drew a nebulous connection between the natural world and the human spirit. The path to understanding your own mind lay in the beauty of the world, from the clouds to the flowers. Everyday language and a focus on lowlife characters in poems like *The Old Cumberland Beggar* (1800) severed Wordsworth from the Augustan Age.

Two for the price of one *Lyrical Ballads* (1798) collected some of the best early work by Wordsworth and Coleridge. Initially ridiculed, today the volume is seen as the landmark early work of British Romanticism.

Samuel Taylor Coleridge. Where Wordsworth explored English beauty, his close friend Coleridge used more otherworldly settings. He didn't write much, but what he did was vivid and dreamlike. Early on he wrote *The Rime of the Ancient Mariner* (1798), a supernatural tale about an old sea dog who kills an albatross and suffers the consequent karma.

The punk poet Samuel Taylor Coleridge's best poems were done and dusted in three years, the period when he was closest to William Wordsworth. A clergyman's son, he dropped out of Jesus College, Cambridge, and joined the army to pay off drinking debts. As a young man he planned to found Pantisocracy, a utopian society in Pennsylvania, but it never happened. By his late 20s he was addicted to opium and his best poetry was behind him.

Romantic poets: the second wave

George Gordon, Lord Byron. The quintessential Romantic in word and deed, Byron raged against society's failings. The solitary heroes of his verse drifted moodily through the fractured world, weighed with guilt about some undisclosed misdeed. Childe Harold was the first, appearing in a series of *Pilgrimage* poems (1812-18). The unfinished *Don Juan* (1823) was Byron's best work, jabbing at hypocrisy and greed with its portrayal of the famous rake. Byron's influence was huge: Continental readers, in particular, relished his work.

Cutting louche
By the standards of any age, the sixth Lord Byron was a charismatic devil. He was always in the midst of some torrid affair, from the Greek boy of an early Mediterranean trip to the married women that caught his eye later on. He had a child by his wife, but soon tired of marriage and pursued a series of affairs. One spurned lover, Lady Caroline Lamb, who famously described Byron as "mad, bad and dangerous to know",

accused him of incest with his half sister. The scandal forced Byron to flee Britain in 1816 and he never returned. He joined the Greek struggle for independence from the Ottoman Empire, spending £4,000 of his own cash on refitting their navy, but died before he had the chance to fight.

I know what you did last summer
Byron, Shelley, Mary Wollstonecraft Godwin (soon to be Shelley's

wife) and another writer, John Polidori, spent the summer of 1816 together at the Villa Diodati on the shores of Lake Geneva. The creative vibes, encouraged by sullen weather and by Byron's suggestion that they all write a ghost story, bore Mary's *Frankenstein* and Polidori's *The Vampyre*, the first English portrayal of the naughty bloodsucker.

Live fast, die young

Keats died from tuberculosis in 1821, aged just 25, while living in a house next to Rome's Spanish Steps.

Shelley drowned when his schooner, *Don Juan*, sank in a storm off the Italian coast in 1822, aged 29. Conspiracy theories abound.

When **Byron** died from a fever, aged 36, in 1824, Westminster Abbey refused to inter the remains of a man with such a scandalous reputation.

Percy Bysshe Shelley was the most politicised of the later Romantic poets. Brilliantly attuned to the tensions of the age, he was a rebel with multiple causes. Family, faith, monarchy and meat (he was a veggie): it all stirred Shelley's bile. He was kicked out of Oxford for championing atheism. *Queen Mab* (1813) hammered the clergy and the *Mask of Anarchy* (1819) called the working class to revolution after the Peterloo Massacre of 1819.

John Keats. The most sensuous of the Romantic poets wrote long narrative verse, rich with imagery. He used the perceived romance of medieval and classical times to explore love and beauty. Keats' *Odes* talked of transience and contrasts – of how love emerges from pain, life from death and sadness from joy. *Ode to a Nightingale* (1819) and *Hyperion* (1818-19) were among the highlights of a tragically short career.

Read all about me
Autobiographies – or salacious personal accounts at least – became popular in the later Romantic period. The psychologically engrossing *Confessions of an English Opium Eater* by Thomas De Quincy, one of the best, did exactly what it said on the cover.

Novelists in the Romantic era

Novelists in the early 19th century weren't as distinctively Romantic as the poets. Walter Scott packed his stories with conflict and heroism and carried aspects of Romanticism but was more significant for his huge popularity than his involvement in the genre. The period also nurtured Gothic Romantic prose. Ann Radcliffe established the appeal of psychological dread in novels like *The Italian* (1797), and Mary Shelley took it to new heights with *Frankenstein* (1818).

One of the best-loved writers in British literature

J. Austen

(1775-1817)

Jane and Walter: the novel's first superstars

In many ways Jane Austen clashed with the prevailing Romantic spirit. She usually avoided the big issues of the day – war in Europe, the rights of man and all that – and observed, instead, the minutiae of life in a narrow band of rural society. Expert at characterisation and the psychology of relationships, she conveyed emotions that readers could (and still can) identify with. A young woman was always at the heart of the story. It began with *Sense and Sensibility* (1811) and ended with *Northanger Abbey* (1817), published posthumously.

Sir Walter Scott's novels came after a successful career writing narrative Romantic poetry. Unlike Austen, he didn't comment on contemporary society; he found his turmoil in the past, establishing the historical novel with his series of Waverley books, named after the first, *Waverley* (1814), about a turncoat English soldier in the Jacobite Rebellion. Scott also chose the Norman era (*Ivanhoe* (1819)) and the Edinburgh riots of 1736 (*The Heart of Midlothian* (1818)) for settings. His heroes were worldly wise, aware that life wasn't simply about trouncing the opposition and that big events impacted on small lives. Scott's novels made him the first living international star of literature.

Social services: Victorian literature

The flamboyance of Romantic literature was tempered by realism in the Victorian age, by the urge to deal more directly with the social issues of the day. With the novel in huge demand, authors turned their sights on the working classes. As the Victorian period wore on, the novel, echoing the timbre of the times, got darker, preoccupied increasingly with the seamier side of life and moral and social decay. Fiction became phenomenally popular. Novels, both good and bad, were devoured by the newly literate middle classes.

Books in bits
Victorian novels were often first published in monthly instalments, a trend started by Dickens. Serialisation made new work more affordable to more people.

Five(ish) Victorian novelists you should be reading

Charles Dickens. The pre-eminent Victorian novelist wove satire and caricature around serpentine plots. His 15 novels began with *The Pickwick Papers* (1837) and finished with *Our Mutual Friend* (1865), his style growing more sober and complex with age. Dickens picked at society's festering sores – in the workhouses, asylums and factories – tugging away at public scruples, but his prime talent was for characterisation. From the grotesque Fagin in *Oliver Twist* (1838) to the loveable Joe Gargery of *Great Expectations* (1861), his creations leap off the page, even now, 150 years on.

William Makepeace Thackeray. In Thackeray, Dickens had his closest rival. He too explored a form of realism and he too caricatured the upper middle class. Thackeray's writing also got darker as it matured. However, he highlighted social strife using a historical rather than contemporary setting, most famously in *Vanity Fair* (1847-48), set amid the Napoleonic Wars.

The Brontë sisters.

Dickens and Thackeray had a stab at the female psyche, but the sisters from Yorkshire really opened it up, even if they did have to

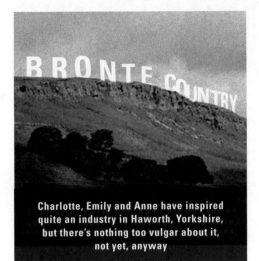

Charlotte, Emily and Anne have inspired quite an industry in Haworth, Yorkshire, but there's nothing too vulgar about it, not yet, anyway

adopt male pseudonyms to secure publication. Each of their best novels – *Jane Eyre* (Charlotte (1847)), *Wuthering Heights* (Emily (1847)) and *The Tenant of Wildfell Hall* (Anne (1848)) – recalled the Romantic tradition, with their love and despair, yet each also examined the realities of life.

George Eliot. No author picked the Victorian psyche apart quite like George Eliot (real name Mary Ann Evans). She wrote of provincial life, pushing realism forward with a rare grasp of human nature. *Adam Bede* (1859), *The Mill on the Floss* (1860) and *Middlemarch* (1871-72) all pitted the individual, their strengths, failings and hopes, against the expectations and actualities of society.

Thomas Hardy. The Dorset novelist came later in the Victorian era, bringing a new degree of naturalism to the novel. His starkly sketched characters, fighting the fickleness of class, gender and bad weather in deepest Wessex, were hostages to fate. *Tess of the D'Urbervilles* (1891) was Hardy distilled, its heartfelt study of an agrarian labourer enough to put anyone off love or farming for life. He gave up novels after critics called *Jude the Obscure* (1895) blasphemous and obscene, so damning was it of Victorian convention.

Dickens' voice of experience

Dickens was put to work in a London boot-blacking factory aged 12, pressed into service by his parents' dire financial straits. It didn't stop his father (whose spirit lived on as Mr Micawber in *David Copperfield*) being jailed for debt. Such beginnings informed Dickens' writing, although he apparently hated discussing his childhood. As a young man he worked as a journalist, submitting social sketches to *The Evening Chronicle* under the pseudonym Boz. From there he graduated to serialised stories. He and his wife, Catherine Hogarth, were never well suited, although they yielded ten children before going their separate ways. A mistress, the actress Ellen Ternan, took up the slack. Dickens cheated death in the Staplehurst rail crash of 1865, his being the only first-class carriage not to plunge off a bridge. He died of a stroke five years later. Dickens' appeal in his own lifetime eclipsed that of any previous author. And so it remains today; he's still regarded as the most popular of Britain's novelists.

They call him the Irish Dickens
Ulsterman William Carleton picked through even grimier subject matter than Dickens, relaying the details of rural life in 19th century Ireland, including the horrors of the Great Famine. Like Dickens, Carleton explored the human character to its dreadful depths and joyous heights. *The Black Prophet* (1847), published at the famine's height, was amongst his best.

First class Trollope
Novelist Anthony Trollope wrote around 3,000 words before breakfast each day and then went off to work for the Post Office. A man of many talents, he's credited with introducing the pillar box to Great Britain.

Victorian wonderland
While many Victorian authors tapped into society others did their best to avoid it, writing fantasy or adventure stories. Lewis Carroll was the most successful. The maths lecturer, real name Charles Lutwidge Dodgson, wrote *Alice's Adventures in Wonderland* (1865) and *Through the Looking Glass* (1872), ostensibly for children but carrying enough satire and verbal wit for the adult. They were John Lennon's favourite books.

Vanity Fair (1847-48) William Makepeace Thackeray. Orphan girl Becky Sharp pulls herself up the social ladder in Thackeray's satire on early 19th century England.

Wuthering Heights (1847) Emily Brontë. The most emotive of Victorian novels was an expertly structured maelstrom of love, anger and death. Stirring stuff.

Jane Eyre (1847) Charlotte Brontë. Jane negotiates a series of setbacks – fire, a mad wife locked in the attic and much more – to secure happiness with the dubious Mr Rochester.

Chronicles of Barsetshire (1855-1867) Anthony Trollope. A series of six novels set in the West Country with recurrent characters; the first great novel sequence of English lit.

Woman in White (1860) Wilkie Collins. Victorian Gothic horror par excellence, tinged with psychological realism and truly unpleasant baddies.

Great Expectations (1861) Charles Dickens. Humble Pip goes off to be a gentleman, but money and love aren't all he'd hoped for in one of Dickens' most twisting, didactic novels.

Middlemarch (1871-72) George Eliot. Multiple plots in a provincial Midlands town, linked by matrimonial strife and the constraints of class.

The Strange Case of Doctor Jekyll and Mr Hyde (1886) Robert Louis Stevenson. The dichotomy of good and evil masterfully coined in one hideous character.

Tess of the D'Urbervilles (1891) Thomas Hardy. The best of Hardy's rural realism: a clever but poor woman is wronged and marginalised by various sanctimonious men.

Dracula (1897) Bram Stoker. Irishman Stoker wrote bits of the chilling epistolary tale in Whitby, setting for the appalling Count's arrival in Britain in a box.

Mythology, depression and some gentle whipping: Victorian poetry

Victorian verse was a motley affair. Much of it fed off Romanticism, still pursuing that emotive, highly subjective worldview. But there was social conscience in there too, its lugubrious voice seeking out the real world more directly than the Romantics ever did. Other Victorian poets, notably Edward Lear and Lewis Carroll, wrote nonsense to great acclaim. Many of the era's prose authors got involved in poetry, Emily Brontë and Robert Louis Stevenson to name two.

Five Victorian poets you should have heard of

Alfred, Lord Tennyson. The titan of Victorian poetry played with the rhythm and sounds of words, creating dreamy, smooth verse. He borrowed the Romantics' imagery in long mournful monologues dealing with classical mythology and Arthurian legend, as in the *Idylls of the King* (1859-85). Tennyson's reputation nosedived after his death, although all agreed on the beauty of *In Memoriam A.H.H.* (1849), a haunting elegy to a dead friend.

Robert Browning. Browning took Tennyson's dramatic monologue to new intellectual heights. Using a range of characters (or 'masks'), Browning explored the darker side of human nature and society. *My Last Duchess* (1842), about a wife-murdering diplomat, was greedily received. Browning's style was deliberately clunky in comparison to the smooth intonation of Tennyson.

Elizabeth Barrett Browning. Better regarded by Victorians than her husband, Robert, Elizabeth poeticised the issues of the day and, particularly, how they affected women, but, like Mr B, used characters to mask her own voice. Her verse was often long; *Aurora Leigh* (1857), about a female author, has novel proportions. *Sonnets from the Portuguese* (1850) chronicled her love for Robert.

Matthew Arnold. Arnold has been seen as the bridge between Romanticism and Modernism. He took the disillusionment of the later Victorian age to new depths, notably in the beguiling *Dover Beach* (1867), a harsh reflection on the state of modern life, relieved only by his hope for love. Part of it was written on his honeymoon.

Algernon Swinburne. Caught up in the Aesthetic movement and learning from the French Symbolists, Swinburne gave late Victorian poetry a sensuality and verve that embraced sadomasochism, death and atheism, all wrapped in eloquent rhyme. The critics weren't happy. *Atalanta in Calydon* (1865) was his first big success.

In praise of Kipling
In 1907 poet, novelist and short story writer Rudyard Kipling became the first English language writer to win the Nobel Prize for Literature. He remains the youngest man to take the prize – he was 41. Kipling later rejected a knighthood and the Poet Laureate job.

In search of the new: Modernism

Writers in the early 1900s responded to the changing world. The old certainties of the universe seemed to have slipped: Darwin's *On the Origin of Species* (1859) was questioning the Old Testament, the cast-iron layers of society appeared suddenly fluid and Freud was poking around in the subconscious. It all contributed to the growth of Modernism and, in literature, to tireless innovation. British literature continued to flourish but most writers followed their own path, rarely beholden to any wider movement. Increasingly they turned inward, losing that confident, structured sense of the external world and dealing instead with the more personal experiences and emotions of the individual.

Five early 20th century novelists that stick in the memory

Rudyard Kipling. An Englishman born in Bombay, Kipling set his books during the Raj. Some have condemned his accounts of India under British rule as racist; others suggest he was being satirical. Most, however, are agreed on Kipling's gift for narrative. *The Jungle Books* (1894 and 95) and *Kim* (1901) were his best novels.

E.M. Forster. Forster's fluid prose framed England's failure to create colonial utopia in *A Passage to India* (1924). His earlier novels, *A Room with a View* (1908) and *Howards End* (1910), detailed clashes of a different kind, between protocol and abandon, materialism and spirituality.

A pocalypse XL

Marlon contemplates the horror of
the largest t-shirt
of his career

Joseph Conrad. A Polish émigré who took British citizenship, Conrad brought his experiences of travel to the novel, exploring how the individual copes (or doesn't) with pressure. *Nostromo* (1904) and the novella, *Heart of Darkness* (1902), its dark jungle mirroring the soul, were thoroughly Modernist.

D.H. Lawrence. Tired of modern life and its materialism, Lawrence, like Forster, sought out the elemental. Human relationships, snubbing the codes of class and gender, filled his best novels, *The Rainbow* (1915), *Women in Love* (1921) and *Lady Chatterley's Lover* 1928).

The horror. The horror. Joseph Conrad's *Heart of Darkness* follows a European sailor journeying into the African jungle to find the barbarised Mr Kurtz. The novella inspired Francis Ford Coppola's Vietnam War film, *Apocalypse Now* (1979).

Virginia Woolf. Woolf traded events and settings for the realm of the individual. She developed the avant-garde stream of consciousness technique: characters poured out inner thoughts (sometimes random, sometimes progressive) and generated a storyline of multiple parts. Sublime imagery bolstered novels like *Mrs Dalloway* (1925) and *To the Lighthouse* (1927).

'What a shining discourse on class'.
Oh, just read us the sexy bits...
Lady Chatterley's Lover, with its four-letter words and candid description of love between the aristocratic Constance and a lowly gamekeeper, was banned on publication in 1928. A well publicised trial in 1960 – E.M. Forster appeared as a witness for the defence – lifted the ban and the book was finally sent out to the shops. It sold out immediately, shifting 200,000 copies in one day. Within a year it had sold two million, outperforming the Bible.

"There shall be in that rich earth a richer dust concealed..."
The Soldier by Rupert Brooke

The father of sci-fi Woking's favourite ex-resident (his Martians landed near town in *The War of the Worlds*), H.G. Wells, wrote his science fiction novels at the tail end of the 19th century but their Modernist slant was more at home in the early decades of the 20th. *The Time Machine* (1895), *The Invisible Man* (1897) and *The War of the Worlds* (1898) – not bad for three years' work – were, of course, imaginative chunks of science fiction, but they also pre-empted the Modernists' urge to rip up the old order, visualising new worlds, however bleak.

The First World War poets

The First World War was sharply chronicled in poetry. It began well enough, with Rupert Brooke's *The Soldier* (1915) patriotically calling men to arms, but the mood blackened when Siegfried Sassoon, Robert Graves, Isaac Rosenberg and Wilfred Owen began writing about life in the trenches. Sassoon satirised the officers blithely sending thousands over the top in *The General* (1917), before Wilfred Owen, writing under Sassoon's tutelage in hospital, considered the wider futility of war in *Dulce et decorum est* (1917). Owen died in battle a week before the war's end.

"WHAT PASSING-BELLS FOR THESE WHO DIE AS CATTLE? ONLY THE MONSTROUS ANGER OF THE GUNS."
Anthem for Doomed Youth (1917), Wilfred Owen

Turn left at the 1930s: the Auden Group of poets

American-turned-Englishman T.S. Eliot dominated Modernism in early 20th century poetry. He expressed distaste for the industrialised world in *The Waste Land* (1922), using the symbolism of mythology in a hugely influential 'fragmented' poem that leapt wildly between settings and timeframes. A new generation of poets took Eliot's disenchantment forward in the 1930s, even if they didn't adopt his radical styling. The Great Depression and the rise of fascism gave them plenty to write about. Four (who earned the group nickname MacSpaunday) stood out:

W.H. Auden. He asked his audience to contemplate the times in which they lived; *Spain* (1937) pointed them in the direction of the Spanish Civil War, its implications and deeper questions of good and evil. In later life Auden took American citizenship and his elegant, fluid poetry swapped politics for religion.

Stephen Spender. Spender drew attention to the labour movement during the fiscal meltdown of the 1930s. In *Vienna* (1934) he threw the spotlight on a socialist uprising; in *The Pylons* (1933) he tries to comprehend the march of electricity across the landscape.

W H Auden (1907-1973)
Memorable Lines

Cecil Day-Lewis. Lewis, a Communist through parts of the 1930s (MI5 kept a file), began with calls for greater social conscience before turning to more traditional themes. He wrote crime novels under the pseudonym of Nicholas Blake to fund his poetry. Much later, in 1968, he was made Poet Laureate. His son, Daniel, would win two Oscars for acting.

Louis MacNeice. Socially aware yet the least politically defined of the 30s poets, MacNeice was born and raised in Northern Ireland. His poetry was witty, his gift lying in the meld of childhood images and a sense of foreboding. The short but lyrical *Snow* (1935) was his most popular poem. He also wrote radio plays for the BBC.

Potty mouthed poet
The Ilkley Literature Festival in Yorkshire has been going strong since 1973, when aging W.H. Auden was star speaker at the inaugural event. Auden didn't put on a stellar performance. Discovered in a cupboard clutching an empty bottle of whisky just before going on stage, he then read very quietly, refusing requests to speak up. Once the applause had died down at the reading's end he finally raised his voice to say: 'And now you can all fuck off'. With that he wandered off into the rainy night, apparently only stopping to tell a schoolboy with an autograph book to 'piss off'.

The great escapes
The Big Read survey conducted by the BBC in 2003 revealed J.R.R. Tolkien's *The Lord of the Rings* as the 'Nation's Best-loved Novel'. Third place fell to another, albeit more recent, fantasy trilogy, *His Dark Materials* (1995-2000) by Philip Pullman. Terry Pratchett, another contemporary author in the fantasy genre, has sold over 50 million books, the bulk of which have been in the amusing, satirical Discworld series. When Pratchett was diagnosed with early-onset Alzheimer's disease in 2007 he described the news as 'an embuggerance'.

Mid century mixed bag for the novel

Modernism never held a truly firm grip on the British novel. Instead, the mid 20th century (and the decades since) supported a wash of styles and themes. Some authors tackled political and social concerns, most plainly the rise of authoritarianism. Others, however, escaped to fantastical new worlds, like J.R.R. Tolkien in his sprawling trilogy *The Lord of the Rings* (1954-55). Belfast-born C.S. Lewis (the C.S. lengthens out to Clive Staples but he was known to friends as Jack) spent most of his time writing books on theology (he was an Oxford don), but found fame with a science fiction trilogy based around the travels of an English linguist to Mars and Venus. Lewis confirmed his renown with the *Chronicles of Narnia* (1950-56), a series of seven fantasy books, ostensibly ripping yarns for kids but containing a strong element of Christian allegory (which Lewis always claimed was secondary to the entertainment factor). Other writers followed the Victorian tradition and hoped merely to keep the pages turning; *Whisky Galore* (1947) by Scottish author Compton Mackenzie was a highpoint for popular literature. Daphne du Maurier (*Rebecca* (1938)), L.P. Hartley (*The Go-Between* (1953)) and P.G. Wodehouse (the *Jeeves* series (1919-74)) are all still widely read.

The three most influential novelists of the mid 20th century

Evelyn Waugh. Waugh was deeply influenced by his conversion to Catholicism in 1930. Prior to that he ridiculed high society and public school life expertly in *Decline and Fall* (1928); afterwards the posh, decadent Catholics of *Brideshead Revisited* (1945) were endearingly human and redemptive. In both periods his work pulsed with satire. Waugh also wrote war novels like *Men at Arms* (1952), inspired by his Second World War commando days.

George Orwell. No author communicated post-war paranoia better than the man born Eric Blair in India in 1903. The allegorical *Animal Farm* (1946) pondered the pitfalls of Stalinism using a clique of power hungry pigs, while *Nineteen Eighty-Four* (1949) commented more overtly on totalitarianism with its expertly coloured story of life with Big Brother and Newspeak.

Graham Greene. A Catholic like Waugh, Greene stuffed his novels with ethical paradoxes. His anti-heroes often seem close to salvation despite their flimsy morals; the first, Pinkie, central to Greene's formative novel, *Brighton Rock* (1938), was downright evil. Greene followed up with a series of thinking man's thrillers, each with its anxious, seedy setting and each with its stressed, morally lightweight protagonist. *The Power and the Glory* (1940) and *The Heart of the Matter* (1948) were amongst the best.

"IT WAS A BRIGHT COLD DAY IN APRIL, AND THE CLOCKS WERE STRIKING THIRTEEN."
Opening line of *Nineteen Eighty-Four*, George Orwell

The writer, the whirlpool and the one legged man
George Orwell wrote *Nineteen Eighty-Four* (1949) on Jura, an isle in the Inner Hebrides. He nearly died when his boat capsized crossing the island's treacherous Gulf of Corryvreckan, famous for its whirlpool. Orwell's brother-in-law, Bill Dunn, a farmer with one leg, smothered himself in sheep fat and became the first (and only) person to successfully swim the gulf...in 1984.

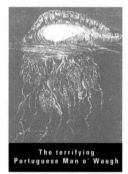

The terrifying
Portuguese Man o' Waugh

Waugh feels the burn
Evelyn Waugh's first big publishing success, *Decline and Fall*, recalled a short, unhappy career in teaching. He was sacked from one teaching job for trying to have his way with the school matron, while another posting pushed him to attempt suicide. Waugh's autobiography recorded how he swam out to sea in a bid to end it all but turned back after being stung by a jellyfish.

Larkin on top
A 2003 survey by the
Poetry Book Society
named Philip Larkin as
the nation's favourite poet.
It also revealed Larkin's
The Whitsun Weddings
(1964) as Britain's
favourite poem.

"ONE: I AM A
WELSHMAN;
TWO: I AM A
DRUNKARD;
THREE: I AM A
LOVER OF THE
HUMAN RACE,
ESPECIALLY OF
WOMEN."
Straight talking from
Dylan Thomas

Dylan on the juice
Dylan Thomas regularly
boasted of his capacity
for ingesting booze.
Apparently he was an
alcoholic from his teens
and a regular, not always
pleasant drunk presence
in Swansea's pubs. He
liked the notional lifestyle
of the romantic, plastered
poet. Alcohol is usually
blamed for his death,
aged 39, in New York, in
the midst of a reading
tour. However, one recent
biography concluded that
Thomas died not from
the drink but from a
physician's failure to
diagnose pneumonia,
instead prescribing a
lethal dose of morphine to
combat the DTs. Whatever
the truth, the official cause
of death was given as
chronic alcohol poisoning.

Post-war poetry fights the tide

British poetry isn't the force it once was. In fact verse,
the original voice of literature, has been steadily
declining in popularity for the last century. Blame has
been apportioned: the inaccessibility of Modernist poetry
in the early part of the century and the unstoppable rise
of the novel. However, a clutch of post-war poets have
achieved greatness:

Dylan Thomas was the first. After the experimental
Eliot and politicised Auden, Welshman Thomas
expressed the joy and sorrow of life and the natural
world with flamboyant metaphor. Lost innocence was
often a theme, his inspiration drawn from childhood.
Sometimes complex, almost surreal, but often pleasingly
simple, his verse struck a chord. *Do not go gentle into
that good night* (1951), written as his father lay dying,
was among his finest poems. (See section 4.2.3. for
more on Thomas.)

Philip Larkin, part of The Movement, a poetic collective
bored with highbrow lit, reacted against Dylan and
was dubbed anti-Romantic. Heavy with irony, his verse
offered a down-to-earth appraisal of modern life in
colloquial language but also tackled the big life issues,
namely love. *The Less Deceived* (1955), Larkin's second
collection of verse, cemented his reputation.

John Betjeman, at work from the 1930s to the 80s,
was almost as popular as Larkin. Like Larkin he brought
wit as well as an innate sorrow to nostalgic, accessible
poetry about the everyday stuff of life.

Ted Hughes, who succeeded Betjeman as Poet
Laureate in 1985, was less cosy. Collections like *Hawk
in the Rain* (1957) were about wild, unsentimental

1. Identity: the
foundations
of British culture

**2. Literature
and philosophy**

3. Art, architecture
and design

4. Performing
arts

5. Cinema,
photography
and fashion

6. Media and
communications

7. Food and drink

8. Living culture:
the state of
modern Britain

nature, selfish in its savagery. Later work, particularly the *Birthday Letters* (1988) that addressed his relationship with wife Sylvia Plath, whose suicide in 1963 many had blamed on Hughes, reached a wide audience.

Seamus Heaney, still writing today, is the most prestigious contemporary poet in the British Isles (from Northern Ireland, he became an Irish citizen in 1972). He began with rural Irish life in the collection *Death of a Naturalist* (1966) but moved on to write about the Troubles, albeit shot through with a mystical, Gaelic heritage, in the likes of *North* (1975). More recently, Heaney's translation of *Beowulf* (1999) was a bestseller. He was awarded the Nobel Prize for Literature in 1995.

...and six modern British poets you should know about

Roger McGough, one of the Liverpudlian 'pop poets' of the 1960s, remains popular for light, socially aware verse, even if highbrow critics are less moved.

Carol Ann Duffy writes of contemporary society with wit and accessibility. A recent collection, *Rapture* (2005), explores the progression of a love affair. Duffy's *Prayer* (1993) was recently voted the nation's second favourite poem.

Andrew Motion, the current Poet Laureate, is renowned for articulating destruction and loss. *Regime Change* (2003) voiced displeasure at the invasion of Iraq.

Paul Muldoon, from County Armagh, won a Pulitzer for *Moy Sand and Gravel* (2002), typical in its experiments with metre, its puns and visions of his homeland.

"ME? I THOUGHT, OBE ME? UP YOURS, I THOUGHT."
Benjamin Zephaniah, of Jamaican descent, told *The Guardian* newspaper about being honoured by the 'Empire'

The national poets
English monarchs have always had their appointed minstrels but Charles II was the first to officially install a Poet Laureate. The latest incumbent, Andrew Motion, is the first to have a set term of office, ten years, instead of a job for life. The Welsh created a similar post in 2005. The National Poet for Wales holds the job for one year; Gwyneth Lewis was the first, and made her mark with the massive inscription on the Wales Millennium Centre in Cardiff. In Scotland they have the Scots Makar, a term drawn from court poets of yore and applied since 2004 to the national poet, appointed for three years by the Scottish Parliament. Scotland's foremost contemporary poet, Edwin Morgan, was a shoo-in for a first go at the job.

A "BLOODY
DISASTER."
Doris Lessing on winning
the Nobel Prize for
Literature in 2007

Wendy Cope's witty observational verse has seen her mentioned alongside Larkin and Betjeman. A debut collection, *Making Cocoa for Kingsley Amis* (1986), sold bucketloads.

Dividing lines
Northern Irish novelists
in the later 20th century
were drawn inevitably –
but not exclusively –
to the themes of
sectarianism. Bernard
MacLaverty enjoyed
acclaim for books like
Cal (1983), a haunting
love story pushed and
pulled by the Troubles.
Before MacLaverty,
Brian Moore, a Belfast-
born novelist who spent
most of his adult life in
North America, dealt
with religious division
and alcoholism in *The
Lonely Passion of Judith
Hearne* (1955). But
Moore's oeuvre was
rangy; he also wrote the
screenplay for Alfred
Hitchcock's *Torn Curtain*,
an experience he hated,
likening it to 'washing
floors'.

Benjamin Zephaniah. A poet, novelist, singer and friend to Nelson Mandela, Zephaniah has chronicled the life of a black man in modern Britain with great insight and humour.

Post-war fiction: the ten writers to read first

Diversity has been the watchword of the post-war British novel. Amongst the deluge of fiction unleashed over the last 60 years much, of course, has fused itself to the concerns of its era. So, *Money: A Suicide Note* (1984) by Martin Amis speaks of 1980s greed and Irvine Welsh's *Trainspotting* of 1990s drug culture. However varied, any half decent précis of later 20th century British fiction should feature the following ten writers:

Kingsley Amis. Amis was associated with a movement of sorts: the Angry Young Men that criticised post-war society. His 'campus novel' (a genre set in universities) *Lucky Jim* (1954) unveiled a caustic talent for satire. Later, his treatment of a pensionable bunch of South Wales booze hounds, *The Old Devils* (1986), won the Booker Prize.

William Golding. For Golding it was all about human nature. Marooned kids in *Lord of the Flies* (1954) provided searing allegory for man's darker traits. He too won the Booker, for *Close Quarters* (1980), but also added the Nobel Prize for Literature in 1983.

Muriel Spark. Spark spent 50 years picking at society, darkly, wittily exploring good and evil. *The Prime of Miss Jean Brodie* (1953), about an eccentric Scottish schoolmistress, was disturbing and hugely popular.

1. Identity: the
foundations
of British culture

2. Literature
and philosophy

3. Art, architecture
and design

4. Performing
arts

5. Cinema,
photography
and fashion

6. Media and
communications

7. Food and drink

8. Living culture:
the state of
modern Britain

Doris Lessing. She broke through with *The Golden Notebook* (1962), innovatively structured and hailed a feminist classic, and later wrote science fiction, a move that bore the *Canopus in Argos* series (1979-83). Nobel came knocking in 2007.

Iris Murdoch. Murdoch, a philosophy lecturer, brought rigorous intellect to novels exploring love, morality and tragedy amid everyday life. *Under the Net* (1952), about a struggling author, was her first; *The Sea, the Sea* (1978) won the Booker.

John Le Carré. Britain's leading spy writer, real name David Cornwell, has intrigued with complex, flawed characters since his first big success, *The Spy Who Came in From the Cold* (1963). *The Constant Gardener* (2001), a thriller, confirmed he still had 'it' four decades later.

Beryl Bainbridge. Early on she mixed morbidity with humour in *The Bottle Factory Outing* (1974), based on her own early adulthood, and later turned to historical fiction with *The Birthday Boys* (1991), based on Scott's trip to Antarctica.

Anthony Burgess. Burgess went on a creative bender when he hit 40, generating everything from literary criticism to symphonies. *Earthly Powers* (1980), reading like a review of the 20th century, may have been his best novel but *A Clockwork Orange* (1962) became more famous after Kubrick's film.

V.S. Naipaul. Born in Trinidad of Indian origin and resident in Britain since the early 1950s, Naipaul is noted for technically brilliant outspoken novels on colonialism. *A House for Mr Biswas* (1961), about an anglicised Indian in the West Indies is considered his best. Has been knighted, Bookered and Nobelled.

Martin Amis. Kingsley's son, and heir to his brutal mockery, is loved and loathed in roughly equal measure. Martin broke through with *The Rachel Papers* (1973); *London Fields* (1989), set in a London faced with nuclear annihilation, also went down well.

Agatha Christie has sold roughly two billion (yes, two billion!) books. Only the Bible has clocked up more sales.

The magic touch
J.K. Rowling's *Harry Potter* novels have sold more than 400 million copies. Late in 2007, a handwritten Rowling book, *The Tales of Beedle the Bard*, sold at auction for £1.95 million.

What's the latest for the novel?

British fiction has maintained its variety into the 21st century. Drug culture, ethnicity, science fiction, fantasy, religion, crime, history: whatever your bag, someone will be writing it and writing it well. For sheer weight of books sold, no one of late has come close to J.K. Rowling, author of the Harry Potter series that held children and adults alike rapt until their conclusion in 2007 with *Harry Potter and the Deathly Hallows*. Other publishing success stories have burned more slowly; witness Louis de Bernières' *Captain Corelli's Mandolin* (1993), which showed how 'literature' could still find a wide, popular audience. Any list of great contemporary British writers will also feature (may even be topped by) Ian McEwan. He describes shocking life-changing incidents before dissecting the fallout in eloquent prose. Scottish author Iain Banks has carved a similarly peerless niche with imaginative, satirical anti-heroes, while countryman Irvine Welsh has waded through Scottish social murk in the likes of *Trainspotting* (1993). Zadie Smith (*White Teeth* (2000) and Monica Ali (*Brick Lane* (2003)) both explored multicultural London with brilliant, human stories. Others have poked around in history for their humanity: Pat Barker (*Regeneration Trilogy* (1991-95)) and Sebastian Faulks (*Birdsong* (1993)) used the First World War, while Sarah Waters plundered a seamy Victorian London for the crime novel *Fingersmith* (2002), connecting with a huge readership.

Three great British book prizes

The Man Booker Prize for Fiction. Britain's top book award includes authors from the UK, the Commonwealth and Ireland. Even getting on the shortlist will boost sales. The winner gets £50,000.

The Somerset Maugham Award. Initiated by Maugham in 1947, and awarded to an author under 35. The winner receives £6,000 to spend on foreign travel. Kingsley Amis (*Lucky Jim*) and John le Carré (*The Spy Who came in from the Cold*) both won it.

The Orange Broadband Prize for Fiction. Given solely to female authors since 1996; Helen Dunmore and Zadie Smith have both felt the benefit of the £30,000 cash award.

Five excellent 21st century novels

The Amber Spyglass (2000) Philip Pullman. Pullman's final instalment of *His Dark Materials*, the fantasy trilogy with an enormous popular following.

Atonement (2001) Ian McEwan. A teenage crush kick-starts a contemporary classic spanning seven decades.

The Curious Incident of the Dog in the Night-time (2004) Mark Haddon. The narrator, a child with Asperger's syndrome, investigates a canine homicide.

On Beauty (2005) Zadie Smith. Race, class and infidelity through the eyes of two conflicting families, written, Smith said, in homage to Forster's *Howards End*.

Labyrinth (2005) Kate Mosse. An adventure story that divides its time between modern day and Middle Ages France.

Keepy-Uppy with Jeremy Bentham

Bloody students

Bentham gets ahead

On Jeremy Bentham's death in 1832 his body, as dictated in his will, was dissected in front of his students. The head was shrunk and a wax replica placed atop his skeleton. This was dressed in his clothes and eventually put on display alongside the preserved head in a large glass fronted cabinet in University College London. And there it remains, although his real head had to be removed from the cabinet because of the inevitable student pranks.

2.2 Philosophy

Did you even know that Britain had a back catalogue of great thinkers? The likes of Hume, Bentham and Russell are strangers in most British households. Perhaps the French philosophers' guile with self-promotion has obscured the British talent for musing. It's a shame because there's much to ponder.

1. Identity: the foundations of British culture

2. Literature and philosophy

3. Art, architecture and design

4. Performing arts

5. Cinema, photography and fashion

6. Media and communications

7. Food and drink

8. Living culture: the state of modern Britain

Prime cuts: the
Francis Bacon story
Francis Bacon entered
Trinity College,
Cambridge, aged 12 and
was a regular in Queen
Elizabeth's court by 15.
He was knighted by
James I in 1603 and had
worked his way up to
Lord Chancellor by 1615.
Frequently in debt,
despite his stature,
Bacon was disgraced in
1621 after admitting to
corruption and spent the
rest of his life in the
lonely pursuit of study.
He didn't marry until
well into his 40s, tying
the knot with 14-year-
old Alice Barnham
after a three-year
engagement. Bacon died
of pneumonia in 1626,
aged 65, apparently
taken ill while stuffing
a chicken full of snow,
keen to investigate the
preservative effects
of cold.

The average Briton shows little appetite for abstract thought. The concept of 'philosophy' itself is remote to most – it feels irrelevant to real life, the preserve of dusty academics. Philosophy just isn't sexy. Perhaps the lack of strong British figures in contemporary philosophy is to blame. Yet there's much for the Brit to be proud of: go back over the last 500 years and you find the nation has produced cerebral giants, figures who shaped the Enlightenment, brought social reform and pushed civil liberties.

Science? Isn't that the devil's work?

If the French bow to Descartes as their paternal sage then Britain tugs the forelock for Francis Bacon. He was the first thinker to look much beyond the deductive Aristotle, turning instead to the inductive, empirical style that would become a consistent thread of British philosophy in the following centuries. Bacon demanded a methodical, scientific approach to life in an age when many still considered science heretical. He studied the world, working to establish a set of natural laws. And so Bacon's importance lay as much in devising a methodology for philosophy as for pushing any particular brand of thought. Indeed, he's often seen him as a key figure in the scientific revolution that shaped the modern era. His best work turned up in *The Advancement of Learning* (1605) and *Novum Organum* (1620).

Hobbes' choice: do you want a punch-up or a dictator?

Like Bacon, his one-time personal secretary Thomas Hobbes questioned religion. He pushed determinism, suggesting that man has the freedom to do as he pleases; that he determines his own fate, even if God, ultimately, is responsible for his creation. From this he inferred that all behaviour is based on self-interest, on survival. And this, he concluded, leads to interminable conflict (he was writing during the English Civil War period) unless we resign ourselves to the governance of some autocratic, unaccountable ruler (a compromise sometimes called Social Contract Theory). Hobbes duly proffered a secular state, dismissing the concept of rule by divine right. It all gushed forth in his major work of literature, *Leviathan* (1651), a book that saw him labelled the father of political philosophy.

Hobbes on tour
Hobbes went on several 'Grand Tours' around Europe in the early 17th century, meeting Galileo, René Descartes and Pierre Gassendi along the way.

You live and learn: Locke and the Empiricists

Bacon's inductive approach unfurled amid the wider growth of science – not least Isaac Newton's articulation of laws on gravity and motion – influencing the next generation of British philosophers in the 17th and 18th centuries. They became known as the Empiricists. Englishman John Locke was their first hero. Where Bacon, Hobbes and Newton envisaged laws of society and nature, Locke saw laws of knowledge. He proposed that everything we know, our 'ideas', aren't innate. Instead, they're acquired through experience, and that experience begins as sensory (what we see, touch etc) but is nurtured by reflection (what we come up with in our heads). This (in simplified form) is empiricism. Locke explained all in *An Essay Concerning Human Understanding* (1690). He also wrote anonymously but brilliantly on political theory, contradicting Hobbes with a progressive package of reason and tolerance, adding fuel to early Enlightenment fires and inspiring the likes of Swiss thinker Jean-Jacques Rousseau.

Northern lights: the Scottish Enlightenment

While England had Newton and Locke, Scotland had its own intelligentsia, an 18th century middle-class elite that featured writers (Robert Burns and Tobias Smollett), engineers (James Watt) and even geologists (James Hutton). The Scottish Enlightenment, as it became known, is also remembered for its philosophers. They were inspired by Francis Hutcheson, an Ulsterman working in Scotland, who was persuasive with his brand of moral philosophy, convinced that man could find the right path using an innate moral compass. The work of Hutcheson's disciples, squeezed into five decades from the 1740s, would have global repercussions, influencing the likes of Immanuel Kant and Karl Marx.

Three thinkers from the Scottish Enlightenment

"BEAUTY IS NO QUALITY IN THINGS THEMSELVES: IT EXISTS MERELY IN THE MIND WHICH CONTEMPLATES THEM."
David Hume

David Hume A generation after Locke came Edinburgh-born David Hume, posthumously recognised as the leading British philosopher of the 18th century, perhaps ever. He echoed Locke's Empiricist footfall, using the principles of empirical thought to open up the human mind. But for Hume, knowledge born of experience was unreliable. Habitual experiences and sensations lead us to predict or rationalise, to build 'causation', but genuine knowledge of what will actually occur in life is impossible. Hume conceded that we have to live by what we know of cause and effect (of what will probably happen), but a scepticism about the ability to actually prove anything underlay his philosophy. His moral philosophy talked a lot about perception: people are only as good or as evil as the individual perceives, and, taken to the extreme, the idea of the self (your own identity), the external world and God are subjective constructs.

1. Identity: the foundations of British culture
2. Literature and philosophy
3. Art, architecture and design
4. Performing arts
5. Cinema, photography and fashion
6. Media and communications
7. Food and drink
8. Living culture: the state of modern Britain

He laid most of it down in the three heavy volumes of *A Treatise of Human Nature* (1739-40), published to general disinterest in Britain but revisited later when Hume found fame in France as a key figure of the Enlightenment.

Adam Smith Smith was a polymath, better remembered today as an economist than as a philosopher. However, he was a close friend and ally to Hume, and began his progressive work with moral philosophy. In *The Theory of Moral Sentiments* (1759) he suggested people are guided in morality by an internal 'sympathy' for the emotions of others. He went on to write *The Wealth of Nations* (1776), a first recognition of the free market economy, fuel to Marxist fires and, many have said, the foundation of modern economics.

Thomas Reid Reid, a minister's son from Aberdeen, agreed with Hume that our ideas about life, self and the world are assumptive, based on reasoning that we can't actually prove. However, in conflict with Hume, his Common Sense school of thought decided that while we can't prove it through causation, the external world must exist as a concrete entity. It's there isn't it? We can see it, feel it and smell it. He made statements about the nature of life based on common sense: I am a conscious being; I have some control over my actions; nature follows certain predictable patterns. Read all about it in *An Inquiry into the Human Mind on the Principles of Common Sense*, published in 1764, the year he succeeded Adam Smith as Professor of Moral Philosophy at Glasgow University.

Revolution of words
While the French took up arms with their Revolution at the end of the 18th century, in Britain the forces of social and political change chose pen over sword. They bore some landmark texts, most notably Thomas Paine's *The Rights of Man* (1791) and Mary Wollstonecraft's *A Vindication of the Rights of Women* (1792). Wollstonecraft's husband, William Godwin, came up with the *Enquiry Concerning Political Justice* (1793).

Majority rules: Utilitarianism

David Hume's later moral philosophy explored utility, the idea that actions are useful if they serve the greater good and happiness of society. In the late 18th and early 19th centuries the Utilitarian movement pushed the principle. Two Englishmen, Jeremy Bentham and John Stuart Mill, got most involved. Bentham felt the pleasure of the individual to be dependent on the general happiness of society; so the best course of action in politics, economics or social reform is usually whatever pleases most people. In his *Introduction to the Principles of Morals and Legislation* (1789) he suggested that pleasures should be quantified, weighed up before the right action could be taken. Mill diverged from Bentham slightly. He decided that it was the type of pleasure, rather than the quantity, that should determine decisions. Many of the Utilitarian movement also fell within the bounds of the Philosophical Radicals, a group led by Bentham that successfully pushed for social and economic reform in Parliament.

It's all in the mind: the Brits do Idealism

In the late 19th and early 20th centuries British philosophy was strongly swayed by Idealism, the thought mode that proved so potent in Europe a century before, directed by the Germans Immanuel Kant and Georg Hegel. Idealism held that objects, places and time only exist when they're perceived. If you're not thinking about them, do they continue to exist? The name Idealism stems from this primacy for 'ideas' over physical realities. To some it sounded irrational, ungodly even, but it's a very hard philosophy to actually disprove. The British variant rejected,

1. Identity: the
foundations
of British culture

**2. Literature
and philosophy**

3. Art, architecture
and design

4. Performing
arts

5. Cinema,
photography
and fashion

6. Media and
communications

7. Food and drink

8. Living culture:
the state of
modern Britain

among other things, Utilitarianism. F.H. Bradley was the big noise. Like Hegel, he placed mind over matter, asserting that we can only be certain of reality and everything that comprises it – what he called the Absolute – if it is known to the mind; independently, reality, or any part of it, doesn't exist. *Appearance and Reality* (1893) explained all. J.M.E. McTaggart was more extreme in *The Nature of Experience* (1927), suggesting that the mind alone exists. Everything else – time, space, cheesecake – isn't real.

Analytical philosophy and the mighty atoms

British Idealism faltered in the first decades of the 20th century. Reputations, most notably Bradley's, were crushed by an emergent generation of analytical thinkers. A reappraisal and renewed understanding of language was central to their work and, they felt, crucial to the development of thought. Be very careful about how you express your thoughts, they said, because the simple grammar used can have a huge bearing on what you're actually saying, making it ambiguous or imprecise. Bertrand Russell led the pack, dismissing metaphysics in favour of a philosophy that reduced everything down to its simplest components. In *Principia Mathematica* (1910-13) he attempted (but didn't quite manage) to show how all mathematics could be expressed in formal, logical terms. Russell also pursued logical atomism, suggesting that the world can be broken down into a series of basic facts, or 'atoms', from which everything can be constructed. G.E. Moore was another British analytical philosopher of the same era, keen on promoting common sense in the methodology of philosophy.

"EVERYTHING IS VAGUE TO A DEGREE YOU DO NOT REALISE TILL YOU HAVE TRIED TO MAKE IT PRECISE."
Bertrand Russell

'Hey Russell, what are you rebelling against?' Waddya got? Bertrand Russell didn't lock himself away in academia. He got stuck into the 20th century, using his platform as a respected thinker and mathematician to lobby on humanitarian issues. In 1916 he was fined £110 and stripped of his Trinity College Fellowship for pacifism, but refused to pipe down and earned a six-month stretch in Brixton Prison two years later. Russell returned to prison for a week in 1961, aged 89, for stirring up the public at an anti-nuclear protest. He was soon back on his hobby horse, fulminating against the US role in the Vietnam War, Israeli aggression in the Middle East and human rights abuses in the Eastern Bloc. Other life achievements included meeting Lenin in 1920 (he wasn't overly impressed), winning the Nobel Prize for Literature in 1950 and surviving a plane crash that killed half the passengers on a flight to Norway in 1948.

In 1987 the elderly,
flimsily framed A.J. Ayer
met Mike Tyson at a
party. The story goes
that the boxer was
behaving deplorably
toward a young model,
Naomi Campbell, when
Ayer stepped in and told
him to desist. "Do you
know who the fuck I am?
I'm the heavyweight
champion of the world,"
offered Tyson. "And I,"
responded Ayer,
"am the former
Wykeham Professor of
Logic. We are both pre-
eminent in our field. I
suggest we talk about
this like rational men."
And apparently they did.

Three 20th century philosophers to chew on

A.J. Ayer Bertrand Russell's analytic philosophy travelled abroad, shaped the so-called Vienna Circle of thinkers and then returned to Britain in the shape of logical positivism under the guidance of A.J. Ayer. He published *Language, Truth and Logic* (1936) at the age of 26, exploring the idea that philosophical problems are only meaningful if they can be solved by logical analysis. And so he attacked entire genres of thought like metaphysics and theology, and continued to do so through much of the 20th century.

Karl Popper An Austrian who took British nationality after fleeing the Nazis, Popper pushed his falsification theory. Preoccupied particularly with science, he argued that hypotheses could and should be falsified by simple observation; it only takes one contradiction to prove something wrong, but infinite agreements to prove it right. He was also renowned for work criticising totalitarianism, voiced in *The Open Society and Its Enemies* (1945).

Isaiah Berlin Berlin, a Latvian Jew, came to London with his family as a child in 1921. Friend and rival to A.J. Ayer, he became known for his *Two Concepts of Liberty* (1959), a theory that revived British political philosophy with its distinction between negative and positive liberty. He pursued myriad lines of enquiry like a good pluralist, but the call for tolerance, for liberty, was a common factor, always coloured by the tumultuous century in which he lived. Later Berlin developed value pluralism, the concept that different values can conflict with each other yet still have equal validity.

1. Identity: the
foundations
of British culture

2. **Literature
and philosophy**

3. Art, architecture
and design

4. Performing
arts

5. Cinema,
photography
and fashion

6. Media and
communications

7. Food and drink

8. Living culture:
the state of
modern Britain

1. Identity: the
foundations
of British culture

**2. Literature
and philosophy**

3. Art, architecture
and design

4. Performing
arts

5. Cinema,
photography
and fashion

6. Media and
communications

7. Food and drink

8. Living culture:
the state of
modern Britain

3 Art, architecture and design

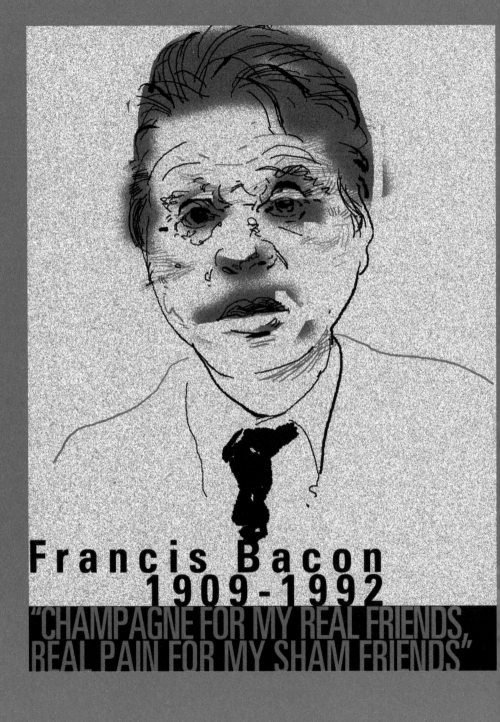

Francis Bacon
1909-1992
"CHAMPAGNE FOR MY REAL FRIENDS,
REAL PAIN FOR MY SHAM FRIENDS"

3.1 Art and design

British art has often been undervalued, labelled as conservative or imitative. True, it was a slow starter, but talk of underachievement, about isolated, solitary artists, is exaggerated. In Turner and Constable we find the first modern artists no less, while contemporary British art, with its knack for conceptualisation, is in fine fettle.

3.1.1 Foreign aid: the early personnel of painting

The primitives

They might not have hung it over the fireplace in a frame, but the Bronze Age Beaker People nevertheless made some of the first British art. They decorated ceramics and made ornaments from gold, silver and copper, rendering simple designs of horizontal bands. Often they buried their best work with the dead. Celtic art, produced around Britain from 500BC, was more sophisticated; its swirling curvaceous patterns in stone and metal were abstract – even cryptic – rather than figurative. Celtic art remained an important strand of British culture throughout the Middle Ages, particularly in Scotland and Ireland, making the transition to illuminated manuscripts in the seventh century and accruing elements of Christianity and Scandinavian design along the way. Texts like the *Lindisfarne Gospels* (c.715) established a tradition of Insular Art, a post-Roman style that blended Anglo-Saxon colour and animal forms with Celtic (in particular Irish) motifs in a manner largely unique to the British Isles. As for the Romans, they brought their figurative Classicism but little survives in Britain bar the odd bust and mosaic.

Begged, borrowed and stolen: medieval art

Little of the above can be described as truly native. Celts, Romans, Saxons – they all brought their skills from abroad, even if designs took new directions in Britain. The borrowing continued with the Normans. Romanesque (12th century) and then Gothic (13th and 14th centuries) both originated across the Channel. When religious art collided with Anglo-Saxon forms a recognisable English Romanesque style emerged, all thick black lines, blocks of solid colour and exaggerated, abstract figures. Monasteries did all the

---

British art: the key dates

1395 The Wilton Diptych shows how great British religious art was before Henry VIII got involved.

1632 Anthony van Dyck arrives in Britain and paints the aristocracy very well indeed.

1732 The first great British name of art, William Hogarth, creates *A Rake's Progress*.

1768 Portraitist Joshua Reynolds is the first president of the Royal Academy of Arts.

1821 The first great age of British art finds John Constable painting *The Hay Wain*.

1834 J.M.W. Turner paints the Houses of Parliament as they burn. Was it the birth of modern art?

1848 The pre-Raphaelite Brotherhood of Painters set up their easels.

1945 Francis Bacon makes the first of his distinctive animalistic paintings.

1992 Damien Hirst's dead shark steals the Young British Artists' first show.

1. Identity: the foundations of British culture 2. Literature and philosophy **3. Art, architecture and design** 4. Performing arts 5. Cinema, photography and fashion 6. Media and communications 7. Food and drink 8. Living culture: the state of modern Britain

hard work. Teams of professional artists worked on illuminated manuscripts with richly coloured 'carpet' pages, while carved ivory and sculptural detail on the grand churches of the age offered artists greater room for expression.

Gothic evolved from Romanesque, advancing the role of naturalism in art; the figures looked increasingly like real people, their gowns like real cloth. The highpoint of English Gothic art has traditionally been seen as the Wilton Diptych (c.1395-99). As per the International Style of later Gothic painting, this two-piece marvel was daubed in tempera on wooden panels, painted as a mobile altar piece. Delicate and colourful, the panels' beauty is undimmed six centuries on. King Richard II kneels humbly before Paradise with its insouciant, strawberry blond angels. An English masterpiece no doubt, although experts now concede it may have been painted by a French artist. Today it hangs in the National Gallery.

Oh Henry, what have you gone and done?

When Henry VIII fell out with the Catholic Church and pulled the plug on the monasteries, he sabotaged the driving monetary and spiritual forces of British art. Popish idolatry was now strictly off the menu, and the royal court took over from the Church as the prime creative arena. The distant European Renaissance remained just that – distant – and for the next 200 years native art struggled for direction. The important painters working in Britain were foreigners, many pushed across the Channel by the Reformation in Europe. Each inspired a clique of British hopefuls, none of whom quite matched their masters' verve.

Well the ears are definitely van Dyck... By the time Antonis van Dyck had become Sir Anthony van Dyck, ennobled by Charles I, he was a very busy man. The commissions flooded in from the English aristocracy, eager to mine the artist's talent for painting a sitter with stately dignity. He took on a number of assistants who would paint the less crucial parts of a portrait from dressed dummies. He didn't even always paint all of the head. Many have argued that he cheapened the portraitist's art in the process, particularly as subsequent artists followed his example.

Two foreign giants of early modern British art... and their flunkies

Less is ...
Minimalist sketch of
Sir Thomas More
(1478-1535)

Hans Holbein the Younger. He came to England from Basel on the Rhine and stayed for more than a decade, becoming court painter to Henry VIII in 1536. Besides supplying portraits of prospective brides for Henry, Holbein generated the thick-necked image of the King that made it through to modern times, although his portrait of the stubbly, bob-haired chancellor Thomas More (1527) is perhaps better known. Holbein was lauded for his detailed, muted rendering of personality, greatly influencing the first really important English painter, Nicholas Hilliard. Hilliard painted Elizabeth I and her clique from the 1570s, specialising in the miniature portrait. Hilliard's pupil, Isaac Oliver maintained the fine English miniature tradition into the early 17th century.

Anthony van Dyck. Portraiture remained the art of choice under the Stuarts, but was shaken up by Flemish artist van Dyck. His portraits were expressive, suggestive of personality even when their mood seemed slightly glum. His work shimmers in a manner not dissimilar to that of his great teacher, Peter Paul Rubens. Van Dyck became court painter to Charles I in 1632 and his style, so good at flattering royalty, inevitably faltered under Cromwell. Sir Peter Lely, a Dutchman, carried van Dyck's legacy after the Restoration, developing the master's style with a rich texture as court painter to Charles II. Lely's series of listless ladies, the *Windsor Beauties* (early to mid 1660s), were typical.

Early modern sculpture

Like painting, sculpture in Britain relied on foreigners for most of its excitement before the 18th century. Anonymous British artists had been sculpting tombs since the Middle Ages, but their work bore little invention. Florentine Pietro Torrigiano was the first big foreign name, although his rich golden sarcophagus for Henry VII (1512), still in Westminster Abbey, failed to push its Renaissance style out to the rest of British art. Grinling Gibbons, an exceptionally gifted woodcarver employed by Sir Christopher Wren to work on St Paul's Cathedral in the 17th century, had an English father but was actually Dutch. By the 18th century, a Frenchman, Louis François Roubiliac, was stealing the show with dramatic Baroque busts that turned up in various English churches, not least Westminster Abbey.

Pietro packs a punch
Pietro Torrigiano, perhaps the most skilled sculptor working in 16th century Britain, was famous back in Italy for breaking Michelangelo's nose in an art school bust up.

Small wonders
The painter of miniatures, or limner, was in great demand in the Elizabethan period. It was a tradition that drifted over from the Low Countries but in England produced its own master, Nicolas Hilliard. Another Brit, Samuel Cooper, took over his mantle in the Stuart era. The miniatures were often commissioned by ruff-wearing dandies, who would have themselves painted full length, tights and all, looking all moody and lovelorn. They would then send the results to the lucky object of their affection; in the manner of a really egotistical, needy Valentine's Card.

Roses are red,
Violets are blue.
Don't I look lovely?
I'm too good
For you...

World, this is Britain calling… look at my lovely painting
Finally, in the 18th century, British art began growing
its own. Collectors were used to paying out on work
by the foreign artists of the day, but in the mid 18th
century they began to buy British (it was still much
cheaper), encouraged by the appearance of
homegrown art in public spaces and the founding of
the Royal Academy of Arts in 1768, which finally gave
artists a classical training of the sort taken for granted
in France and Italy. Momentum grew, initially in
portraiture and later in the new favourite genre,
landscape. As Gainsborough, Turner, Constable and
others emerged, the world began paying attention to
British art.

William Hogarth
(1697 – 1764)

Hogarth on the offensive
William Hogarth was the first really big name.
A law unto himself, he ignored the prevailing
appetite for portraiture. Instead, he engraved
and then painted edifying scenes of political
corruption and social strife. His most famous
were *A Rake's Progress* (1732-33), a series of
paintings framing the unhappy fate of a
morally bankrupt merchant's son. The artist
convinced himself that this was what a
British audience would respond to, what they
would buy: they needed art with a moral
message. Hogarth, who also painted more
standard portraits and family scenes, packed
his work with colour and character yet, pigeonholed as
an engraver, failed to earn the respect of his peers.

1. Identity: the   2. Literature   3. Art, architecture   4. Performing   5. Cinema,   6. Media and   7. Food and drink   8. Living culture:
foundations   and philosophy   and design   arts   photography   communications   the state of
of British culture   and fashion   modern Britain

Face value: the golden years of British portrait painting

The century after 1750 was the great age of British portraiture. England and Scotland both produced a number of significant practitioners, most following the mode set by the leading portraitist of the age, Joshua Reynolds. The timing was just right, with Britain's growing upper class clamouring for the kudos that a stately portrait stirs. As for the artists, most would probably have preferred painting something more interesting, but the money in portraiture wasn't half bad. By the time the last great portrait painter of the age, Thomas Lawrence, put down his brush in 1830, British artists were beginning to impress in Europe.

The big three portrait painters of the 18th century

Joshua Reynolds, the genteel Devonian, travelled to Italy as a young man in 1749 and the Renaissance rubbed off. He began painting sitters in a dramatic, almost mythological light, echoing the lofty 'Grand Manner' of Raphael, Titian et al. At odds with the scruffier style of Hogarth a generation before, it set the trend for 18th century British portraiture. He tried to capture something of the sitter's character, their interests or their career through setting, expression or the objects at hand (from dogs to archery bows). It's this rendering of personality, rather than a knockout talent with the brush, which impresses with Reynolds. He retired in 1789, aged 66, when he went blind in one eye.

Thomas Gainsborough was Reynolds' great rival. While Reynolds' portraits were stage managed for drama, Gainsborough's were light, graceful and real. Largely self-taught, he was a natural, expertly

The man of a thousand horses

George Stubbs occupies his own niche in British art history, renowned as the artist who painted horses. He made hay out of the fact that getting a horse in your own portrait attested to wealth in the later 18th century, although also managed to produce a number of oils with equine content alone. Stubbs spent much of his early adulthood dissecting animals, eventually publishing *The Anatomy of the Horse* (1766) to wide acclaim. His horses were painted out hunting, mingling with their owners or being devoured by lions; in short, if it neighed, out came the easel. In the likes of *Whistlejacket* (1762) he painted champion racehorses.

rendering flesh and cloth with animated brushstrokes. Landscapes crept into his portraits revealing a joy at painting nature. And while painting faces paid the bills, when he got the chance Gainsborough sketched elegantly composed (and, in truth, rather unrealistic) rural scenes.

Allan Ramsay predated Reynolds and Gainsborough by a decade, one of various talented artists wrapped up in the Scottish Enlightenment. More in the Reynolds mould, he too travelled to Italy and painted with similarly grand solidity, although like Gainsborough he had a knack for shimmering cloth. Appointed Royal Painter by George III in 1761, Ramsay gave up painting for writing in 1773 after he fell off a ladder and hurt his right arm.

A brush with the classics Scottish painter Gavin Hamilton was the leading British artist of neo-Classicism, a genre that left most British art cold whilst it was being received with rapture in early 19th century France. Yorkshireman John Flaxman was another neo-Classicist; an Academy man through and through, he was best known as a sculptor. Both artists perfected their craft in Rome.

And the award for the best painting of a bird in an air pump goes to... Joseph Wright of Derby was an important 18th century portraitist, recording the great Midlands industrialists of his era. But he did much more than just faces. In the 1760s he began painting his 'Candlelit Pictures', naturalistic interior scenes brilliant in their use of chiaroscuro.

His best effort was *An Experiment on a Bird in the Air Pump* (1768), subject matter that also betrayed Wright's fascination with the scientific advances of the Enlightenment. Later, after a fruitful trip to Italy (Vesuvius obligingly erupted while he sketched), Wright set about painting landscapes.

The Romantic British masters

As the 19th century dawned the attendant Romantic spirit, so bountiful in literature, dished up a creative windfall for landscape artists. Painting a rural scene hadn't been deemed credible art before but the elemental mood of Romanticism legitimised the study of nature. Watercolour, a relatively new medium quickly completed in situ, lent the genre a hand. Through landscape, for the first time the viewer really got to see what the British artist was feeling as much as seeing. In short, it was the beginning of modern art. A Welshman, Richard Wilson, was the first Brit to concentrate on landscape, although he approached the subject in a precise, rather emotionless way. However, he had some influence on the two artists that would dominate the period. Both, variously, have been called the most important painter in British history:

John Constable wanted to paint his native Dedham Vale with truth, to convey how changes of light, weather or season affected the view. An inheritance from his father, a wealthy mill owner, allowed him to do so without ever actually selling a landscape painting. He sketched in summer and then spent winters in London, completing large, studied oils from those freer, impressionistic prelims. Today his paintings might bring docile pastoral bliss to mind but in their day, with their dabs and flecks and their modest subject made grand, they were radical. In Britain his loose brushstrokes got a mixed reception; it was the French who really went for Constable, and who, via the art of Eugène Delacroix and later the Impressionists, secured his posthumous fame.

Big in France
The Hay Wain (1821), a watery Suffolk scene like most of his best paintings, won Constable the Gold Medal when it was shown at the 1824 Paris Salon. The artist himself never actually made it across the Channel.

Constable referred to the flecks of white that covered his canvases in his later career as 'my snow', used to express movement, light and feeling.

Turner's twin
Later in life, hounded by scathing critics, Turner invented an alter ego, an identity into which he could escape in life and paint. His concocted conjoined twin, Admiral Puggy Booth, was free to work as outlandishly as his name might demand. Turner spent his final years as Booth, living incognito in Chelsea.

Joseph Mallord William Turner, wigmaker's son, was born a year before Constable in 1775. He walked the wilder side of the Romantic spirit, painting violent storms, churning seas and ghostly sunsets in oils and watercolours. Early on he was exact, joining Constable in a faithful, classical rendition of landscape for the likes of *Tintern Abbey* (1795). However, later paintings bore emotive swirls of paint, blurring water, land and sky to convey the drama of a storm or the heat of fire. Some of it verged on abstraction. *Stormy Sea with Blazing Wreck* (1835-40), its flashes of light and dark only suggestive of the subject within, was typical. The Academy loved most of his work (while largely indifferent to Constable's) but critics struggled with the raw, imprecise nature of his later paintings. Turner's remarkable grasp of light and shade would influence the French Impressionists a generation on.

Blighty's best
Turner's *The Fighting Temeraire* (1839), the old warship backed by a glassy sunset, was voted the Greatest Painting in Britain in a 2005 public poll by BBC Radio 4 and the National Gallery. Constable's *The Hay Wain* came second.

Landscaping goes flat
East Anglia's placid scenery seduced the early landscapists. Gainsborough was born in Suffolk and returned in adulthood, incorporating the gentle terrain into his portrait paintings. Constable came from East Bergholt on the Essex/Suffolk border, and would paint the landscape for the rest of his life, even in absentia. In the first decade of the 19th century the Norwich School grew up in Norfolk around the watercolourists John Crome and John Sell Cotman, its painters absorbed by landscapes both foreign and local.

EAST ANGLIA

Angels in Peckham? Of course Mr Blake… just step this way please

William Blake was the great visionary of the Romantic world. He didn't paint from life, relying instead on imagination in an era when artists weren't recognised for self-expression. Tigers, angels and dragons all poured out onto the canvas. They were born, said Blake, of regularly experienced visions. He'd been seeing unusual stuff since boyhood when he encountered a tree filled with angels on Peckham Rye. Blake used the strong lines of medieval art but also borrowed from the Renaissance, exaggerating mystical figures with the Mannerism of Michelangelo. He was anti-authoritarian, experimental and solitary in his work and he got short shrift as a result. The world wasn't ready for Blake – many called him mad – and his professional output was limited to book engraving. Many of his illustrations were created to accompany his own poetry (see section 2.1.4. for more on Blake's verse). Blake was working on a series of plates to illustrate Dante's *Divine Comedy* when he died in 1827. His reputation only gathered momentum 50 years later, and today Blake is considered a pivotal contributor to British art.

In the raw talent
William Blake and his wife Catherine moved to Lambeth in 1790. They clearly felt relaxed in their new homestead: a visiting friend found the pair naked in the garden reading Milton's *Paradise Lost.* "It's only Adam and Eve, you know," commented Blake.

Dadd does for dad
Richard Dadd became much admired for his paintings of fairies in the Victorian era. However, he found true fame when he went mad in his mid 20s and stabbed his father to death. After 20 years in Bedlam hospital, Dadd eventually ended up in Broadmoor, the 'criminal lunatic asylum', where he produced much of his best work.

Proceed with caution: art under the Victorians

While French painters fed on the expressive work by Constable and Turner in the mid 19th century, British artists looked away. William Powell Frith, the big name painter of the time, was typical with his conservative, detailed studies of an ordered society behaving like it bloody well should from the drawing room to the racecourse. The social change and grit of industrialising Britain barely featured on the canvas. Instead, paintings tended to moralise, instructing the new middle classes on what their aspirations should be.

William Powell Frith, master of the Victorian crowd scene, had quite a crowd of his own. He lived in Bayswater with his wife Isabelle and their 12 children, but also kept a mistress, Mary, and seven supplementary kids about a mile down the road. Isabelle only became aware of William's duplicity when she saw him posting a letter near their house one day when he was supposed to be on holiday in Brighton.

Turning back the clock with the Pre-Raphaelites

The Pre-Raphaelite Brotherhood of painters formed in 1848 as a clandestine association under Dante Gabriel Rossetti, son of an Italian refugee. As the name intimated, the school looked back to early Renaissance art and the medieval period, to the time before Raphael, an artist popular with 19th century neo-Classicists. They tuned in to a Victorian nostalgia for the pre-industrial age and the Aesthetic Movement that felt beauty alone was adequate motivation for art. In technique, artists like Rossetti, John Everett Millais and William Holman Hunt aimed for a crisp realism, while subject matter drew on religious, Arthurian and medieval themes, often inspired by some work of literature. But their efforts to resurrect the pre-Raphael world, to manufacture naivety, haven't withstood modern criticism, and the Brotherhood's art has often been dismissed as sentimental and artificial.

In its own era, the Pre-Raphaelite taste for somnolent scenes of women and nature suffocated anything more radical in British art for the rest of the 19th century. However, Rossetti's friend William Morris took the idealised medieval aesthetic into the design world in the 1880s with the Arts and Crafts Movement. Morris, a committed socialist, shared his wife with Rossetti.

New beginnings

At the end of the 19th century a small group of British artists embraced the new. Inspired by the French Impressionists and reacting against the conservatism of the Royal Academy, they formed the New English Art Club in 1886. The Americans John Singer Sargent and James McNeill Whistler were both involved, but the most radical painters were English. Walter Sickert and Wilson Steer came closest to mirroring the loose style of Impressionism. Alas, the Club quickly factionalised and the impetus stuttered, even while their annual exhibitions continue right up to this day. One dissident faction, the so-called Glasgow Boys, flourished, bringing a touch of social realism to rural Scottish scenes throughout the 1890s. James Guthrie and John Lavery were among the head Boys.

From cubes to dead sharks: art over the last century

Conservative club: Edwardian art

A few cliques flicked paint at the British art establishment in the early 20th century, most conjuring some slant on the Post-Impressionism flourishing in France. Of the more significant collectives, the Camden Town Group earned most attention. Led by Walter Sickert, he of the New English Art Club, the subscribers exhibited their mix of Impressionist, Post-Impressionist and Cubist work in the three years before the First World War. The Bloomsbury Group, featuring Scottish painter Duncan Grant and his sometime lover, textile artist Vanessa Bell, also had a stab at the avant-garde of the Post-Impressionists, Matisse in particular. Similarly, the prosaic landscapes of Northern Irish painter Paul Henry were forward-thinking in their veracity. However, they swam against the general current of British art in the Edwardian period which, led by the Americans James McNeill Whistler and John Singer Sargent, idled in pleasing but unchallenging portraiture.

The Vorticists stir things up… a bit

One small group of British artists did generate something genuinely avant-garde in the years before the First World War. The Vorticists formed in London in 1914, gathered by painter, writer and all-round agitator Wyndham Lewis. He printed a magazine-cum-manifesto, *Blast*, which ripped into the mannered tastes of early 20th century British art, and an exhibition of artwork followed. Vorticist paintings took the angular lines of Cubism (developing in France) and used them to frame modern, mechanised Britain.

Throw in Mrs Lavery and it's a deal
Portraitist John Lavery, son of a failed Belfast publican, was perhaps the first nationally significant artist to emerge from the north of Ireland. He became a respected pillar of the Royal Academy and was knighted in 1918. Yet the society painter maintained a keen interest in the cause of Irish independence, even loaning his London house to the Irish delegation that negotiated the Anglo-Irish Treaty in 1921 and included first leader of the Irish Free State and IRA man, Michael Collins. The Irish government showed their gratitude by placing Lavery's portrait of his second wife, Hazel, on the Irish pound note. Historians have pondered whether Michael Collins showed his by having an affair with the painter's wife.

Hues who: the Scottish Colourists
The Scottish Colourists took their inspiration from Paris, from the Post-Impressionists and in particular the Fauvist style of Matisse, imitating his vibrant colours. Four painters were involved: Samuel Peploe, John Duncan Fergusson, Leslie Hunter and Francis Cadell. The quartet produced still life and landscape paintings, charmed in particular by the western isle of Iona. The Scottish Colourists went almost unnoticed when they exhibited in the 1920s and 30s but today their importance in the history of British art – theirs being a rare native take on Modernism – is often noted.

French fry
Painter and critic Roger Fry staged two exhibitions of French Post-Impressionist painting in London, in 1910 and 1912. The art establishment guffawed and most of the public who visited left bemused, but for circles like the Bloomsbury Group, Fry became a hero of the avant-garde.

Parallels also existed with the Italian Futurist movement although Lewis claimed originality for his merry band. Vorticism was radical and exciting but it didn't last. The First World War soon called the main protagonists away, and once the fighting was done few wanted to linger over the machine age celebrated in Vorticist paintings. Some have suggested the brief movement was as close as Britain got to the avant-garde in the 20th century.

Lone masters: art between the wars

British art seemed timid after the First World War, worried perhaps by a sense of triviality in the wake of such a conflict. While Continentals picked up Modernism once more, Britain remained hesitant. Significant innovators did emerge over the subsequent four decades but they tended to work in isolation. For many, the human figure, however distorted, provided an ongoing obsession. A few kindred spirits did pool their creativity: Picasso's abstract expressionism found English patronage in the Unit One group of artists in St Ives, Cornwall, while painters like Stanley Spencer, Augustus John and Lucien Freud gently twisted the conventions of figurative art. Francis Bacon did most to corrupt tradition with his grotesque portraits. Unit One disciple and war artist Paul Nash later gave a British landscapist's perspective on surrealism, while a neo-Romantic style emerged with John Piper, another war artist, playing with drama and colour in landscape.

The five British artists of the mid 20th century you should know about

Stanley Spencer set biblical episodes amid the cosy village life of his own interwar Britain, shocking contemporary audiences. In the Second World War he painted industrial toil in shipyards on the Clyde, while his

122

later work grew increasingly erotic. Nude paintings of his second wife roused the Royal Academy president to prosecute for obscenity. Whatever the subject, his figurative style was dependably accurate.

Henry Moore was the pre-eminent British sculptor of the 20th century. Having explored early South American art in the 1920s, Yorkshireman Moore turned to abstraction a decade later. Picasso gave him a starting point and he progressed from indeterminate shapes to bulging, smooth female forms that directed his work right into the 1980s. His huge reclining forms were, he said, born of nature and they duly felt at home placed in the landscape.

Moore's friend **Barbara Hepworth** also bought into abstract modes, but used them to express landscape more than figures. Working in metal, wood and stone, she made smooth, tactile sculpture. Hepworth's shapes became distinguished by their use of holes, or what she called 'abstract negative spaces', carved smoothly into the sculpture. Her best known work is probably *Single Form* (1963), resident at the United Nations building in New York. She died in a fire at her St Ives studio in 1975.

Francis Bacon was the most important British painter of the 20th century. He had no formal art training but toured the galleries of Paris, Berlin and London in early adulthood, inspired particularly by Picasso. In 1945, aged 36, he submitted *Three Studies for Figures at the Base of a Crucifixion* (1944), an unnerving meld of human and animal forms, for display in London. It brought overnight fame. He was a figurative painter but his portraits disturbed with their visceral, torn shapes, their figures 'deformed and then reformed' as

"WHEN I'M DEAD, PUT ME IN A PLASTIC BAG AND THROW ME IN THE GUTTER."
Francis Bacon instructs the barman at The Colony Room club

Live fast, die old: Francis Bacon
Francis Bacon was born to English parents in Dublin in 1909. It wasn't a happy childhood; he was kicked out of the familial home in his early teens after being discovered dressed in his mother's underwear. Bacon destroyed most of his early paintings, made in the 1930s while working in London as an interior designer. When the Second World War broke out, invalided out of service by asthma he went into the Civil Defence Corps. Bacon drank and gambled through much of his life and cultivated a debauched reputation, particularly at his favourite drinking haunt, The Colony Room in Soho. His sex life, pursued predominantly with men, also became the stuff of legend. He once professed a sexual attraction to his father, and apparently slept with the uncle that chaperoned a trip to swinging Berlin in the late 1920s. By the 1960s he'd taken to crawling Soho's bars in fishnets, a leather overcoat and make up. He died in 1992, laid out by a heart attack while visiting friends in Madrid.

Bacon once said. Some paintings perverted the classics, notably his screaming rendition of Velazquez' unbending Pope Innocent X. Open, wailing mouths were a recurring theme. Bacon was also in the habit of painting faces near lumps of meat, hinting at the physiological similarities.

Lucian Freud, grandson of Sigmund, migrated to Britain from Nazi Germany as a boy. Taking much from the style of Stanley Spencer, he developed a realist, prosaic approach to the human figure, daubed with thick strokes. The older he got, the more human his figures became; their lumps and bumps offered up without much charity. They sat, impassive, usually naked, in increasingly grubby, unglamorous rooms. Widely acknowledged as a highly accomplished artist, Freud continued to paint in the 21st century. In 2008 his portrait of a sleeping, naked Jobcentre supervisor became the most expensive piece of art by a living painter, selling at auction for £17.2 million.

Pop goes the easel

Britain flirted with Pop Art in the 1960s, its artists rebelling against the inaccessibility of abstract expressionism with something more resonant of reality. Richard Hamilton was the first Brit to sign up. In fact, Hamilton was the first Pop Artist anywhere, his photo collage *Just What Is It That Makes Today's Home So Different, So Appealing?* (1956), with its bodybuilder and stripper ensconced in their consumerist living room, was typical of the humour and everyday references that Pop Art would strive for. Peter Blake was another who placed consumer products in his art, mixing them with celebrity images, stripes and target shapes. He's best known for the cover of The Beatles' *Sergeant Pepper's Lonely Hearts Club Band* (1967). Scotsman Eduardo Paolozzi was the significant sculptor of Pop Art, although he went on to create abstract and then more figurative work. But David Hockney is the artist that

1. Identity: the   2. Literature   **3. Art, architecture**   4. Performing   5. Cinema,   6. Media and   7. Food and drink   8. Living culture:
foundations   and philosophy   **and design**   arts   photography   communications   the state of
of British culture   and fashion   modern Britain

did most after graduating from Pop Art, ultimately becoming the prime painter of late 20th century Britain.

From radical to national treasure: David Hockney
Bradford's famous son dabbled with abstract expressionism in the late 1950s before turning to Pop Art briefly in the early 60s. In 1963 he was profoundly influenced by a visit to California and began producing more realist work; the images of serene swimming pools and bronzed figures were reminiscent of snapshot photos. By the 1970s his paintings had grown in their naturalism. *Mr and Mrs Clark and Percy* (1970-71), a rather stilted domestic scene of married couple and cat, was typical and popular. Hockney's work has often been concerned with his own sexuality, from crudely drawn figures aside bites of text like 'queer' and 'unorthodox lover' to the sculptured

Bridget deceives the eye
Bridget Riley developed wavy abstract patterns in the 1960s, creating illusions of light and movement. It was christened Op Art and given a niche of its own.

male physiques of his Californian paintings. More recently he has turned to landscape, producing an enormous painting of Yorkshire, *Bigger Trees Near Warter* (2008), for the Tate Britain gallery.

Love it or loathe it but don't ignore it: contemporary British art
Contemporary British art has no defining style. Conceptual art has been important since the 1970s, but can turn the public off with its emphasis on ideas over aesthetics. Critics claim British artists are too concerned with the avant-garde and with personal motifs; that their art serves a very narrow audience. In this, it differs much from the conservative spirit of a century ago but little from contemporary art anywhere else in the world. And yet Britain has working artists that have become household names, and the discussion of art spreads well beyond the slim bounds of its own community.

The Academy
loses its head
In 2006, artist David
Hensel visited the Royal
Academy to see his
sculpture, *One Day
Closer to Paradise* – a
laughing head on a flat
slate base, on display.
All he found was the
base it was supposed to
stand on, no sculpture.
A judging panel had
assumed the two pieces
were separate (they
were delivered in two
bits) and decided the
plinth was better. "The
base was thought to
have merit and accepted;
it is currently on display.
The head has been safely
stored ready to be
collected by the artist,"
explained an Academy
spokeswoman.

The rise of the Young British Artists (YBAs) in the 1990s did much to raise the profile of contemporary art. Often referred to as Britart, theirs wasn't a specific school; instead they shared exhibition spaces, an interest in conceptual art and a talent for self-publicity. Damien Hirst cooked up the YBA's signature dish, *The Physical Impossibility of Death in the Mind of Someone Living* (1991), or 'that dead shark in a tank of formaldehyde' as most people called it. By 1997 the Royal Academy was showing their work. Not everyone loved it. Critics, tabloids and the public often took issue, convinced they were being conned by the likes of Tracey Emin's *My Bed* (1999) installation (the exhibit was Emin's unmade bed). In 1999, Stuckism evolved in reaction to the YBAs, placing the emphasis back on figurative art. In 2003 they displayed an exhibit entitled *A Dead Shark isn't Art* at their Shoreditch gallery. Whatever the reaction, it's hard to deny that the YBAs have given modern British art an energy that it maintains today. Beyond the conceptual art of the YBAs, the most popular British artist of recent years has been Jack Vettriano, a miner's son from Fife dismissed by critics but popular with the public for paintings with a thick, noir-like feel. Vettriano's *Singing Butler* (1992) print sells more postcards and posters than any other work by a British artist.

The Turner Prize

Britain's most famous contemporary art award is the Turner Prize, given to artists aged under 50. Named after the 19th century landscapist, the prize is famously controversial. Recent recipients have included Martin Creed, whose 2001 exhibit featured a room in which the light went on and off, and Simon Starling, the 2005 winner who converted a shed into a boat, sailed it down the Rhine and then converted it back into a shed and displayed it as a work entitled *Shedboatshed*. Good or bad, the Turner Prize always provokes debate on the state of British art.

1. Identity: the   2. Literature   **3. Art, architecture**   4. Performing   5. Cinema,   6. Media and   7. Food and drink   8. Living culture:
foundations   and philosophy   **and design**   arts   photography   communications   the state of
of British culture   and fashion   modern Britain

Five big artists of contemporary British art

Damien Hirst He began with suspended and dissected dead animals – shark, sheep, cow and pig – intended, Hirst explained, to discuss mortality rather like Francis Bacon did, not to shock. He moved on to paintings of coloured spots, one of which went to Mars in 2003, daubed on the side of the Beagle 2 probe. More recently *For the Love of God* (2007) was a platinum skull adorned with more than 8,000 diamonds. It sold for £50 million. Hirst uses a number of assistants in 'factory' workshops to create his art; the concept rather than the execution, he insists, is the creative part.

Rachel Whiteread Another of the YBAs, Whiteread raised interest with the Turner-winning *House* (1993), in which she cast the entire inside space of an East End terraced house in situ as a work of art. Much of her portfolio has involved such casts, comprising 'negative space' like the inside of a room or a box.

Gilbert and George The inseparable duo, whose appearance as suited gents belies a renegade approach to art, started with performance art, creating *The Singing Sculpture* (1970) for which they coated themselves in gold paint and mimed to a Flanagan and Allen song. These days they're better known for giant, colourful canvases, frequently featuring photos of the boys themselves and often 'enlightening' with the use of nudity, bodily fluids and provocative titles like *Naked Shit Pictures* (1995). Despite their persistent strangeness the 'national treasures' tag doesn't seem inappropriate.

Basin instinct
Loutish behaviour on booze and drugs used to gain Damien Hirst as much attention as his art. He received much coverage, for instance, for urinating in the sink of a Soho club.

Open or wrapped?
Damien Hirst created his shark in a tank of formaldehyde for art patron Charles Saatchi, who offered to buy whatever the artist wanted to make. He paid £50,000 for it in 1991. (A *Sun* newspaper headline at the time read '£50,000 for fish without chips'.) Saatchi sold the piece in 2004, apparently for around £6.5 million.

"EACH OF OUR PICTURES IS A VISUAL LOVE LETTER FROM US TO THE VIEWER,"
George Passmore (of Gilbert and George)

The drugs do work
Damien Hirst became the world's most expensive living artist in 2007 when *Lullaby Spring* (2002), a stainless steel medicine chest containing brightly coloured pills, sold for £9.65million. Sotheby's, the auctioneer, referred to the work "tackling the intrinsic frailty and vulnerability of life". Later in the year *For the Love of God*, his diamond encrusted skull, sold for five times that amount.

Tracey Emin The *enfant terrible* of contemporary British art (even in her 40s), another of the YBA gang, Emin brings a strong autobiographical thread to work in multimedia. *Everyone I Have Ever Slept With, 1963-1995* (1995) was true to its title, comprising a tent embroidered with a roll call of folk who'd shared her bed. More recently Emin's work has featured ambiguous slogans, writ large in neon or scrawled on bed sheets. In 2007 she daubed 'One Secret is to Save Everything' against a backdrop of swimming sperm on a large flag displayed in London's Jubilee Gardens.

Anthony Gormley The prime sculptor of 21st century Britain deposits human forms in public spaces. He talks about trying to represent the space occupied by the body rather than the body itself. *Angel of the North* (1998), a rusty 20-metre high figure with a 54-metre wingspan stands overlooking the A1 in north-east England, while a series of 100 faceless life-size figures, *Another Place* (1997), recently took up permanent residence on Crosby Beach on Merseyside. Like many of Gormley's sculptures, *Another Place* was made from moulds of his own body.

Laughing all the way to the Banksy

Some call Banksy the most exciting contemporary painter in Britain. A graffiti artist, he sprays subversive wit on public and private walls, using a distinctive stencilled style. He's the master of the visual one liner: here two policemen enjoying a snog, there the Mona Lisa pointing a bazooka or children saluting a Tesco bag up a flagpole. A key to Banksy's success has been his anonymity. The continued mystery over his identity (despite the best efforts of the tabloids) has generated a sizeable Banksy myth. He made his name in London and his home city, Bristol, but in recent years Banksy has gone international. He went to Venice Beach, Los Angeles, and wrote 'Fat Lane' on the sidewalk, and painted windows in Israel's West Bank barrier. He's even had a gallery show and released a coffee table book, somehow maintaining anonymity. Today, you can pay six figures for a genuine Banksy, even while London councils still scrub his work off their walls.

Culture? Can't get enough of it

An *Art Newspaper* survey revealed recently that seven of the top 30 most visited galleries and museums around the world were British. They attracted 22.5 million visitors in 2007, significantly more than their French or American equivalents. Tate Modern got twice as many visitors as the MoMA in New York, while the Kelvingrove Art Gallery and Museum in Glasgow pulled in more punters than the Uffizi in Florence.

"IF YOU'RE GOING TO DAMAGE SOMEONE'S PROPERTY, IT'S GOOD TO SHOW A BIT OF DEDICATION TO IT. JUST SLAPPING IT UP SEEMS A BIT RUDE."
Banksy

Glasgow spooks out
Scotland's late 19th
century creative vibe
bore the Glasgow Four,
an arty quartet blending
elements of Celtic,
Japanese and Art
Nouveau design in
stylised motifs. They
were an intimate bunch,
comprising architect
Charles Rennie
Mackintosh; his wife-to-
be, the painter and glass
engraver Margaret
MacDonald; her sister
Frances, skilled in
textiles, metalwork and
graphics; and Frances'
husband-to-be, James
Herbert McNair, a skilled
painter and furniture
designer. Not everyone
loved the Four; they were
also dubbed the Spook
School after a fondness
for Celtic hobgoblins and
the like.

From Chippendale to Arts and Crafts: great moments in early British design

Peer back beyond the modern era and you find a few standout moments of British design; occasions when functionality colluded with form and elevated everyday objects beyond the norm. There's always been what you'd call craftsmen. The 18th century had a selection: from the 'big three' furniture designers, Thomas Chippendale, Thomas Sheraton and George Hepplewhite, to the 'father of English potters', Josiah Wedgewood, and Scottish interior designer-cum-architect Robert Adam. But the relationship between beauty and utility found new vigour, perhaps surprisingly, in the industrial age of mass production. The Great Exhibition of 1851 was a landmark event, not simply for Joseph Paxton's stunning Crystal Palace but also for the objects, from clocks to coffee roasters, exhibited within its vast glass and cast iron body.

A decade later the Arts and Crafts Movement emerged, inspired by the motifs of nature and a rather idealised notion of craftsmanship. The anti-utilitarian theory of John Ruskin and the Gothic throwback architecture of Augustus Pugin played their part, even while the furniture makers, architects and decorative artists of Arts and Crafts often employed mechanisation in their methods. Leading light William Morris comes closest to fulfilling our image of the 'designer'. Morris & Co produced furniture, wallpapers, fabrics and tapestries, many with the twisting, organic patterns that are still in print today. The Arts and Crafts Movement stretched into the early 20th century, strongly influencing Art Nouveau and carrying figures like Charles Rennie Mackintosh, architect, interior designer and decorative artist, and Charles Robert Ashbee, founder of the Guild of Handicraft, within its broad ranks.

Ooh Pearl, I do like your sofa...does it come in Bakelite?
Britain was something of a bystander to the avant-garde
modernism that swept Europe and the USA in the 1920s
and 30s. And yet its influence rippled, much dissipated,
into British homes in the shape of sleek furniture,
curvaceous radios and rectangular fireplaces. Syrie
Maugham became a big, early British name in top-end
interior design, working for the likes of Noël Coward and
Wallis Simpson. She was fixated with white (furniture,
fabric, walls, books), occasionally mixing in bits of colour
to dramatic effect. Syrie picked up the surname in a short-
lived marriage to the largely homosexual writer Somerset
Maugham; her maiden name was Barnardo, passed from
her father Thomas John Barnardo, founder of the
Barnardo's charity for destitute children. The streamlined
shapes of modernism infiltrated homes further in the
1930s, with Bakelite telephones, geometric three-piece
suites, veneer sideboards and chrome lighting. All such
items have become highly collectable in the 21st century
as the desire for true antiques has waned.

Conran leads Britain into the light
As post-war austerity lightened, the 1951 Festival of
Britain played a role in normalising modern design for the
average Brit. They began to appreciate that chairs, bins,
lights and other functional objects were suitable targets
for style, that they were integral to the new consumer
society. Design, its reach extending into numerous
aspects of life – industry, interiors, advertising – became
an accepted wing of creativity. On the home front, one
man in particular knocked on the front door to offer
guidance. Terence Conran, designer and entrepreneur,
opened the first Habitat shop on London's Fulham Road
in 1964, selling a 'lifestyle' that mixed Scandinavian
simplicity, ethnic roughage, repro classics and pop art –
shoppers could buy everything from duvets to bean bags

1. Identity: the   2. Literature   **3. Art, architecture**   4. Performing   5. Cinema,   6. Media and   7. Food and drink   8. Living culture:
foundations   and philosophy   **and design**   arts   photography   communications   the state of
of British culture   and fashion   modern Britain

to the chicken brick. Conran has been an important figure in British design ever since; the one designer, perhaps, that most Brits could actually name. In the 1980s and 90s, Conran was also credited with sparking Britain's modern day revolution in restaurant dining.

Five icons of British design

London Tube map. Humble Harry Beck's 1931 map, inspired by electrical circuit diagrams, rejected scale and geographical accuracy for clarity. He got five guineas for his trouble.

Telephone box. The red variety, with its crown insignia, multiple windows and domed roof was designed by Giles Gilbert Scott in the 1930s. It seems destined to live on, in spite of lamentable redesigns and the rise of the mobile.

Anglepoise lamp. A modest marvel designed by George Carwardine in 1933 to mimic the movement and balance of the human arm. Its simple functionality has since acquired an 'industrial' chic.

Concorde. Alright, it was a joint effort with the French, but the pointy nosed, triangular star of supersonic travel won its place in British hearts in the 1960s. Retired in 2003, Concorde still topped a BBC poll of design icons three years later.

The Mini. Alec Issigonis' aptly named car first hit the road in 1959, dreamt up as a petrol saver after the Suez Crisis hit. It became a key ingredient of swinging 60s Britain; the Beatles bought one each.

Who are the important contemporary British designers? Is 21st century Britain as 'design aware' as, say, France or Italy? Probably not. But it's not far behind. Stores like Habitat, interior design magazines, TV shows and Swedish style goliath IKEA have spoon-fed Britain's burgeoning middle classes a dose of style, even if it is rarely avant-garde. Perhaps James Dyson is the most radical designer of recent years, although his is very much a function-led approach. His bagless vacuum cleaner, finally put into production by Dyson himself in 1993 after 5,000 prototypes and numerous rejections from the major vacuum manufacturers, has become both iconic and lucrative – Dyson is a billionaire. His more recent successes include the Airblade hand dryer, worthy of mention not least because it does actually dry your hands. Perhaps of more aesthetic interest are the likes of Jonathan Ive, the principal designer at Apple Inc. lauded for his involvement in the iMac and the iPod. Another, Tom Dixon, former design director at Habitat, began welding his own furniture in the 1980s when an Italian manufacturer took up his waif-like S-bend chair. Dixon only entered the design world after a motorcycle accident in his early 20s forced him to quit art school. The Mirror Ball light is another of his successes. Jasper Morrison has also produced some memorably simple, unobtrusive furniture, while also designing mobile phones, bus stops and more. He calls his style 'utilism'.

"I JUST THINK THINGS SHOULD WORK PROPERLY."
James Dyson

3.2 Architecture

Britain has a rich trove of architecture. Even after Hitler and the post-war planners had done their worst, the Saxon churches, Gothic cathedrals, Tudor palaces, Georgian squares and Victorian stations still singled Britain out for special praise. Even some of the modern stuff is breathtaking.

1. Identity: the
foundations
of British culture

2. Literature
and philosophy

3. Art, architecture
and design

4. Performing
arts

5. Cinema,
photography
and fashion

6. Media and
communications

7. Food and drink

8. Living culture:
the state of
modern Britain

3.2.1 Picking through the ruins: ancient British buildings

Do those curtains come in stone? Furniture in the stone houses of Skara Brae was made, like the walls, of stone. Beds, dressers and even watertight tanks where inhabitants stored fishing bait all utilised the local rock. The prime source of their meagre wood supply was the Atlantic Ocean, which coughed up driftwood from North America.

The largest lump of Roman Britain
The largest single surviving piece of freestanding Roman architecture in Britain belongs to Viroconium, a ruined Roman town that thrived in Shropshire. It's a wall with a hole in it, once part of the cold pool in a complex of baths.

Set in stone: prehistoric architecture

Poke around in 'British' architecture before the Norman invasion and you find crumbling lumps. Farthest back are the mysterious chunks of rock that make up Britain's 900 surviving megalithic stone circles, dating from around 3,000BC. Dolmens, piles of earth and lineal standing stones also characterise Britain's prehistoric landscape. The earliest recognisable dwellings date from the same era. Skara Brae, Orkney's squat beachside village, is by far the best-preserved Neolithic settlement in Europe.

Empire building: the Romans in Britain

There isn't much Roman architecture left in Britain even though they built forts, aqueducts, baths and entire towns. Today we're left with chunks of brick, stone and cement – don't expect soaring Corinthian columns. However, the passing of years and walls hasn't dimmed the impressiveness of floor mosaics in the Roman palace at Fishbourne, near Chichester, a site that was once similar in scale to Buckingham Palace. Aside from the hot and cold tubs of Roman Bath (sections of which remain), most of the rest of Roman Britain comprises broken walls, notably at the Roman town of Silchester, in Berkshire, the amphitheatre in Chester and, most spectacularly, in the surviving stretches of Hadrian's Wall in northern England, a structure dating to 120AD. The symmetry and order of the Romans' architecture wouldn't be seen in Britain again for another 600 years after their departure.

136

1. Identity: the foundations of British culture   2. Literature and philosophy   **3. Art, architecture and design**   4. Performing arts   5. Cinema, photography and fashion   6. Media and communications   7. Food and drink   8. Living culture: the state of modern Britain

A knack for Angles

For all we know the Anglo-Saxons built towering gherkin-shaped office blocks. Unfortunately, if they did, they built them with wood and the Vikings burned them down. We do know they introduced the open hall house to the British landscape in the fifth century, its wooden structure comprising one large room open to the rafters, fire burning in the middle. The design would find continued use in Britain for a thousand years. And we also know that here, in the newly Christianised kingdoms of Anglo-Saxon Britain, the first native ecclesiastical architecture grew up. Their taste for roughly hewn stone churches lives on in over 50 extant buildings in modern day England. They're all pretty small; the Normans flattened or rebuilt anything of a decent size.

Towering over the Vikings

While large swathes of mainland Britain rolled over and let the Vikings have it their way, over in Ulster the monasteries built soaring round towers to keep the longhairs at bay. Many of the surviving examples date to the 10th century – the 28-metre-tall cone-topped beauty in Antrim is probably the best.

The five best bits of pre-Norman architecture in Britain

Skara Brae The 5,000-year-old stone-slabbed affair dramatised by Orkney weather was mothballed by a sand dune for centuries and only revealed in 1850.

Hadrian's Wall. The Emperor's second century 73-mile long boundary with the Scots once stood six metres tall. Today its best bits are a third of that height, abutted by fragments of the forts that once regulated the border.

The Roman baths of Bath The best British remnant of Roman leisure time is found in Bath. The original stuff – the columns and heating system – only survives below knee height, but faithful recreation of the rest gives a good idea of what the Romans had.

Bathtime 60-400 AD

Church of St Peter-on-the-Wall Bradwell-on-Sea, Essex. This simple stone box is 1,300 years old. A windswept perch overlooking the North Sea lends stirring atmosphere.

St Andrew's Church Greensted, Essex. The only surviving wooden Anglo-Saxon church (the oldest wooden building in Europe no less) was restored in the 19th century, gaining dormer windows in the process.

Towering ambition: the master masons

Medieval churches didn't have architects in the modern sense. Instead there were master masons who developed and shared their styles and techniques, some achieving significant prestige. Labourers were often unskilled, plucked from the local community and sometimes put to work unpaid as a condition of serfdom. They worked high up on scaffolding and accidents were no doubt common. The master mason building Canterbury Cathedral, William of Sens, was replaced in 1178 when he fell from scaffolding.

Britain is strewn with churches. Most of the country's oldest buildings were constructed for worship, and tens of thousands still stand despite the vagaries of religious taste. From the modesty of the medieval village church to the pomp of St Paul's Cathedral, Britain simply wouldn't be Britain without its ecclesiastical architecture.

Look, I've got a massive Romanesque church, I'm clearly very important

William the Conqueror wanted to wipe the Saxon slate clean. Churches and abbeys, in the most, were replaced or reshaped with a Norman variant of Romanesque, the solid style of rounded arches, stout walls and barrelled vaults popular on the Continent. The British version, usually referred to as Norman rather than Romanesque, drifted over the Channel before William arrived. A wave of building in the 11th and 12th centuries bore monumental cathedrals. They weren't simple expressions of faith; these buildings reflected the political power of bishops, abbots and the new Norman overlords. Chevrons, waves and animal heads, all carved in stone, were common design motifs. In the 12th century the Norman style spread west to Ireland and north to Scotland, although its finest hour came just short of the border, at Durham. Perched on a sizeable rock, side by side with its Norman castle, Durham's cathedral is the most spectacular in England with its patterned piers and soaring ribbed ceiling.

Points of interest: the magnificence of Gothic

Norman architecture shone for a century before progressing to something more delicate, more technically astute: Gothic. It too came from mainland Europe, where rounded Romanesque arches became pointed and fat walls and piers lost weight, their girth reduced by the innovation of flying buttresses and ribbed vaults that directed weight to the ground more efficiently. But while the French and Germans built their cathedrals high, in Britain the master masons (under strict orders from the priests) went for length, building extended naves. Gothic stretched from the end of the 12th century to the start of the 16th, evolving as it went. Britain's Gothic adventure is usually carved into three sequential styles, each of which can often be found, jumbled, within the construction of a single church:

Early English (late 12th to 13th centuries). Pilfered from France despite the name, Early English was all about the pointed arch and tall, undecorated lancet windows that swapped Romanesque's gloom for heavenly light. Solid pillars were replaced with thin stone shafts, clustered around columns. Salisbury Cathedral brought it all together brilliantly.

Decorated (first half 14th century). The brief Decorated period lived up to its name. Windows gained tracery, their frames delicately carved and bisected by thin vertical bands of stone and topped with trefoils. Carved and painted wall designs appeared while structural innovation reached stunning new heights. Decorated Gothic was often tagged onto existing churches in bits and pieces; Ely and Exeter cathedrals fared particularly well.

Perpendicular (late 14th to mid 16th centuries). Perpendicular's prime style concern was vertical lines. It quietened the flamboyance of the Decorated period with huge pointed windows and lithe stone piers. Tracery became increasingly delicate. The most staggering achievement was the fanned vault, which allowed for flatter roofs and wowed

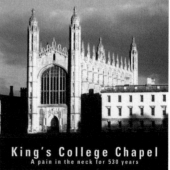

King's College Chapel
A pain in the neck for 530 years

visually with geometric tendrils of stone. The 530-year-old fanned ceiling at King's College Chapel, Cambridge, still guarantees a stiff neck and slackened jaw. In smaller churches, Perpendicular introduced fine wooden roofs.

Boxing clever: Renaissance churches

By the time the Tudors were on the throne, the great age of British church building had passed. The new Church of England adopted or destroyed the buildings of pre-Reformation faith but rarely replaced them. A small clutch of churches absorbed the Renaissance spirit in the 17th century, sharing the continental taste for Classicism. The church of St Paul in Covent Garden is the finest example. Begun in 1631 by Inigo Jones (named architects were on the scene by that time, and Jones was the first of great significance), St Paul's Church introduced Britain to the Tuscan portico with its no-nonsense columns and recalled Romanesque with round arched windows. Jones travelled to Italy, absorbed the tenets of classical design – it was all about getting things in proportion – and aligned them in England with changing modes of worship. People needed to focus on the preacher, and the boxed shapes of Roman architecture served the purpose well.

1. Identity: the
foundations
of British culture

2. Literature
and philosophy

3. Art, architecture
and design

4. Performing
arts

5. Cinema,
photography
and fashion

6. Media and
communications

7. Food and drink

8. Living culture:
the state of
modern Britain

Wren's church building binge

Inigo Jones didn't build much but he was highly influential. Cromwell and co kept up the lean years for ecclesiastical architecture during the Commonwealth, but once they'd gone Jones' classical designs spurred the first decent wave of church building since the Reformation. London's calamitous 1666 fire helped out, creating the opportunity for major redevelopment. One architect, Christopher Wren, dominated the rebuild. By the time he was at work in the 1670s, the style of pillars and domes, copied reverently from Rome and then elaborated and exaggerated, had been dubbed Baroque. Wren is usually credited with 52 London churches in the later 17th century, although he had considerable help from assistants. Around half survived the Blitz in the Second World War. St Stephen's in Walbrook is the most elaborate. It's got the dome that would later loom large in Wren's masterpiece, St Paul's Cathedral. Built between 1675 and 1710 to a commission from Charles II, the cathedral has a medieval floor plan but is dominated by that large Classical hemisphere. The pillars, porticos and statues add up to Britain's finest Baroque church.

"READER, IF YOU REQUIRE A MEMORIAL, LOOK AROUND YOU."
Inscription on Christopher Wren's tomb in St Paul's Cathedral

The church shaped like a house

In post-Reformation England the Church was content to revamp Roman Catholic buildings for Protestant services but in Scotland and Ireland the Presbyterians, more extreme in their taste for simple services and a good Bible reading, built new structures for the job. Many, like St Columba's in Burntisland, Scotland, built in 1592, resembled a large square house with a tower. The idea that a church should be shaped like a meeting hall has persisted with minority denominations in Scotland, Ireland, England and Wales ever since. Baptists, Unitarians, Methodists and Quakers have built churches that reflect the architectural foibles of their period, from the soft early Georgian elegance of John Wesley's Methodist New Room in Bristol to the Victorian mock Baroque of David Bryce's Unitarian Church in Edinburgh.

Congratulations have a moon

Christopher Wren only became an architect in his 30s. Before that he was a highly esteemed scientist, counted among the founders of the Royal Society and admired by Isaac Newton for work that included the first injection of a substance into the bloodstream (the lucky patient was a dog). When Charles II was restored to the throne, Wren presented the King with a large-scale model of the moon.

Christopher Wren's Baroque cathedral of St Paul's is the fifth church to stand on its London site.

He was always going to
be interesting with a
name like Augustus
Welby Northmore Pugin,
and it's true that the
architect of the Gothic
revival, born in 1812,
stuffed a lot into his 25-
year career. He began
with furniture design,
churning out chairs for
George IV at Windsor at
the age of 15, went on
to interior design,
political writing and
then architecture.
His work was guided
by conversion to
Catholicism, aged 23.
Pugin looked to restore
Britain's faith in its own
architecture, and
specifically the Gothic
style that had built
medieval Catholic
cathedrals across the
country. His talent didn't
forestall a brief stay in
prison for debt. A first
wife died, and a second
and third bore children
that would follow in his
professional footsteps.
In 1851 Pugin was taken
to Bedlam, an asylum
for the insane, possibly
poisoned by the mercury
he was prescribed for an
eye problem. He died a
year later, aged 40.

Taking the mock: Georgian and Victorian churches

The Georgians didn't build any great cathedrals.
Instead they assembled a few neo-Classical parish
churches, some Baroque, others born of the Palladian
style that took hold of grand house building in the
early 18th century (see section 3.2.3 for more). The
Victorians maintained the fondness for things past but
reacted against the formality of neo-Classicism with
neo-Gothic churches. They built loads, working hard
to ensure Britain's rapidly expanding industrial towns
were kept in check with religious instruction of all
denominations. A few cathedrals went up. In Truro,
Cornwall, the darkly Gothic affair was the first Anglican
cathedral since Wren's St Paul's. Augustus Pugin
was the prime church architect of the Victorian age.
He did most to reinvigorate the medieval spirit of
Gothic church building with soaring spires and pointed
windows, although he's more famous today for
co-designing the Palace of Westminster with
Charles Barry.

1. Identity: the
foundations
of British culture

2. Literature
and philosophy

**3. Art, architecture
and design**

4. Performing
arts

5. Cinema,
photography
and fashion

6. Media and
communications

7. Food and drink

8. Living culture:
the state of
modern Britain

Mixing medieval and modern: 20th century churches

New churches in the early 20th century plodded on with the medieval revival, driven in particular by Scottish architect Ninian Comper with his weakness for Perpendicular Gothic. A few pursued other trends, notably William Lethaby in 1902 when he built an idiosyncratic Arts and Crafts church in Brockhampton, Herefordshire, complete with thatched roof and concrete vaults. A couple of late 20th century cathedrals braved Modernism, notably at Coventry where Basil Spence used blocky shapes and modern materials to recreate the feel of a tall Gothic structure alongside the ruins of the medieval church blown up by the German air force in the Second World War. Liverpool's Metropolitan Cathedral was less concerned with continuity, taking a radical circular design. Some said it was an architectural response to the city's other cathedral, the mighty sandstone neo-Gothic Anglican effort (the largest in Britain), designed by 22-year-old Giles Gilbert Scott and begun in 1904. Others called it Paddy's Wigwam, referring to the tent-like structure and its large Irish Catholic congregation.

"TO WALK FROM THE RUINS OF THE OLD CATHEDRAL INTO THE SPLENDOUR OF THE NEW IS TO WALK FROM GOOD FRIDAY TO EASTER, FROM THE RAVAGES OF HUMAN SELF-DESTRUCTION TO THE GLORIOUS HOPE OF RESURRECTION."
John Irvine, Dean of Coventry Cathedral

Key styles and periods

Mid 11th to early 13th century:
Normans build 'motte and bailey' and stone castles.

13th to early 14th century:
concentric castles.

16th century:
Tudor palaces and prodigy houses.

Late 17th to early 18th century:
Baroque.

Mid 18th century:
Palladianism.

Late 18th century:
neo-Classicism.

Early 19th century:
Regency and Scottish Baronial.

Mid 19th century:
the height of Gothic Revival.

Late 19th century:
Queen Anne and the Domestic Revival.

Here for keeps: early Norman castles

If you see a large, grassy mound in the middle of an English or Welsh town, looking rather forlorn round the back of Burton's, it's probably a motte, an earthwork built up by the Normans to support a wooden castle. The wooden topping will be long gone but these structures were crucial to securing the Normans a toehold in Britain. Their job done, they were soon replaced with stone structures. William the Conqueror dished out land to local lords who protected their patch with these chunky stone behemoths, at the heart of which was the keep, a fortified central tower. There were two main types: the shell keep, essentially a protective wall enclosing wooden buildings; and the hall keep, a multi-storied building with defence downstairs and a great hall, living quarters and chapel somewhere on the floors above. A century after William conquered, Britain had around 2,000 such castles.

Four imposing Norman castles

The White Tower. The formerly whitewashed hall keep at the heart of the Tower of London was built on William's orders and finished in 1097. Rudolf Hess, Adolf Hitler's deputy, was the last person to be imprisoned in the Tower, incarcerated there for four days in 1941.

Orford, Suffolk. Only the hall keep of the 1160s remains but it's a beaut, with 18 sides, a 90ft (27m) high view out to the North Sea and its very own merman legend.

Cardiff. A shell keep with 12 sides constructed circa 1200 as one of the mighty Marcher castles built by Anglo-Norman lords trying to control Wales.

Carrickfergus. The most intact Norman castle in Northern Ireland, surrounded on three sides by Belfast Lough, only gave up its role as a garrison in 1928.

The great castle building age

Britain's castle building bonanza peaked in the late 13th century. Beleaguered by recalcitrant tribes, Edward I recruited French castle design maestro, James of St George, to reinforce his authority. Edward's castles were built in the new concentric style, a design probably picked up on Crusade in the Holy Land: two or three walls were better than one, arranged in ever decreasing rings around central buildings. The first, begun in 1268, was a grey giant in Caerphilly, South Wales, still pleasingly intact today and second only to Windsor as Britain's largest castle. The best appeared in disputed border regions. Northumberland and Scotland bore dozens but the finest appeared in North Wales. With much of England and Wales subdued to the Crown, the great age of castle building was over by the 14th century. Only the fractious Scottish border regions and unruly Ireland kept up the building work. In Scotland they had pele towers, in Ireland tower houses, both of them with living quarters arranged above a defensive ground floor.

Old castles never die…

Not all of England's Norman castles were emasculated by the relative peace that descended over the country some time in the 14th century. Many were put to service again in the 17th century as strategic strongholds in the Civil War (the pounding they took explains why so many are in ruins). Dover's Norman castle saw action in the Napoleonic Wars with troops housed in barracks tunnelled underneath the 12th century structure. The same tunnels were put to service again in the Second World War, converted to use as a command centre and underground hospital. The evacuation of British and French troops from Dunkirk was masterminded from within the warren.

Three medieval castles built to last

Caerlaverock. A rare triangular affair in Dumfries and Galloway actually built c.1277 by the Scots to resist Edward I. It didn't quite do the job.

Beaumaris. The last, biggest and best of Edward I's castles in North Wales is still staggering. Considered the apogee of British medieval military architecture.

Smailholm Tower. A pele tower built in the Scottish Borders by the Pringle family in the 15th century. Locals would huddle inside when the English came calling.

Hampton Court

On the defensive: the Welsh bastides
When James of St George built Edward's stock of north Welsh castles he often incorporated bastides. These fortified towns had their origin in Gascony, France, where the English king had considerable 13th century influence. In Conwy much of the old bastide wall remains, interspersed with 21 towers. They were built not for the Welsh, but for English settlers in need of protection from understandably grouchy locals.

"HARDWICK HALL, MORE GLASS THAN WALL."
Early 17th century rhyming couplet

Pile drive: the time of great houses

Large decorative houses replaced castles in Tudor England. No one really needed ten-foot thick stone walls anymore. And as builders turned to brick and Henry VIII gave Church cash to the favoured few, a secular building boom ensued. Designs were often eclectic: Gothic, Renaissance and Flemish motifs could all appear in one building, but, in common, new builds rarely kowtowed to prevailing European trends. Henry VIII built his own collection of sumptuous palaces characterised by tall redbrick gatehouses and twisting chimneystacks. The palaces of Hampton Court and St James are the best preserved. Elizabeth I had a different impact. She didn't build her own palaces but she did ensure that anyone who might put her up for the night would do so properly. Palatial houses were assembled simply on the off chance that she might visit, and some lay unused when she never showed. They became known as prodigy houses. Burghley House, begun in 1555, in Lincolnshire, was better than most, its uncoordinated pale stone mash of castellation, cupola and balustrade undeniably dazzling. While houses built toward the end of Elizabeth's reign, Burghley included, maintained this mismatch of styles, they did begin playing with the symmetry of Classical design. Longleat in Wiltshire and Hardwick Hall, Derbyshire, both designed by Robert Smythson, got the ancient proportions just right.

Scotland does the Renaissance

Scotland's pugnacious clans ensured that defence remained pertinent to castle design longer there than in England, and the tower house (the lanky, defensive child of the pele tower) remained popular into the 17th century. However, Scotland was also more tuned into the Renaissance than England. Under the Stuarts, particularly James V with his preference for French wives, grand Scottish houses picked up elements of French Renaissance design in the 16th century. Stirling Castle, with its sumptuous façade, is usually considered the finest example of Renaissance architecture in Britain.

146

| 1. Identity: the foundations of British culture | 2. Literature and philosophy | **3. Art, architecture and design** | 4. Performing arts | 5. Cinema, photography and fashion | 6. Media and communications | 7. Food and drink | 8. Living culture: the state of modern Britain |

Back to the Classics

Inigo Jones and Christopher Wren warmed Britain up for Classicism in the 17th century, and while architects couldn't quite leave Gothic alone, they spent much of the next 200 years plugging away at the Ancients, going through three phases:

Baroque (1660-1720). Two men dominated the sensual curves, straight lines and overblown decoration of secular Baroque. Nicholas Hawksmoor was trained by Christopher Wren and put his education to good use at Easton Neston, an idiosyncratic Northants country house begun in 1695. Hawksmoor also collaborated with the other great British Baroque architect, John Vanbrugh. The pair worked on Castle Howard in Yorkshire, and Blenheim Palace, the finest Baroque pile in Britain.

Palladianism (1720-60). Association with the Tories, the deposed Stuarts and their despised French friends sullied Baroque's good name, and the Georgian era dawned with a new generation of architects. It was the age of the Grand Tour, the ritual European jolly that introduced Britain's young nobs to the Classical 'correctness' of Roman building. Architects looked back to Inigo Jones and in doing so found the 16th century buildings of Andrea Palladio. Palladianism dominated British architecture for 50 years, depositing correct, classically-proportioned and somewhat stiff buildings. Facades were generally flat save for the odd portico, but inside the buildings were more ebullient. Holkham Hall in Norfolk, begun by William Kent in 1734, is the apotheosis of Palladianism. The style also found approval in Ireland, where it kept a purer form than in England but added fancier, rococo style interiors. Castle Coole in County Fermanagh was a high point.

Neo-Classicism (1760-90). Eschewing the rules of Palladianism, neo-Classicism was more decorative, more concerned with Classical motifs than with exact proportions. Scotsman Robert Adam was the chief architect and Kedleston Hall, Derbyshire, the high point of his

Britain's first Classical building

The Queen's House in Greenwich was Britain's first wilfully Classical building (others like Burghley and Longleat merely bore elements of Classicism). It was built by Inigo Jones in the early 17th century for two successive queens of England. Inspired by Andrea Palladio's use of Classical proportion, Jones came up with the 'double cube' shape.

147

The two giants of neo-
Classicism, Robert Adam
and William Chambers,
didn't limit themselves
to a pastiche of ancient
Rome. They took liberally
from other periods and
locations too. Chambers
designed the ten-storey
Chinoiserie Pagoda in
Kew Gardens, while
Adam converted a
rambling house at
Culzean in Ayrshire into
a romantic, medieval
style castle with
battlements and turrets.

achievements. He tended to remodel rather than build
from scratch. A master of interiors, Adam drew on first-
hand experience of domestic architecture in Pompeii
and Herculaneum. The south front of Kedleston was
modelled on the Arch of Constantine in Rome.
Commentators said he brought 'movement' to buildings,
drawing out columns and pushing back niches to enliven
the flat, monumental feel of Palladianism. The other great
British neo-Classicist was William Chambers, another
Scot, responsible for Somerset House in London in 1776.

It's just like being in Athens (no, really):
Regency architecture
Politically, the Regency period lasted from 1811 to 1820,
the years when Prince George played proxy king for mad
dad George III. However, in architectural terms, Regency
expands to include the first 30 years of the 19th century,
a period when elegant neo-Classicism spilled from the
grand residences into town houses and even town
planning (see section 3.2.5 for more). Neo-Classicism
also twisted toward ancient Greece. Wealthy Brits began
digging around in Greece and absconding back to Britain
with whatever ancient remains they unearthed, inspiring
a cultural fascination with all things Greek. Appropriately
enough, the British Museum, custodian of the Elgin
Marbles, is the most arresting structure of the Greek
Revival. Designed by Robert Smirke in the 1820s, the
façade with its regimental Ionic order of columns was
typical of the movement's measured pomp. The
popularity of the Greek Revival in Scotland, at home
amid the Scottish Enlightenment, brought Edinburgh its
'Athens of the North' subheading. William Henry Playfair
was the prime architect, writing Hellenistic elegance into
the likes of the Royal Scottish Academy.

1. Identity: the
foundations
of British culture

2. Literature
and philosophy

3. Art, architecture
and design

4. Performing
arts

5. Cinema,
photography
and fashion

6. Media and
communications

7. Food and drink

8. Living culture:
the state of
modern Britain

However, Regency wasn't all about Classicism. Elsewhere George IV's love of frippery unleashed a 'cult of styles'. The exotic eastern flavour of Chambers' Pagoda at Kew reached an incongruous zenith in the King's Royal Pavilion in Brighton. Built over seven years from 1815 by John Nash, the onion domes and latticework outside speak of Indian and Islamic design while the opulent interior has a strong oriental flavour.

Crystal Palace
The controversy smoulders to this day

I knew moving south of the river was a mistake

Stupid barbeques

A palace made of glass Joseph Paxton's epic Crystal Palace was built for the Great Exhibition of 1851, assembled in Hyde Park in just six months. Constructed from wrought and cast iron and 25 acres of glass, the mile-long structure was a triumph of Victorian innovation. Dismantled and moved to Sydenham after the exhibition, the Crystal Palace burned down in 1936 – the sound of the roof crashing down could be heard five miles away.

Past masters: Victorian architecture

Regency's style clash grew into the pastiche parade of Victorian architecture. Gothic eventually overshadowed Classical in the battle of the revivals but was often used in tandem with other styles – neo-Classical, Elizabethan and the Renaissance modes of France, Venice and Italy – in the space of one building. The grandiose styles of the past encountered the new wealth of the present, conveyed in magnificent warehouses, railways stations and arcades. Even factories began to acquire elaborate Greek, Gothic or Italianate facades. John Marshall hid his Leeds linen

Scotland picked up the revivalist Victorian mood and built large decorative castles in the Baronial Style. 'Stick a cone on it' seemed to be a key philosophy: porches, turrets and even bay windows were adorned with 'candlesnuffers'. The style reached a climax at Balmoral Castle, Queen Victoria's Deeside hideout.

mill behind an Egyptian Revival frontage in 1838. We can only guess whether the workers putting in 72-hour weeks appreciated the interpretation of Edfu's Temple of Horus. Despite the stylistic bunfight, Victorian architecture can be hewn roughly into three periods:

Early Victorian (1830-50). Gothic – deemed the only genuine English style – was in the ascendancy. A backlash against industrialisation led by the critic John Ruskin directed an obsession with the aesthetics of an idealised medieval Britain. Messrs Barry and Pugin (see section 3.2.2 for more) captured the pointy, rather heavy Gothic style in the Houses of Parliament. Thomas Cubitt and Prince Albert proved, however, that eclecticism still reigned with the Italianate Osborne House, built on the Isle of Wight in the 1840s.

High Victorian (1850-70). The overblown ornamentation of Gothic reached its height with architect George Gilbert Scott at the helm. The neo-Gothic St Pancras Station Hotel in London was one of his finest buildings. The station itself, opened in 1868, was also stunning, its patterned bricks and latticed ironwork typical of the pride and grandeur the Victorians brought to public buildings. It recently emerged, beaming, from a lengthy revamp to take on the role of London's Eurostar terminal.

Late Victorian (1870-1900). Gothic was losing out to a more homely, domestic style by the 1870s. The Arts and Crafts movement, itself born of that Victorian yearning for a simplified past, provided the inspiration. Architecturally, Arts and Crafts evolved into the Queen Anne or Domestic Revival style, a light mix of red brick, gables and floral motifs that had little to do with the actual Queen Anne of the 18th century.

3.2.4 In and out of love with Modernism: 20th century builds

One step forward, two steps back
The rustic whiff of Arts and Crafts lingered into the 20th century. Among its progeny, the Domestic Revival's unchallenging vernacular style of traditional methods and roughcast render would end up plastered along suburban avenues for decades to come. Charles Voysey and Edwin Lutyens were the key vernacular architects, although Lutyens soon turned from domesticity to Classicism, sparking an Edwardian neo-Baroque movement dubbed the Wrenaissance: while the Continent swooned over Art Nouveau, under Lutyen, Britain regressed 200 years. One rare work of innovation did slip through the conservative net, it too owing some debt to Arts and Crafts. Charles Rennie Mackintosh's Glasgow School of Art mixed the organic curves of Art Nouveau with Scottish tower house vernacular and functional, geometric style. It was a pioneering British take on the Modernism that would shape 20th century European architecture.

The Mac
The heart of Glasgow's
Art School campus
designed by
Charles Rennie Mackintosh

Reluctant Modernists
While Le Corbusier and Gropius followed Mackintosh's functionalist lead abroad, in 1930s Britain little could dent the prevailing Classicism dominated by Lutyens. The location of Britain's most progressive interwar efforts speak of Modernism's perceived worth: the Penguin Pool and Gorilla House at London Zoo were both designed by Russian émigré Berthold Lubetkin in the early 1930s.

I've had better holidays...
In 1914 Charles Rennie Mackintosh rented a house in Walberswick, drawn to the Suffolk coastal village as a watercolourist (he was more than just an architect) in search of the light. However, locals called in the army when they became suspicious of the way he would walk with a lantern along the shore in the evening. When Mackintosh began ranting in a thick Glaswegian brogue he was arrested on suspicion of being a German spy. He spent a week in prison before the confusion was cleared up and he fled sunny Suffolk.

151

Lubetkin went on to explore the social function of architecture with Highpoint One, a seminal north London apartment block that pursued the Modernist love of a straight line and reinforced concrete. Art Deco, the more decorative side of Modernism, found its best British form in the lidos and cinemas that latched on to a 1930s thirst for public leisure.

Concrete bungle: the New Brutalists

Modernism broke through in the 1950s, even while it was rarely mind blowing. The 1951 Festival of Britain showcased modern architecture with radical, temporary builds on London's bombed out South Bank. One still remains, Leslie Martin's Festival Hall, a first British brush with large-scale Modernist architecture. The public grew to accept (if not love) its angular concrete and glass body. Cityscapes across Britain grew tall concrete blocks in the following 20 years but few stirred much admiration. Modernism's unforgiving corners were pushed further by the New Brutalist school, convinced they could find social harmony with raw, blocky structures. Peter and Alison Smithson led the mode that generated shopping centres, public buildings and flats. The public struggled to swallow that much concrete, and many such builds have since been torn down. However, recent reappraisal has found something to love in the New Brutalist style.

Some buildings, like Ernö Goldfinger's 1972 landmark Trellick Tower (once described as 'Colditz in the sky') in west London, have even gained listed status, while contemporary British architects have returned to bare concrete.

Et tu, Brutalism?
Portsmouth's reviled (and doomed) Tricorn Centre

1. Identity: the
foundations
of British culture

2. Literature
and philosophy

3. Art, architecture
and design

4. Performing
arts

5. Cinema,
photography
and fashion

6. Media and
communications

7. Food and drink

8. Living culture:
the state of
modern Britain

The High-Tech Rogers and Foster show

Bare concrete was out of fashion by the 1980s. For many, whatever the perceived social merit, the Le Corbusier style just didn't work with an overcoat of British drizzle. Architects of the later 20th century turned instead to glass and steel. Richard Rogers and Norman Foster, knights and household names both, are the world-famous trailblazers of the High-Tech style. Rogers made his name incorporating the mechanics of a building – pipes, elevators and girders – into its external aesthetics. His 'inside out' Lloyd's Building in London has been lauded since its 1986 inception. Foster has also been concerned with transparency, using recurring plate glass segments and exposed metal beams. His first major triumph was the amorphous Willis Faber and Dumas building in Ipswich, radical on its 1975 initiation for a tinted glass shell, inscrutable in daylight but revealing at night. The lurching glass beehive of the Greater London Authority building beside the Thames (once referred to as the 'glass testicle' by then mayor Ken Livingstone) has seen the Foster style develop into the 21st century.

Rebuilding the Baltic
Norman Foster's Swiss Re Building, or 'the Gherkin', was built on the site of the Baltic Exchange, an Edwardian masterpiece all but destroyed by an IRA bomb in 1992. What remained of the Exchange was boxed up and bought for £800,000 in 2006 by two Estonian businessmen intent on reconstructing the century-old building in the middle of Tallinn.

Protection racket: listed buildings
The British listed building scheme protects anything of significant architectural interest – on the grounds of age, decoration or historic importance – from destruction or unsympathetic alteration. There are three Grades (I, II* and II) covering the 500,000 or so listed properties in Britain (Scotland has an A, B and C system). Almost everything built before 1700 gets automatic listing, as do most buildings constructed between 1700 and 1840.

"BRITAIN GETS THE ARCHITECTURE IT DESERVES. WE DON'T VALUE ARCHITECTURE, WE DON'T TAKE IT SERIOUSLY, WE DON'T WANT TO PAY FOR IT AND THE ARCHITECT ISN'T TRUSTED."
David Chipperfield, winner of the prestigious Stirling Prize for architecture in 2007, gives his opinion to *The Times*

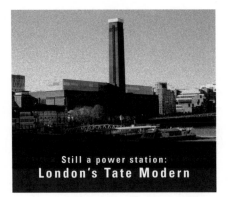

Still a power station:
London's Tate Modern

What do the British people think of their modern architecture? In 1984 Prince Charles stood in front of RIBA (the Royal Association of British Architects) and talked about how modern architects "consistently ignored the feelings and wishes of the mass of ordinary people in this country". The appalled black-tied audience dismissed HRH as an ill-informed amateur, but he articulated what a lot of ordinary Brits felt: that modern architecture was self-indulgent, unattractive and poorly planned. Things have changed somewhat in the past two decades, thanks largely to the renunciation of gaunt concrete structures. A number of successful builds, from Foster's Gherkin to Herzog and de Meuron's reinvigoration of Bankside Power Station as the Tate Modern, have acclimatised the public to more radical architecture. After a perfunctory period of ridicule, most new landmark buildings acquire a nickname and a place in public affections.

Five great buildings of contemporary Britain

Eden Project by Nicholas Grimshaw. The most futuristic build in Britain sits like giant frogspawn in a former Cornish quarry.

Maggie's Centre Kirkaldy by Zaha Hadid. Black and pointy outside, light and curvy inside; from the Baghdad-born British architect.

Swiss Re Building by Norman Foster. Britain's most popular piece of recent architecture rises 180 metres above the City of London like a cosmic vegetable.

Gateshead Millennium Bridge by Wilkinson Eyre. The lithe double arcs on the Tyne move, appearing to wink as the ships pass underneath.

National Assembly for Wales by Richard Rogers. Cardiff Bay's parliament is transparent and ecologically conscientious. And it's got a wonderfully wavy wooden roof.

154

1. Identity: the   2. Literature   3. Art, architecture   4. Performing   5. Cinema,   6. Media and   7. Food and drink   8. Living culture:
foundations   and philosophy   and design   arts   photography   communications   the state of
of British culture   and fashion   modern Britain

Rural vernacular architecture

Rural vernacular architecture before the 20th century
was dictated by the local climate, building materials
and agriculture. Each region had its own style.
In modern housing, such nuances have all but gone,
replaced with a homogenous new-build format across
the country. Thankfully, plenty of the older stuff
survives outside the main urban areas.

Stone cottages
Britain's stone houses were built mainly in the north
and west. Yorkshire has its granite, Cumbria, Wales
and Cornwall their slate, the Cotswolds its honey-
coloured limestone and Northumberland a red
sandstone. Further east, flint and clunch (a chalky rock)
are both used in East Anglia. Roofs were sometimes
built of stone too, although thatch was more likely.
Upland areas had longhouses, two storey affairs with
people at one end and their animals and crops at the
other. Scottish, Irish and Welsh crofts had a similar
partition but were reduced to one long, low storey
with a room at either end.

Timber-framed houses
Where there was no local stone, medieval Britons built
timber-framed properties, filling the gaps with cob
(mud and straw). Box-shaped hall houses were at the
grander end of timber-framing, their central hall flanked
by two-storeyed living quarters. They're found all over
southern England, East Anglia and the Midlands.
Cheaper versions just had the hall. Cruck houses were
simpler, constructed from two curved timbers propped
up to support both walls and roof.

1. Identity: the
foundations
of British culture

2. Literature
and philosophy

**3. Art, architecture
and design**

4. Performing
arts

5. Cinema,
photography
and fashion

6. Media and
communications

7. Food and drink

8. Living culture:
the state of
modern Britain

Urban vernacular architecture

The Victorians

Lured from the countryside in their millions, the new working class of the industrial revolution took up residence in the brick terraces of burgeoning factory towns from Belfast to Birmingham. A fireplace in each room, rudimentary plumbing, sash windows and a small yard were typical features. In Wales, long ribbons of terracing appeared in the coal mining Valleys. The Scots saw the worst side of Victorian urban living: they built up as well as along, creating multi-storied tenement flats with communal stairways and yards. The tenements rapidly turned into overcrowded slums. Large amounts of Britain's Victorian terracing was flattened in the 1950s and 60s to make way for wider roads and high-rise blocks of flats.

Out in the burbs

When town centres became overcrowded in the early 20th century and housing crept out to new suburbs, domestic architecture was led by the Victorian Arts and Crafts movement. Semi-detached replaced terrace and nostalgia set in with mock beams (the so-called Tudorbethan style) and pebbledashed render. Modernist builds in the 1960s and 70s spawned featureless housing estates on the edges of towns and high-rise blocks in the centres. A decade later, the half-hearted modernism was gone, replaced by a confused pastiche. The Tudorbethan style refuses to die; faux beams still find their way onto modern housing estates, although a scaled down Regency style reigned on mass new builds through the 1990s. With a chronic housing shortage looming, local authorities are now turning to lowish-rise flats, for which a tentative modernism is being employed. Ecological concerns are making a painfully slow impact on new developments in the 21st century.

1. Identity: the   2. Literature   3. Art, architecture   4. Performing   5. Cinema,   6. Media and   7. Food and drink   8. Living culture:
foundations   and philosophy   and design   arts   photography   communications   the state of
of British culture   and fashion   modern Britain

Best laid plans

The random pattern of most British town centres, still guided by medieval street plans, belies a modern preoccupation with planning, with presenting domestic architecture in communal, ordered ways. The Georgians were the first to plan large clusters of housing, and planners and architects have been collaborating ever since, setting out terraces, squares and whole towns. In a more general sense, attempts by planners to accommodate the motorcar ruined historic town and city centres in the later 20th century. Innumerable medieval buildings were simply knocked down in the quest to make town centres more profitable; replaced with shopping precincts and car parks that removed any aspect of local charm.

"YOU HAVE TO GIVE THIS MUCH TO THE LUFTWAFFE: WHEN IT KNOCKED DOWN OUR BUILDINGS IT DID NOT REPLACE THEM WITH ANYTHING MORE OFFENSIVE THAN RUBBLE. WE DID THAT."
Prince Charles

Four memorable plans

Georgian: Bath. Transformed from village to grandiose spa town in the early 18th century by John Wood and his son. The Circus and Royal Crescent remain inspiring.

Victorian: Saltaire. Built around a Yorkshire textile mill in 1853 by enlightened industrialist Titus Salt, Saltaire had neat gritstone terraces, bathouses and a hospital.

Arts and Crafts: Hampstead Garden Suburb. Created a century ago as a model village on the fringe of soot-shrouded London. Other 'garden suburbs' followed suit.

Modern: Alton Estate. A New Brutalist mix of high-rise blocks, maisonettes, parkland and social strife on the edge of London; one of many concrete complexes built to remedy the post-war housing shortage of the 1950s.

4 Performing arts

4.1 Music

Music is the precocious talent of contemporary British culture, and has been since the 1960s. Multicultural, global, cool – is there a better advert for the modern nation? But there's much more to British music than backbeats, iconic riffs and the Winehouse beehive; it also harbours a rich folk and classical repertoire.

4.1.1 Folk stories: traditional music

Mention 'folk' music to many Brits and they'll groan, turn and run. The modern variant suffers from an image problem, as famous for weird beards and chunky knits as for its distinctive sound. But those in the know are appreciative of Britain's folk heritage, and while modern folk has been around since the 1950s, the traditional sort traces its roots back beyond the Middle Ages. This was the music of the common people; the love songs, work songs, lullabies and dance tunes of the peasantry, passed from generation to generation. The songs and tunes evolved and mutated over time, and those that survive are impossible to attribute or date, which, of course, is part of their charm. Scotland, Wales and England each have their own styles and traditions.

Don't point that thing at me In the Jacobite Rising of 1745, pipers accompanied the Highland armies into battle, their deafening noise striking fear into English hearts – a response it can still induce today. Following the defeat of Bonnie Prince Charlie at Culloden in 1746, the playing of the Great Highland Bagpipe was effectively outlawed. One piper, James Reid, was hanged because his bagpipe was deemed 'an instrument of war'.

Scotland

Britain's northern territories have a proud folk music tradition, from the Gaelic waulking songs sung by tweed makers and puirt a beul (improvised nonsensical 'mouth music') of the Highlands and Islands to the ballads of the Lowlands and Borders, all accompanied by the fiddle, bagpipe, whistle and clarsach (small Celtic harp). Scotland has always been big on piping: the Great Highland Bagpipe has become emblematic and piobaireachd, the classical music of the bagpipe, instantly recognisable. The Scottish tradition evolves still, pursued in the local mods (festivals of Gaelic music) and by groups like the Tannahill Weavers and the Battlefield Band.

Northern Ireland

The old counties of Ulster share in the wider Irish rituals of Gaelic music. Here, more than anywhere else in the UK, traditional music remains a regular feature of life, even while the legendary pub sessions featuring guitar, fiddle, bodhrán (shallow goatskin drum), squeezebox and flute actually began with Irish expats in English pubs. The most prominent Gaelic folk band from the north in recent years has been Altan. In Northern Ireland specifically, the Scots and English plantation settlers of the 17th century brought ballads that remain part of the folk repertoire. The Ulster Scots tradition of marching bands, featuring pipe (or flute) and giant lambeg drum, also remains strong. World conquering flautist James Galway blew his first flute in a Belfast band.

Wales

The self-proclaimed 'Land of Song' is famed worldwide for the male voice choirs that live on in the former mining communities of South Wales; the ruddy-faced gents of the Treorchy and the Morriston Orpheus choirs are considered masters of the craft. To the north and west of Wales, instruments like the crwth (six-stringed lyre) and the pibgorn (wooden pipe), and the performing of simple, vernacular penillion songs can be traced back to the 12th century, to the first eisteddfods, the spirited contests of music and poetry. Penillion were sung to the accompaniment of the Welsh triple harp (a harp with three rows of strings), the instrument most commonly associated with Wales. The traditions live on: Robin Huw Bowen and Llio Rhydderch are internationally acclaimed Welsh triple harp players and the annual National Eisteddfod of Wales is a major cultural event.

Competitive culture
The eisteddfod has become an important element of resurgent Welsh identity. Apparently, the tradition dates back to 1176 when Lord Rhys held a musical showdown in his Cardigan castle, although the current Welsh language format seems to have emerged in a 19th century revival. The biggest is the International Eisteddfod, held annually in Llangollen, North Wales.

England

Pre-Christian festivals and ceremonies, like the Furry Dance in Cornwall, the Nutter Dance in Lancashire (both spring things) and apple tree wassailing in Somerset, often provided the initial inspiration for English folk music. From the 16th century, popular songs detailing the exploits of heroes and villains were printed on sheets known as broadsides and sold on the streets. One of the earliest recorded 'broadside ballads' is *A Lytel Geste of Robyne Hood* (c.1506). Traditional English instruments include the fiddle, concertina and Northumbrian pipes (a bagpipe blown with bellows), of which Kathryn Tickell is a well-known modern-day exponent. England also harbours a strong tradition of sea shanties, the sailors' work songs. Some are still performed, notably by the Fisherman's Friends of Port Isaac, Cornwall.

Sumer is Icumen in. An English secular round (a single melody for multiple voices each starting at a different point) discovered in Reading Abbey and dating from around 1240. It features in the cult movie *The Wicker Man* (1973).

Scarborough Fair. The song has existed in many forms over the centuries. In it, a former lover is asked to perform a set of impossible tasks in order to be taken back. Simon & Garfunkel's arrangement featured in Mike Nichols' film *The Graduate* (1967).

Suo Gan. A traditional Welsh lullaby of uncertain date, *Suo Gan* remains in regular performance today, and appeared in the Steven Spielberg film *Empire of the Sun* (1987).

English folk: the giant panda of music

By the end of the 19th century, the English folk song was an endangered species, lost in the new urban sprawl and shoved aside by music hall. But folk had its protectors: Cecil Sharp and a small group of enthusiasts from the Folk Song Society set about collecting, transcribing and cataloguing folk songs from around the country. Sharp, a composer and music teacher, gathered thousands of songs, often adding his own clumsy piano parts. Significantly, he encouraged others to join in, most notably the composer Ralph Vaughan Williams, whose work would bear a large debt to the English folk song.

In post-war Britain, the English folk song needed rescuing again. A second revival occurred in the 1950s and '60s, instigated almost single-handedly by Ewan MacColl (real name Jimmie Miller), a communist, playwright and singer/songwriter. He founded London's Ballads and Blues Club and, in reaction to the rise of

American folk, introduced a draconian policy demanding that performers only play songs from their own country. Suddenly, folk clubs were popular; for a few years they were even considered cool. Peggy Seegar, an American who became MacColl's third wife, and for whom he wrote his masterpiece *The First Time Ever I Saw Your Face* (1957), Shirley Collins, and Martin Carthy were also instrumental to the revival. By the 1960s folk was fusing with rock 'n' roll. *Folk Roots, New Routes* (1964) by Shirley Collins and Davey Graham is usually considered the landmark album, while Steeleye Span, the jazz-influenced Pentangle, Fairport Convention and The Incredible String Band, a psychedelic Scottish outfit, were also important. Alas, the boom was short-lived – by the mid 1970's, folk rock had become regularly self-indulgent and unwittingly ridiculous.

Maybe this time: contemporary folk

In 1981 folk music changed its name. The International Folk Music Council was reborn as the International Council for Traditional Music, perhaps because the very mention of the word 'folk' conjured that image of a beard, a jumper and an ear with a finger in it. Yet while the Scots, Irish and Welsh now appear to cherish their traditional folk music, in England the negative stereotypes persist. However, there is some hope. In recent years, English folk music has undergone a revival (yes, another one) with young musicians like Seth Lakeman and Kate Rusby, neither of whom has a beard, playing traditional English music with energy, confidence and pride.

Dirty secrets
Ewan MacColl's *Dirty Old Town* (1949) is still a jukebox regular, usually in versions recorded by The Dubliners and The Pogues. Many mistakenly assume it's an Irish song, but the town in question was actually Salford, MacColl's birthplace. Salford City Council (it's not actually a town) objected to the indictment of their ward yet subsequently knocked much of the place down and started again. As for MacColl, he led an eventful life. MI5 kept a file on his communist activities in the 1930s and leaned on the BBC in an effort to suppress his work. He deserted the army in 1940 and didn't resurface until after the war when he mysteriously escaped prosecution. He was married three times and fathered five children, one of whom, Kirsty MacColl, was a successful songwriter herself until she was killed in a scuba diving accident in 2000.

165

Five contemporary folk artists worth a listen

Eliza Carthy. The daughter of folk musicians Martin Carthy and Norma Waterson is an acclaimed singer and fiddle player. *Anglicana* (2002) was a highpoint.

Seth Lakeman. Dynamic singer, songwriter and fiddle player from Devon who mixes traditional folk with the occasional modern beat. *Kitty Jay* (2004) and *Freedom Fields* (2006) were both critically acclaimed albums.

Kate Rusby. A singer/songwriter known as 'The Barnsley Nightingale', Rusby plays traditional and original folk songs. Had a top ten single with *All Over Again* (2006), a duet with Ronan Keating.

Show of Hands. Singer/songwriter Steve Knightly and multi-instrumentalist Phil Beer (they do have beards) play mainly original folk material. *Lie of the Land* (1995) was hailed a masterpiece.

Laura Marling. Another singer/songwriter, this one more in the American folk tradition of Joni Mitchell and Neil Young. The debut album *Alas I Cannot Swim* (2008) won a coveted Mercury Music Prize nomination.

A GOD OF SMALL THINGS
Yorkshire's own Jake Thackray (1938-2002)
Possibly the most underrated
person ever to pick up a guitar
and write a song...

1. Identity: the foundations of British culture   2. Literature and philosophy   3. Art, architecture and design   **4. Performing arts**   5. Cinema, photography and fashion   6. Media and communications   7. Food and drink   8. Living culture: the state of modern Britain

Britain has never been able to boast a Mozart, Beethoven or Bach, and in any list of legendary classical composers only one Brit, at most, will make an occasional appearance in the top ten – and that's usually the one who was really a German. But don't tune out just yet; classical music has played its part in shaping modern British culture and a number of composers merit closer inspection.

The early years

First things first, where did British classical music come from? The origins lie in the monophonic (single melodic line) liturgical plainsong and Gregorian chant of the early Middle Ages, which, with the later organum and motet (both polyphonic – having more than one part), dominated medieval music. It all informed the work of John Dunstable (or Dunstaple), the first great British composer, in the early 15th century. Most of Dunstable's manuscripts, an important musical link between the medieval and Renaissance eras, were torched in the Dissolution of the Monasteries, and much of the surviving repertoire was pieced together from fragments discovered in Europe. His best-known work is a motet – *Veni Sancte Spiritus – Veni Creator* (15th century).

Mad for the madrigal

Polyphonic music continued its development in the Renaissance era, aided by the appearance of new instruments like the viol and the virginals (an early harpsichord). Henry VIII's almighty rift with Rome upped the importance of royal patronage and, while most music remained religious in nature, there was a growing demand for more secular stuff. The major composers of the 16th and early 17th centuries included John Taverner, Orlando Gibbons and William Byrd, but perhaps the most

Three reasons why
Henry Purcell is not dull

His *Music for the
Funeral of Queen Mary*
(1695) was used as the
title music for the
Stanley Kubrick film
A Clockwork Orange
(1971).

His music was a major
influence on The Who's
legendary guitarist, Pete
Townshend.

He may have died of
chocolate poisoning
(although TB seems
more likely).

important was Thomas Tallis whose *Spem in alium*
(c.1570), a forty-part motet, is considered a
masterpiece. By the later 16th century, the English
madrigal was all the rage. They were light, melodic,
secular songs, usually for three to six unaccompanied
voices, and any composer worth their keep had a few
up their sleeve. Few did better than Thomas Morley,
although today his *Now is the Month of Maying* (1595)
actually reads like a prime example of just how banal
the English madrigal could be:

"Now is the month of maying,
When merry lads are playing,
Fa la la la la.
Each with his bonny lass,
Upon the greeny grass,
Fa la la la la."

Finally, someone really good: the Purcell years

When the political turmoil of Civil War and the
Protectorate finally ebbed, music in the late 17th
century was illuminated by the brief brilliance of Henry
Purcell, considered by many to be the greatest of all
British composers. Purcell was an exceptional organist
and, as a composer, his sheer inventiveness and
mastery of the Baroque form commanded the
admiration of all his contemporaries. He produced a
great body of work including music for the church,
the theatre and royalty. He died at the age of 36 and
was buried in Westminster Abbey next to the organ.
Purcell's one opera, *Dido and Aeneas* (1689), featuring
the famous *Dido's Lament*, is considered his best
work.

1. Identity: the   2. Literature   3. Art, architecture   **4. Performing**   5. Cinema,   6. Media and   7. Food and drink   8. Living culture:
foundations   and philosophy   and design   **arts**   photography   communications   the state of
of British culture   and fashion   modern Britain

He might be German, but he's our German:
the age of Handel

The leading figure of 18th century British music was undoubtedly George Frideric Handel. Born in Germany, with his name spelled slightly differently, he moved to London in 1712, aged 27, and later became a British subject. Influenced by Purcell and Italian composers like Corelli, Handel's many operas and oratorios displayed a deceptive simplicity, bringing great fame, wealth and popularity during his lifetime. Mozart, Beethoven and Bach all apparently admired his work. Little is known of Handel's private life except that he ate and drank to excess and had a very, very bad temper. The fact that he never married has drawn speculation about his sexual orientation. He's best remembered for his *Water Music* (1717) and *Music for the Royal Fireworks* (1749), orchestral works written for Kings George I and George II (also both German) respectively, and for his supreme achievement, *Messiah* (1741), the oratorio with which his name will always be associated. Another notable composer of the period was Thomas Arne whose *Masque of Alfred* (1740) featured the ever popular song *Rule, Britannia!*

1. Identity: the
foundations
of British culture

2. Literature
and philosophy

3. Art, architecture
and design

**4. Performing
arts**

5. Cinema,
photography
and fashion

6. Media and
communications

7. Food and drink

8. Living culture:
the state of
modern Britain

Flags at the ready
The Proms, founded in 1895, is an eight-week classical music festival held every year at the Royal Albert Hall. The highlight is the last night – a more informal evening with lots of flag waving and stirring tunes like *Jerusalem* and *Land of Hope and Glory.*

Mr Holst, Mr Holst…
Gustav Holst hated signing autographs. The story goes that, when asked, he would hand out a typed statement reading: "I do not give out autographs".

The land without music?

In the title of a 1904 book, Oscar Adolf Hermann Schmitz, a German critic, described Britain as *Das Land Ohne Musik* (The Land Without Music). He may have had a point. Since Handel's death in 1759, Britain's contribution to classical music had been negligible. However, Schmitz's condemnation was ill timed: the 20th century saw a renaissance in British music that incorporated a new nationalist style. It also bore four great British composers:

Edward Elgar

Despite having no formal training in composition, Elgar progressed from a job as bandmaster at Worcester and County Lunatic Asylum to being the first British-born composer in 200 years to achieve international recognition. He came to prominence with his first major orchestral work, *Enigma Variations* (1899) – the enigma being that the fourteen variations are on an original theme that is never heard. Elgar's greatness, some say his Englishness, lies in a use of bold melodic themes set against a brooding, nostalgic melancholy. An oratorio, *The Dream of Gerontius* (1900), is considered his finest work and his *Pomp and Circumstance March No. 1* (1901), otherwise known as *Land of Hope and Glory*, brings the house down every year at the Proms.

Gustav Holst

Born in England of Swedish extraction, Holst was a highly original composer, the master of orchestration who drew on influences as disparate as English folk songs and madrigals, Hindu mysticism and the avant-garde sounds of Stravinsky and Schoenberg. He was also fascinated by astrology, the study of which provided the inspiration for his most famous work (although he never considered it his best), *The Planets* (1914-16), a seven-movement orchestral suite.

Vaughan Williams

Ralph (weirdly rhymes with 'safe') Vaughan Williams is considered to be the most characteristically English of composers. He rejected most foreign influences, infusing his music instead with the moods and rhythms of native folk songs and the work of 16th century English composers. His rich, plaintive style evoked the essence of the English countryside, so much so that Stravinsky said his *Pastoral Symphony* (1921) was "like staring at a cow for a long time" – a little kinder perhaps than fellow composer Elisabeth Lutyens who christened it "cow pat music". Williams is best known for *A Sea Symphony* (1910) and *A London Symphony* (1913), and for his concerto *The Lark Ascending* (1914) featuring that famous, ethereal solo violin.

Benjamin Britten

Britten was, to date, the last of the great British composers. His dexterity and inventiveness, particularly as a vocal composer, brought him international fame on a par with Elgar. He's best remembered for the opera *Peter Grimes* (1945), the orchestral work *The Young Person's Guide to the Orchestra* (1946), and *War Requiem* (1961), a large scale orchestral and choral work featuring the poetry of Wilfred Owen. He wasn't a fan of the 'Englishness' of the previous generation of composers, although he did arrange folk songs for his partner, the tenor Peter Pears. Throughout his life, Britten's homosexuality and his pacifism were well known. However, few were aware of his obsessive, though innocent, relationships with a procession of 13-year-old boys.

"IT IS CRUEL, YOU KNOW, THAT MUSIC SHOULD BE SO BEAUTIFUL. IT HAS THE BEAUTY OF LONELINESS AND OF PAIN: OF STRENGTH AND FREEDOM. THE BEAUTY OF DISAPPOINTMENT AND NEVER SATISFIED LOVE. THE CRUEL BEAUTY OF NATURE, AND EVERLASTING BEAUTY OF MONOTONY."
Benjamin Britten on cheerful form

And did those feet... Hubert Parry isn't among the best-known composers but he is held responsible for the 20th century renaissance of British classical music. A choral composer of some repute, he was also Director of the Royal College of Music where he tutored Holst and Vaughan Williams. He's notable for composing the choral song *Jerusalem* (1916), viewed by some as preferable to *God Save the Queen* as an English national anthem. Parry set William Blake's poem to music at the request of Robert Bridges, the Poet Laureate, to inspire the troops during the First World War.

171

Minority rule: British classical music in the 21st century

Ever since Britten was buried in Aldeburgh, Suffolk, in 1976 (Peter Pears joined him ten years later), British classical music has struggled to live up to its invigorated reputation. John Taverner, a direct descendant of the 16th composer of the same name, and Peter Maxwell Davies have produced well-received works, but nothing of any real magnitude has emerged. Classical music does have its place in modern British culture, but perhaps not in the way its advocates would hope. It's used in TV commercials and at various sporting events, and the average Brit may well watch the Last Night of the Proms on television (if there's nothing else on), but, in truth, it remains a minority, largely middle-class affair – respectable music for respectable people.

Three British orchestras

The Royal Scottish National Orchestra. Formed in 1891 as the Scottish Orchestra, gaining royal patronage a century later.

The Hallé. Britain's oldest surviving symphony orchestra, founded in Manchester by Sir Charles Hallé in 1858.

London Symphony Orchestra. The LSO was founded in 1904. The esteemed Hans Richter and Edward Elgar were the first two principal conductors.

Ever since rock 'n' roll first swaggered ashore in the 1950s, cockily trailing a comb through its lustrous quiff and setting dull post-war Britain alight, music has been an intrinsic element of popular British culture. It's up there with the great daily topics for discussion: counted alongside the weather, the government, sport or sex as worthy of idle prattle. Perhaps it's the one thing Brits know for sure that they do as well as anyone else in the world.

"GUITAR GROUPS ARE ON THE WAY OUT, MR. EPSTEIN." Decca Records executive Dick Rowe to Brian Epstein as he turns down The Beatles in 1961. Oops...

It came from over the water

When Elvis Presley, Jerry Lee Lewis and Buddy Holly seduced British youth in the 1950s, the native music industry was quick to try and cash in on that American sound. Tommy Steele and Cliff Richard both ran on the 'Britain's answer to Elvis' ticket, but for all their moody posturing and the excellence of Cliff's first single, *Move It* (1958), they were soon exposed as pale imitations of the real thing. Perhaps of greater significance was the skiffle boom that arose at the same time. Lonnie Donegan was the figurehead and his single *Rock Island Line* (1955) typified the form: skiffle was fast, basic, country-tinged rock 'n' roll played with acoustic guitars, washboards and the odd homemade tea chest bass. Skiffle's simplicity, and the fact that most of the instruments could be found in the kitchen, encouraged teenagers to form their own bands. A few of them would, in the next decade, change the history of popular music.

Jazz banned
It's a bitter irony that the organisation set up to care for British musicians, the Musicians Union, played no small role in stunting the growth of homegrown jazz. In a misguided attempt to protect its members' jobs, the union effectively banned American musicians from performing in Britain from the mid 1930s until 1956. Some argue that watching Charlie Parker and Dizzy Gillespie playing in the flesh and in their prime would have given British audiences more of a passion for jazz.

All what jazz

It may have its devotees and the odd dedicated venue here and there – Ronnie Scott's in London stands out – but modern jazz has only ever drawn a minority interest in Britain. However, while home-grown talent hasn't been abundant, a few noteworthy figures have graced the jazz stage: saxophonist Johnny Dankworth and pianist Stan Tracey are veterans of the jazz scene and have always commanded respect – Tracey's album *Under Milk Wood* (1965) is regarded a highlight of British jazz; the 1970s brought the acclaimed avant-garde music of pianist Keith Tippett and saxophonist Evan Parker; and in recent years saxophonist Courtney Pine has come to the fore, fusing jazz with modern elements like drum 'n' bass.

Stan the Man
Stan Tracey scattering chords like shale at Ronnie Scott's

Mop top gets chop

When Ringo Starr admitted in 2008, with some degree of honesty (or naivety), that he missed nothing about his home city of Liverpool, the angry local response came soon after: the city woke to find its foliage sculpture of The Beatles missing Ringo's head.

It was the 60s, man

The union of rock 'n' roll, skiffle, drugs, 45rpm singles, sex, class consciousness and moptopped baby boomers launched a seismic cultural movement in the early 1960s. Britain owes its lofty place in the pecking order of modern music to this period, an era when British guitar bands, crooners and starlets sold the verse/chorus/middle eight format to the world and, in particular, to the United States. Of course, some bands were more important than others...

The Beatles

Liverpudlian skiffle band The Quarrymen changed their name to The Beatles in 1960 and went on to sell over a billion records. After the band were signed to Parlophone records in 1962 by George Martin, the producer with whom they formed a lasting relationship, the singles *Love Me Do* (1962) and *Please Please Me* (1963) soon followed and 'Beatlemania', with its screaming, clawing girls and ringing record shop tills, swept Britain. What made The Beatles so great? They were inventive and rebellious (although their 'long' hair looks quite short in retrospect), but, above all, in John Lennon and Paul McCartney they had a songwriting duo par excellence. When music entered its psychedelic phase in the mid 60s, the influence of drugs and Indian spiritualism became more evident in The Beatles' sound. Recording techniques became more innovative, while their songwriting grew increasingly sophisticated, producing some of their finest work on the albums *Revolver* (1966) and *Sgt. Pepper's Lonely Hearts Club Band* (1967). Internal friction split the band up on 10th April 1970, with McCartney apparently the first to walk. He and Lennon went on to have successful solo careers, although neither could eclipse the achievements of The Beatles, acknowledged 40 years on as the world's most successful group.

The Fabs, suited and booted in '64. Their instant hold on the American market still seems completely fantastic

So The Beatles were quite good then? The Beatles had 17 No.1 singles in Britain, enjoying a total of 69 weeks at the top spot. *Please Please Me* (1963) was the first; *The Ballad of John and Yoko* (1969) the last. In the States they managed 20 chart toppers. In April 1964 they held all five top positions in the Billboard Hot 100, and a remarkable 12 positions in all. And they've clearly still got it, 40 years after their demise: *The Beatles 1*, an album featuring all their chart topping singles, made the No.1 spot itself in Britain for nine weeks in 2000.

... and The Stones

The only songwriting partnership to rival Lennon and McCartney in the 1960s belonged to Dartford boys Mick Jagger and Keith Richards. The pair had both briefly played skiffle but The Rolling Stones formed in 1962 with their roots firmly in rhythm and blues.

The Beatles
and The Stones
It's difficult to overstate
the musical and cultural
impact of The Beatles
and The Rolling Stones.
Their fans – in Britain
and around the world –
dressed like they did,
wore their hair the same
and took the same
drugs. Their music has
been an influence –
direct or not – on almost
every band since.
The songs are still heard
everywhere you go; their
greatest hits on every
pub jukebox. Even today,
those of a certain
vintage (and some
younger) will still define
themselves by
allegiance to either.
The Beatles or The
Stones. And the ripples
spread a long way from
home. The 'British
Invasion' of the mid
1960s that saw The
Beatles, The Stones and
other British bands like
The Yardbirds and The
Animals dominate the
American Billboard
charts was surely the
apogee of 20th century
British cultural clout.

Early releases covered American R&B songs, but by 1965 they were writing their own material, developing a distinctive style with the raw energy of Richards' guitar and an arrogantly lazy rhythm section. Success followed, with the singles *(I Can't Get No) Satisfaction* (1965), *Get Off My Cloud* (1965) and *Paint it Black* (1966) all hitting No.1 on both sides of the Atlantic. With Jagger's snarling vocals and menacing persona, The Stones were seen as dangerous; the dark to The Beatles' light. Later songs like *Sympathy for the Devil* (1968) simply stirred parental anxiety. The band maintained their status and record sales throughout the 1970s, achieving eight consecutive No.1 albums in the USA. The albums *Let it Bleed* (1969) and *Exile on Main Street* (1972) are considered their best. Somewhat implausibly, The Rolling Stones are still going: playing sell-out stadium gigs over 45 years after they formed.

Two other important 60s bands

The Who. Following early hits *I Can't Explain* (1965) and *My Generation* (1965), The Who became famed for their dynamic, often destructive live performances, with the frenzied drums of Keith Moon and the trademark 'windmill' guitar-playing of Pete Townshend (a trademark that regularly made his right hand bleed). The epic single *Won't Get Fooled Again* (1971) and *Tommy* (1969), the first rock opera, featuring the single *Pinball Wizard*, were Who highlights.

The Kinks. The Kinks came to prominence with the No.1 single *You Really Got Me* (1964). The song's distorted guitar riff would be echoed in the heavy rock and punk bands to come. Singer Ray Davies was perhaps the most distinctly English writer of his generation; songs like *Waterloo Sunset* (1967) would inspire many future British bands, most notably Blur.

1. Identity: the   2. Literature   3. Art, architecture   **4. Performing**   5. Cinema,   6. Media and   7. Food and drink   8. Living culture:
foundations   and philosophy   and design   **arts**   photography   communications   the state of
of British culture   and fashion   modern Britain

Does that sequinned blouse come in electric blue? How do you follow the 1960s then? With sequin-spangled trousers, five-inch platform heels and men in make-up, as if you even have to ask. The glam rock of the early 1970s was polished, Stones-like guitar music played by an eclectic range of artists, from the pouting, slinky T-Rex to the progressive, arty Roxy Music – their albums, *Electric Warrior* (1971) and *Roxy Music* (1972) respectively, are highly regarded. The most significant figure to emerge from glam rock was David Bowie.

David Bowie sings another folksong from Alpha Centauri

Bowie added a sense of theatre to music, paving the way for the spectacular live shows gig-goers have come to expect from contemporary bands. The albums *Hunky Dory* (1971) and *The Rise and Fall of Ziggy Stardust and the Spiders from Mars* (1972) make required listening. While Bowie and co wowed as much with aesthetics as tunes, at the other end of the spectrum Van Morrison was all about the music. Northern Ireland's savoured favoured son found critical solo success at the end of the 1960s with the wandering folky mysteriousness of *Astral Weeks* (1968), and remains lauded for his incomparable vocals: the lungs may be from Belfast but the voice box resides somewhere in the Mississippi Delta.

Car wash
There is a famous rock myth that The Who's eccentric drummer, Keith Moon, drove a Rolls Royce into the swimming pool of the Holiday Inn in Flint, Michigan in 1967. Moon always strongly refuted the story – claiming the car was a Lincoln Continental.

A day in the life
John Lennon was assassinated at 11pm on 8th December 1980 at the entrance to the Dakota building (where he'd lived with Yoko Ono for seven years) in New York by Mark David Chapman, a crazed fan who shot him in the back four times. Chapman, who'd asked Lennon for an autograph earlier in the day, was carrying a copy of J.D. Salinger's novel *The Catcher in the Rye* (1951) at the time of the shooting. He'd written "This is my statement" inside.

"YOU MUST UNDERSTAND THAT IT'S NOT A WOMAN'S DRESS. IT'S A MAN'S DRESS."
David Bowie explains away a challenging outfit

Fishy stories

The saga of British rock music is strewn with (mostly) apocryphal stories involving groupies, hotel rooms, drugs and the like. Have you heard the one about Mick Jagger, Marianne Faithfull and a Mars Bar; or Led Zeppelin, a young groupie...and a mud shark? Perhaps it's best not to ask. Other tall tales include Keith Richards' claim that he had his blood replaced in a Swiss clinic, the one about Mama Cass choking to death on a ham sandwich in her London flat (she actually died from a heart attack, although it *was* in the same room where, four years later, The Who drummer Keith Moon would die after taking too many prescription pills) and the story of how The Beatles enjoyed a sly spliff in the Buckingham Palace toilets before collecting their MBEs.

Elton, Freddie and friends: the other types of 1970s rock

While glam rock was camping its way up the singles chart, its less effeminate cousins were selling albums by the bucket load. Hard rock bands like Black Sabbath, Deep Purple and Led Zeppelin played heavy, blues-influenced rock music and introduced the world to the now obligatory long guitar solo, tight jeans and screaming lead vocal. The Led Zep albums *Led Zeppelin IV* (1971) and *Physical Graffiti* (1975) were monumentally successful; the former featured *Stairway to Heaven* (1971) – frequently cited as a 'best rock song ever' contender.

Progressive (prog) rock was perhaps more intricate, inventive and conscious of its own artistic depth, with keyboards a major feature of bands like Yes, Genesis, and Pink Floyd. They showed off their musical talents in epic songs strewn with time and key changes. Genesis' *The Lamb Lies Down on Broadway* (1974) moved many, while Pink Floyd's *The Dark Side of the Moon* (1973) is one of the most successful records of all time, having sold 40 million copies worldwide. Another hugely popular group of the mid 1970s, Queen, were a mixture of heavy, glam and prog rock. *A Night at the Opera* (1975) is considered their finest album, and not just because it featured Britain's third best-selling single of all time, *Bohemian Rhapsody*. The band maintained their commercial success until singer Freddie Mercury's death from AIDS in 1991. Finally, Reginald Kenneth Dwight (or Sir Elton Hercules John as he's also known... or the Winner from Pinner (take your pick)) found his form in the 1970s with expertly crafted piano rock. So far, he's sold over 200 million records; the best of which has to be the album *Goodbye Yellow Brick Road* (1973).

Anarchy in the UK: the rise and fall of punk

Punk exploded out of the urban decay of mid-1970s Britain, rebelling against the bloated music industry of the day and against society as a whole. With The Sex Pistols and The Clash at the fore, punk was rock music stripped of all sophistication. It was angry and anarchic, and was played very fast, very loudly and usually very badly. Following the release of The Sex Pistols' single *Anarchy in the UK* (1976), punk blazed a controversial trail across Britain. Its anti-establishment, 'do-it-yourself' philosophy inspired a disaffected generation to form their own bands. A few were successful but most disappeared without a trace. Punk found a particularly receptive crowd in Northern Ireland, where bands like The Undertones and Stiff Little Fingers gave the province its most fruitful period of modern music. By the time The Sex Pistols' bass player, Sid Vicious, died of a heroin overdose in 1979, punk had burnt itself out. But its spirit permeated British culture, influencing hairstyles, fashion and music – as bands like The Libertines and Arctic Monkeys proved – well into the 21st century.

I swear I was there
On June 4th 1976, The Sex Pistols played at the Lesser Free Trade Hall in Manchester in one of the most influential gigs of all time. Thousands of people claim they were there, even while the audience numbered about 35. Among those who actually did attend were The Buzzcocks; members of what would become Joy Division, The Fall and The Smiths; and, so he says, Mick Hucknall of Simply Red.

Five important punk bands

The Sex Pistols. Fronted by Johnny Rotten, they courted scandal at every opportunity. An infamous television interview in 1976 prompted *The Daily Mirror* headline: "THE FILTH AND THE FURY!"

The Clash. The most political of the early punk bands. Their first single, *White Riot* (1977), called on the white working class to take to the streets.

The Damned. The band have the distinction of releasing the first British punk single, *New Rose*, on October 22nd, 1976.

The Buzzcocks. The *Spiral Scratch* EP (1977), released on their own New Hormones label, included the punk anthem *Boredom*.

Siouxsie and the Banshees. In true punk style, they performed their first gig despite having no songs to play.

The 80s scene

2 Tone, named after the Coventry record label responsible for most of the releases, combined Jamaican ska music (calypso-tinged rhythm and blues) with an urban punk sensibility for uplifting, insistent dance music. The Specials, Madness and The Beat were the big names, and The Specials' *Ghost Town* (1981) was probably the stand out track. Another clique, the New Romantics, appeared in the early 1980s wearing outlandish clothes and laughable make-up. The music was synthesiser-driven, heavily influenced by Bowie and shamelessly pretentious. Spandau Ballet and Duran Duran were the main protagonists. Other 80s bands weren't so easily categorised. The Police emerged out of the punk scene, but weren't really a part of it. *Synchronicity* (1983) is considered the best among their albums, which have sold more than 50 million worldwide. Dire Straits weren't part of any scene either but their presence is hard to ignore. The album *Brothers in Arms* (1985) was staggeringly successful. The Jam, a modish blend of anger and sharp suits, were another important band in the late 1970s and early 80s. Frontman Paul Weller is still making well-received music today.

Leave it, Mam! I'm trying to sing, isn't it?

TOM: THE EARLY YEARS at home practising his stage act in mirror with a vacuum cleaner as microphone. Lots of aspiring stars do it. It's not unusual.

Tom and Shirley – didn't they do well By 2007 Tom Jones had amassed £190 million, while fellow Welsh singer Shirley Bassey had sold 135 million records. Not bad for a miner's son from Pontypridd and a Tiger Bay teenage mum. Neither had an easy start in life. Bassey's father, a Nigerian sailor, walked out when she was two, and she grew up with six older siblings in the notorious dockside district of Cardiff. By 17 she was pregnant and working as a waitress. As for old snake hips, as a child in Ponty he was confined to bed by tuberculosis for a year. He left school aged 15 with no qualifications and worked variously as a labourer and door-to-door vacuum cleaner salesman before fame came knocking.

180

Northern souls: the Manchester scene

Manchester became a focal point for British music in the latter half of the 1980s. The Smiths' simple, naked musical style, and their name itself, was a reaction against the pomposity of the New Romantic trend. Their sound relied heavily on the inspired, jangling guitar of Johnny Marr and on the talent of singer Morrissey whose lyrics had their own unique blend of maudlin wit and emotional depth – the album *The Queen is Dead* (1986) stands out. The Stone Roses and Happy Mondays arose from the drug-fuelled, all-night rave culture of the 'Madchester' scene in the late 1980s to produce some of the most important music of the period. Albums like The Stone Roses' eponymous 1989 debut and the Mondays' *Pills 'n' Thrills and Bellyaches* (1990) introduced psychedelic and dance elements to the basic rock format – both have stood the test of time.

Top one, nice one, get sorted: the dance revolution

Whatever your pleasure – house, acid house, techno, jungle, trance, garage – electronic dance music and the attendant club scene have been potent forces in British culture since the late 1980s. From underground beginnings, each scene has had its influence on mainstream pop and rock music with its use of computer-based recording and sampling techniques. The nature of clubland music, its tunes spliced into one continuous stream of music, made stars of club DJs like Pete Tong, Sasha and Danny Rampling. Perhaps the most significant artists emerged from the Bristol trip hop scene. Trip hop used the breakbeats and samples of electronic dance but slowed them right down; anyone trying to dance to it was in trouble. The down-tempo moodiness of the genre is best experienced on Massive Attack's *Blue Lines* (1991) and Portishead's *Dummy* (1994).

The wizard of Moz
Former Smiths singer Morrissey, a solo artist since 1987, is in danger of graduating from 'enigma' to 'national treasure': in 2006 he came second in a BBC poll of top living British icons, ahead of Paul McCartney and David Bowie.

"THE SMITHS HAPPENED BECAUSE I HAD WALKED HOME IN THE RAIN ONCE TOO OFTEN."
Morrissey

The Britpop years

Looking back, it feels like the dominant trend in 1990s popular music was Britpop, even while British music had become a hugely varied beast. The Britpop tag was applied to a number of bands, notably Oasis, Blur and Pulp, who took their influences (sometimes very obviously so) from British bands of the 1960s and 1970s, sang about life in modern Britain and wrapped it all up in a Union Jack (Cool Britannia crowed the newspapers). Oasis' *(What's the Story) Morning Glory?* (1995), *Park Life* (1994) by Blur and *Different Class* (1995) by Pulp are among the classic albums of the era.

NOEL GALLAGHER
BRITPOP'S GREATEST DIPHTHONG

Big noises in the contemporary music scene

British music proceeds through the new century as it did through the last. It's diverse, daring, inventive – all the things that have made it such a global cultural force. Fads come and go with alarming speed – new rave, emo, electropop, dance punk – just read the *NME* for whatever's new. Good old guitar bands remain a key part of the story: Coldplay are among the glitterati of world rock, even if they haven't broken much new ground since their debut album *Parachutes* (2000). Other bands like Franz Ferdinand, Snow Patrol, The Libertines and the punk-influenced Arctic Monkeys have made an important impact, and Radiohead remain out front in terms of innovation.

Hip hop has made inroads into the charts in recent years, led by American artists but restyled by British acts like Dizzee Rascal and Kano, who also draw rap, dancehall, garage and other elements of urban music – a vital force in modern British culture – into their work. Perhaps the unexpected revelation of the later Noughties has been the rise of the female singer/songwriter. Amy Winehouse, Adele and Duffy have reshaped listening habits with smoky, soulful vocals that, however derivative, repeatedly impress. Both Winehouse and Adele attended the Brit School, a performing arts college which, along with reality TV shows like *Pop Idol*, *Popstars: The Rivals* and *The X-Factor* (which generously coughed up Girls Aloud, Leona Lewis (another Brit School graduate) and Will Young), perhaps proves that modern pop stars are made not born. The Brit-led reality TV talent show format has been sold around the world, a source of national pride or shame depending on your outlook.

Five British music festivals

Glastonbury
Held most years in June, in Somerset, it is the world's largest performing arts festival. Set in 900 acres of farmland, or mud, depending on the weather.

Aldeburgh
A programme of predominantly classical music unfurls on the Suffolk coast each June. Most of the action actually happens in the converted maltings at Snape.

Creamfields
Dance music reigns in Cheshire each August, in the festival baby of Liverpool superclub, Cream.

WOMAD
Festival of world music that's been going on in the West Country each July since 1982. Spin-off WOMAD fests now occur around the world.

Edinburgh Jazz and Blues
The biggest such fest in Britain usually starts swinging at the end of July.

A flavour of the 21st century: five albums

Parachutes
(2000) Coldplay.

Up the Bracket
(2002) The Libertines.

A Grand Don't Come For Free
(2004) The Streets.

Whatever People Say I Am, That's What I'm Not
(2006) Arctic Monkeys.

Back to Black
(2006) Amy Winehouse.

Boys and girls
The 1990s witnessed the rise and, hankies at the ready, the fall of the boy band and the girl group. With irritatingly catchy hits like *Back For Good* (1995) and a young Robbie Williams in their ranks, Take That became pin-ups for prepubescent girls nationwide (not to mention their sizeable gay following) while The Spice Girls sold an unbelievable 55 million records worldwide after hitting the big time with their debut single *Wannabe* (1996).

4.2 Theatre, dance and comedy

A playwright for all eras, William Shakespeare still looms large in British theatre a good 400 years after he was at work. However, the late 20th century brought a new golden age, a time when Pinter, Stoppard, Hare, Bennett and others reinvigorated the British stage. Now, if only they could get more people to actually visit the theatre…

Pete, you can play third shepherd...
Perhaps the origins of British theatre lie around the fire, with some hammy minstrel giving his all to the drama of *Beowulf*. But who knows – maybe they just delivered it deadpan instead. Liturgical dramas, played out from the tenth century onward, offer more solid evidence for theatre. Monks turned ritual into theatre, aware that the people were more likely to grasp scripture when it was acted out. The Passion (at Easter), Magi (Christmas) and Annunciation (March) were all regularly performed. Liturgical drama in church became commonplace in the Norman era, shaped increasingly into structured plays. Guilds began taking over the acting duties, the laymen working with the Church to get the narrative right. The lives of saints also made for popular drama, although the Reformation left few extant saints' plays. While Christianity loomed large in early medieval theatre, it didn't monopolise completely: often, the old pagan rituals were woven into biblical stories. You couldn't, for example, guarantee that a priest wouldn't process down the village street carrying a large (fake) phallus, incorporating an old pagan fertility rite into the Easter pageant.

Theatre, the new rock 'n' roll
By the 15th century, drama was an important part of British cultural life (even while staging was still a relatively ad hoc affair) with performances delivered in everyday spaces rather than dedicated theatres. Venues might include the village church, a market place or patch of open ground. Northern England was particularly fond of processional theatre in the summer, with the action carried or wheeled through town on a series of mini stages. In winter, theatre moved indoors, sometimes staged in the local manor house where the gentry would be seated at a high table at one end of the hall and the plebs sat and stood at the other. In all instances, the drama was less 'them and us' than today; the audience would often become involved in the play, and local figures were frequently characterised on stage.

Play list: the key genres of medieval drama

Mystery plays. Full-blown biblical epics told from Creation to Last Judgement and often run over days. Towns in England had their own mystery play 'cycles': versions from York (comprising 48 pageants), Chester and Wakefield survive almost intact. Guilds of craftsmen acted out the different parts, the parable often relating to their trade – so, for example, the shipwrights would take charge of Noah and the Flood. This association with the guilds engendered the 'mystery' name, derived from *mysterium*, a Latin word meaning handicraft.

Morality plays. The didactic child of mystery plays, they pitched vice against virtue (personified with different characters) and made sure that morality romped home with the mortal soul. *Everyman*, dating to the late 15th century, is the most famous example.

Interludes. Performed as a *digestif* between courses at a banquet, or within the acts of a larger play, interludes were usually secular skits; amusing, sometimes farcical diversions that often satirised local public figures. Others followed the morality format.

Folk Plays. By the late 15th century, the green tights of Robin Hood were a standard fixture of the theatre wardrobe. Tied in to pagan spring celebrations, the outlaw story made for popular drama, touring around England and Scotland to the accompaniment of morris dancing and archery competitions. Henry VIII took part in Robin Hood plays as a young man, before the story of subversion against the Crown began to rankle and the genre was suppressed and superseded by the story of St George.

Stage presence: the dawn of the theatre

British drama mushroomed in the 16th century, rapidly evolving from the didactic morality/mystery mode of old into the secular, professional and terrifically creative strand of British culture that rose to a crescendo with William Shakespeare. The impetus for staging drama moved from the Church to the nobility, a transition spearheaded by Henry VII with his small troupe of court actors. Wealthy lords followed his lead, retaining their own players or employing the troupes-for-hire that travelled the country. Outside noble circles, drama moved into innyards (courtyards attached to inns), before finally, in 1576, Britain acquired its first purpose built theatre since Roman times, constructed by actor James Burbage in Shoreditch under the instruction of the Earl of Leicester. Leicester called it, perhaps under pressure for a decision, The Theatre. Others soon followed, reaching stylish heights in 1599 when Burbage's sons built The Globe, an octagonal three-tiered marvel in Southwark.

Prelude to a golden age

With the stage set, drama progressed to fit the new venues. Classical themes dribbled in from the Renaissance and the medieval format of interludes and folk plays fed a new secular style. At the same time, the mystery cycles slowly declined, their demise hastened by association with Catholicism in the Reformation. Professional playwrights emerged, writing for similarly professional companies of actors. The earliest memorable play (that survives) was a comedy, *Ralph Roister Doister* (c.1553), written by Nicholas Udall in the style of Roman playwright Terence and performed by his pupils at Eton College. The first tragedy came soon after: *Gorboduc* (1562) was written by Thomas Sackville and Thomas Norton, and its story about succession strife probably didn't impress the young Elizabeth I, for whom it was first performed. *Gorboduc* was also the first British play in blank verse, a novelty that freed actors from the constraints of rhyming couplets. These, the first true British plays, were shown up for their lack of sophistication by what came next – the golden age of British theatre, or British Renaissance theatre as it's sometimes called.

Shakespeare: was he really that good?

William Shakespeare began his career in theatre as an actor, playing alongside Richard Burbage in the Lord Chamberlain's Men, one of a handful of professional companies. As a writer he found early success with poetry but turned, in his mid 20s, to concentrate on writing plays. The *Henry VI* trilogy were probably the first, written between 1590 and 92. Over the subsequent 20-year period Shakespeare wrote 37 plays. The first decade, the 1690s, bore history plays, consumed with the lives of *Henry V* (1599), *Richard III* (1591) and the rest, thoughtful comedies like *Much Ado About Nothing* (1598) and the tragedy of *Romeo and Juliet* (c.1594). Some say his later work was shaded by the deaths of his son, his father and the Queen, and the second decade was certainly defined by the solemn, self-destructive giants of *Macbeth* (c.1606), *Hamlet* (c.1600), *Othello* (1602-03) and *King Lear* (c.1605), although ended with tragicomedy in his final solo play, *The Tempest* (1610).

Shakespeare's supreme talent was for psychology, for shaping believable characters with strengths and flaws, with the love, hate and ambition that we recognise as immutably human traits. Such was their universality that Lady Macbeth's guilt and Hamlet's complex melancholy still resonate clearly today. Shakespeare brought these emotions to

Villain of the piece
Early English playwright Nicholas Udall, headmaster at Eton, was hauled up before the college council in 1541, accused of stealing college silverware. He denied the charge but unexpectedly confessed instead to sodomising two of his pupils. Less prestigious figures would have hung but Udall was given a year in prison. Six years later he embarked on a new career as a vicar.

Flat hunting with William Shakespeare

Phrases
first found in
Shakespeare

Bated breath
(The Merchant of Venice)

Green-eyed monster
(Othello)

Wild-goose chase
(Romeo and Juliet)

Milk of human kindness
(Macbeth)

Pound of flesh
(The Merchant of Venice)

What the dickens
*(The Merry Wives
of Windsor)*

"THE REMARKABLE
THING ABOUT
SHAKESPEARE IS
THAT HE IS REALLY
VERY GOOD, IN SPITE
OF ALL THE PEOPLE
WHO SAY HE IS VERY
GOOD."
Robert Graves

life with his use of language, manipulating the blank verse or spinning out the metaphor to enhance a character or situation. Throw in the twisting plots, made navigable by those strong, distinct protagonists, and a talent for both comedy and deep tragedy, and you have the secrets of Shakespeare's enduring popularity. It took a century for the posthumous reputation to gather pace, to rise significantly above his contemporaries, but today there is no higher deity in the pantheon of British culture. No one has been quoted more or performed more on stage, the inspiration for composers, artists and writers; a direct influence on everyone from Charles Dickens to Giuseppe Verdi and Sigmund Freud.

Dramatis personae: Shakespeare, the man

We know little of Shakespeare's religion, politics or true sexual leanings; a few public certificates are all that survive to comment on his life. There aren't even contemporary portraits. We do know that he was born to a Stratford-upon-Avon glovemaker and his wife in 1564, the third of eight children. By the age of 18 he was married to Anne Hathaway, the 26-year-old farmer's daughter carrying his child. Twins added to their Stratford brood two years later, in 1585, but by 1592 it seems William was living in London, earning his money from the theatre. He wasn't chasing publication – any plays that did find print did so without his participation, and the first folio of his work only appeared in 1623, seven years after his death. He made his money (which amounted to quite a bit) not from royalties or commissions but from his shares in the Lord Chamberlain's Men (elevated to the King's Men when James I came to the throne) and their theatres, The Globe and The Blackfriars. Shakespeare retired to Stratford sometime around 1613 and died from who knows what three years later, famously leaving his

1. Identity: the   2. Literature   3. Art, architecture   **4. Performing**   5. Cinema,   6. Media and   7. Food and drink   8. Living culture:
foundations   and philosophy   and design   **arts**   photography   communications   the state of
of British culture   and fashion   modern Britain

'second best bed' to his wife in the will. By 1670 the Shakespeare lineage had died out, but the name lives on in his hometown today in museums, on tea towels ('Out Damned Spot!' they read) and in the Royal Shakespeare Company.

If you only see five Shakespeare plays, see these

Hamlet. The prince wrestles with love, hate, guilt and more as he moves to avenge his father's death. Many call it Shakespeare's finest four hours.

Romeo and Juliet. Young lovers torn apart by old family grievances.

Macbeth. Dastardly but human, Shakespeare's murderous Scottish king descends into madness.

A Midsummer Night's Dream. A comedy of interwoven plots that blur real and fantasy worlds but remain concerned with love.

Henry V. The finest of his history plays lauds the King's stirring military success.

Playboys: two of Shakespeare's contemporaries

British theatre flourished in the Elizabethan and Jacobean eras. Inn yards and the new purpose-built theatres, capable of holding as many as 3,000 people, were packed with audiences drawn from all sectors of society. The ravenous appetite for drama was sated by a raft of playwrights (all of them poorly paid for their work) that worked alongside Shakespeare. Two writers among the many have stuck in the collective memory:

Christopher Marlowe. Born in the same year as Shakespeare but at work earlier, Cambridge-educated Marlowe was a tragedian, the author of emotional, often bombastic plays who pioneered the use of blank verse as an expressive tool of drama. Passionate, amoral

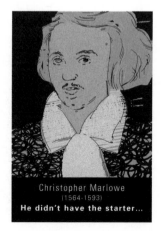

Christopher Marlowe
(1564-1593)
He didn't have the starter...

"ALL THEY THAT
LOVE NOT TOBACCO
AND BOYS ARE
FOOLS."
Christopher Marlowe

Jonson cheats
death...twice
In 1598 Ben Jonson
killed actor Gabriel
Spencer during a duel
over some unrecorded
quarrel. Tried at the
Old Bailey for murder,
Jonson escaped the
gallows by pleading
'benefit of clergy', a
get-out usually granted
to clerics but extended
to Jonson because he
could read Latin. He
served a short prison
sentence, had his
possessions seized and
was branded on the
thumb.

heroes, doomed to fail by over-ambition, drove all six of his plays. *The Tragical History of Doctor Faustus* (c.1590) was his best work, while *Edward II* (c.1591) was a big influence on Shakespeare's history plays. Marlowe, although popular as a writer, was adjudged a rake in his own time and was denounced variously as a heretic and a homosexual. Historians have enjoyed claiming him a government spy, employed to snitch on Catholics even though he seems to have been an atheist. Marlowe died fighting over a bill in a Deptford tavern, aged 29.

Ben Jonson. Born a decade after Shakespeare, his friend and rival, Jonson is remembered best as the author of darkly satirical drama. *Volpone* (1606), a story of greed and misogyny in Venice, cemented his reputation as a comedic writer but *Bartholomew Fair* (1614) is of as much interest today with its amusing snapshot of Jacobean London. Beyond writing for commercial theatre, Jonson created witty masques (a masked mix of poetry, music and dance) for James I's court. Unlike Marlowe and Shakespeare he stuck quite firmly to the classical precepts of playwriting.

Only the spelling mars
Ben Jonson's otherwise beautiful epitaph

1. Identity: the
foundations
of British culture

2. Literature
and philosophy

3. Art, architecture
and design

**4. Performing
arts**

5. Cinema,
photography
and fashion

6. Media and
communications

7. Food and drink

8. Living culture:
the state of
modern Britain

Theatre in the blood

English Renaissance theatre didn't simply fizzle out in the generation after Shakespeare and Jonson. Instead John Webster, a late contemporary, fed a Jacobean taste for tragedy with his talent for bloody revenge drama. His disturbing masterpiece *The Duchess of Malfi* (1614), in which the titular Italian toff is murdered by her own brothers, is still regularly performed today. The other standout work of early 17th century theatre is John Ford's *'Tis Pity She's a Whore* (1633), another Italian-set sequence of heinousness, with incest the prime sin. And then the curtain fell on British theatre's golden age. Puritans began fulminating against the immorality of drama and when Civil War broke out, the theatres were closed and remained so for almost 20 years. The Puritans also banned Christmas and maypole dancing, the cheery old sods.

Acting up

The political tensions of Elizabethan England leaked into the theatre, the authorities fearful that new plays could rouse large theatre audiences to rebellion. And so each new play had to go before the Master of the Revels who ensured the work wasn't too morally or politically provocative. Any writer deemed to have crossed the line could end up in prison. Ben Jonson was incarcerated in 1597 after *The Isle of Dogs*, a play he co-authored with Thomas Nashe, appeared on stage. Alas the play, and any hint at what made it so naughty, hasn't survived, but it must have been pretty bad – the Privy Council banned all other theatre for most of that year.

In good company

Some theatre companies roamed the country in Elizabethan and Jacobean England; others performed in their own London theatres, where two particular troupes ruled the roost. The Admiral's Men were owned by early theatre mogul Philip Henslowe, resided at the Rose Theatre in Southwark and became associated with the plays of Christopher Marlowe. Their leading man, Edward Alleyn, was the best paid actor of the era – he retired to a £10,000 plot in Dulwich. At The Globe theatre the Lord Chamberlain's Men employed the services of Shakespeare as an in-house writer. Richard Burbage, the first man to take the leads in *Hamlet*, *Othello* and *King Lear*, was the primo thespian. The leading comic actor of the Lord Chamberlain's Men, William Kempe, is better remembered today for morris dancing from London to Norwich on an epic 'Nine Days' Wonder'.

Restorative powers: drama bounces back

Charles II lifted the Commonwealth ban on theatre in 1660. Companies
called initially on the Renaissance repertoire but new work soon appeared,
generating the Restoration drama that would stretch beyond Charles'
reign into the early 18th century. It began with tragedy, the restrained
classical variant inspired by French dramatist Corneille, at its most
effective in British hands with Thomas Otway, who brought a powerful
pathos to an often stiff genre with *The Orphan* (1680) and *Venice
Preserv'd* (1682) before apparently choking on a lump of bread and dying
wretchedly poor, aged 33. John Dryden, poster boy for the Augustan Age,
is actually better remembered than Otway, celebrated for Restoration
tragedies like *All for Love* (1678) even while his withering poetry was
probably more accomplished (see section 2.1.3. for more on Dryden).

Well mannered: Restoration Comedy

So much for tragedy; Restoration drama found its true form in comedy.
It too was inspired by Continental theatre, notably French playwright
Molière, but added a wry British humour. The comedy of manners, as the
prevailing genre was called, played up to theatre's new, predominantly
well-heeled audience with intricate plots woven around some social or
sexual scandal among the genteel set. The outlandish characters and
witty, frequently crude dialogue were often as important to the comedy
of manners as the layering of plot and subplot. A typical example might
involve a sharp, irrepressibly randy London rake enjoying carnal knowledge
(just offstage but conveyed via heavy double entendre) with the eager-to-
experiment wife of some repressive aristocratic idiot. Subplots, including
the rake's genuine affections for a virtuous young maiden, fill in the gaps.
It might all sound rather vapid but the depiction of fashionable high
society, its sexual mores recently liberated from Puritan control, would
have struck a chord with the late 17th century smart set.

1. Identity: the
foundations
of British culture

2. Literature
and philosophy

3. Art, architecture
and design

**4. Performing
arts**

5. Cinema,
photography
and fashion

6. Media and
communications

7. Food and drink

8. Living culture:
the state of
modern Britain

The Restoration Comedy playwrights

George Etherege. Proffered a reputation with *She Would if She Could* (1664), the first Restoration comedy, and confirmed it with *The Man of the Mode* (1676), based on real London characters like the rake John Wilmot (see 2.1.3. for more on him).

William Congreve. Restoration theatre's best playwright wrote *Love for Love* (1695) and *The Way of the World* (1700) before giving up, aged 30, when tastes turned against licentious comedy.

William Wycherley. Few picked apart the codes of marriage and sexual morality like Wycherley. The sharpest of the Restoration comedy satirists, his best play was *The Country-Wife* (1675), in which a rake feigns impotence in order to bed rich adulterous women.

George Farquhar. The Londonderry man gave up acting after stabbing a colleague with what he thought was a pretend sword; his move into writing bore plays that sparkled with verbal dexterity and humour. *The Recruiting Officer* (1706) and *The Beaux' Stratagem* (1708) were his best.

"HEAVEN HAS NO RAGE LIKE LOVE TO HATRED TURNED, NOR HELL A FURY LIKE A WOMAN SCORNED."
From William Congreve's *The Mourning Bride* (1697)

The stage door opens to women

When theatre revived in 1660, it lost the broad audience of the Shakespearean era. Theatregoers were drawn almost solely from the upper classes, who used the new proscenium-style theatre (with its protruding stage, pit, gallery and boxes) for illicit liaisons and parading as much as watching drama. The paucity of venues precluded most people from attending, with the dozen or so pre-Civil War London theatres replaced by only two. More encouragingly, British theatre finally allowed women on stage. Former orange seller, probable prostitute and bit on the side to Charles II, Nell Gwyn, was the most famous, but Elizabeth Barry is usually deemed more accomplished. Women also began to emerge as playwrights. The superior female dramatist of the Restoration period was Aphra Behn, lauded for *The Rover* (1677), a comedy of manners.

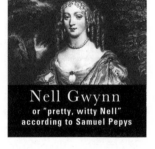

Nell Gwynn
or "pretty, witty Nell"
according to Samuel Pepys

Betting on Barry
In an era when
audiences were rapt
at the sight of females
on stage, Elizabeth
Barry stood out with
passionate, forceful
performances, often
played opposite the
leading male actor of
the day, Thomas
Betterton. He wrote that
Barry brought "success
to plays that would
disgust the most patient
reader". She did comedy
– notably as Mrs Loveit
in Etherege's *The Man
of the Mode* – but was
at her best in Thomas
Otway tragedies,
bringing a genuine
psychological depth to
the roles. No doubt
she drew on her own
life experiences as the
mistress of John
Wilmot, the libertine
Earl of Rochester.
Sources suggest it was
Rochester who trained
her for the stage, taking
on the job for a bet.

"AN INSPIRED
IDIOT"
Politician and writer
Horace Walpole on
Oliver Goldsmith

Under the Irish influence: 18th century theatre

When the ribald laughs of Restoration Comedy slipped from fashion in the early 1700s (hastened by moralising pamphleteers), British theatre entered a subdued century. Some advances were made: London theatres increased in number and playhouses in towns like Lancaster, Bristol and Ipswich pushed drama out to the provinces; and in David Garrick, Britain found its most famous star (apparently the first to whom the word was applied) of the stage, the first actor to pursue naturalism over elaborate declamation. But it wasn't a golden era. Audiences were as likely to watch Italian opera as they were a British play. Indeed Italian opera helped generate one of the period's favourite genres, the 'ballad opera' of popular songs and satire that peaked with John Gay's *The Beggar's Opera* (1728).

Scotland produced a rare, notable playwright in John Home, whose *Douglas* (1756) was a popular tragedy, but the finest drama on British stages in the later 18th century belonged to a couple of Irishmen. Oliver Goldsmith and Richard Brinsley Sheridan reacted to the so-called 'sentimental' comedy of the mid 18th century and revived the comedy of manners, albeit minus the Restoration rude stuff. Goldsmith's *She Stoops to Conquer* (1773), still in repertoire today, is a class-clash farce set over the course of a single day. Sheridan, perhaps the greater playwright, is also still regularly performed. He immersed himself in London's West End, taking a stake in the Drury Lane Theatre where, aged 23, he produced his memorable romcom muddle, *The Rivals* (1775). For all its sophistication, the drama of Sheridan et al was less pivotal in upping audience figures than pantomime and farce. By the end of the 19th century the masses were back, and Britain's burgeoning theatres were seating more than 2,000 at a time.

1. Identity: the
foundations
of British culture

2. Literature
and philosophy

3. Art, architecture
and design

**4. Performing
arts**

5. Cinema,
photography
and fashion

6. Media and
communications

7. Food and drink

8. Living culture
the state of
modern Britain

Two 18th century acting legends

David Garrick. Sometimes credited with single-handedly reviving Shakespeare's reputation, Garrick shone as Richard III and Hamlet. An occasional, average playwright himself, Garrick was also instrumental in bringing realistic scenery, lighting and costume to British theatre. For the role of Hamlet he designed a stunt wig that, aided by string, stood magically erect in response to the ghost of Hamlet's father. However, his legacy remains grounded in a talent for intensity, naturalism and timing on stage. The Garrick Theatre in London's West End bears his name.

Sarah Siddons. The eldest of 12 Kemble children, celebrated as a great acting dynasty, the prime British actress of the 18th century was a dab hand at tragedy (she never played comedy). Siddons honed her craft on the Yorkshire theatre circuit before moving to Drury Lane and astonishing audiences with the way she 'became' a character. They were particularly keen on her Lady Macbeth.

Who threw that?
Edmund Kean was the like the Brando of the early 19th century, electrifying audiences as Shylock, Othello and Hamlet, and even travelling to New York for the role of Richard III. "By God he is a soul," said Byron. But it all started going wrong for Kean, something of an unstable megalomaniac, when he was cited for adultery in a divorce case and compelled to pay damages of £800. The public turned on the actor and audiences began booing and lobbing fruit. He took to drink and drugs, collapsed on Covent Garden stage in 1833 and died soon after, aged 44.

Age of excess: melodrama and farce in the 19th century

As theatre audiences broadened in the 19th century, serious drama struggled for attention. Instead, the crowds that poured into new 'illegitimate' theatres (unsanctioned by the state) opted for melodrama, derivative of gothic tragedy and the stormy moods of Romanticism. With dramatic music, elaborate scenery and the new (smelly and dangerous) marvel of gas lighting, it was quite a show. Melodrama dominated the 19th century stage with its stock cast of two-dimensional characters – hero, villain, old crones and comedy figures – caught up in some violent excitement, be it a shipwreck or a killing spree. *A Tale of Mystery* (1802) by Thomas Holcroft, adapted from a French play, was among the first and most famous, but an Irishman, Dion Boucicault, produced the best (and least overwrought) efforts for the British stage. The high drama spotlighted the contribution of actors and theatre managers as much as

This is an absolute farce... Once Brandon Thomas' *Charley's Aunt* got on stage in the 1890s it refused to budge, breaking all records for longevity with a run of 1,466 performances.

Dame academy Pantomime attached itself resolutely to British theatre in the Victorian era. Advances in stage machinery, lighting and costume brought new colour to old folk stories like *Jack and the Beanstalk* and *Dick Whittington*. The shows could be enormous; Drury Lane impresario Augustus Harris put over 500 on stage for an 1882 performance of *Sinbad the Sailor*. Popular at Christmas, the panto – in contrast to melodrama and music hall – has survived to the modern era.

playwrights, and Edmund Kean was star turn, remembered for scaring audiences witless with his Shylock in *The Merchant of Venice*. Farce, not unconnected to the histrionics of melodrama, had been part of British drama for centuries but reached a peak in late Victorian theatre with *Charley's Aunt* (1892), Brandon Thomas' ludicrous story of Oxford undergraduates, mistaken identities and gentle transvestism.

The Irish influence returns

A handful of writers bucked the 19th century trend for melodrama and farce. Scottish playwright Joanna Baillie wrote intimate, psychological drama at odds with the taste for grand spectacle, while others clutched at the realist style popular on the Continent. Thomas Robertson was the trailblazer, writing and producing social comedies with prosaic conversational dialogue and everyday characters. Such was the attention to detail, to naturalism, in plays like *Society* (1865) and *Caste* (1867) that Robertson's heirs talked of 'cup and saucer' drama. Followers included Arthur Wing Pinero, with 'problem plays' like *The Second Mrs Tanqueray* (1893), a work sympathetic to the Victorian woman's lot. Pinero and co are rarely revisited today but they paved the way for George Bernard Shaw, the Irishman who mixed comedy with campaigning on the British stage, shedding light on issues like prostitution (*Mrs Warren's Profession* (1893)) and religious hypocrisy (*Major Barbara* (1905)). He had trouble with the censors but was crucial in wresting British theatre away from more frothy Victorian fare. *Pygmalion* (1913), about a London flower girl plucked from the gutter, became Shaw's best-known work, thanks in part to a 1950s Broadway (and later, Hollywood) revamp as *My Fair Lady*. Another Irishman, Oscar Wilde, shared Shaw's talent for humour in plays like *The Importance of Being Earnest* (1895), a briskly witty satire on late Victorian society still regularly performed in Britain today.

"A little bit of what you fancy does you good!"
Marie Lloyd

We're 'avin a knees up: music hall

The Victorian love of spectacle launched theatre's unpretentious cousin, music hall – the leap from ballad opera, burlesque and melodrama to a genre that combined song, comedy and novelty acts wasn't huge. The music halls themselves, found predominantly in London, evolved from pubs with sideshows into purpose-built venues. London got its first, The Canterbury, in 1852. Each show would feature a dozen or more acts, from Jules Léotard, swinging around on a trapeze in his stretchy all-in-one, to Harry Champion singing *Boiled Beef and Carrots* or Kaufmann's Cycle Beauties, a group of swimsuited lovelies with a talent for formation bike riding. Music hall was riotously popular for half a century but declined after the First World War, outlived by the revue, a more refined cabaret-style show.

Opera with laughs: Gilbert and Sullivan

Opera, ballad opera and the tradition of the 'extravaganza' (elaborately staged fairy tales popularised by prolific playwright James Planché) all contributed to the Victorian operetta. And nobody did a Victorian operetta quite like Gilbert and Sullivan. Librettist W.S. Gilbert and composer Arthur Sullivan were fairly ordinary in isolation but together they wrote 14 immensely popular comic operettas between 1871 and 1896. Around half are still in regular performance even while the political and social issues that Gilbert satirised are often alien to the modern audience. You can pretty much guarantee that somewhere in Britain tonight an audience will be watching a G&S operetta: *The Pirates of Penzance* (1879), *HMS Pinafore* (1878) and *The Mikado* (1885) are the most likely candidates.

"WHY, IF I WAS TO TRY AND SING HIGHLY MORAL SONGS THEY WOULD FIRE GINGER BEER BOTTLES AND BEER MUGS AT ME. THEY DON'T PAY THEIR SIXPENCES AND SHILLINGS AT A MUSIC HALL TO HEAR THE SALVATION ARMY."
Singer Marie Lloyd, renowned for a nudge, a wink and a double entendre

Coward goes for the jocular

Britain laboured with the naturalism moving through European theatre in the late 19th and early 20th centuries. Audiences found the plays of Henrik Ibsen and Anton Chekhov hard work and, despite the best efforts of Pinero and Shaw, theatregoers fell instead under the spell of light comedy and farce. Composer, actor and writer Noël Coward, dressing-gowned to the nines, struck the right note after the First World War, reviving the comedy of manners with a dose of moral decadence. Conceived one sleepless night and written in four days, *Private Lives* (1930) was perhaps his finest comedy; its tale of a divorced couple reunited inadvertently on respective honeymoons rich with Coward's droll dialogue. Novelist Somerset Maugham also succeeded with the comedy of manners, while Ben Travers churned out the Aldwych farces of the 1920s: humorous, astutely arranged plays named for the theatre in which they debuted. Of the few writers that produced something more serious, J.B. Priestley stood out, messing with time frames in *Dangerous Corner* (1932) and *Time and the Conways* (1937).

A naughty 60s ladder

It's not how big your ladder is, it's how you carry it

You Won't Always Be on Top, a building site comedy by Henry Chapman, fell foul of the Lord Chamberlain's censorship policy in 1959 for, amongst other things, using a workman's ladder at a 'suggestive angle'.

Private lives: Noël Coward

Noël Coward, a piano tuner's son from Teddington, was the Midas of pre-1950s showbiz. Musicals, plays, screenplays, songs, skits – he wrote the lot, but also acted, sang, directed and danced on stage and screen. Coward never openly confessed his homosexuality, although many of his plays offered clue enough. An affair with the married Prince George, Duke of Kent (fourth son of George V), lasted two decades. He squirmed while his extravagant lifestyle was criticised during the Second World War, unable to reveal that he was in fact in the employ of MI5.

Coward counted Winston Churchill, Laurence Olivier and Queen Elizabeth the Queen Mother among his friends but could be notoriously bitchy, and his fragile ego splintered in the 1950s when critics roasted his later work. Coward also wrote some of the most popular songs of the interwar period.

His now oft-parodied baritone singing is perhaps best remembered in *Mad Dogs and Englishmen* (1932), a satire on the British colonial stereotype, a title only eclipsed by *Don't Let's Be Beastly to the Germans* (1943), a piece of wartime satire that backfired and was banned by the BBC.

Working-class heroes

Public funding helped establish the National Theatre (a more English than British affair) after the Second World War and also strengthened the provision of playhouses and companies outside London, exploiting a deep pool of native writing and acting talent. The first playwrights to break with convention were dubbed the Angry Young Men. In 1956, John Osborne wrote *Look Back in Anger*, and its protagonist Jimmy Porter became the first in a line of disillusioned working-class figures in British theatre, the alienated heroes of what was dubbed 'kitchen sink' drama. Playwrights like Bernard Kops, Arnold Wesker and Shelagh Delaney, with the intense *A Taste of Honey* (1958), joined Osborne in criticising the establishment and the social inequalities inherent in British society. The kitchen sink writers were a varied bunch, most of whom rejected the Angry Young Man tag (or 'Woman' for Delaney). Even while they worked, more traditional theatre limped on under the pen of Terrence Rattigan, whose *The Deep Blue Sea* (1952), written in the 'well made' style that conformed to strict technical principles, was a genuine highlight of post-war theatre.

Worthy of an encore: modern British theatre

The Angry Young Men didn't bequeath an abundance of great plays but they did open the door to something new. Activism, improvisation, feminism, surrealism: each had its time on the British stage in the 1960s, 70s and 80s, a period when experimentation and healthy funding drove a renaissance in British theatre. Drama finally became less London-centric as the new Arts Council pushed cash out to regional repertory companies, built new theatres or resurrected old playhouses. Scotland, for so long marginalised when it came to drama, also found a voice; the crucial play was John McGrath's *The Cheviot, the Stag and the Black, Black Oil* (1973), which, although written by an English playwright, told the story of an exploited Scotland, from the Highland Clearances to the closure of Clyde shipyards.

Fluctuations in funding – cut in the 1980s but boosted in the 1990s – may have dimmed the good times somewhat, but British theatre remains in comparatively good health. Indeed, when judged against theatre in much of the world, the British variant thrives. London's West End declaims its

In celebration
of bugger all
Dylan Thomas expended most of his talent on poetry but left perhaps his greatest legacy in the shape of a radio play. *Under Milk Wood* (1953) is set in Llareggub (read it backwards), a seaside Welsh village that, while fictitious, was probably based on Laugharne in Carmarthenshire, where Thomas lived in the early 50s. It begins while the inhabitants are asleep; we learn about the dreamed passions and obsessions of Captain Cat, Organ Morgan, Dai Bread and others. When they wake, the audience watches each go about the daily routine in the knowledge of their concealed, intimate imaginings. Thomas submitted the play to the BBC in 1953, apparently unfinished, but died before they aired it the following year. *Under Milk Wood* moved later to both stage and screen, although Richard Burton's narration for BBC radio in 1963 is the most memorable version.

role as a global hub for drama old and new (nowhere debuts more new shows each year), regional audiences are growing and British stage actors, from Ian McKellen to Judi Dench, Maggie Smith and Ewan McGregor, are still the benchmark of thespian quality. Only the occasional negative voice suggests that West End theatre relies too heavily on such stars to draw the punters. Beyond the West End, generous funding has boosted regional theatre over the last decade.

The big three playwrights of post-war British theatre

Harold Pinter. Influenced by Absurdist Irish playwright Samuel Beckett, Pinter emerged in the late 1950s. His plays were preoccupied with memory, shocking with their portrayal of lost idylls and use of prosaic settings. Typically, a Pinter play has an undercurrent of menace; this and the subtle, plausible use of language – with pauses and gaps conveying more than dialogue itself – have generated their own genre, 'Pinteresque'. *The Caretaker* (1960), *The Homecoming* (1965) and *Betrayal* (1978) were among his best. Pinter also acted and directed. He was awarded the Nobel Prize for Literature in 2005 and the top French accolade, the Légion d'honneur, in 2007 (the French seemed particularly appreciative of his appetite for politicised debate) a year before his death.

Tom Stoppard. The intelligent but accessible talent of modern British playwriting chips away at metaphysical and ethical themes without ever growing stodgy. His breakthrough play, *Rosencrantz and Guildenstern Are Dead* (1967), established the mix of humour, surrealism, humanity and philosophy: its leading duo buffoon their way through life, stumbling periodically on some existential truth, while the Shakespeare play from which they're drawn (and ultimately by which they're bound), *Hamlet*, unravels in the background. Typically for Stoppard, the characters come to life amid the disorder of colliding worlds. Later work became more politicised, concerned particularly with human rights in the old Eastern Bloc, although *The Real Thing* (1982), one of his best, deals with love, art and life in general. Stoppard also works on screenplays, notably *Shakespeare in Love* (1998) and *The Bourne Ultimatum* (2007).

Tom Stoppard

Tom Fun: When Harold Pinter was lobbying to have London's Comedy Theatre renamed the Pinter Theatre, Stoppard wrote back: "Have you thought, instead, of changing your name to Harold Comedy?"

Alan Ayckbourn. The most prolific, consistently popular writer of modern British theatre has been picking Middle England apart since the 1960s. A 'serious humour' lies at the heart of plays that turn on the failure of human relationships and, in particular, on the foibles and miserable black humour of life in the suburbs. Some of it's farce, although Ayckbourn's work appears to darken as he ages. His first big success came with *Relatively Speaking* (1967), establishing the blueprint of mistaken identities, extramarital treachery and comedy. He's written over 70 plays, many of which had their opening night in his Scarborough theatre, marched on to the West End (and Broadway) and then toured the country in perpetuity.

"I WANT TO DEMONSTRATE THAT I CAN MAKE SERIOUS POINTS BY FLINGING A CUSTARD PIE AROUND THE STAGE FOR A COUPLE OF HOURS."
Tom Stoppard

Best of the rest: the other modern British playwrights
you should know about

Joe Orton. Wrote subversive black comedies about sex and death in the 1960s, of which *Entertaining Mr Sloane* (1964) and *Loot* (1965) stood out. Orton was murdered, aged 34, with a hammer by his long-term lover Kenneth Halliwell.

Caryl Churchill. Has written socially conscious plays about women, sexual politics and greed since the late 1950s. *Top Girls* (1982), about women compromising to win power in two male dominated worlds, is among her best.

David Hare. Another social commentator, Hare has set his plays in contemporary Britain, relaying a satirical dismay at post-war failings in *Slag* (1970) and *Pravda* (1985), a stab at domineering media barons.

Brien Friel. The most successful Northern Irish playwright of the 20th century set much of his work in rural Ireland. Plays like *Translations* (1979) and *Dancing at Lughnasa* (1990) explore identity through the tensions of change and British rule.

Peter Shaffer. Wide-ranging playwright who moved from *Five-Finger Exercise* (1960), a neat slice of domestic meltdown, to *Equus* (1973), a psychological piece about a teenager who blinds half a dozen horses.

Michael Frayn. Journalist and novelist who first impressed in drama with *Noises Off* (1982), a farce within a farce: like much of his work, it spoke of man's failed but unbending efforts to impose order on the world.

Alan Bennett. A distinct, playful voice in British theatre for 40 years, Bennett reveals his own dark humour in a variety of settings, from the royal court in *The Madness of George III* (1991) to a Yorkshire school in *The History Boys* (2004).

The rise of the directors

Directors are deemed as important to modern British theatre as writers and actors. They gather the components of a play – lighting, costumes, approach to the script, cast, direction and so on – but are seen as auteurs as much as co-ordinators. Peter Brook led the post-World War Two charge, directing the Royal Opera House by the time he was 22, and was followed by the likes of Joan Littlewood, renowned for left-wing theatre in the 1950s and 60s, and Peter Hall, the most influential figure of recent years. Hall founded the Royal Shakespeare Company in 1960 and went on to direct the National Theatre. Younger directors of note include Sam Mendes and Nicholas Hytner.

Three knights and two dames: the best of British stage talent

Laurence Olivier. He had a reputation for hamming it up but Olivier remains the giant of 20th century theatre, best remembered for his physical, highly technical approach to the great Shakespearean roles.

John Gielgud. Another master of Shakespeare, Gielgud's style – and in particular his versatile voice – was light and graceful compared to Olivier's. He also took on modern roles by the likes of Pinter.

Peggy Ashcroft
(from a sketch by Mervyn Peake in 1937) won an Oscar for *A Passage to India* at 77 years of age

Ralph Richardson. As accomplished in modern roles as in the Shakespearean staples. He worked alongside his good friend Gielgud on many occasions.

Peggy Ashcroft. The leading British actress of the 20th century stage found stardom opposite Olivier and Gielgud in *Romeo and Juliet* in 1934. A rare outing in film 50 years later, in *A Passage to India*, bagged an Oscar.

Judi Dench. A generation younger than the rest, Dench has served much of her time on stage with the Royal Shakespeare Company. Her turn as Lady Macbeth in a minimalist production of 1976 left critics agog.

The beauty of Bennett

Alan Bennett has probably considered scribbling 'National Treasure' as a sobriquet on his passport: as an actor, author, playwright (for stage, radio and television) and screenwriter he's almost universally loved: a totem for modern British culture no less. A butcher's son from Leeds, Bennett began as the understated player in *Beyond the Fringe*, a funny stage revue, but has gone on to reach a wider audience than his comedy troupe colleagues. It's often said that Bennett himself looms large in his work, with its dry voice, heavy with irony and burdened by some inner disappointment. He's probably best known for two series of *Talking Heads* (1988 and 1998), the poignant television monologues from unassuming characters with murky but typically human depths. But a radio play, *The Lady in the Van* (1990), based on the itinerant woman who took up residence in Bennett's driveway for 15 years, perhaps speaks best of the idiosyncratic, humane, funny and humdrum blend that shapes his work.

Saved from the censor Edward Bond's play about a group of South London thugs, *Saved* (1965), turned on the scene where a baby is stoned to death. It ended up on stage at the Royal Court Theatre despite an interdict from the censor. The subsequent prosecution ultimately brought an end to the Lord Chamberlain's long-standing and outmoded powers of censorship over British theatre.

As the beast wakes Belfast playwright Gary Mitchell has carved a successful career writing plays about his home city, and in particular the working-class Loyalist neighbourhood of Rathcoole. However, his portrayal of local colour in the likes of *As the Beast Sleeps* (1998) stirred the ire of local Loyalist paramilitaries who threatened his family, blew up his car and, eventually, told the entire Mitchell clan they had four hours to leave their homes or be killed. Today, Mitchell lives in hiding somewhere in Northern Ireland.

Three contemporary playwrights worth watching

Patrick Marber. Found fame initially as a comedian but shines today as a playwright, notably as the author of *Closer* (1997), a modern tragedy of intimacy and betrayal. He also won plaudits for the screen adaptation in 2004.

Georgia Fitch. Acclaimed on arrival with *adrenalin... heart* (2002) and then praised more recently for *I Like Mine with a Kiss* (2007), the witty story of two friends who both fall pregnant on the cusp of 40.

Roy Williams. Slang, urban patois and familiar situations bring a fresh reality to Williams' gritty drama. The brilliant *Sing Yer Heart Out for the Lads* (2002), found xenophobia and racism in a London pub on the day of an England-Germany football match.

Emerging traditions: modern theatre in Scotland and Wales
After a century or so of deliberation, Scotland launched its National Theatre in 2006. As yet it doesn't have a building, but the associated company has already worked on more than 50 new productions for the Scottish stage, with Iraq War drama *Black Watch* (2006) deemed the most successful by merit of its transition to theatres outside Scotland. The National Theatre is the latest achievement for an emerging Scottish theatre tradition, a mode of intense contemporary drama that counts writers Liz Lochhead, David Harrower and David Greig among its leading lights. Harrower's *Knives in Hens* (1995), the disturbing story of a rural murder, is a particularly standout example of modern drama from a Scottish playwright. Alas, Wales doesn't yet have an equivalent tradition – they're still debating the merits of a National Theatre. However, in Sherman Cymru is does have a progressive company that pushes new work in both Welsh and English.

In tune with the public: the rise of musicals

It may have the Shakespearean tradition, the finest stage actors in the world and progressive playwrights, but the most successful wing of modern British theatre is the musical. Composer Ivor Novello succeeded Gilbert and Sullivan in the early 20th century, leading a golden age of West End operettas and musicals with shows like *The Dancing Years* (1939), in which he also starred, before Rodgers and Hammerstein, Bernstein et al dragged everyone's attention away to Broadway. But the West End struck back in the 1970s and 80s, led by Andrew Lloyd Webber's big budget musicals. It began with *Joseph and the Amazing Technicolour Dreamcoat* (1968) and has continued with *Cats* (1981), *The Phantom of the Opera* (1986) and others. Critics suggest Lloyd Webber has regressed musical theatre, enslaving characterisation and plot to catchy tunes. His productions have also been sniffily dismissed as too global, as unidentifiable with 'British' theatre. Perhaps it depends on your measure of success – no doubt the stats for *The Phantom of the Opera*, having played in 25 countries to over 100 million people and with box office takings of nearly £2billion, will be success enough for Lloyd Webber.

Who goes to the theatre today? Theatre attendance in Britain is relatively healthy. Audience levels have remained consistent for the last 20 years, with about one in four people going to see a play each year. However, it's an aging audience: the under 40s don't flock to the theatre in any great number. If they do, it's more likely for stand-up comedy or a musical – spurred on by reality TV shows that pick the leads in new shows – than plays. 'True' theatre still suffers somewhat with an image problem – many erroneously assume that the genuine article will be 'difficult'.

Edinburgh's big fest
The biggest event on the Scottish theatre calendar, the Edinburgh Festival, staged in August, is actually various different festivals combined. The International Festival of Music and Drama, at its heart, does what its name suggests, while the misleadingly named Fringe turns out to be the largest arts festival in the world.

Playing the fuel: Ivor Novello
Ivor Novello spent four weeks in prison during the Second World War, jailed for fraudulently acquiring petrol coupons for his Rolls Royce. An attempt to bribe the officer delivering the summons didn't help his cause. Years before, Novello had been something of a matinee idol on both stage and screen, as well as the

composer of songs forever associated with the 'lost generation' of the First World War: *Keep the Home Fires Burning* (1914) is the best remembered. These days Brits are more likely to associate Ivor Novello with the song writing awards that bear his name, won by everyone from Eric Clapton to Amy Winehouse and Iron Maiden.

It says here that youput
your left leg in...
In 1651, John Playford
published *The English
Dancing Master*, a 'how
to' guide to more than
100 traditional English
dances. The manual
enjoyed regular reprints
over the next 75 years.
Cecil Sharp gave it
another print run in the
early 20th century.

In step with tradition

'Traditional' British dance is a rather woolly genre; its
bounds drawn without much discrimination and inclusive
of folk dancing, the ceilidh, country dancing and pretty
much anything pre-20th century that didn't involve a tutu.
England, Scotland, Wales and Northern Ireland each have
their 'traditions' and each, in turn, has its own regional
specialities, from the Welsh border morris men with their
blackened faces, to the clog stompers of Lancashire.

England

Dance was popular with the masses in medieval England,
and individual routines like the *Sir Roger de Coverley* and
the *Jenny Pluck Pears* would have been known to most.
They, like the broad range of styles, from morris to country
to square, are now usually grouped under the 'folk' banner.
The dances fell from fashion in the industrial age and
would have been lost but for the efforts of composer
Cecil Sharp in the early 20th century. He travelled around
recording (and prudishly doctoring) the music and moves
of dances that were all but extinct, initiating a revival that
continues into the 21[St] century. The nearest most English
people get to participating in traditional dance these days
is at a barn dance, a hoedown of choreographed moves
led by a caller and their band.

The old routine: three traditional English dances

Abbots Bromley Horn Dance. Staffordshire folk balance deer antlers on their
shoulders while dancing. First recorded in the 13th century.

Rapper Sword Dance. Specific to Northumberland and County Durham: take five
miners, give each a two-handled sword and watch them bob and weave. Dates back
about 200 years.

Maypole Dance. Young maidens cavort around a large wooden pole (it's a fertility rite)
on May Day, weaving ribbons into a pretty pattern. Probably has Pagan origins.

208

1. Identity: the
foundations
of British culture   2. Literature
and philosophy   3. Art, architecture
and design   **4. Performing
arts**   5. Cinema,
photography
and fashion   6. Media and
communications   7. Food and drink   8. Living culture:
the state of
modern Britain

Scotland

The ceilidh (say 'kay-lee', despite the spelling) is a Celtic evening of music and dance. The band strikes up with fiddle, accordion and bodhrán, a caller shouts the moves and the group, usually paired up in a line but sometimes arranged in a ring, follow the energetic steps. Dances once varied between Highlands and Lowlands, although the modern era uses a fairly universal repertoire featuring *The Gay Gordons* and others. Scottish country dancing is ceilidh's refined, slightly earnest cousin. Its roots are less folksy, grounded instead in the studied moves of the Renaissance court. Reels, jigs – both skippy, fast-paced dances – and strathspeys – a more sedate affair (thetune to *Auld Lang Syne* is used for one) – are the main variants. A third Scottish discipline, Highland dancing, usually performed solo in competition at Highland games, may be the oldest of all Britain's native routines. It's a fast, complex blur of skips and steps, more in tune with ballet than ceilidh or Scottish country dancing. *The Highland Fling*, originally performed on a shield by victorious warriors, is the most famous sequence.

Northern Ireland

Sharing Scotland's Celtic heritage, traditional dancing in the north of Ireland centres on the ceilidh (or céilí as it may be written in Ireland). But the region also pursues step dancing (*Sean-nós* in Irish Gaelic (this actually translates as 'old style' and also refers to a type of singing)). Usually performed solo, it's the famously up-tempo form that finds the feet going hell-for-leather while the upper body remains largely impassive. In Northern Ireland, the Irish heritage of *Sean-nós* has the inevitable sectarian connotations and it remains a predominantly Nationalist pastime. Scottish Country Dancing is also popular in Northern Ireland, carried along by the Ulster Scots connection.

Culture with bells on
Even in 21st century England and Wales, morris dancing remains an iconic, idiosyncratic and frequently mocked branch of national culture. Morris men are still regularly sighted at village fetes or outside pubs in summer. Most draw on regionally specific styles of dance, from the Border (that's the England/Wales border) to the Cotswold to the Molly (East Anglian). In common, the dances tend to be all-male affairs, and usually incorporate bells on trousers, flailing handkerchiefs, whooping and some form of prop – from sticks to antlers and swords. As for the origins of 'morris', it's usually taken as a bastardisation of 'Moorish', an association with North Africa that remains unexplained.

"...DANCING IS PRACTICED TO REVEAL WHETHER LOVERS ARE IN GOOD HEALTH AND SOUND OF LIMB..."
Thoinot Arbeau, writing in 1588

Wales

Like England, Wales lost most of its folk dances in the industrial age: the strong non-conformist chapels did their best to stamp out anything so depraved. The surviving routines are often hybrid affairs comprised of remnants of Welsh dance and elements of the morris and other styles. They're usually watched at the local eisteddfod rather than joined, performed rather formally in the 18th century dress of petticoat, apron, shawl and even tall stovepipe hat – all cherished as symbols of Wales' renewed national identity. Only one Welsh dance tradition appears undiluted (even while other nations have their equivalents) – clog dancing. The Welsh variant evolved among farmers and quarry workers, its complicated steps and tricks (some of them like the high kicks of the Cossack) pursued solo in competition.

Movers and shakers
While everyone from ditch-dwellers to lords loved to boogie back in medieval times, moves were nevertheless indicative of social standing. The early modern multitude got their kicks from traditional folk dances with pagan roots, but in royal circles they called on a more refined repertoire. The Elizabethan period saw processional dances imported from the Continent; decorous routines like the pavane, a slow stately affair, became popular on ceremonial occasions and at posh parties. Only the volt, in which the man hoists his lady high in the air, authorised any degree of grappling with an opposite number. Queen Elizabeth led by example, using dance for daily exercise. She apparently danced the gaillard, a lively mix of leaps and bounds, six or seven times each morning.

An understudy's story: British ballet
Englishman John Weaver played a role in ballet's
formative years. His London *ballet d'action* in the early
18ᵗʰ century explored how the moves of classical ballet
could portray emotion. But the innovation was short lived.
British ballet went off the boil, and for 200 years simply
borrowed from the Continent with its composers,
choreographers and dancers. Only in the early 20ᵗʰ
century did the foreign imports finally inspire native
success when two former Ballet Russes dancers, Marie
Rambert (Polish) and Ninette de Valois (Irish – her real
name was Edris Stannus), established the companies that
would become, respectively, Ballet Rambert and the Royal
Ballet. Frederick Ashton was the big British choreographer
of the 20ᵗʰ century, his best work emerging during a long
tenure at the Royal Ballet. In 1963 he created *Marguerite
and Armand* for Margot Fonteyn, Britain's prima ballerina,
and Rudolf Nureyev – the first night inspired 21 curtain
calls. Fonteyn (born Margaret Hookham) only retired from
the Royal Ballet in 1979, aged 60. Only Darcey Bussell,
herself recently retired, has achieved anything like the
same level of interest in the years since.

Matthew Bourne, famous for an all-male *Swan Lake*
(1995) and a ballet adaptation of the film *Edward
Scissorhands* (2005), is the current big noise in
choreography. Today, ballet struggles somewhat with
public image. It suffers accusations of elitism, while the
difficulty in actually doing it precludes the enjoyment of
participation that popularises other dance forms. The film
Billy Elliot (2000) stirred popular interest in ballet and no
doubt got more children dancing, but it's going to take
more than a movie to get the masses through the theatre
doors. For all that, the Royal Ballet, based at the Royal
Opera House in Covent Garden, remains internationally
celebrated.

1. Identity: the   2. Literature   3. Art, architecture   **4. Performing**   5. Cinema,   6. Media and   7. Food and drink   8. Living culture:
foundations   and philosophy   and design   **arts**   photography   communications   the state of
of British culture   and fashion   modern Britain

In 2006 the National Campaign for the Arts produced *The Dance Manifesto*, claiming dance as the fastest growing art form in Britain. Their figures had one in ten Brits attending dance performances, and nearly five million participating themselves. The popularity of television shows like *Strictly Come Dancing*, and the attendant growth in ballroom participation, would seem to support the claims.

Movement for change: modern dance

Modern dance thrives in Britain. It's lively, uninhibited and varied, featuring elements of tap, ballet, hip-hop, ballroom, Latin and the rest – there is no distinct 'national' style. The foundations were laid in the 1960s and 70s, guided by the London Contemporary Dance Theatre that produced choreographers like Richard Alston and Siobhan Davies, both of whom went on to form their own progressive companies. The growth has continued over the last 20 years, with a number of interesting choreographers and companies at work. Among them, Lea Anderson has built a reputation for converting everyday movement into dance, and Akram Khan is eulogised for blending Western contemporary dance with the Kathak dance form of south Asia. Khan has his own company, one of various progressive outfits that keep Britain at the forefront of the contemporary scene. Random Dance, resident company at Sadler's Wells, London, led by choreographer Wayne McGregor, has done much to strengthen the cause with emotive, beguiling moves that look as painful as they do radical. The Rambert Dance Company is another important force, its ballet origins redirected toward modern dance in the 1980s. Wales has its own national contemporary dance company, Diversions, resident at the Wales Millennium Centre in Cardiff (or the Armadillo as locals call it).

212

| 1. Identity: the foundations of British culture | 2. Literature and philosophy | 3. Art, architecture and design | **4. Performing arts** | 5. Cinema, photography and fashion | 6. Media and communications | 7. Food and drink | 8. Living culture: the state of modern Britain |

The great tradition of larking about

Britain's comic preferences are well rooted – class, sex, scatology, politics and vanity have all been used to raise a laugh for centuries. General buffoonery was big back in medieval days, the slapstick, juggling and riddling of actors and jesters unfurling in market squares, halls and the royal court. Shakespeare featured the fools in his plays, although relied on irony, ridicule and the odd bit of smut for the actual humour in his work. Class generated much of the mirth in the Restoration comedy of manners, a genre that chuckled on into the 20th century, while the 19th century music hall tradition gave birth to stand-up comedy, the medium against which British comics still test their mettle; the successful usually funnel on into sitcoms, sketch shows and films. Modern comedy is an integral part of the British cultural jigsaw and its stars, the equal of any in the world, generate a public profile to rank alongside actors and musicians. If you can't regurgitate a *Little Britain* catchphrase, discuss what happened in last night's *Gavin and Stacey* or do *that* David Brent dance then you might as well just look at the floor.

Jonson in good humour
17th century playwright Ben Jonson took a scientific approach to comedy. Renaissance thought recognised the four 'humours' of the human character, controlled by the levels of blood, phlegm, yellow bile and black bile present within the body. An imbalance of the humours exaggerated certain personality traits, created caricature and, therefore, comedy in Jonson's characters. Aside from this 'comedy of humours', Jonson also mastered satire with aplomb.

Have you heard the one about British stand-up?

For a century British comedians have learned to swim (or sink) in the perilous waters of stand-up. Variety and music hall established the pre-Second World War mode of 'cheeky chappie'-style routines peddled by George Formby and Max Miller, their acts a mix of double entendres, songs and bad outfits. When music hall died in the 1960s, the gagmen moved to working men's clubs, and Les Dawson and, later, Lenny Henry, plied mother-in-law jokes, impersonations and wry observation. The seamier end of the club circuit supported acts like Bernard Manning, notorious for his mix of smut and racism. Meanwhile, Peter Cook's Establishment Club in Soho stood in sharp contrast with its politicised satire.

Max Miller
(1895 – 1963)
"I'm filthy with money – I'm filthy without it!"

An alternative stand-up scene emerged in the folk clubs of the 1970s where Billy Connolly and Jasper Carrott mixed funny songs with observational gags, but the real revolution in British stand-up came in the 1980s. The first dedicated comedy clubs gave vent to a new generation of alternative, politicised (Thatcher was PM), punkish and irreverent acts who fancied themselves the children of American comic Lenny Bruce. Alexei Sayle, Dawn French, Jo Brand, Ben Elton and Rik Mayall were all among the new crowd. And British stand-up has built on this alternative tradition ever since; most cities and large towns have some form of comedy venue and the majority of British comedians pass through the stand-up school of hard knocks on their way to success. The blunt political stuff of the 1980s has lost its edge, replaced by a post-PC mode that draws more on traditional gag-led comedy (albeit with a heavy dose of irony). Eddie Izzard (a surreal, gifted rambler), Peter Kay (old school observational stuff) and Russell Brand (articulate and wide-ranging) rank high amongst the 21st century generation of stand-ups.

Jo Brand

"The quickest way to a man's heart is with a penknife through his breast pocket."

Instant classics: sketch shows and sitcoms

They might cut their teeth in stand-up, but most British comedians reach their audience through the small screen or radio. The sketch show has always been popular: after *The Goon Show* got things rolling on radio in the 1950s, the genre enjoyed a 60s and 70s telly heyday when *The Morecambe and Wise Show*, *The Two Ronnies* and *Monty Python's Flying Circus* were all in their prime. *The Catherine Tate Show* and *Little Britain* keep the medium going today by caricaturing everyday folk, from the only gay in a small Welsh village to a potty-mouthed granny. Sitcoms reach even more viewers. Depressive genius Tony Hancock set the bar in the 1950s with *Hancock's Half Hour*, a Galton and Simpson-penned radio – and then TV –

show set around the daily disappointments of its priggish antihero. The same writing duo created *Steptoe and Son*, a TV long-runner in the 1960s and similar to *Hancock* in its fatalism. The skewed domestic setting has been a sitcom staple ever since, from the mainstream farce of *Terry and June* (1980s) to the dysfunction of *Fawlty Towers* (1970s) and *Absolutely Fabulous* (1990s) and sofa-based subtlety of *The Royle Family* (late 1990s). Class played its hand in others: *The Good Life* (1970s) had a bourgeois pleasantness and *Whatever Happened to The Likely Lads* a working-class pathos (1970s), while *Only Fools and Horses* (1980s and 90s) won hearts with its dreaming market trader. More recently, Ricky Gervais twisted the sitcom into a fly-on-the-wall mockumentary with his toe-curling turn as David Brent in *The Office* (2002-03), an instant classic.

Ricky and Stephen
The long and
the short
of Brit
Com

Wiley old Barker
The Two Ronnies – that's Ronnie Barker and Ronnie Corbett – made popular, mainstream, punchline-led comedy for 20 years. A number of their sketches were supplied through the post by the elusive writer Gerald Wiley. The 'fork handles' sketch, recently voted amongst the funniest on British TV, was one of his. In the early 1970s the reclusive Wiley called everyone connected to the show to a Chinese restaurant where his identity would be revealed – when Ronnie Barker stood up and confessed, they thought he was joking. But eventually the penny dropped. Fearful of foisting his material on Corbett, Barker had chosen to write anonymously instead.

Three sketch shows you should have seen

Monty Python's Flying Circus (1969-74). Five Oxbridge graduates and an American created farcical, surreal comedy that did away with punchlines in favour of segued sketches and abrupt endings. Old ladies, Nazis, Spanish Inquisitors: the Pythons took on many guises.

The Morecambe and Wise Show (1961-83). Tall, bespectacled funnyman Eric Morecambe and his short, hairy-legged straightman Ernie Wise were the most popular double act Britain has produced. Their 1977 Christmas show drew 28 million viewers.

Not the Nine O'Clock News (1979-82). The sketch show variant of the 1980s alternative comedy scene mixed observation and satire. The stars, Griff Rhys Jones, Rowan Atkinson, Mel Smith and others, became the prime cast of British comedy for the next decade.

Taking the peace
The most popular
home-grown comedy on
Northern Irish TV sets
in recent years was
Give my Head Peace, a
sitcom that satirised
the sectarian divide and
the paramilitaries via
the members of two
comically dysfunctional
families. A pilot episode,
*Two Ceasefires and a
Wedding*, lampooning
the hackneyed 'love
across the divide' story,
hinted at the style.
The show ran for ten
years before ending
in 2008. Detractors
wondered whether it
simply reinforced the
negative stereotypes,
but most people just
laughed along.

Five sitcoms worth the licence fee

Dad's Army (1968-77). That rare thing – a sitcom generally agreed to have stood the test of time with its portrayal of a bungling, elderly Home Guard unit in the Second World War.

Yes, Minister (1980-88). Satire on the machinations and doubletalk of modern politics, with Paul Eddington's MP (and later PM) controlled by Nigel Hawthorne's Machiavellian permanent secretary. It was Margaret Thatcher's favourite show.

Blackadder (1983-89). Rowan Atkinson's sardonic historical figure, sketched by writers Ben Elton and Richard Curtis, ran for four series, each set in a different century.

Only Fools and Horses (1981-2003). Wheeling, dealing but never quite achieving, Del Boy and Rodney Trotter shaped the show that was voted Britain's best ever sitcom.

Phoenix Nights (2001-). Peter Kay is Brian Potter, wheelchair-bound impresario of a Bolton working men's club: the perfect introduction to a distinctly northern brand of humour.

A talent for satire

Britain has always had a pleasingly irreverent approach to the great and the good, and satire – with its irony, exaggeration and wit – has been a mandatory strand of humour since the days of Dryden and Hogarth. Modern satire really got going with the satire boom of the early 1960s. *Private Eye*, a fortnightly magazine that still seems to delight in its libel court jollies, began downsizing political and celebrity ego, while its one time editor Peter Cook did something similar on stage in *Beyond the Fringe*, joined by Dudley Moore, Alan Bennett and Jonathan Miller. Cook's audacious impersonation of a maladroit Prime Minister Harold Macmillan garnered particular notoriety. *That was the Week that Was* (also known as *TW3*), fronted by David Frost and scripted by everyone from John Cleese to

1. Identity: the
foundations
of British culture

2. Literature
and philosophy

3. Art, architecture
and design

**4. Performing
arts**

5. Cinema,
photography
and fashion

6. Media and
communications

7. Food and drink

8. Living culture:
the state of
modern Britain

Peter Cook (1937-1995)
Dudley Moore (1935-2002)

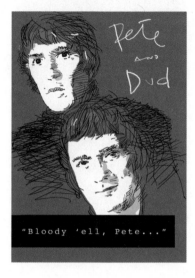

"Bloody 'ell, Pete..."

Dennis Potter and John Betjeman, also featured in the 60s satire boom. A second wave emerged in the 1990s, with TV panel show *Have I Got News For You* the leading light; its wry analysis of the week's news representing a softer approach than the acerbic putdown-via-puppet methods of 1980s show, *Spitting Image*. It's a short leap from the wit of satire to the skewed imitation of parody, a genre that found intelligent, often surreal life in the 1990s with *The Day Today*, a spoof news show with Chris Morris' intense anchorman, and *Knowing Me, Knowing You...With Alan Partridge*, Steve Coogan's chat show send up. *Da Ali G Show*, the Sacha Baron Cohen effort that also featured a certain Borat, and *Bo Selecta!*, both TV productions, have fed the British hunger for mockery in the 21st century.

The comedians' comedian

If you're searching for the Maharishi of modern British comedy, perhaps you should focus on Peter Cook. He began writing and performing for the Footlights, the Cambridge student troupe, before leading the satire boom of the early 1960s, but is perhaps more famous for his partnership with Dudley Moore in *Not Only But Also*. When Cook slipped from the heights in the 1970s, his life was directed increasingly by alcoholism, and his death, aged 57, in 1995, was attributed largely to a drink problem. Many said he'd wasted his talent, but Cook's influence has been immense, cited as a guiding light by everyone from *Monty Python* to *The Young Ones* and Chris Morris. Stephen Fry, perhaps the sharpest wit of contemporary Britain, called Cook "the funniest man who ever drew breath". A 2005 Channel 4 poll of comics judged him the top 'Comedians' Comedian', ahead of Groucho Marx and Eric Morecambe.

Autograph please, Mister Hockney

Alan Bennett faces an occasional occupational hazard

5 Cinema, photography and fashion

Michael Caine

60s heartthrob (even in a cardigan). Real name: Maurice Micklewhite.

Quite a lot of people know that

5.1 Cinema

British cinema has been a mixed affair. Korda and Hitchcock shone in the 1930s, David Lean oversaw a golden age and New Wave directors later established social realism as a fine perennial genre. However, elsewhere, British cinema has relied on individual gems, films that are hailed as epochal but later revealed as isolated treasures.

Talent unmasked:
the BAFTAs
The BAFTA Film Awards
are Britain's answer to
the Oscars, dished out
each February to the
high achievers of cinema
from all nationalities.
BAFTA itself is the
British Academy of Film
and Television Arts,
established in 1947 (the
telly part was actually
added later and has its
own awards ceremony)
by a pool of directorial
talent that included
David Lean, Alexander
Korda and Carol Reed.
Reed himself directed
the Best British Film in
the first three years of
the awards. The iconic
golden masks that serve
as BAFTA gongs were
designed in 1955 by US
sculptor Mitzi Cunliffe.

British cinema has travelled a rocky road. Periods of success, triumph even, have been curtly followed by years in the doldrums. The 1930s nurtured Alfred Hitchcock and Alexander Korda, and a golden age came a decade later, packing out cinemas with David Lean epics and Ealing comedies. In the 1960s, the New Wave directors established social realism as a perennial, praiseworthy strand of British film. But either side of such spurts, homegrown cinema has relied on individual gems, films that are hailed as epochal but usually revealed in retrospect as isolated treasures. We shouldn't be surprised at the mixed fortunes. English language cinema is dominated by the star-driven industry in Hollywood, and Britain's ensemble affairs struggle to compete with America's cultural and economic might. However, despite the hard luck stories, films like *Nil by Mouth*, *The Full Monty* and *Atonement* have played a crucial role in shaping the cultural landscape of modern Britain. They present a diverse cinematic tradition that while distinctly 'British' has no overriding style. From Mike Leigh's realism to the escapism of Bond, the suspense of *The Third Man* or the culture-clash gay romance of *My Beautiful Laundrette*, British cinema is nothing if not eclectic.

Who goes to the cinema and what do they watch? Cinema audiences have steadily increased in Britain over the last 20 years, creeping up from a 1984 nadir when only 54 million tickets were sold all year. These days the figures have levelled out at around 160 million admissions a year. Ten times that number went to the

1. Identity: the
foundations
of British culture

2. Literature
and philosophy

3. Art, architecture
and design

4. Performing
arts

**5. Cinema,
photography
and fashion**

6. Media and
communications

7. Food and drink

8. Living culture:
the state of
modern Britain

movies in 1946, before television became so distracting. Around half the British cinema-going public is aged under 25, although this statistic is falling, with the over 45s taking an increasing share of seats. Perhaps these demographics help to explain why Brits are far more likely to watch a Hollywood film than anything native. The number of British films in the cinemas varies, but usually equates to around one in five on show. Some years are better than others; for example, in 2006, a bumper year for British film, a third of all box office receipts came-from homegrown cinema. Even while a third of films released in Britain are in a foreign language, the greatest number in Hindi, they account for little over three per cent of total box office revenue.

Five film festivals

London Film Festival
The oldest show in town has been running each October since the 1950s.

Raindance Film Festival
Britain's biggest independent film fest showcases movies from around the world in the West End each autumn.

Dead by Dawn
Edinburgh drinks down a bloody brew of horror movies every April.

Viva! Spanish and Latin American Film Festival
Hispanic movies every March in Manchester.

Black International Film Festival
An October mix of film, music and live arts in Birmingham.

Mighty Blighty: recent British Oscar winners

Sam Mendes.
Best Director for *American Beauty* in 2000.

Julian Fellowes.
Best Original Screenplay for *Gosford Park* in 2002.

***Wallace & Gromit: the Curse of the Were-Rabbit*.**
Best Animated Feature Film in 2006.

Helen Mirren.
Best Actress for *The Queen* in 2007.

Daniel Day-Lewis.
Best Actor for *There Will Be Blood* in 2008.

Kate Winslet.
Best Actress for *The Reader* in 2009.

Danny Boyle.
Best Director for *Slumdog Millionaire* in 2009.

There was a tragicomic air to William Friese-Greene's life. He took out more than 70 patents on inventions that were forward thinking but often technically inept. A cigarette card photo printing machine and his involvement in early X-ray were rare triumphs. He claimed to have sent details of his failed 'Biophantascope' to Thomas Edison, later credited with the invention of the film camera, but Edison denied all knowledge. His enthusiasm as an inventive dabbler brought periodic financial strife, including a spell in prison for borrowing while bankrupt. William would no doubt have enjoyed *The Magic Box* (1951) a biopic that wildly exaggerated his role in the birth of film: an all-star cast including Laurence Olivier and Richard Attenborough couldn't stop the film foundering at the box office. Friese-Greene died while speaking at a meeting of film moguls in 1921.

William, it was really nothing

Everyone remembers the Lumière Brothers and their flickering projection of a train, but did the Englishman William Friese-Greene beat them to the first moving image? If he did, unfortunately he was the only person who saw it. His 'Biophantascope' machine, patented in 1889 (six years before the Lumières' first film), took four or five photos per second, captured on film rolling behind the shutter. Alas there's no concrete record to suggest that he could successfully project the results, and the genuine invention of cinematography probably happened elsewhere. Whatever its origins, when film got going Britain was mesmerised. Audiences in the early 20th century were rapt by the work of foreign film companies, particularly the French Pathe and Gaumont studios that were churning out newsreels and silent movies.

Britain's first big film-makers

Britain began building its own studios in the Edwardian era, led by an influx of American technicians and actors. Will Barker and Cecil Hepworth were the first major homegrown figures. From his Ealing studio, Barker made silent historical epics; and they were epics – *Jane Shore* (1916) used 5,000 extras. By contrast Hepworth's films were modest. One of his earliest filmic projects recorded Queen Victoria's funeral in 1901, but he really made his mark with *Rescued by Rover* (1905). It cost £7/13/6 to make (the cheapest British film ever according to *The Guinness Book of Records*), involved various members of Hepworth's family and featured a child being rescued by the star, Rover, a collie. Believe it or not, the use of cinematic narrative by Hepworth and co-director Lewin Fitzhamon, conveying drama through edited shots rather than a procession of staged acts, proved revolutionary. The public lapped it up and Rover returned for a sequel. Hepworth made films into the 1920s, by which time his radical style had become old hat.

Talkies and quickies

Britain's early film industry struggled through the 1920s, stifled by the economic and creative dominance of Hollywood. In 1927, Parliament passed the Cinematograph Films Act demanding that cinemas show a set quota of British films. Initially it was 7.5 per cent of output, raised to 20 per cent by the mid 1930s. However, instead of fostering an industry of self-sufficient Hollywood-style studios, the act created a glut of 'quota quickies', uninspiring films produced to make up the numbers. Against the odds, two highly celebrated directors emerged in the 1930s:

Alfred Hitchcock delivered the first British talkie, *Blackmail* (1929), a crime thriller with the provocative mix of fear, violence and blond heroines that would recur throughout his long directorial career. Another Hitchcock effort, *The 39 Steps* (1935), developed the motifs brilliantly with the story of an innocent man on the run in Scotland. Hitchcock left for Hollywood in 1939 although he would periodically return to Britain, using it as a backdrop for his American films.

Alexander Korda, a Hungarian émigré, was initially signed by Paramount to produce quota quickies but did much more, establishing his own London Film Productions to produce and direct *The Private Life of Henry VIII* (1933). The elegantly made film was a global success and its star, Charles Laughton, bagged an Oscar.

First on the scene
Ealing Studios stake a claim as the world's oldest still in use, originally unveiled as a four-acre plot by William Barker in 1902. In more recent times *The Cruel Sea* (1953), *The Ladykillers* (1955) and *Shaun of the Dead* (2007) were all shot there.

"THERE WAS NOTHING OF COURAGE IN WHAT I DID. IT WAS ALWAYS JUST A LARK FOR ME. ... I WAS SUCKLED ON AMYL ACETATE AND REARED ON CELLULOID."
Cecil Hepworth

Hepworth hits hard times
The fledgling film industry was a precarious business. Even Britain's first true filmic maverick Cecil Hepworth found his studio in receivership by 1924. The original negatives of Hepworth's films were melted down for their silver content.

Fighting the filth
In 1916 the British Board of Film Classification compiled a list of things that wouldn't be tolerated in film. It included such depravity as:

• The unnecessary exhibition of under-clothing
• Excessively passionate love scenes
• The exhibition of profuse bleeding

"BLONDES MAKE THE BEST VICTIMS. THEY'RE LIKE VIRGIN SNOW THAT SHOWS UP THE BLOODY FOOTPRINTS."
Alfred Hitchcock

Hitchcock: the boy that made the man
Alfred Hitchcock, Hollywood giant, was born a chicken dealer's son in Leytonstone, East London. Biographers have noted how childhood events influenced his filmmaking style. A ten-minute spell in a local police cell, apparently arranged by his father after some wrongdoing, is used to explain his later fascination with falsely accused characters. As for his preoccupation with controlling mothers, famously realised in Mrs Bates of *Psycho* (1960), look no further than his own mum: she made Alfred stand at the foot of her bed each night, recounting the events of the day.

Welsh grit
The first Welsh talkie was Ifan ab Owen Edwards' *Y Chwarelwr* (*The Quarryman*) (1935), the rather romanticised story of life in a slate-mining community.

A string of Korda hits followed, admired as much for production quality as narrative, and he put the likes of Laurence Olivier and Vivien Leigh on screen.

Despite the best efforts of Hitchcock, Korda and co, the British film industry was dogged by financial gaffes and poor production standards in the 1930s. The American studios moved in and began running things, producing 'British' classics like *Goodbye Mr Chips!* (1939) with its kindly retired teacher in the mood for a flashback.

The five early British films you should watch

The Lodger: A Story of the London Fog (1926) Alfred Hitchcock.
If you're going to watch a silent British film, watch this one, young Hitchcock's serial killer story starring Ivor Novello.

The Private Life of Henry VIII (1933) Alexander Korda.
Korda's brilliant dissection of the big bearded one is among the most commercially successful British films ever made.

Nell Gwyn (1934) Herbert Wilcox.
Leading pre-war actress Anna Neagle stars as the Cockney girl with the ear (and other bits) of the King.

The 39 Steps (1935) Alfred Hitchcock.
The best of Hitchcock's pre-Hollywood films starred Robert Donat, caught up with a dangerous blonde.

Pygmalion (1938) Anthony Asquith
and Leslie Howard. Can you make a lady from a 'heap of stuffed cabbage leaves'? Leading man Leslie Howard attempted to find out.

Reality bites: the wartime experience
British cinema took an unexpected turn during the
Second World War: it improved significantly. The
'make do' mantra of the war years dispatched 1930s
extravagance, but while manpower and facilities were
reduced quality climbed as a more realist style of
film-making developed. It originated in documentary,
a mode developed in the 1930s by John Grierson,
famous for his work on *Night Mail* (1936), in which a
chugging score by Benjamin Britten and W.H Auden's
monotone verse enlivened the journey of a Royal Mail
train from London to Scotland. When documentary
passed realism onto film, the wartime current
inevitably created gentle propaganda. Some of it was
highly watchable; in *Went the Day Well?* (1942), a
British village was overrun by German troops,
eventually repelled by fierce housewives. Other realist
films had more humdrum content. *This Happy Breed*
(1944), adapted from a Noël Coward play and directed
by David Lean, studied the 'ordinary' interwar lives of
a squabbling family in Clapham. The war years also
saw the first pairing of Michael Powell and Emeric
Pressburger, known collectively as 'The Archers'.
Theirs would become a director/writer partnership
responsible for 19 British films. One of the earliest,
The Life and Death of Colonel Blimp (1943),
established their 'difference'. Its unflattering appraisal
of the British character – romantic but stunted – was
set in contrast with a likeable German officer. Winston
Churchill decided the film was unpatriotic and tried to
halt production.

How Welsh
was my valley?
The film version of
Richard Llewellyn's book
*How Green Was My
Valley* was released in
1941. America enjoyed
the movie's recollection
of a Welsh pit village
childhood, awarding five
Oscars, including Best
Picture. But perhaps
that was because the
film was Hollywood
made. The characters
were actually played
by a mix of English,
American and Irish
actors and the movie
was shot in Malibu
Canyon, California. Even
so, to many it's still *the*
'Welsh' film.

1. Identity: the
foundations
of British culture

2. Literature
and philosophy

3. Art, architecture
and design

4. Performing
arts

**5. Cinema,
photography
and fashion**

6. Media and
communications

7. Food and drink

8. Living culture:
the state of
modern Britain

Big days at the box office
Once cinemas learned
to operate around the
disturbances of German
air raids, film became a
welcome relief in the
lives of wartime Brits.
Audience figures in the
1940s reached an all-
time high. In 1946, 1.6
billion tickets were sold
at 4,709 cinemas. From
this era, *Spring in Park
Lane* (1948), a class-
clash romcom starring
Anna Neagle, remains
the most watched British
film of all time with 20.5
million tickets sold.

Nothing lean about the Lean years

Film's wartime maturation initiated a golden age of British cinema that lasted into the 1950s. Eclecticism ruled with a roll call of historical, contemporary and comedic movies. David Lean was the shining directorial force. His *Brief Encounter* (1945), written by Noël Coward and starring Trevor Howard, is a classic, even while the clipped accents and stiff upper lips raise a smile today. Another Lean effort, *Great Expectations* (1946), starring John Mills, is arguably the best film adaptation of Dickens yet. Carol Reed challenged Lean's supremacy with *The Third Man* (1949), a slice of British *noir* from the pen of Graham Greene that saw Orson Welles skulking around war-torn Vienna. If the polls are to be believed then *The Third Man* stands out as the golden age film most appreciated by a modern audience. Powell and Pressburger were prolific in their own enjoyably experimental field. The dark psychology of *Black Narcissus* (1946), set in a remote Himalayan convent (but filmed in London), produced something that few other golden age flicks managed, eroticism. In the early 1950s the fresh memories of war were mined for material, producing a series of epic movies like *The Cruel Sea* (1953) and *The Dam Busters* (1955).

The Ealing comedies

Ealing Studios
Taken in 1939

The series of comedies produced by Ealing Studios in the decade after the Second World War were peculiarly native affairs; a blend of self-mockery, cynicism, black humour and blokes in frocks. *Passport to Pimlico* (1949), about a London street that declares independence, was one of the first, typical in its gentle subversion, followed rapidly by the likes of *Kind Hearts and Coronets* (1949), in which one man sets about murdering an entire, disparate family to acquire a dukedom. *The Ladykillers* (1955) was a final triumph, its gang of ruthless criminals brilliantly incongruous in the confines of a small English lodging house. Its star, a goofy-toothed Alec Guinness, became the leading Ealing comedy light. In *Kind Hearts and Coronets* he played all eight members of the ill-fated d'Ascoyne family, and later took on the impossibly nice, utterly British bank robber of *The Lavender Hill Mob* (1951).

"WE ALWAYS WERE ENGLISH AND WE ALWAYS WILL BE ENGLISH, AND IT'S JUST BECAUSE WE ARE ENGLISH THAT WE'RE STICKING UP FOR OUR RIGHT TO BE BURGUNDIANS!"
Connie Pemberton,
Passport to Pimlico

If you only watch ten golden age films, watch these

Henry V (1944) Laurence Olivier. Agincourt and all that; Olivier starred, produced and directed in a thinly camouflaged but stirring slice of wartime propaganda.

Brief Encounter (1945) David Lean. Golly gosh, they're both married but can't keep their hands off each other. Fatal attractions consume Celia Johnson and Trevor Howard.

Great Expectations (1946) David Lean. A young John Mills plays Pip in Lean's magnificently murky mix of Gothic mansions and graveyards.

A Matter of Life and Death (1946) Powell and Pressburger. RAF pilot David Niven hovers between life/earth and death/heaven after bailing out; bizarre but brilliant.

Brighton Rock (1947) John Boulting. Ominous adaptation of Graham Greene's crime thriller that cast Richard Attenborough as edgy gang leader Pinkie.

Black Narcissus (1947) Powell and Pressburger. Anglican nuns set up shop on a remote Himalayan hilltop and grapple with repressed desire and madness. Brilliantly creepy.

Whisky Galore (1949) Alexander Mackendrick. Hebridean Islanders battle to stash a cache of shipwrecked whisky in an early Ealing comedy.

The Third Man (1949) Carol Reed. An American writer played by Orson Welles searches for a fixer in Vienna, encountering a famous twangy musical motif every time he finds him.

The Cruel Sea (1952) Charles Frend. The Royal Navy fight back German U-boats in a classic British war movie, filmed documentary style.

The Ladykillers (1955) Alexander Mackendrick. A little old lady unwittingly outmanoeuvres Alec Guinness' blackly funny criminal gang.

Dashing young bow
The impossibly precocious Orson Welles, aged about eleven, probably

Come hither
with your zither
Director Carol Reed
apparently heard zither
player Anton Karas
strumming away in a
Viennese pub and
recruited him to score
the music for *The Third
Man*. One particular
section became known
as *The Harry Lime
Theme* (after Orson
Welles' character) and
spent 11 weeks at the
top of the US Billboard
charts in 1950.

Three great British actors of the golden age

Laurence Olivier. Brought his Shakespearean stage talents to the screen in
Henry V and *Hamlet* (1948), for which he won best actor, director and picture
gongs at the Oscars.

Deborah Kerr. Scottish rose who cut her teeth on the likes of *Black Narcissus*
before moving on to conquer Hollywood, writhing memorably on the beach with
a damp Burt Lancaster in *From Here to Eternity* (1953).

Alec Guinness. The versatile giant of the Ealing comedies won his Best Actor
Oscar for a role in *Bridge on the River Kwai* (1957). However, he would become
best known, to his clear disappointment, as Obi-Wan Kenobi in *Star Wars* in
the 1970s.

1. Identity: the
foundations
of British culture

2. Literature
and philosophy

3. Art, architecture
and design

4. Performing
arts

**5. Cinema,
photography
and fashion**

6. Media and
communications

7. Food and drink

8. Living culture:
the state of
modern Britain

Life stories: Free Cinema

As the big studios struggled in the mid 1950s a new, independent strain of film-making gathered pace. A group of young documentary makers established Free Cinema, a movement that held six programmes between 1956 and 1959. Like the Angry Young Men writing for theatre, the figures of Free Cinema were irreverent toward the Establishment and bored with the old social and sexual mores. Lindsay Anderson and Karel Reisz were the key film-makers, but Free Cinema also showed work by the likes of Roman Polanski and French New Wavers François Truffaut and Claude Chabrol. In common, their work documented the stuff of everyday life, free (they felt) from the orthodoxies of traditional film-making. Shooting on location using hand-held 16mm cameras, they made documentaries like *We are the Lambeth Boys* (1957), a Karel Reisz film that followed a group of south London teens.

"THESE FILMS WERE NOT MADE TOGETHER; NOR WITH THE IDEA OF SHOWING THEM TOGETHER. BUT WHEN THEY CAME TOGETHER, WE FELT THEY HAD AN ATTITUDE IN COMMON. IMPLICIT IN THIS ATTITUDE IS A BELIEF IN FREEDOM, IN THE IMPORTANCE OF PEOPLE AND IN THE SIGNIFICANCE OF THE EVERYDAY."
Free Cinema film programme, 1956.

Sinking feeling: New Wave cinema

Free Cinema led directly to the New Wave of British film in the late 1950s and early 1960s. It took the social realism of those documentaries and made drama from it, cutting into the marrow of workin-class life. The warts and all subject matter saw the genre christened 'kitchen sink'. Anderson and Reisz both went across from Free Cinema to New Wave, joined by another director, Tony Richardson, graduate of the playwright's school, who had a hand in more New Wave films than most. There was a continuity of technicians too, notably with cameraman Walter Lassally. *Room at the Top* (1958), directed by Jack Clayton, lifted the veil first when working-class Joe was torn between clawing his way up the social ladder and cosying up to the French woman he falls in love with. Its popularity paved the way for a rash of kitchen

sink dramas dealing with 'real' issues like abortion
(*Saturday Night and Sunday Morning* (1960) and
delinquency (*The Loneliness of the Long Distance
Runner* (1962). New Wave had fizzled by 1964 but the
trend for liberalism was set and social realism would
reappear over the coming decades, as would the likes
of Albert Finney, Alan Bates and Rita Tushingham, the
new breed of British actors that got their break in the
kitchen sink.

Sex and spooks: cinema in the 1960s
New Wave's progressive spirit lingered through the
1960s but tended as much toward sexual as social
freedom. *Alfie* (1966) was popular but very much of its
time; its woman-chasing wideboy, played with aplomb
by Michael Caine, soon felt a feminist backlash.
The permissive mood found its way into period pieces
too, notably in Ken Russell's *Women in Love* (1969) –
as famous for its nude fireside wrestling between
Alan Bates and Oliver Reed (for which both actors
apparently got drunk) as for its quality. Kitchen sink grit
returned toward the end of the decade, realised in the
directorial work of Ken Loach whose *Kes* (1969) dealt
brilliantly with the struggles of a working-class
Barnsley boy.

Britain also cultivated cinematic genres in the 1960s
that were destined to run for years. The James Bond
leviathan took its first step with *Dr No* (1960) and
broke into a run with *Goldfinger* (1964), Sean Connery
taking charge of the outrageous baddies and trite one-
liners. A subtler spy genre adapted the novels of Len
Deighton, with Michael Caine starring in *The Ipcress
File* (1965). Hammer Films maintained a prolific series
of mannered horror flicks, begun in the late 1950s and
strung out into the 60s with sequels that invariably

*1. Identity: the
foundations
of British culture*   *2. Literature
and philosophy*   *3. Art, architecture
and design*   *4. Performing
arts*   **5. Cinema,
photography
and fashion**   *6. Media and
communications*   *7. Food and drink*   *8. Living culture:
the state of
modern Britain*

starred Peter Cushing (as Baron Frankenstein) or Christopher Lee (as Dracula). And then there were the *Carry On!* films, ribald low budget comedies with little in the way of narrative but a continuity of actors and lowbrow jokes. They stretched to a run of 29 films between 1958 and 1978. Critics grimaced but the public were enthusiastic; *Carry on Camping* was the top earning film in Britain in 1969.

"HAVE LOVE WITHOUT MEANING, HAVE MURDER WITHOUT GUILT, HAVE THE DAZZLE AND THE MADNESS OF LONDON TODAY..."
From the trailer for *Blow-Up*

Ten 1960s films you need to watch

Peeping Tom (1960) Michael Powell. Disturbing serial killer film initially condemned but later lauded as unique in style and content.

Saturday Night and Sunday Morning (1960) Karel Reisz. 'Don't let the bastards grind you down' said kitchen sinker Albert Finney. A fine New Wave effort.

Lawrence of Arabia (1962) David Lean. An enigmatic Peter O'Toole impressed in Lean's visually stunning desert drama. It won seven Oscars.

Billy Liar (1963) John Schlesinger. Kitchen sink does comedy as lowly Tom Courtenay fantasises about a grander role in life.

Tom Jones (1963) Tony Richardson. A period drama with its mind in the permissive 60s; led enjoyably by Albert Finney as the titular rogue.

Goldfinger (1964) Guy Hamilton. The third Bond film set the format: choreographed fights, sardonic wit, M, Moneypenny, Q and girls like Pussy Galore.

Alfie (1966) Lewis Gilbert. Michael Caine's philanderer loves 'n' leaves his way toward a flimsy moral comeuppance. It was a big hit on release.

If... (1968) Lindsay Anderson. Free Cinema graduate Anderson peeled back the layers of the British public school and found hypocrisy, rebellion and violence.

The Italian Job (1969) Peter Collinson. An unchallenging but popular classic; Michael Caine pulls off an audacious heist in Turin under the cover of a football crowd.

Kes (1969) Ken Loach. Yorkshire lad Billy Casper finds escape from his dry working-class life via kestrel fancying. Not as sentimental as it sounds.

"YOU WERE ONLY SUPPOSED TO BLOW THE BLOODY DOORS OFF."
Michael Caine, *The Italian Job* (Brits recently voted it their favourite film one-liner)

British film has lurched from peak to trough throughout the last four decades. While cinema is in reasonable health at present, overall the bad times seem to outstretch the good. There's no shortage of British talent: in front of the camera Ewan McGregor, Keira Knightley and co are global stars, while behind it, directors like Paul Greengrass and Ridley Scott have flown the flag in Hollywood. But funding – or the lack of it – is a consistent bugbear, exacerbated by the marketing and distribution shortfalls that can prevent good films from actually reaching an audience.

Sex, drugs and the knights who say 'ni': 1970s cinema
British cinema endured some lean years in the 1970s. A Hollywood recession rippled out across the Atlantic, collaborating with Government funding cuts to stifle the industry. The rare good films that did surface were dogged by notoriety. Nicholas Roeg's *Performance* (1971) blurred thriller and psychedelia with Mick Jagger in the lead role. It raised eyebrows with its three-in-a-bath activities but has been acknowledged more recently as complex and brilliant. Violence and misogyny were the prime offenders in *A Clockwork Orange* (1971) and *Get Carter* (1971). In Scotland Bill Douglas laboured away on a trilogy of absorbing socially real films based on his own life in the coalmining town of Newcraighall; *My Childhood* (1972) was the first. The Monty Python crew began making films with *Monty Python and the Holy Grail* (1975), a work that wears well in comparison with the lame sex comedies of the era, notably the *Confessions* series that shone fame's torchlight on Robin Askwith's buttocks.

"THE MOST TRAGIC EPISODE IN BRITISH CINEMA, BUT ALSO, WEIRDLY, THE MOST MEMORABLE... IT WAS TEN YEARS BEFORE THE BRITISH AUDIENCE WOKE UP AND REALISED THAT SEX COMEDIES WERE ABSOLUTE SHIT."
The Guardian

Set to slow-mo: film in the 1980s

The cinematic drought lingered through the 1980s. TV had stolen much of cinema's audience, as well as most of its studios. 1981 was a low point; only 24 British films were made, fewer than in any year since 1914. Despite the gloom, the decade produced a few sporadic gems. Richard Attenborough directed his way to an Oscar with the saint-in-sandals epic, *Gandhi* (1983), and the Academy also threw plaudits at *Chariots of Fire* (1981), the stirring Olympic period piece that today, with its interminable slo-mo, feels a bit daft. While it wasn't a golden era the 1980s did nurture a stock of interesting directors, names that would hang around for the next 20 years. Stephen Frears impressed with *My Beautiful Laundrette* (1985) with its race, sexuality and class issues. For Bill Forsyth, the big break came with amusing adolescent angst in *Gregory's Girl* (1981); for the offbeat Derek Jarman it was with a deft biopic of *Caravaggio* (1986) complete with typewriters and calculators in the artist's 17th century world. Peter Greenaway roused interest with a succession of image conscious films, notably the flesh and food fest *The Cook, The Thief, His Wife and Her Lover* (1989).

Other British directors made more of a mark in Hollywood. Ridley Scott's *Blade Runner* (1982) and Alan Parker's *Mississippi Burning* (1988) were two of the more memorable Brit-directed American affairs; both directors had started out making adverts for television. While funding crises, TV tussles and the temptation of Hollywood weakened British film in the 70s and 80s, one genre weathered the storm: James Bond continued to perform at the box office, even when the title role passed to Roger Moore and the mood drifted toward self-parody.

"THE OLD FASHIONED IDEA OF THE NARRATIVE, SIT IN THE DARK, HOLLYWOOD CENTRED, BOOKSHOP CINEMA IS FINISHED. IT DIED ON THE 31ST SEPTEMBER 1983 WHEN THE REMOTE CONTROL WAS INTRODUCED TO THE LIVING ROOMS OF THE WORLD."
Director Peter Greenaway

Going to the
movies in Welsh
A handful of excellent
films shot in the Welsh
language have emerged
in recent years, in line
with a resurgence of the
national tongue. *Hedd
Wyn* (1992) is the best,
accruing an Oscar
nomination for Best
Foreign Language Film
with its moving story of
a poet sucked into the
savagery of the First
World War. *Solomon
and Gaenor* (1998), a pit
village love story set in
the same era, was also
well received.

The 1990s revival

The sporadic triumphs of British cinema grew in number in the 1990s. Period pieces performed well at the box office led by Merchant Ivory Productions (American James Ivory directed and Indian Ismail Merchant produced) with the likes of *Howards End* (1992) and *The Remains of the Day* (1993). Jane Austen's middle-class machinations also transferred well to screen, with Ang Lee's *Sense and Sensibility* (1995) making a sizeable profit worldwide. But for financial success nothing beat *Four Weddings and a Funeral* (1994), with Mike Newell directing Hugh Grant's bumbling Englishman: it cost $5 million to make and recouped about $245 million. A mini wave of self-deprecatory comedies followed, with engaging if predictable films like *Brassed Off* (1996) and *The Full Monty* (1997) underscoring their colloquial humour with a sense of social desperation. Director Danny Boyle painted his own plucky underclass in the likes of *Trainspotting* (1996), a stand out, funny and occasionally surreal adaptation of Irvine Welsh's novel about Edinburgh junkies. And then there were the culture clash gems of *Bhaji on the Beach* (1993) and *East is East* (1999), both exploring second generation migrant lives with poignant humour.

Keeping it real: social grit at the cinema

Films like *Trainspotting* and *The Full Monty* represent the popular, palatable fringe of the social realism that still gnaws at British cinema. The genre lay dormant for a decade or so after the successes of New Wave, reliant on television to keep it alive, before returning to the big screen in the 1980s under the direction of Mike Leigh. Leigh's character-led films chart moral and social decline, heavy with the discord of post-war Britain. His working methods – incorporating improvisation and the actors' own life experiences – heighten the realism and emotional depth when they come off. *Secrets and Lies* (1996), in which a woman goes in search of her birth mother and finds a dysfunctional familial mess, and *Vera Drake* (2004), about a 1950s back street abortionist, are among Leigh's best. Ken Loach has returned periodically to social realism after the success of *Kes* in the 1960s, notably

1. Identity: the   2. Literature   3. Art, architecture   4. Performing   5. **Cinema,**   6. Media and   7. Food and drink   8. Living culture:
foundations   and philosophy   and design   arts   **photography**   communications   the state of
of British culture   **and fashion**   modern Britain

in *Riff Raff* (1990) and *Sweet Sixteen* (2002). Like Leigh, he rarely presents an actor with a completed script, hoping to heighten the spontaneity with genuine surprise. Gary Oldman, better known as a Hollywood actor, wrote and directed *Nil By Mouth* (1997) based on his own childhood in a south London council house, while Shane Meadows has developed the everyday story tradition in more recent years, impressing with *This is England* (2006), about a boy struggling for identity after his father dies in the Falklands War.

"WE'VE GONE ON HOLIDAY BY MISTAKE"
Withnail
(*Withnail and I*)

1970-2000: ten films you need to watch

Don't Look Now (1973) Nicholas Roeg. But I can't help it. Chilling, beguiling tale of a couple in Venice trying to forget about the murder of their daughter.

The Long Good Friday (1979) John MacKenzie. Classy example of the overworked British gangster genre with Bob Hoskins playing the gangland boss.

Monty Python's Life of Brian (1979) Terry Jones. 'He's not the messiah, he's a very naughty boy'. The best effort in the Python cinematic canon.

Gandhi (1982) Richard Attenborough. Ambitious but well worth a look for the cinematography and for Ben Kingsley's excellent lookylikey.

Withnail and I (1986) Bruce Robinson. Two out-of-work actors in the 1960s leave Camden for a holiday in the Lakes; witty, well scripted and peerless.

Four Weddings and a Funeral (1993) Mike Newell. Hugh Grant bumbles his way into Andie MacDowell's drawers. Funny, touching and worthy of its acclaim.

Secrets and Lies (1995) Mike Leigh. A family unpicked, with its drinking, white, working-class mum confronted by the black daughter she gave up for adoption.

Trainspotting (1996) Danny Boyle. Ewan McGregor battles heroin addiction in a dark, funny gem of a film, the best British effort of the 1990s.

The Full Monty (1997) Peter Cattaneo. Redundant Sheffield steel workers decide the path to self-respect lies with male stripping; unexpectedly warming.

Shakespeare in Love (1998) John Madden. A refreshing break from the usual costume drama with Tom Stoppard's modern, funny script. Made with American cash, it won seven Oscars.

Best of British: contemporary cinema

Today, British film is enjoying one of its periodic booms, thanks in part to increased funding (not least from the National Lottery) and generous tax breaks on production costs. Many ostensibly British productions, the *Harry Potter* series among them, are actually joint efforts, incorporating foreign cash but using British talent in front of and behind the camera. The current variety of work is impressive, and the reliance on romcoms, costume dramas and geezer gangster flicks seems to have passed. Stand out films like *The Constant Gardener* (2005), a joint effort with the US, Germany and Canada that adapted John le Carré's novel about an ethically suspect pharmaceutical company at work in Africa, and *Atonement* (2007), have won recognition from the movie arbiters in Hollywood. There wasn't a dry palm in the house for *Touching the Void* (2003), a Bafta-winning documentary about two men's mountaineering grief. Its director, Kevin Macdonald, then turned to feature films and excited with *The Last King of Scotland* (2006), featuring a characterisation of Idi Amin that was, by turns, charming and raging.

Trainspotting director Danny Boyle continues to make interesting films; *28 Days Later* (2002) brought zombie horror back from the dead with a stylish, disturbing vision of apocalyptic London, and *Slumdog Millionaire* cleaned up at the 2009 Oscars, winning eight awards including Best Picture and Best Director. Michael Winterbottom is another directorial force, his prolific, eclectic turnover of movies including the likes of *24 Hour Party People* (2002), a pleasingly eccentric biopic of Tony Wilson and the Manchester music scene. The older boys have also found more mainstream success; Stephen Frears won Oscar nominations with *The Queen* (2007), and Ken Loach the Palme d'Or at Cannes with *The Wind that Shakes the Barley* (2006). Even James Bond basks in the positive glow of 21st century British cinema, smartly reinvented with Daniel Craig in the role for *Casino Royale* (2006).

Instant classics: five great 21st century British films

Enduring Love (2004) Roger Michell. Subtle, disturbing vision of Ian McEwan's novel about a man whose life crumbles after witnessing a ballooning accident.

Wallace & Gromit: The Curse of the Were-Rabbit (2005) Nick Park. The most popular film ever made about one (plasticine) man, his dog and a giant vegetable competition.

This is England (2006) Shane Meadows. A 12-year-old boy has to choose between good skinhead and bad skinhead, and finds himself in a violent, confused world.

Hunger (2008) Steve McQueen. The stark, true story of Bobby Sands and the IRA hunger strikes of 1981 retold with a certain restraint and some stunning acting.

Slumdog Millionaire (2008) Danny Boyle. A poor Mumbai teen is arrested on suspicion of cheating his way through *Who wants to be a Millionaire*. Gripping stuff.

5.2 Photography

Photography has helped shape the world view of Britain since the 1960s when David Bailey shot the beautiful people and Tony Ray-Jones snapped seasiders sipping a cuppa. But the nation's role in photography goes back much further, right back to the days when assiduous Victorians tinkered about in sheds with tubs of acid.

Let there be light (oh, and a bit of dark too…)
Britain was right there at the dawn of photography,
at the forefront of 'fixing the shadows' as they called
it. In 1839 Henry Fox Talbot took the age-old camera
obscura trick, threw in some new chemicals and
produced the first paper negative, of an oriel window
in Lacock Abbey, Wiltshire (a location used more
recently for filming the *Harry Potter* series). His hobby
developed with images of nature and architecture
(haystacks, doorways and the like). Photographic
technology improved rapidly in the Victorian era, while
the medium was seen increasingly as an art form.
Cameras were faster by the 1870s, and available to
the multitude by the end of the century thanks to the
push-button innovations of Kodak.

Five(ish) famous Victorian photographers

David Octavius Hill and Robert Adamson. The Scottish duo (Hill the artist;
Adamson the scientist) chose the calotype for portraits of famous Scotsfolk, but
also snapped Edinburgh cityscapes and the prosaic fishing communities nearby.

Oscar Gustave Rejlander. The Swede who found his way to Wolverhampton in
the 1850s was the first great art photographer. He spliced multiple images to create
large, allegorical scenes.

Lewis Carroll. Better known today as an author, Carroll was fascinated by
photography, taking thousands of images of people, including loads of young
Alice Liddell, inspiration for *Alice's Adventures in Wonderland*.

Julia Margaret Cameron. One of the first to capture character (rather than dead
pan portraiture) using soft focus, theatrical settings and the like. Famous sitters
including Charles Darwin and Alfred, Lord Tennyson felt the benefit.

Peter Henry Emerson. Emerson eschewed the contrived snaps of contemporaries
and talked up photography as documentation, fond in particular of capturing rural
Norfolk in the 1880s. He later changed tack completely and advocated photo
manipulation.

Have camera will travel

It didn't take long for travel photography to develop. Roger Fenton was one of the first practitioners, although his images of British soldierly life (minus the dying – he was employed as a propagandist by the Government) in the Crimea in the 1850s have more often seen him labelled the first photojournalist. Others journeyed simply to record the exotic. Samuel Bourne took some memorable shots of India and the Himalayas in the 1860s; who knows what Brits back home would have made of his photos of the Taj Mahal. Scotsman John Thomson went to the Far East in the same decade, snapping Sumatran villagers, Siamese royalty and the jungle smothered temple of Angkor Wat. Later he took up residence in Brixton and photographed London's poor, one of the first to document British penury with a camera. But perhaps the most famous adventuring Victorian snapper was Francis Frith. He photographed Egypt and the Middle East in the 1850s, before returning to England to establish a photo factory that churned out millions of prints of virtually every town in Britain. They were sold to the masses as postcards, many of which you can still buy today. And then there's Linnaeus Tripe, an army officer who photographed India and Burma in the 1850s, worthy of mention on name alone.

If it's good enough for the Queen...
When Oscar Gustave Rejlander first displayed *The Two Ways of Life* (1857), a large print comprising 32 merged photos, some slated the work as indecent. The allegorical image featured one man looking to a life of virtue, with its religion and charity, and another surveying topless women and other symbols of vice. Exhibitors at the Edinburgh Photographic Society apparently covered the naughty half when it went on show. However, any negative opinions were largely rearranged when Queen Victoria bought a copy for her beloved Albert.

"PHOTOGRAPHY
IS NOT A SPORT.
IT HAS NO RULES.
EVERYTHING MUST
BE DARED AND
TRIED."
Bill Brandt

Picture imperfect: the British talent for photojournalism

The adoption of photography by the media industry in the early 20th century spurred its role as a documentary tool. Photojournalism came to the fore, pushed forward by smaller, easy to use cameras, and in Britain *Picture Post* magazine printed the new visual narrative for a massive audience. First published in 1938, within a couple of months it was selling well over a million a week. Some notable photographers shot for *Picture Post*. Bert Hardy covered the Blitz with his trusty Leica and went on to capture the Allies' advance across Western Europe, from D-Day to the liberation of Bergen-Belsen. Bill Brandt, the best-known British photographer of the interwar years, also contributed to *Picture Post*. Born in Germany to a British father, Brandt too covered the Second World War, although concentrated as much on society as soldiers. Before the conflict he'd shot the poor and the rich of London; after it he photographed brooding landscapes and stretched, sculptural nudes. His portraits featured everyone from Ezra Pound (1928) to Peter Sellers (1963). A third *Picture Post* man, Humphrey Spender (brother of poet Stephen), confirmed Britain's mid century prowess for photojournalism. Surreptitiously he captured life in the industrial north, working for the Mass Observation project, an anthropological study of working-class England. Spender did everything he could to ensure spontaneity, even hiding a camera in his rain mac. His photos of 'Worktown' (actually Bolton disguised) were seminal in their ordinariness.

Fashions and faces: Beaton, Bailey and Rankin

As Britain pursued its passion for photojournalism in the mid 20th century a more affected genre of photography also evolved, set to explode in the 1960s. It embraced fashion, advertising and high society (in short, the beautiful people) and found its outlet in magazines like *Vanity Fair*, *Harper's Bazaar* and *Vogue*. Cecil Beaton bore the torch with staged, glamorous images of Marlene Dietrich, Audrey Hepburn and the royals from the 1920s through to the 60s.

"I NEVER CARED FOR FASHION MUCH, AMUSING LITTLE SEAMS AND WITTY LITTLE PLEATS: IT WAS THE GIRLS I LIKED."
David Bailey, former partner of Jean Shrimpton, Catherine Deneuve, Marie Helvin…

After a post-war lull, Beaton's influence emerged in the 1960s with a group of photographers that distilled the spirit of swinging Britain. East End boys David Bailey and Terence Donovan led the pack, moving in the same circles as the musicians, actors and socialites they photographed. Bailey shot The Beatles, the Kray Twins and model Jean Shrimpton in a style that, while mindful of Beaton's, was edgier; its situations minimalist and less contrived. Like Bailey, Donovan worked primarily in monochrome and shot a similar array of 60s faces. Both moved from fashion and portraiture to advertising campaigns and filming TV commercials. Others like Lewis Morley (his shot of Christine Keeler, naked on a chair, became iconic), Norman Parkinson and Lord Lichfield (who had a way with royals) operated in the same milieu in the 1960s and 70s. Fashion/portrait/society photography still thrives in Britain today. Nick Knight and Corinne Day have been the big names in fashion in recent years, involved in editorial shoots for the likes of *Vogue* and *i-D Magazine*, as well as framing some memorable ad campaigns. In the 1990s, Day was accused of fostering 'heroin chic' by shooting pallid models in drab locales. In portraiture, Rankin has become internationally famous, perhaps the best-known British photographer of modern times – the Bailey of his generation if you like. His polished, commercial portfolio features everyone from Kate Moss to the Queen, usually shot against a white backdrop.

"I DON'T DO PHOTOJOURNALISM ANY MORE BECAUSE, FRANKLY, NOBODY REALLY WANTS IT."
Don McCullin

Occupational hazard When Don McCullin was covering the war in Cambodia in 1970 his Nikon camera stopped the bullet from an AK-47, probably saving his life.

Record makers: the modern crop of photojournalists

Even while *Picture Post* bowed out of publication in 1957, Fleet Street flourished and the documentary genre continued to produce excellent British photographers throughout the later 20th century. Some stuck with the social truths of urban Britain, as pioneered by the likes of Humphrey Spender; others looked to rural communities or followed in Bert Hardy's footsteps and went overseas for their real life stories.

Five important documentary photographers of recent times

Tony Ray-Jones. Little referenced these days but hugely important for recording the customs and habits of 1960s Britain. With cups of tea by the seaside and the like, Ray-Jones represented the other side of the 60s coin to Bailey and Donovan. He died of leukaemia, aged 31, in 1972.

Martin Parr. Followed the Ray-Jones format but threw in satire, tapping the values, clichés and disappointments of everyday English life, from ill-fitting outfits at a wedding reception to a series of 'bored couples'. More recently he's worked for Magnum Photos, world leaders in photojournalism.

Fay Godwin. Godwin recorded human relationships with landscape. She photographed the traditions of rural life and how they were changing in the 1970s and 80s, passing visual comment on environmental abuses and the limits on public access to the land.

Don McCullin. Perhaps the greatest British war photographer of the later 20th century. He began with a north London street gang, his own, in 1958, moved on to the war in Vietnam and then documented the

246

troubles in Northern Ireland. The honesty of his photos convinced the British Government to refuse him entry to the Falklands in 1982.

Chris Killip. Shooting in monochrome in the 1980s, Killip eloquently caught the downsides of Thatcherism, particularly in the mining communities of the North East. He also turned his hand to landscape, not least that of his native Isle of Man. These days he lectures at Harvard.

What and who: modern art photography

The distinctions between documentary, fashion and portraiture on one hand and 'art photography' on the other can be fuzzy. All photography is art, right? And the work of Rankin and Nick Knight, who often manipulates his images in the manner of a modern day Rejlander (he would have loved the digital age), is sometimes referred to as fine art photography, as are the landscapes of James Ravilious. The cultural powers-that-be recognise the connections: Richard Billingham took photographs of places he'd visited as a child, most of them waste ground, and won a Turner Prize nomination in 2001. There are, however, contemporary British photographers who work overtly in the manner of the artist, contriving and staging the subject for record as a piece of art. Helen Chadwick made use of animal parts, food, fluids and her own image in the 1980s, and exhibited *Opal* (1996), photos of dead human embryos, shortly before dying prematurely from a viral infection. Matt Collishaw, often lumped together with the Young British Artists (see section 3.1.5. for more on the YBAs), creates collages of flowers, humans and fairies, but came to fame in 1997 with a large close-up of a fresh bullet hole in someone's head. Another YBA and Turner prize nominee, Sam Taylor-Wood, shot *Crying Men*, portraits of actors in tears. Daniel Craig, Jude Law and Steve Buscemi all turned on the waterworks.

Snap judgements
In 2008 the Metropolitan Police launched a poster campaign urging the public to watch out for terrorists with cameras. 'Thousands of people take photos every day. What if one of them seems odd?' read the text. Civil liberties campaigners weren't impressed.

5.3 Fashion

Fashion plays a weighty part in the story of contemporary British culture. Open-minded and unbound by proscriptive tradition, it's an absorbing blend of eccentricity and formality. Sharp tailoring, a venerable textiles industry and innovative fashion designers have all contributed.

1. Identity: the
foundations
of British culture

2. Literature
and philosophy

3. Art, architecture
and design

4. Performing
arts

**5. Cinema,
photography
and fashion**

6. Media and
communications

7. Food and drink

8. Living culture:
the state of
modern Britain

National costumes

There are certain subtleties of style between the regions of 21st century Britain. Some observers point to a north/south fashion divide for women: generalisations are usually a mistake, but Manchester, Leeds and Newcastle are said to have a more dressy, glam style than London and the south with their casual femininity. In the realms of traditional costume you're on safer ground: certain conventions demand acknowledgement:

Scotland

The callow traveller might assume that every man north of the border goes about his daily business in a kilt. They don't. But they will don the national dress of kilt, waistcoat, sporran (the small furry pouch hung around the waist) and brogues at the slightest ceremonial excuse. The humble wraparound (which evolved 200 years ago from the 'great plaid', a shoulder-draped affair) has played its part on the catwalk, notably in Vivienne Westwood's 1993 collection, *Anglomania*, with its mini-kilt. The Lochcarron Textile Mill in Scotland created a special tartan for Westwood, named the 'McAndreas' after her third husband. Military regulation famously dictates the kilt an underwear-free zone (the true origin of the phrase 'going commando' perhaps?).

Wales

The Welsh national costume is a rather faux affair. Fearing the loss of Welsh national identity in the 19th century, not without justification, Lady Llanover led the drive to create a national dress. Based on the countrywear of the time it features a flannel petticoat worn under an open-fronted bed gown, an apron, a red shawl and a kerchief or cap. The tall 'chimney' hat was added later, in the 1840s. The ensemble only really appears at public events; people don't slip it on for a trip to the supermarket. The practice of carrying babies in a shawl is a genuine Welsh tradition.

England

By contrast, England has no national dress, pre-fabricated or otherwise. There are, however, certain recognisably English uniforms, from the Beefeater's costume – the scarlet and gold suit, stockings and round brimmed black hat worn by the keepers of the Tower of London (and an English Miss World contestant) – to the red tunics and bearskins of the Queen's Foot Guard and the white shirts and knee breaches of morris men.

Fashion history: greatest hits

The **Elizabethan** era, with its brocades, jewels and elaborate hats, was a sucker for style. Rich men wore ruffs, breeches, doublets, cloaks and an occasional codpiece, while women endured the corset, farthingale (hooped petticoat) and brocaded gown. Dress was governed by social standing, and fashion faux pas were even criminalised. In 1574 the Queen set dress codes in law: only royal garb could be trimmed with ermine; lesser nobles had to make do with fox or otter. Anyone violating the Sumptuary Clothing Laws could face fines and the loss of property, title and even life. The masses had a go at imitating the styles of court but used much cheaper materials.

In the **Regency** period women wore neo-classical, high-waisted 'empire silhouette' dresses that allowed for a low, square neckline and short puff sleeves. For men, breeches were tight as hell, coats had tails, waistcoats were double breasted and linen shirts were finished off with an elaborate cravat, playing right into the hands of the new fashion victim, the dandy.

Fashion was still bowing to social convention in **Victorian** Britain. Well-to-do women found their rears enlarged by steel-framed bustles and their waists reduced by brutal corsetry. Legs were sensed not seen; even bathing costumes covered the entire body. Men's clothing sobered after its Regency jaunt, governed now by dark colours and sharply cut frock

Look out, it's the fashion police
A sumptuary law of 1571 dictated that everyone over the age of six wear a woollen cap on Sunday and holy days, all in an effort to boost the English wool industry. In 1795 Prime Minister William Pitt the Younger introduced a tax on wig powder. The well-to-do and their servants, among whom the wig (short for 'periwig') was an 18th century fashion essential, paid a guinea a year for their whitening powder. The tax hastened the wig's demise. These days they're still worn by barristers, judges and some governmental dignitaries – a hairy hangover from the days when they needed a disguise to ensure safety.

coats. Umbrellas offered a useful key to social status; the wealthy owned a brolly, while the majority rented one in wet weather or simply did without. Eyeglasses were used as fashion accessories rather than visual aids; often they didn't even have lenses. The Victorian age also saw the advent of haute couture, in which fragile gauze dresses decorated with flowers and ribbons were worn once or twice and then cast aside because they soiled and crushed so easily. Of course, little of this style troubled the masses, who wore rough but restrictively formal clothes for the daily routine.

Trendsetters: phases of 20th century fashion

Fashions changed rapidly throughout the 20th century. Sewing machines, synthetic fibres and youth culture all played a part in the century that democratised modes of dress. Today, certain decades are remembered for a particular look, while the derivative, recycling mode of modern fashion means that each period has its cultural resonance for the average Brit. Certain fads and phases live longer in the memory than others:

Edwardian Lady. A final fling for old school elegance initiated the S-bend silhouette, achieved with a corset that forced hips back and busts forward, and the long, tight and aptly named hobble skirt. Fancy blouses were de rigueur; the less wealthy used appliqué, lace, faggoting and pin tucks to emulate detailed high couture. The Edwardian blouse returned with vigour in the first decade of the 21st century. Merry Widow hats, of wide brim and feathered trim, were named after the popular Edwardian operetta.

Flapper Girl. Sporting short hair (the bob), shortish shift dresses, snug cloche hats and flat chests (often bandaged into submission), the flapper girls strove for a boyish look in the 1920s. A cigarette in a long holder usually completed the ensemble. The uncomplicated construction of the flapper dress led women to make their own, narrowing the disparities of fashion between classes.

Make do and mend. In wartime Britain pillowcases became shorts or blouses, and leather soles were replaced with cork. Siren Suits and Kangaroo Coats could be zipped in a hurry, their roomy pockets quickly filled with essentials on the way to the air raid shelter. In 1941 the government introduced Utility Clothing, taking charge of production and outlawing anything too fancy – pockets and turn-ups were both restricted in an effort to save material. The CC41 label attached to the mass-produced designs gained an ironic, collectable fame.

Teddy Boys. Take a long jacket with a velvet collar, some drainpipe trousers, a narrow tie, a duck's arse quiff (as the tall hairstyle was called) and a pair of brothel creepers (thick-soled suede shoes) and you've got the first real uniform of youth rebellion. Teddy boys emerged in the 1950s and kickstarted the fashion revolution of the following decade with its mods, rockers and hippies. As for the name, it derives from a taste for Edwardian ('Teddy') jackets.

Biba, Mary Quant and the miniskirt. Despite the egalitarian mien of the early 1960s, designer fashion remained restricted to the wealthy. Biba changed all that in 1964. It was a London fashion boutique that sold the latest European looks at a fraction of designer prices. The Biba brand became hugely successful, and other, similar ventures followed, including Miss Selfridge, a groovy spin-off from the Oxford Street department store. Meanwhile Mary Quant lopped inches off hemlines, introducing every British girl to the miniskirt (even while it was actually invented by André Courrèges). Quant herself became a fashion icon, sporting a sharp Vidal Sassoon 'five-point' haircut. Trousers began to flare late in the decade.

1970s. The most vibrant decade of recent British fashion had an anything goes feel. Early on, hippies popularised kaftans, Macramé bags and Afghan coats. The flares of the late 1960s widened out to bell-bottom proportions before high-waisted straight trousers and platform soles stepped into view. It was only a short leap to the lycra trousers and stretch sequin tube tops of disco. Even blokes got involved, suddenly (and briefly) comfortable with outrageous sideburns and tightly crotched trousers. By the end of the decade, punk was reining in the flare,

Quantifying Quant
By the end of the 1960s, an estimated seven million women owned a Mary Quant garment.

Costume king
Photographer and designer Cecil Beaton won Oscars for his costume design on *Gigi* (1958) and *My Fair Lady* (1964). Similar efforts on Broadway secured four Tonys.

customising jackets and causing offence with rude t-shirts. Punk's influence would be long ranging. Mohican haircuts, spikes and ripped fabric shocked initially but were later adopted by the mainstream.

Fashion coming up from the streets

Savile Row. Mayfair road with a mystical place in men's fashion. It's the bastion of bespoke tailoring, a London street where everyone from Jude Law to Napoleon III has bought a sharp suit. Regency dandy Beau Brummell was the area's first high profile customer.

King's Road. Charles II's private road through Chelsea became a hippy hang out in the 1960s and a hotbed of punk in the 70s, led by Malcolm McLaren and Vivienne Westwood with a boutique called Sex. Today it's all painfully respectable.

Carnaby Street. The Soho street set the trends for Swinging London in the 1960s with boutiques that shaped the 'mod' style. The cutting edge went blunt years ago, although the area retains a number of independent clothes shops alongside the high street giants.

The major British designers of 20th century fashion

Look back to 1857 and it turns out that an Englishman, Charles Worth, initiated haute couture. He opened the first Parisian shop offering set dress designs based on four annual fashion shows; previously, the wealthy had simply suggested designs to anonymous seamstresses. Back in Britain, Norman Hartnell was an important 20th century name, dressing the likes of Noel Coward and Marlene Dietrich in his London salon, before creating the Queen's coronation dress in 1953. A new wave of designers mixed nonconformism with slick tailoring in the 1960s, drawing their inspiration from street fashion and establishing London as a sartorial hub. They were led by Mary Quant and Zandra Rhodes, who set up her own London boutique in 1969 selling radical print designs and who would develop punk fashion with reversed seams and jewelled safety pins. Vivienne Westwood was the other grande dame of punk clothing (and now an actual dame). She's been shocking and entertaining in equal measure since the early 1970s. With slogan t-shirts (one showed a swastika), underwear as outwear, penis cufflinks and vertiginous platforms, few have challenged fashion precepts as often or as successfully. The 1980s was the decade of Katherine Hamnett, who flogged the t-shirt slogan for years (remember Choose Life or Frankie Says Relax?), and Bruce Oldfield, Barnardo's boy turned celebrity couture hero, dressing everyone from Princess Di to Diana Ross. Paul Smith also cultivated a glowing reputation, taking the classic men's suit and throwing in splashes of colour – he calls it 'Savile Row meets Mr Bean'. Smith, like Oldfield, Hamnett, Westwood and Rhodes, is still making clothes.

> "I'M NOT TRYING TO DO SOMETHING DIFFERENT, I'M TRYING TO DO THE SAME THING BUT IN A DIFFERENT WAY."
> Vivienne Westwood

The assault on Paris: contemporary designers
British designers have been chipping away at the Parisian fashion fortress for years, building up London as a comparative force, but they've taken a more invasive approach of late, invited in by the famous couture houses. John Galliano (actually a Gibraltarian) was the first, taking up the head designer's role at Givenchy in 1995 and then at Christian Dior a year later. His designs often have a theatrical, fantastical quality. East End taxi driver's son Alexander McQueen crossed the Channel a year later, succeeding Galliano at Givenchy. He later joined Gucci, broadening a reputation for shocking, subversive statements carried along on exemplary tailoring (he learned the trade on Savile Row). One of his earliest catwalk collections, Highland Rape, offered comment on British involvement in Scottish history. The third Brit in Paris was Stella McCartney, daughter of a certain Beatle, who worked for fashion house Chloé, pursuing a talent for femininity and sharp tailoring. These days she's got her own label. A lifelong vegetarian, McCartney refuses to use leather or fur in her designs. Back on home turf, Matthew Williamson (bright, kaleidoscopic dresses), Giles Deacon (powerful glamour) and Scotsman Christopher Kane (wildly eclectic – he said a 2007 collection was based on elements of Scarlett O'Hara and Rambo) are all important contemporary designers.

The Macintosh. After 20 years of experimentation with softened rubber and wool, Charles Macintosh's Glaswegian firm finally manufactured their first waterproof coat in 1824.

The Burberry Gabardine coat. A closely woven waterproof twill created predominantly for Hampshire farmers by Thomas Burberry in 1879; the Burberry style – with its beige and red check – has become world famous.

The Barbour jacket. So durable that disciples often bash it against a wall to soften up the initial stiffness. Ever present in the Sloane Ranger's 1980s wardrobe, they remain popular with the country set.

The cardigan. The pullover with perks, made fashionable by James Brudenell, 7th Earl of Cardigan, while fighting in the Crimea. He led the charge of the Light Brigade at Balaclava, after which the woollen headgear is named. If only he'd been as good at war as he was at knitwear.

Wellington boots. The cobbler to the first Duke of Wellington played around with the Hessian boot, and bravo, a soft calfskin star was born – hard wearing in battle, comfy for the drawing room and great for wanging (it's a sport). The vulcanised rubber variant arrived in the mid 19th century.

Modern uniforms: fashion stereotypes

Sloane Ranger (Sloanes). Ex-public school types, named for Sloane Square in Chelsea. Male variant sometimes called Hooray Henrys.
Uniform: look for tracksuit bottoms tucked into Ugg boots, scruffy ponytails, upturned collars and pashminas on girls, and loafers with jeans, an open collar shirt and maybe even a tweed jacket thrown in for males. Tan shoes, boating-jackets and sleeveless puffers straddle the gender divide.
Brands: Barbour, Jack Wills, Abercrombie & Fitch.
Ambassadors: William and Harry Windsor.

Chav. Derogatory term for 21st century youth of low socio-economic class, blamed for many of society's ills. *Uniform:* gold jewellery (hooped earrings, thick neck chains), white trainers (in 'prison white', so clean they look new), clothes with prominent logos, hooded tops (or hoodies) and baseball caps. Look out for the 'council-house facelift' on girls – gelled hair pulled back in a tight bun. *Brands:* Burberry, Yves Saint Laurent bags, sports brands (particularly Kappa, Reebok and Adidas). *Ambassadors:* footballers, WAGs (footballers' 'wives and girlfriends') and rappers.

East London Cool. Hard-to-define clique who, despite appearances of casualness and the thrift store/fancy dress chic, sport a highly calculated look. *Uniform:* constantly changing, but likely to sit comfortably on the border between ugly and cool. Skinny jeans, plimsoll-type trainers and scruffy hair usually a given. *Ambassadors:* Brit pack musicians, fashion students, London It girls, Russell Brand, Bob Geldof's children.

Five British style icons

Twiggy. That's Lesley Hornby to her parents. Epitomised 1960s style with a waif silhouette, long lashes, bug eyes and modish bob.

Kate Moss. She gets dressed (skinny jeans, waistcoats etc) and the rest of Britain copies, as they have done for nearly 20 years despite drug scandals and wayward lovers.

Princess Diana. Dressed by various British designers, Diana morphed from Sloane Ranger to elegant icon, influencing women's fashion in the 1980s and 90s.

David Beckham. The footballer has been a rare male fashion icon for years; for a while his haircuts were front page news.

Bryan Ferry. The Roxy Music frontman, renowned for a sharp suit, helped lead British men from the sartorial dark ages back in the 1970s and 80s

6 Media and communications

6.1 Media

Britain has a love-hate relationship

with its media. Press, TV, radio –

the public slurps them all up

greedily, yet each has its image

problems and none is exempt from

mistrust or even contempt.

6.1.1 Reverting to type: national and regional newspapers

Whilst the newspaper industry in Britain hasn't been unaffected by the rapid growth of the Internet, relatively speaking it thrives. The biggest selling paper, *The Sun*, still shifts over three million copies a day; more than any other in the English-speaking world. The industry is lively and competitive and supports a wide range of titles, representing all but the most extreme political views and obscure interest groups.

The British press: key dates

1549 First British 'news letter', *Requests of the Devonshyre and Cornyshe Rebelles*.

1621 *Courant*, the first recognisable English newspaper, rolls off the presses.

1690 *The Worcester Postman* becomes the first regularly published paper (it's still going today).

1702 *The Daily Courant*, a single page of two printed columns, launched as the first British daily.

1785 *The Daily Universal Register* is born, changing its name three years later to *The Times*.

1855 The abolition of the tax (or 'stamp') on newspapers makes them affordable to the man in the street. *The Daily Telegraph* becomes the first penny national.

1904 Alfred Harmsworth reinvents the *Daily Mirror*, launching the tabloid format in the process. The 'red top' tabloids really take off in the 1940s.

1980s The nationals leave Fleet Street, spiritual home of British newspapers, for east London amid bitter conflict with trade unions.

1994 *The Daily Telegraph* becomes the first national British newspaper to make daily content available online.

The nationals: you are what you read

Each national newspaper in Britain has its mores, has a culture and identity that reflects and reinforces what the reader considers their place in British society to be. Size still matters in this respect: there's a general split between broadsheets and tabloids. When people talk about the 'tabloids', it's usually shorthand for a newspaper blending big headlines, lurid photos and sensational, conjectural stories. The 'red tops' (*The Sun*, *Daily Star* et al) are the most extreme. Broadsheets (*The Times*, *The Independent*, *The Daily Telegraph* etc), double the size, are more restrained, valued for their measured political and financial news. Confusingly, most of the broadsheets now publish a 'compact' edition, similar in proportion to a tabloid. If they can't see the size but can see the title, the casual British observer can make some reasonably educated guesses about a person based on whether they're carrying a copy of *The Guardian* or the *Daily Mail* (see below for more). But, beyond the perceived connotations of class, education, wealth and so on, perhaps the most important thing about the national press in Britain is its relative freedom – even if it is, on occasion, the freedom to print absolute cobblers.

You can't fool all the people all the time
In 2007 a BBC World Service poll revealed that only 29 per cent of Britons felt their media were doing a good job of reporting news accurately.

Best of the press: Britain's big newspapers

The Sun/News Of The World

A pair of tabloids owned by Rupert Murdoch's News International that dwarf their nearest rivals. Traditionally right-leaning, both nevertheless supported Tony Blair and New Labour. Political bias aside, they're best known for scantily clad women, strong opinions and high profile news 'scoops'.

Daily Mail/Mail On Sunday
Part of Associated Newspapers, these titles are the prim,
proper and generally indignant face of tabloid journalism.
More reserved than *The Sun or Daily Mirror*, they take a
conservative standpoint on the news and are more likely
to feature the royals than a bikini model.

Daily Mirror/Sunday Mirror
Claims to be the original tabloid are disputed, but this left-
leaning newspaper was definitely one of the forerunners and
the dominant force in the field until overtaken by *The Sun* in
the 1970s.

The Times/The Sunday Times
The Sunday edition of this famous broadsheet actually
outsells the daily version by around two to one. Another one
owned by News International, *The Times* features well-
informed news coverage and, at the weekend, a range of
quality supplements.

The Daily Telegraph
The biggest selling daily broadsheet positions itself to the
right of the political centre, presenting British and world
news in fairly sober fashion.

The Guardian/The Observer
The reputation of *The Guardian* and its Sunday sister paper
belies their relatively low sales figures. These are the leading
left-of-centre broadsheets and the term '*Guardian* reader' has
become shorthand for describing middle-class, liberal 'media
types'.

Financial Times
The only daily paper in Britain to carry a blow-by-blow
account of the world markets has been a ubiquitous, salmon-
pink-paged part of the city gent's uniform for a century. Also
the only British newspaper to sell more copies abroad than
on home turf.

1. Identity: the
foundations
of British culture

2. Literature
and philosophy

3. Art, architecture
and design

4. Performing
arts

5. Cinema,
photography
and fashion

**6. Media and
communications**

7. Food and drink

8. Living culture:
the state of
modern Britain

Ragtime: the regional press

No single regional newspaper in Britain competes with the nationals. Scotland's *Daily Record* and *Sunday Post*, if they can be classed as regional, sell slightly under 400,000 copies each and London's *Evening Standard* offloads around 300,000, but beyond these there's a steep drop off in circulation figures. Even *The Western Mail*, which bills itself as 'the national newspaper of Wales', dips below sales of 40,000; *The Scotsman*, in its role as Scotland's 'thinking newspaper', sells around 50,000. In Northern Ireland *The Belfast Telegraph*, the biggest daily, claims a readership of about 75,000. It's a mildly Unionist affair, countered in the province by the lightly Nationalist (and less tabloidy) *Irish News*, which sells just under 50,000 a day. While there are no regional giants in Britain, most cities and large towns will have one, if not two, daily papers. At the very least a district will be covered by a weekly title. The leading regional papers, such as the *Kent Messenger* or the *Express & Star* in the West Midlands, sell around 140,000 copies of each edition.

But it's there in black and white...
The Press Complaints Commission, a board of 17 members drawn from the major publishers, investigates complaints made against Britain's newspapers, although it has no legal powers – the industry is expected to self-regulate. In more extreme cases, the courts get involved. The most notorious abuse of press freedom in recent years related to the reporting of Madeleine McCann's disappearance in Portugal – almost a dozen papers, the *Daily Express*, *Daily Star*, *Evening Standard* and *News of the World* included, paid out thousands in damages after publishing a series of false stories.

"THE *DAILY MIRROR* IS READ BY PEOPLE WHO THINK THEY RUN THE COUNTRY. *THE GUARDIAN* IS READ BY PEOPLE WHO THINK THEY OUGHT TO RUN THE COUNTRY. *THE TIMES* IS READ BY PEOPLE WHO ACTUALLY DO RUN THE COUNTRY. *THE DAILY MAIL* IS READ BY THE WIVES OF PEOPLE WHO RUN THE COUNTRY. *THE FINANCIAL TIMES* IS READ BY PEOPLE WHO OWN THE COUNTRY. ...AND *SUN* READERS DON'T CARE WHO RUNS THE COUNTRY AS LONG AS SHE'S GOT BIG TITS." from TV sitcom *Yes Prime Minister*

| 1. Identity: the foundations of British culture | 2. Literature and philosophy | 3. Art, architecture and design | 4. Performing arts | 5. Cinema, photography and fashion | **6. Media and communications** | 7. Food and drink | 8. Living culture: the state of modern Britain |

The Gentleman's Johnson

Not only was *The Gentleman's Magazine* a publishing first in its own right; in 1738 it also provided Samuel Johnson with his first proper writing job. Doctor Johnson penned semi-fictional reports from Parliament called *'Debates in the Senate of Magna Lilliputia'*. It was illegal to report from Parliament verbatim so Johnson used his own dialogue to present the political issues of the day. (See section 2.1.3 for more on Johnson.)

Knowledge stores: the early magazines

As a publishing term, 'magazine' occurred first in Britain in 1731 with the inaugural edition of *The Gentleman's Magazine*, an amalgamation of pretty much anything Edward Cave, the publisher, thought might interest educated folk. Previously, the word 'magazine' had referred to a place where goods were stored; hence Cave deemed it appropriate for his ragbag digest. Earlier publications with a similar, albeit less developed, format had always been referred to as 'journals'. As magazines developed in the 19th century, the range of titles became increasingly diverse even while most remained true to the 'magazine' name with a wide range of subject matter; some, like *The Spectator* and *The Economist* remain in print. Charles Dickens published 19 editions of his own magazine, *Household Words*, between 1850 and 1859, overseeing every aspect of production. It featured the serialisation of his own novels, notably *Hard Times*, but also included work by other authors, including Elizabeth Gaskell's *North and South*. Later in the 19th century, magazines like George Newnes' *Tit-Bits* and *Answers to Correspondents*, its rival and imitator from Alfred Harmsworth, capitalised on improved literacy standards.

Shelf life: modern British mags

The top selling magazines of 21st century Britain can't compete with newspapers for circulation, but what they lack in bulk they make up for in diversity. The market is dominated by a few major publishers, including Bauer, IPC Media, Northern & Shell and The National Magazine Company, but the breadth of titles is still huge. The dominant sector by far is television listings – Brits are buying the likes of *TV Choice*, *What's On TV* and the *Radio Times* in vast quantities. Large international titles like *Cosmopolitan*, *Vogue*, *Time* and *National Geographic* all sell fairly well, but are dwarfed by the nation's thirst for televisual guidance. The second most influential group, positioned a long way below the TV guides in sales figures, are women's lifestyle magazines. At the top end of the scale, titles like *Take A Break* and *OK!* cover a mix of celebrity and human interest in varying ratios. *Heat, Closer* and *Grazia* are also worth noting: aimed at younger women they focus more heavily on celebrity gossip (*Heat* in particular will think nothing of devoting four pages to celebrity cellulite). With a notoriety that far outweighs sales figures come the 'Lads Mags'. These include monthlies like *Loaded* and *FHM*, and weeklies *Nuts* and *Zoo*, with their mildly varying quotas of semi-naked female celebs, glamour models and other laddish fare.

Long runners: venerable Brit mags

Tit-Bits Originally titled *Tit-Bits from all the Most Interesting Books, Periodicals and Contributors in the World*, it was a cheap magazine of human interest stories and jokes. Founded in 1881, the title survives as the adult magazine *Titbits International*.

The Spectator Established in 1828, *The Spectator* has close links to both *The Daily Telegraph* and the Conservative Party. Indeed, several former editors have gone on to ministerial roles in Conservative cabinets.

Punch The humorous, satirical magazine *Punch* was founded in 1841, before fading away in 1992. In 1996 it was relaunched by Mohamed Al Fayed, the Egyptian owner of Harrods, but ceased publication once more in 2002.

The Economist It may call itself a newspaper, but this liberal-leaning publication, founded in 1843 to campaign for free trade, looks and feels very much like a magazine.

Tatler Focused on the ins and outs of upper-class British society, *Tatler* was established in 1901 but has its roots in a much earlier publication that ran from 1709 to 1711 and featured contributions from Jonathan Swift.

From Baird to worse

Not all of John Logie Baird's inventions took off as well as television. He's also credited with inventing, amongst other things, glass razors (which shattered and lacerated in equal measure) and pneumatic shoes (which burst). He also once managed to short out the entire electricity system of Glasgow while trying to create diamonds by super-heating graphite.

Reception committee: a Scottish affair

Scotland had a major influence on the emerging television industry in the early 20th century. John Logie Baird is generally credited with creating the first working television set, even while his machine, which he dubbed the Televisor, was quickly superseded. It was another Scot, John Reith, who really shaped the course of the industry. From the moment he joined the fledgling British Broadcasting Company as General Manager in 1922 he stuck to a three-word guiding principle: educate, inform and entertain – an epithet that remains in the BBC mission statement. The most notable watershed event of Reith's tenure at the BBC (there were many) was to push it from privately owned Company to publicly owned and funded Corporation.

Licence to bill

The BBC still looms large in modern Britain as a strangely anthropomorphic cultural force. Britons regard 'the Beeb' in much the same way as they might a favoured elderly relative: much loved, perhaps not cut out for the modern world, but still capable of inspiration. Indeed, another colloquial term for the BBC is 'Auntie'. However, the warm glow comes at a price. You can't own a television set in Britain – even if it's tucked away in a cupboard or hooked up to a subscription only service – without also purchasing a TV licence. The licence fee goes to fund all of the BBC's television, Internet and radio services, which remain entirely free of advertising. But the BBC doesn't monopolise airtime in the way it once did. When the Television Act passed into law in 1954 it allowed for an independent commercial television station, and ITV (Independent Television), a network of regional broadcasters aiming to compete both against the BBC and one another, took up the new role.

Channel 4 were awarded a licence in 1982 with a remit to provide more educational and regional programming, spawning the likes of S4C (Sianel Pedwar Cymru or Channel 4 Wales), broadcasting in both Welsh and English. Channel Five added to the terrestrial TV picture in 1997.

Square-eyed monsters and the digital age

The Brits are avid viewers, up there with the most square-eyed in Europe – your average citizen spends a good two and a half hours a day in front of the old idiot box. But viewing habits are changing, if only to adapt to the increasing number of available channels. The digital age is shaking up the established order. The interloper-in-chief is BSkyB, owned in part by News Corporation (parent company of News International, behind *The Times* and *The Sun* newspapers). Sky TV, as it's simply known to most, operates nearly all of the major subscription services, based largely around Premiership football, major US imports and blockbuster movies. Many other digital services are available via the Freeview system, which aims to replace the traditional analogue service by 2012.

Trust issues
The BBC's reputation for impartiality and independence took a knock in 2004 after the publication of *The Hutton Report*, an independent enquiry into the suicide of Dr David Kelly. Kelly, a UN weapons inspector, was caught in the row between the BBC and the British Government over allegations that a key Government dossier had been doctored to justify the 2003 invasion of Iraq. The BBC was severely criticised, the Director General resigned and the role of the Board of Governors (now abolished) was reviewed.

What's on the box?

BBC One The original British channel and still the most watched carries much of the BBC's flagship news, current affairs and entertainment programming, not least its biggest draw, *EastEnders*. It also gets all the sporting events that the Corporation can afford.

BBC Two A less mainstream version of BBC1. Here you're more likely to find arts programming, new comedy and documentary series.

1. Identity: the
foundations
of British culture

2. Literature
and philosophy

3. Art, architecture
and design

4. Performing
arts

5. Cinema,
photography
and fashion

6. Media and
communications

7. Food and drink

8. Living culture:
the state of
modern Britain

ITV Primetime ITV hosts popular soaps and entertainment shows like *The X Factor* and its principal soaps, *Coronation Street* and *Emmerdale*. Off peak you are more likely to find a mix of syndicated and regional programming.

Big Brother
The popularity of watching egotists with restricted freedom is finally waning after a decade.

Channel 4 Broadcasts a wide range of programmes – a mix of US imports, hard-hitting documentaries and reality TV – but tends to be more 'youth' orientated than the others.

The X Factor
The latest and most enduring version of the reality singing show format has manufactured a few genuine stars, most notably Leona Lewis.

Sky One The flagship channel from BSkyB. Prime time programming consists largely of big budget US imports like *The Simpsons* and *Lost*.

The Apprentice
Gravelly-voiced entrepreneur Alan Sugar hires and fires the hopefuls; each series is received as something of a televisual event.

Prescribed programming

In a TV-obsessed nation, these are the shows you should have seen:

Fawlty Towers The iconic, anarchic 1970s sitcom from John Cleese topped a British Film Institute poll to find the 100 best examples of British TV.

Blue Peter This children's magazine show has been running since 1958, shaping more than a few generations of Britons.

Life On Earth Sir David Attenborough and his brushes with nature are a British institution. This 13-parter was a landmark series in 1979 but for a more recent example try *Planet Earth*.

Play For Today/The Wednesday Play One-off dramas from the 1960s and 70s. The best examples were *Cathy Come Home* and *Abigail's Party*, which helped launch the careers of Ken Loach and Mike Leigh respectively.

Monty Python's Flying Circus Seminal, by turns hilarious and surreal, and a huge international success from the early 1970s.

The national dish

They don't make 'em like that any more

British TV seems to have mislaid its talent for challenging drama. In 2007 just over a quarter of peak time drama on British TV comprised soap operas; police dramas took more than a third of dramatic airtime. Go back ten or 20 years and it was a different story – if you find any of the following three on a thrift store VHS shelf, it's worth making the investment:

Boys from the Blackstuff (1982). Alan Bleasdale set the five-parter about unemployed roadmenders in his home city, Liverpool. For many it offered a jarring indictment of Thatcher's Britain; for others, simply gripping drama.

The Singing Detective (1986). From Dennis Potter, master of the sarcastic, surreal musical mini-series, came the story of a mystery writer confined to a hospital bed and his imagination by a severe skin disease of the same sort that afflicted Potter himself.

Our Friends in the North (1996). Adapted from Peter Flannery's play, the story of four Newcastle friends roamed from the 1960s to the 90s, weaving real political and social stories within.

"CAN'T WE GET YOU ON MASTERMIND SYBIL? NEXT CONTESTANT – SYBIL FAWLTY FROM TORQUAY, SPECIAL SUBJECT THE BLEEDIN' OBVIOUS."
Basil Fawlty,
Fawlty Towers

Britain tunes in: highs and lows of radio

His claim to be the inventor of radio is disputed, but Guglielmo Marconi (an Italian at work in Britain) certainly made some giant leaps forward in the field. By 1897 he was transmitting Morse code signals across Salisbury Plain and in 1901, at Poldhu in Cornwall, he received the first transatlantic radio signal. By 1922 Britain was broadcasting bona fide radio to her public. Although the BBC was the only licence holder, competition soon arrived from stations such as Radio Luxembourg and Radio Normandy, beaming in from the Continent. Radio played a key role in the Second World War, employed by both sides for propaganda and morale purposes. *It's That Man Again,* or *ITMA* as it was more commonly known, a comedy programme broadcast during WWII, is said to have helped maintain domestic morale. 'Lord Haw Haw' was less helpful, broadcasting Nazi propaganda into Britain from the Germany Calling station.

Pirate radio stations including Radio London and Radio Caroline began drawing listeners in the 1950s and 60s. The stations were young and vibrant, based on offshore ships from where they played the new pop music of the time. The BBC reacted by launching Radio 1, employing former pirate DJs like Tony Blackburn and John Peel. Peel went on to become a venerated figure, championing a broad range of new music up to his early death in 2004. These days Terry Wogan, intermittent host of Radio 2's breakfast show since 1972, is the great star of the airwaves, even while Chris Moyles, his early morning counterpart on Radio 1, attracts almost as many listeners.

Treacherous occupation
The Lord Haw Haw name is usually associated with William Joyce, although it was used by several presenters as part of Nazi Germany's wartime radio propaganda. Joyce, born in New York and raised in Ireland, was caught by Allied troops in Germany and executed for treason by the British in 1946.

"I JUST WANT TO HEAR SOMETHING I HAVEN'T HEARD BEFORE."
John Peel

Listening habits and podcasts

Today 90 per cent of Britons regularly listen to the radio, tuning in for an average of three hours a day. There are eight national analogue broadcasters – five from the BBC and three independents – as well as a host of national digital stations. Additionally, every region has its own BBC analogue service, as well as one or more commercial analogue stations. Whilst nominally independent, local radio is dominated by a few large media groups, resulting in a fairly uniform sound around the country. Increasingly, Britons are accessing their radio via podcasts, the downloadable digital files. Licensing laws make it prohibitively expensive for podcasts to include music, so radio shows are edited after broadcast and then made available for users. The lack of musical content means that the most downloaded shows are comedy-based offerings from BBC Radio 4 and some of the digital stations.

Britain's eight national radio stations

BBC Radio 1 By day it's big name DJs playing chart music; of an evening the playlists get more eclectic.

BBC Radio 2 Plays a range of popular music from the 1960s to the present day. Efforts to capture a younger audience went awry in 2008 when presenters Russell Brand and Jonathan Ross were suspended for making lewd comments.

BBC Radio 3 Classical music, jazz, opera and the occasional bit of Shakespeare; average listener age of 57.

BBC Radio 4 A mixture of current affairs, magazine shows, comedy, drama and discussion.

BBC Radio 5 Live Predominantly sports coverage but also broadcasting news and phone-in shows.

Classic FM The name's a giveaway: classical music with an accessible approach. It became Britain's first national commercial radio station when it launched back in 1992.

Virgin Radio Has a rather blokey feel, aiming at people in their 20s and 30s by broadcasting a mix of old and new rock.

talkSPORT Similar to Radio 5 Live in programming but even heavier on the sport.

Goon down in history
Spike Milligan's *Goon Show* left a dazzling legacy. Cited by everyone from the *Monty Python* boys to The Beatles and Prince Charles as an influence, it also bestowed new words upon the English language, not least 'lurgi', coined by Milligan in 1954 to mean an unpleasant but unspecified illness.

Panic stations!
In the event of a national emergency, when radio services are limited, BBC Radio 4 (formerly the BBC Home Service) is the only one that will continue broadcasting.

The ten shows that made British radio

The Archers The gentle rural radio soap has been running since 1950 and is still the most popular show on Radio 4.

Desert Island Discs Features a guest talking about the eight pieces of music they would take to a desert island. First broadcast in 1942, making it the world's longest running radio show.

The Goon Show Spike Milligan's surreal comedy show ran from 1951-1960 and is credited with inspiring bits of *Monty Python's Flying Circus*.

Hancock's Half Hour Tony Hancock's hugely influential comedy found a vehicle on radio before it made the transfer to TV in 1960.

I'm Sorry, I'll Read That Again Popular comedy show of the 60s and 70s, which provided talent for *Monty Python* and *The Goodies* and led to *I'm Sorry, I Haven't A Clue*, which is still going today.

It's That Man Again Starred Liverpudlian comic Tommy Handley, who played the Minister of Aggravation and Mysteries. The title referred to a common newspaper introduction for Adolf Hitler.

Just a Minute A panel show that's been going since 1967, in which contestants try to talk for one minute on a given subject without 'repetition, hesitation or deviation'.

Letter From America Alistair Cooke's weekly reflection on all things American lasted an amazing 58 years, from 1946 to 2004.

The Today Programme An influential Radio 4 news and current affairs programme for early weekday risers. A British institution since 1957.

Woman's Hour A popular Radio 4 magazine show that has been discussing women's interests since 1946.

6.1.5 New media: Britain on the Web

Ta-da! The World Wide Web

A British man gave us the World Wide Web as we know it today. Although the Internet evolved through decades of research and collaboration, it was the work of Sir Tim Berners-Lee that first got it working in synchrony with browsers, servers and websites, or in his words: "I just had to take the hypertext idea and connect it to the Transmission Control Protocol and domain name system ideas and – ta-da! – the World Wide Web." Sir Tim topped a recent list of 'Greatest Living Geniuses' compiled by *The Daily Telegraph.*

Net gains

As a nation, Britain is fairly switched on to the Web. In 2008 the Office for National Statistics confirmed that 16.46 million homes had some form of access to the Internet, which equates to 65 per cent of the total. Over 85 per cent of this access was via broadband. There is, however, a degree of regional disparity, with around 70 per cent of London and the South West online but only 60 per cent of Yorkshire and the Midlands. Two out of every three Brits use the Internet every day. Age also plays a part – 70 per cent of over 65-year-olds confessed to never having been online. Perhaps most interestingly, Internet use seems to be an all or nothing pursuit: a quarter of all Brits said they'd never used it.

Browsing habits

So, when they're online, what are the Brits doing? It seems that searching for information about goods and services and sending and receiving emails are the prime activities. Two-thirds of users also research and book travel on the Net, while around half utilise Internet banking services. Google, Facebook, Windows Live, YouTube and Yahoo generally feature in the top five

Crunch and crumble
As the credit crunch began to bite in 2008, Google reported a 40 per cent surge in the number of people searching out recipes for apple crumble, apparently desperate for comfort food and the frugality of home cooking.

e-democracy in action
In late 2006 Downing Street launched an e-petition website, enabling web users to put their name to a favoured cause. Unsurprisingly, the range of petitions has been broad: one demanded all retired Gurkha soldiers be given British citizenship; another suggested the Government replace the national anthem with the Spandau Ballet song *Gold*.

websites, even while their positioning may vary. When it comes to spending money online, Amazon and eBay dominate. Wikipedia, the collaborative encyclopaedia, is another site usually ranked in the top ten. More people get their news and sport from the BBC's web service than anywhere else. Social networking is very popular amongst the 16 to 35 age group; Facebook is out ahead as the prime portal, but MySpace and Bebo are also significant players. Second Life, the interactive virtual world for which devotees create an alter ego (or 'avatar'), is also popular.

Offbeat online: three quirky sites

holymoly.co.uk A mishmash of celebrity gossip, entertainment news, wit and bile. The site is based around a weekly mail-out and user-generated content such as 'The Rules Of Modern Life'. Not for the easily offended.

nicecupofteaandasitdown.com A celebration of that great British experience: tea, biscuits and a nice sit down. Features 'biscuit of the week' and has branched out, somewhat controversially, to cover cakes.

rathergood.com A window into the surreal side of the British sense of humour. It's a repository for musical parody and animation, featuring such cult classics as The Spongmonkeys and The Viking Kittens.

Belle de Jour The long running, apparently true-life blog from a working London call girl has won various awards, been turned into books and spawned a TV series: *belledejour-uk.blogspot.com*

Guido Fawkes From a political 'insider' who treats all aspects of British party politics with equal measures of dislike and mistrust. A good, well-informed place to get the gossip from Parliament: *order-order.com*

LinkMachineGo A simple idea done well: this regularly updated page of popular culture blog links is a great place to start if you're at a loose end online: *timemachinego.com/linkmachinego*

Scary Duck A witty and personable blog featuring irreverent comment on anything that catches the writer's eye. Example topics, such as shed-related blasphemy and 'Zombie Dave' the office cleaner should give you an idea of what to expect: *scaryduck.blogspot.com*

spEak You're bRanes A response to the ignorance, racism and poor English that some members of the British public impart in the comment or reaction sections of news websites: *ifyoulikeitsomuch whydontyougolivethere.com*

6.2 Communications

By 'communications' we don't mean the coded, 'turned out nice again' nuances of British chitchat. We're talking about the postal service, the roads, the rails, the airports... in fact, all those things the Brits love to beef about when (as is often the case) they haven't 'turned out nice again'.

Dispatching tradition: the postal service

The postal service in Britain is going through a period of significant change. In 2006, after more than 350 years, the Royal Mail lost its monopoly on postal services. At present you'll still be hard pushed to post a letter without their help, but this may not be the case for much longer. Some sort of privatisation for the Royal Mail itself seems inevitable. Today the Royal Mail Group Ltd, transmuted descendant of Charles I's 17th century postal service, is split into three sections: Royal Mail delivers the letters, Parcelforce delivers the parcels and the Post Office runs the network of post offices around the country. The post offices serve as multipurpose retail outlets, often comprising the only local shop in rural areas. Alas, small rural post offices are, by and large, losing money and many are closing down despite the protestations of local users. As a rule the postal service in Britain is good, with around 85 per cent of first-class domestic letters arriving the next day. Over 99 per cent of mail arrives safely: not bad considering the Royal Mail delivers 79 million letters a day.

The stamp with no name
Because Britain was the first country in the world to publish stamps, it's the only one that doesn't have to print its name on them.

Late post
The bafflingly named (but well intentioned) Deceased Preference

Service came up with an interesting statistic in 2008: 59 million items of junk mail are being sent to dead people each year. The problem is apparently much worse in the north of England, with recently deceased Hull residents receiving more mail post-mortem than anyone else.

Britain on the blower

Britain has been enamoured with electronic chitchat ever since Scots-born Alexander Graham Bell moved to North America and set about inventing the telephone in the 1870s. By the 1930s Brits were gabbling away happily in cast iron kiosks, and by the 1960s most homes had their own phone. The dominant force in the British telecommunications industry has traditionally been BT. Formerly part of the Post Office, it was rebranded as British Telecom in 1981 and privatised in 1984. BT's monopoly was actually first broken in 1982, but it still controls the vast majority of the fixed line telephone market in Britain. Although BT is a private company, it's required by law to provide a phone line to all addresses in the UK and to provide public phone boxes. However, the iconic red telephone boxes may soon be a thing of the past. They were already under threat, replaced by more modern glass affairs with wireless Internet access, before the growth of mobile phones accelerated their demise. Between 2002 and 2008, around 30 per cent of all phone boxes were removed and of those that remained, 60 per cent were unprofitable. Of course, these days the mobile phone rules supreme. In fact, 115 per cent of Brits own a mobile phone (i.e. they've got more than one each), compared with 94 per cent across the rest of the EU and 77 per cent in the USA. The five big mobile service providers are Vodafone, O2, T-Mobile, Orange and 3. Vodafone, a British-based company, is the largest mobile phone service company in the world, worth an estimated £75 billion.

Drama by numbers
In each major area code, groups of numbers are reserved for use in films and television shows to prevent any real numbers from being accidentally quoted on screen.

No, really, it's me… it's Gordie
In 2008 it was revealed that Prime Minister Gordon Brown periodically telephoned members of the public who wrote to the Government voicing concerns over the state of the nation. "The PM takes a great interest in correspondence that comes in. He likes to keep in touch with voters who take the trouble to contact him," explained a Downing Street spokesman. The revelation emerged as Labour popularity slumped to a 25-year low.

Calls of nature
A recent survey estimated that the average Briton spends ten months of their adult life on the mobile phone. The same survey revealed that a quarter of Brits will take a call while sitting on the toilet.

Hope you like jammin' too: on the roads
In Britain the car is king. Private vehicle ownership is
high – there were 22 million cars in the country at last
count – and the roads, particularly in the South East,
are amongst the most congested in Europe. While
the road network is extensive and largely free, getting
stuck in a traffic jam has become part of British life.
In recent years, Government efforts to tackle
congestion have reoriented from building wider roads
(which only seems to generate more traffic) to road
pricing for drivers. The Congestion Charge Zone
introduced to central London in 2003 is the first such
big move in the effort to reduce congestion and
pollution in British cities. It remains to be seen
whether the required investment in public transport
will now be made to provide motorists with an
efficient, affordable alternative to the car. At present,
the high price of fuel at the petrol pumps (higher here
than almost anywhere else in the world) is doing more
than anything to change British driving habits. When
they're not parked in a jam, the British, on the whole,
drive much as stereotypes would suggest. Politeness
and respect for other road users are expected and
anything seen as rude behaviour can, paradoxically,
provoke a touch of road rage. Serious road rage is rare,
although the media attention given to high profile
cases of violent attack may suggest otherwise.
Drink driving has become a big social taboo and the
associated penalties are severe.

On and off the rails

Before it was sold off in the mid 1990s British Rail, the national rail company, rivalled the weather as a popular topic of gripe for the public. Nothing much has changed since, although these days the moaning is divided between various separate companies (who run the trains) and Network Rail (who maintain the rails). In fairness to the train companies, the British rail network has been undergoing an extensive programme of repairs and upgrades since the Hatfield rail crash of 2000 exposed a number of flaws. However, trains remain overcrowded and expensive, although punctuality could be worse. In 2008 the Department of Transport acknowledged that rail commuters in Britain sometimes endure carriage conditions which EU law deems unacceptable for sheep, goats, calves and chickens.

Doctor's orders

During the early 1960s the rail network was drastically reduced by the actions of Richard Beeching, then Chairman of British Railways. Popularly known as Doctor Beeching (he had a PhD), his report, *The Reshaping of Britain's Railways* (often referred to as 'The Beeching Axe'), initiated the closure of 7,500 miles of branch line and a third of railway stations.

"BEECHING IS A PRAT!"
"NO, I'M NOT."
Dr Beeching responded with his own pen to a piece of graffiti he found in a station toilet

Giving out the wrong signals

The worst rail crash in British history happened at Quintinshill on the Scottish West Coast Main Line in 1915. A dozy signalman forgot where he'd parked a train and 227 people died in the resulting collision of five (yes, five) trains. Most of the dead were soldiers. The dishevelled troops that survived were mistaken for foreign prisoners of war and stoned by the locals on their journey back to barracks. Because the crash happened during the First World War the censorship measures in place ensured that it went unreported.

Welcome to hell

In the week that Heathrow's much anticipated £4 billion Terminal 5 building opened in March 2008, hundreds of British Airways flights had to be cancelled. The massive new facility went into meltdown, with some 28,000 items of luggage led astray by glitches in the new baggage handling system and inadequate staff training. Escalators wouldn't work and staff couldn't find anywhere to park. "Welcome to hell" read the quickly improvised toilet graffiti. For some it was all too much: supermodel Naomi Campbell was removed kicking, screaming and spitting from a flight after being informed that her bag wouldn't be travelling on the same plane.

"I DID NOT FULLY UNDERSTAND THE DREAD TERM 'TERMINAL ILLNESS' UNTIL I SAW HEATHROW FOR MYSELF."
Dennis Potter

Up in the air

Britain is well served by airports and flight routes, even while the international airports are somewhat concentrated in the London area. Heathrow and Gatwick are major international hubs, with Heathrow the busiest passenger airport in the world. London Stansted and London Luton specialise in low-cost flights to destinations around the UK and Europe. Budget flights have mushroomed in recent years, with EasyJet and Ryanair vying for the biggest share of the market by offering flights at little cost above the basic taxes and fees. However, as fuel prices and green taxes rise, the golden era of budget air travel may be coming to an end. Manchester and Edinburgh are the major northern airports, although limited international flights are available at airports across the country.

Underground, overground

Most towns and cities in the UK have a bus network, and even the most rural of areas will have some form of bus service, however infrequent and unreliable. Several towns and cities, including Manchester, Nottingham, Sheffield, Croydon and Blackpool, have a tram system. Of these, only Blackpool is a long-running traditional tramway, all the others having been resurrected in the last 20 years. The London Underground, which opened to the public in 1863, is the oldest subway train system in the world. Known by Londoners as the 'Tube', it has 268 stations and over

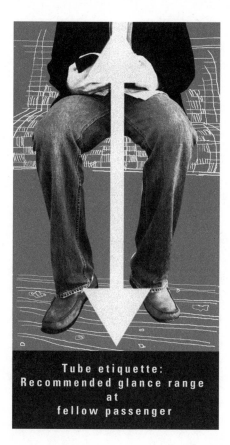

Tube etiquette:
Recommended glance range
at
fellow passenger

250 miles of track, less than half of which is actually under ground. Another notable British subway, Glasgow's, is the third oldest in the world (Budapest is second oldest, in case you were wondering).

7 Food and Drink

7.1 Food

Don't sneer, give it a chance. British food has emerged from its darkest hours and moves forward with an admirable confidence, rediscovering a wealth of traditional produce and ingredients whilst also taking notes and inspiration from Britain's post-war migrant communities.

Of late, Britain has consistently been voted third in the world league tables of fine dining. The San Pellegrino World's Best Restaurants list named six British establishments in their 2008 top 50. Heston Blumenthal's Fat Duck restaurant in Berkshire was voted second best in the world for the third year running.

Past his sell-by date
Former French President Jacques Chirac joked in 2005 that English food was the second worst in Europe (he gave Finland top spot). "You can't trust people who cook as badly as that," he reportedly added. Many in France still refer to British people as 'le rosbif'.

Big day for brown stuff
A recent poll found Worcestershire sauce to be the British foodstuff with the greatest global impact. The brown, runny, fishy, vinegar-based delicacy, produced by Lea and Perrins in the same Worcester factory for a hundred years, isn't really British at all – Lord Sandys, Governor of Bengal, brought the recipe home to England from India in the early 19th century.

All hail the gastro revolution

My how the tables have turned. British cuisine, mocked for so long by foreigners, now ranks among the best on Earth. The last 20 years have transformed the way Brits see their food. Restaurant-goers spend more, are more demanding and more appreciative; aware that their options extend beyond meat and two overcooked veg. The fusion of traditional British food with foreign influences, from Indian to French, Thai to Italian, has been central to its renaissance. But let's not get carried away. Granted, Britain has some of the best restaurants in the world, people are more knowledgeable about cuisine and food has become a key part of national culture, but have attitudes really changed that much? Can we say that British people live and breathe food like the Italians or the French? Do they construct their days around lengthy mealtimes? In truth, probably not. Not yet.

Great moments in British food

1586 Francis Drake brings the humble potato back from the Americas.

1762 John Montagu invents the sandwich.

1847 Joseph Fry mixes cocoa butter and cocoa powder and comes up with the chocolate bar.

1861 *Mrs Beeton's Book of Household Management* is published. Boil your cabbage for 45 minutes she urged.

1890 Frenchman Auguste Escoffier arrives to cook at the Savoy Hotel and introduces the 'brigade de cuisine' system, a structure still used in all the top restaurants today.

1950 Elizabeth David writes *A Book of Mediterranean Food*, introducing olive oil, garlic and other treats to the British diet.

1954 14 years of food rationing comes to an end.

1967 The Roux brothers open Le Gavroche; it became Britain's first Michelin three-starred restaurant in 1982.

2007 Clare Smyth becomes the first (and only) female chef in Britain to run a restaurant with three Michelin stars (Gordon Ramsay at Royal Hospital Road).

Begged, stolen and borrowed: the story of 'British' flavours

For centuries the British diet was directed by invading Europeans. The Romans introduced asparagus, cucumber, peas, pheasant and viniculture, embraced seafood and built the extensive road network that moved food around the country. The Saxons' farming expertise served up wild game and fertile land on which to grow a variety of foods – they were particularly good at herbs. The art of drying and preserving fish was handed down from the Vikings and Danes, and smoked fish and shellfish still taste best in the old Norse heartland of the North East. Having colonised Sicily shortly before appropriating England, the Normans brought spices and recipes from southern Italy and Africa. Crusaders had their first taste of oranges and lemons in the same era, and cinnamon, cloves and ginger, considered suggestive of wealth, appeared in a range of savoury and sweet dishes.

When Britain itself turned colonial overlord, the flavours of foreign lands were assimilated once more, brought back by explorers and traders. Coffee, cocoa, potatoes and tea poured in. Dishes like kedgeree (rice, lentils, onions and egg) and mulligatawny (spicy meat or chicken soup) found an appreciative British audience in the days of the Raj, before complete cuisines from the Indian subcontinent, East Asia and the Caribbean were absorbed into the culture of British food in the 20th century. Ethnic food and ingredients are now readily available in shops, and thousands of international restaurants reflect the diverse British palate.

We're going to need a bigger oven... Elizabeth David's revolutionary 1950s tome *A Book of Mediterranean Food* included guidance on stuffing a whole sheep.

"CHICKEN TIKKA MASALA IS NOW BRITAIN'S TRUE NATIONAL DISH, NOT ONLY BECAUSE IT IS THE MOST POPULAR, BUT BECAUSE IT IS A PERFECT ILLUSTRATION OF THE WAY BRITAIN ABSORBS AND ADAPTS EXTERNAL INFLUENCES." Or so said Robin Cook during his tenure as Foreign Secretary

1. Identity: the
foundations
of British culture

2. Literature
and philosophy

3. Art, architecture
and design

4. Performing
arts

5. Cinema,
photography
and fashion

6. Media and
communications

7. Food and drink

8. Living culture:
the state of
modern Britain

FRYING TONIGHT
Fish 'n Chips

A great British dish (from
Spain and Belgium)
Fish and chips appeared
first in Britain in the
19th century. Jewish
immigrant Joseph Malin
opened the earliest
recorded chip shop in
Bow, East London, in
1860, although Dickens
wrote of a 'fried fish
warehouse' in *Oliver
Twist* 30 years earlier
(there was no mention
of chips). Of course,
they're not really British
at all: the Spanish were
the first to fry fish, and
chips were apparently
born in Belgium.

Knowing your onions: the food provenance factor
The path from field to plate isn't as simple as it might be.
There's been a gulf between genuine wholesome produce
and what the masses actually eat since the days of the
Industrial Revolution when processed food first filled British
bellies. But the situation is slowly changing. Food health
scares, the emergence of an organic market, animal
welfare issues and the carping of celebrity chefs have all
encouraged consumers to investigate the origins of their
food, in essence to return to the values of regional cuisine.
And European legislation is helping out – in 1992 the
European Union created classifications designed to protect
and promote regionally important food products. A
Protected Designation of Origin (PDO) standard recognises
food that is produced, processed and prepared in a given
geographical area using a recognised skill. A Protected
Geographical Indication (PGI) offers proof of a link between
the foodstuff and a specific region in at least one of the
stages of production or preparation. Clotted cream, Orkney
beef and Cornish Yarg cheese are classified PDO; Dorset
Blue cheese and Welsh lamb are PGI.

Name that foodstuff

The sandwich. The gambling habits of the 11th Earl of Sandwich, John Montagu, bore one
of the greatest snack foods ever. Unwilling to leave the card table, he instructed a servant
to prepare some meat between two slices of bread so that he could eat one-handed.

HP sauce. A brown sauce that blends malt vinegar with fruits and spices; created by a
chef at the Houses of Parliament in the late 19th century.

Victoria sandwich. Actually a sponge cake with a jam and cream filling, created as an
afternoon pick-me-up for Queen Victoria.

Marguerite
Patten OBE
"More squirrel, dear?"
Our first (1947) telly chef

Waiter, there's a squirrel in my soup
Marguerite Patten was the culinary doyenne of the 1940s and 50s. She was lauded
for the resourcefulness of recipes like rook pie and squirrel tail soup. Don't laugh –
she's sold 17 million books. In 2007 Marguerite, then aged 94, was presented with a
Woman of the Year award.

1. Identity: the
foundations
of British culture

2. Literature
and philosophy

3. Art, architecture
and design

4. Performing
arts

5. Cinema,
photography
and fashion

6. Media and
communications

7. Food and drink

8. Living culture:
the state of
modern Britain

Caerphilly. Wales' best-known cheese is a mild, white and crumbly affair first made in 1831 in the town of the same name.

Stilton. Blue veined with a soft white texture, believed to have been made first in 1710 at Quenby Hall in Leicestershire.

Stinking Bishop. A soft Gloucestershire cheese, its rind washed in a bitter perry (pear juice), made in the modern age since 1972 but with aged monastic origins. The smell can clear a room.

West Country Farmhouse Cheddar. The only one of the Cheddar range (it comes in many variations) to earn PDO status is made in Somerset, Dorset, Devon and Cornwall.

Crowdie. A soft, fresh Scottish cheese made since the days of the Viking occupation. Crafted from the whey that separates naturally from souring milk.

In 1901, 3,500lbs of cheese was despatched from the village of Cheddar to Captain Scott's ship *Discovery*, which was embarking on an expedition to the Antarctic.

"IT IS CALLED OUR ENGLISH PARMESAN AND BROUGHT TO THE TABLE WITH THE MITES SO THICK AROUND IT THAT THEY BRING A SPOON FOR YOU TO EAT THE MITES WITH, AS YOU DO THE CHEESE." Daniel Defoe writing about Stilton cheese in the early 18th century.

TV dinners

What is it about Britain and TV chefs? Nowhere in Europe devotes more telly time to cooking than the UK. Fanny Craddock (born Phyllis Primrose-Pechey) was among the first, a genuine 'personality' from the 1950s to the 70s. She dressed like Princess Margaret, could swing abruptly from tenderness to wrath and was roundly loved for her fancy French recipes. The recent revelation about her fondness for amphetamines could go some way to explaining the quirky personality. Next came Graham Kerr, the first TV chef with a global reach whose 'Galloping Gourmet' sobriquet revealed him as an entertainer. And the small screen foodies have come in a steady stream ever since. Delia Smith shot to fame in the 1970s and changed the way Brits cook and talk: the 'Delia Effect' brought sales stampedes on everything from prunes to omelette pans while 'Doing a Delia' entered the dictionary. Today, the likes of Jamie Oliver, Nigella Lawson and Gordon Ramsey hold TV audiences rapt across the English-speaking world.

British food has become rather homogenised in the modern era. Travel from Cornwall to Caithness and you'll find similar stuff served up in restaurants, pubs and homes. However, there will be variations based on the local catch of the day – it is an island nation after all – and, if you know where to look, you'll also find the traditional dishes that once directed local diets. In common, the regional foods of Britain are rarely dainty; instead, the damp, tepid climate reared a range of filling, dependable meals. And, as food provenance, food miles (how far your food has travelled to the shop) and organic farming grow in stature, so the humble traditions of good local produce are being revisited.

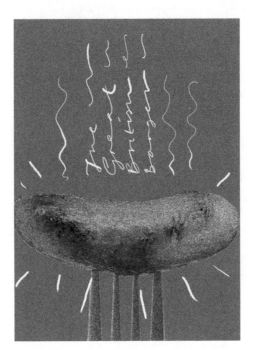

i. Northern England

Food in the north of England is warming stuff, a solid mix of bakes and stews. Oatcakes, parkin (a gingery Yorkshire cake), stotty cake (a flat round loaf from the North East) and curd tarts are all baking staples. Lancashire is home to treacle toffee but more famous for its hotpot, a layered casserole of lamb, potatoes and onions cooked in a glazed terracotta pot. Pickled red cabbage is the traditional hotpot accompaniment. Lancashire, and the town of Bury in particular, also claims black pudding, the fat sausage blend of ox blood, oatmeal, onions and spices, as its own. Yorkshire pudding, a muffin-shaped piece of light batter, has become a nationwide staple, to be served up with roast beef and gravy. Elsewhere, Northumberland still cures its Craster kippers (smoked) the way it did a century ago; coiled Cumberland sausages, flavoured with black and white pepper, remain best married with a buttery mash and rich onion gravy; and the potted shrimps of Morecambe Bay (small brown characters) are about as unpretentious as gourmet grub gets, unless you're into mushy peas (soaked and then simmered with sugar and salt).

A Glasse act
Yorkshire puddings were known as dripping puddings until food writer Hannah Glasse suggested the new name in her 1747 book *The Art of Cookery*. It used to be served with gravy as a first course, but Yorkshire pud is more commonly served alongside roast beef today.

Three great northern foods

Cumberland rum butter. Made in the Lake District since the 19th century, the alcoholic properties also find it referred to as 'hard sauce'.

Eccles cake. A small pocket of pastry filled with currants, named after its Lancashire hometown.

Pease pudding. The dried pea purée was a nationwide staple of old but is now limited predominantly to the North East; usually served with boiled bacon.

ii. Eastern and South East England

The dark soils of Lincolnshire produce one-fifth of the country's food, while East Anglia rears much of the nation's meat and poultry. The east of England is, therefore, perhaps better known for its foodstuffs than its dishes. Grimsby and Lowestoft are the main fishing ports, and if you follow the East Anglian coastline clockwise you encounter Stiffkey Blues (cockles), Cromer crabs, Yarmouth bloaters (herring), Colchester oysters and Southend whitebait; delicacies the lot. The East Anglian saltmarshes also harbour samphire (sea asparagus), picked at low tide from June to September. Inland, vast orchards grow soft fruits, while villages like Tiptree, in Essex, still mash up the produce for fine jam. Roast Norfolk Black turkeys, introduced to England in the early 1500s, Suffolk cured ham and Newmarket sausages are three meaty specialities. Further south, at Whitstable in Kent, the Dredgerman's Breakfast is a gut-busting plate of streaky bacon, shelled oysters and thick bread. On Kent's southern fringe the grazed salty marshes at Romney produce a flavoursome lamb, while sweet southern teeth are sated by the Sussex pond pudding (a steamed buttery blob hiding an entire lemon), Isle of Wight doughnuts and Richmond Maids of Honour (small round cheesecakes).

Return of the Native
Perhaps the Romans made Colchester, or Camulodunum, their first British colony because they adored the oysters that grow nearby – the so-called Colchester Native. Indeed, Pliny the Elder declared oysters to be Britain's sole attribute. After the Romans left in the fifth century so too did the taste for oysters, which came to be seen as a poor man's alternative to meat. These days the Colchester Native thrives again, served up in some of the world's best restaurants.

Keen as...
East Anglia is also associated with English mustard, enjoyed (or endured – it's a hot one) in one form or another since Roman times. Today, the Colman's name is synonymous with the yellow condiment but it was the Keen family who first began making mustard on a commercial basis in 1742. Then, in 1903, Jeremiah Colman began milling mustard at Stoke Holy Cross, just outside Norwich, with mustard seeds grown in the East Anglian fens.

Three great eastern foods

Cromer crab. A north Norfolk legend renowned for its high proportion of white meat. Enjoyed in various recipes but at its best simply boiled and dressed in the shell.

Haslet. A long loaf of seasoned, chopped and cured pork that probably has its origins in Lincolnshire. Usually sliced and served cold.

Melton Mowbray pork pie. More Midlands than eastern perhaps; either way, the combo of chopped pork filling, jelly layer and coat of brown pastry has become a national treasure.

iii. South West England

Sitting in a pub overlooking the spectacular Cornish coast eating the local catch, with its lobster, crabs and mackerel, is one of life's great culinary experiences. Inland, Cornwall and Devon's green pastures are grazed by the Friesians that produce some of Britain's finest dairy products, clotted cream included. And it would be remiss not to mention the Cornish pasty: the reputation of the semicircular folded pie has suffered by many a poor imitation, but when executed well the pasty is a wonderful combination of crisp pastry and moist meaty interior. The West Country can also lay claim to the Cornish saffron cake, Oldbury tart (gooseberry pie) and West Country cream tea. In recent years the region has become a key player in Britain's renewed relationship with organic farming, offering up a vast range of foodstuffs, from apples to Gloucester Old Spot pork.

GIANT CORNISH PASTIE
Ideal snack for hungry surfer

Cream tea etiquette
In Cornwall put the jam on the scone, followed by the cream; in Devon do the reverse.

Pocket-shaped genius
The Cornish pasty originated as a working man's meal, enjoyed as a convenient way of eating hot meat with the fingers. Sometimes meat was put at one end and a sweet filling at the other – a complete meal all in one.

Three great south-western foods

Clotted cream. Milk is slowly heated, cooled and plundered of its cream, which is then heated again until a golden crust forms. In Cornwall they dump it on bread, cover with syrup or black treacle and call it Thunder and Lightning.

Bath chaps. Take a pig's cheek or lower jaw, brine and boil it before coating with breadcrumbs. Eat cold like ham.

Colston bun. A ring-shaped Bristol bun flavoured with dried fruit; named after the local merchant who made a packet trading in the West Indies (slaves included) in the early 18th century.

iv. London

London is the foodie capital of Britain. If you can eat it – and this is food from anywhere in the world – you'll probably find it on sale here somewhere. For native produce, markets like Billingsgate (fish) and Smithfield (meat) have been the largest such trading centres in Britain for centuries. The East End was once known for its jellied eels and meat pies; some of the Eel Pie and Mash houses, dating to the 18th century, have survived, and could be deemed to serve up the most 'authentic' London food. If pie and mash are representative of traditional working-class Londoner grub, then Fortnum & Mason in Piccadilly and Harrods Food Hall in Knightsbridge have ritually catered for the social antipode. Both retain an impeccable pedigree, drawing in the best food from around Britain. But the capital's modern cuisine is defined by its eclecticism. Chinese, Lebanese, Italian, Indian, Polish, Sudanese – the variety of food reflects the diversity of the population.

Three great London dishes of yore

Bubble and squeak. Thrifty dish using leftover cabbage and potato that was once a winter favourite with Londoners. The name derives from the sound it makes during cooking.

Boodle's orange fool. Akin to a trifle (a cold desert layered with sponge cake, fruit, custard, jelly and cream), the fool was a speciality of Boodle's, a gentleman's club founded in 1762.

London Particular. A thick soup made with peas and bacon stock, named after the capital's famous 'pea-souper' fogs.

v. Wales

There's a reason why Wales is famed for its leeks and cabbages – they're among the few veg able to flourish in the harsh Welsh landscape. Both can crop up in *cawl*, a rich broth of vegetables, lamb and bacon that has its regional variations. Pork continues to be a mainstay of the diet and lamb, once considered a luxury, is among the country's most famous exports. Shoals of herring and mackerel swim off the west coast, while across the Gower cockles are gathered, by hand, as they have been since Roman times. Laverbread, or *bara lawr*, a purple seaweed that turns dark green when cooked, is a distinctly Welsh staple, traditionally served alongside Welsh cured bacon, cockles and oatmeal for a man-sized breakfast. Afternoon tea serves up a number of Welsh choices: *bara brith* (a rich fruit loaf), Welsh cakes (a flat scone cooked on a griddle), *teisen carawe* (caraway seed cake) and *teisen mel* (honey cake).

Cheap shots from the English
Ask most Brits to name a dish from Wales and they'll come up with Welsh rarebit (or 'rabbit'), a concoction of stout, cheese, Worcestershire sauce and eggs, usually smeared over toast. However, most Brits would be wrong: the dish seems more likely to be of English origin, the name given as a slight to the Welsh because it contained cheap ingredients.

Three great Welsh foods

Braised faggot. Found in various parts of Britain but thought to have Welsh roots, a faggot is pig offal wrapped in caul fat, the stomach lining.

Glamorgan sausage. Not a tube of meat but a vegetarian effort made with Caerphilly cheese, leeks and breadcrumbs.

Crempog geirch. One of many pancake variants found in Wales, the geirch is made with oatmeal, milk, salt, eggs and butter.

Auld dining companions
The rest of Britain doesn't always appreciate Scotland's edible treasure trove; much of the country's seafood, notably lobster, langoustines and razor clams, is exported to France.

Host your own Burns Supper in five stages

1. Chairman invites 'the company' to receive the haggis, and out it comes, carried aloft, quivering, on a platter and chaperoned by a bagpiper.

2. Chairman then recites Burns' *Address to a Haggis*. When he reaches the line "an' cut you up wi' ready slight" he thrusts at the undefended haggis with a dirk (dagger); everyone applauds and swigs a tot of whisky.

3. And so the feasting begins: cock-a-leekie soup (chicken and leek) for starters, then the haggis with neeps (swede) and tatties (mashed potato), followed by tipsy laird (sherry trifle).

4. Just as the whisky's starting to work someone stands and gives the Immortal Memory speech, eulogising the great Rabbie.

5. Finally, stand – if you can – and join hands to sing *Auld Lang Syne*.

"FAIR FA' YOUR HONEST, SONSIE FACE, GREAT CHIEFTAIN O' THE PUDDIN-RACE!"
Robert Burns' *Address to a Haggis* (1786)

vi. Scotland

The Scottish diet has always been robust. Warming broths were made with porridge, lentils and barley, and the national dish, haggis, immortalised by poet Robert Burns, was guaranteed to fill empty stomachs. Consisting of sheep or calf offal mixed with suet and oatmeal, squeezed into an animal stomach and then boiled, haggis inevitably tastes better than it sounds. The larder north of the border continues to harbour some fine produce. Salmon and trout are found in the clean, cold waters and the Highlands and forests are rich with a variety of game including partridge, grouse, and deer. Aberdeen Angus, a hornless breed of black cow that can be traced back to the 12th century, is world-famous for its beef, while the long-haired Highland cattle also produce good meat. The ostriches that have begun appearing on the moors, farmed for their meat, have a shorter Highland pedigree. Scottish delicacies include Cullen skink (a soup of smoked haddock and potatoes), Arbroath smokies (salted and smoked haddock), grouse stuffed with rowanberries and Aberdeen Angus steak with a whisky sauce. Cranachan, a mixture of toasted oatmeal, whisky, cream and raspberries, is a traditional dessert.

Three great Scottish foods

Mealie pudding. More like a sausage actually: a cream-coloured affair filled with oatmeal, onions and suet.

Clootie dumpling. A bit like the haggis' sweeter cousin: a ball of beef suet, flour, breadcrumbs and dried fruit wrapped in a cloth (or *cloot*) and simmered for hours on end.

Scotch broth. The tradtional versions tended to feature mutton and pearl barley, simmered at length with various herbs, veg and whatever else was to hand.

vii. Northern Ireland

The Northern Ireland kitchen doesn't do delicate. Potatoes and bread have been staples for centuries, mingled with the meat, dairy and seafood that come naturally to the region's fecund landscape. It says much about the cuisine that the province's signature dish remains the Ulster Fry, a heart-stopping plate of bacon, eggs, sausages, black pudding and mushrooms. The Fry is distinguished from its Full English cousin (see section 7.1.3.) by the addition of soda bread farls (a fried, flattened version of the famous Irish bread that mixes flour, baking soda and buttermilk) and potato farls (a similar bread stocked with spuds). Like the rest of Ireland the northern region has a stew of meat, potatoes, carrots and onions, although the choice of meat – steak – distinguishes it from the stew to the south that prefers lamb. One other local speciality, beef sausages, has been drawing southerners across the border for years.

Late riser
Irish soda bread isn't as ancient as you might imagine. Ireland's 'soft' flour – a product of the local climate – had always struggled to rise to the occasion when mixed with the usual yeast, and so bicarbonate of soda was introduced to the mix in the 1840s to beef up Ireland's bread.

Three great foods from Northern Ireland

Champ. Mashed potato featuring chopped scallions (spring onions) and a generous dollop of butter.

Dulse. A red seaweed, air-dried and eaten as a snack or sometimes included in the mix for soda bread.

Yellowman. A dense, chewy honeycomb toffee. Like dulse, it's long associated with the annual Auld Lammas Fair in Country Antrim.

Getting into bad habits

The British diet has been deteriorating for years. One of the longest working weeks in Europe has fuelled the demand for quick and easily prepared food, and so Britain consumes more junk food and ready-made meals than anywhere else in Europe. For many the 'ready meal culture' has become ingrained; the evening meal reduced to a supermarket-prepared dish shoved in the microwave for five minutes. Even while Britain may be working harder, employment and lifestyle are actually becoming more sedentary. The consequences are all too apparent: 60 per cent of adults are overweight and 25 per cent are obese. Scotland has the worst figures by some margin; folks north of the border are second only to the Americans in the obesity tables. In schools across Britain, nutrition and basic cooking techniques have been re-emphasised as part of the national curriculum in a bid to get future generations eating more healthily.

Table talk

Some parenting experts in Britain have forecast a race of 'feral TV dinner toddlers', unable to use a knife and fork and who take their meals from freezer to microwave to bedroom. In a recent National Family Mealtime Survey, only 20 per cent of those polled sat down to dinner together once a week. Of the families that made a habit of eating together regularly, 75 per cent did so while watching TV. Under Tony Blair, the Labour Government pushed its 'Respect' agenda, citing the decline in communal eating as a factor in the breakdown of family life and encouraging families to eat together.

Feast foods

Shrove Tuesday (40 days before Easter). Get out your frying pan and tuck into pancakes sprinkled with caster sugar and lemon.

Mothering Sunday (4th Sunday in Lent). A day to indulge in simnel cake, a rich fruitcake with a layer of marzipan in the middle. In medieval times they ate a light biscuit-like bread that was boiled and then baked.

Easter (March/April). Warm, delicately spiced hot cross buns at the breakfast table on Good Friday, and then lamb as the featured meat on Easter Sunday. Chocolate eggs and bunnies are given to children.

Christmas Day (25th December). Serves up roast goose or turkey accompanied by bread sauce, cranberry sauce, roast potatoes, gravy and vegetables (at least one should be Brussels sprouts, although they were recently voted the most hated vegetable in Britain). Finish with Christmas pudding, a steamed rich and fruity mix, decorated with holly, doused in brandy and then set alight at the table to ward off evil spirits and keep your drunk uncle amused. A silver charm or coin is hidden inside the pudding.

British mealtimes

Breakfast: taken between 7am and 9am during the working week.

Elevenses: 11am, a mid morning pick-me-up with coffee or tea and a biscuit.

Lunch (also called dinner in the north): snatched (more often than lingered over) sometime between noon and 1.30pm. On Sundays the traditional roast will replace the more common weekday snack.

Afternoon tea: not many people do it these days, but the 4pm tray of tea, dainty sandwiches, scones and cake was all the rage in high society up to the later 20th century.

Dinner (more likely to be called tea in the north): the main meal of the day usually happens between 6pm and 8pm.

Habits that come but once a year

Popular history suggests that Henry VIII was the first king to eat turkey on Christmas Day, eschewing the traditional goose in favour of a Norfolk Black. The practice soon caught on. A glass of Christmas cheer (sherry in England, whisky in Scotland) is usually left out for Santa on Christmas Eve. Animal lovers might also leave something carrot-like for the reindeer.

Sunday best

The Sunday roast may trace its origins back to the medieval serfs who worked a six-day week. On Sundays they went to church and then gathered to practise fighting, honing their battle skills in case the lord's land should need defending. The squire rewarded them with ale and a meal of spit-roast oxen.

303

The most important meal of the day

"I never see any home cooking. All I get is fancy stuff."
The words of Prince Philip quoted back in 1962.
However, when a tabloid journalist went undercover in
Buckingham Palace he revealed that, like most modern
British folk, HM's breakfast table features cereal and

ME AND MY BIG MOUTH

Prince
Philip
wishing for
the
occasional
elaborate
breakfast

toast. While weekends, birthdays
and hotel stays may still demand the
traditional 'Full English' of bacon,
eggs, sausage, tomato, mushrooms,
toast, marmalade, tea and coffee,
perhaps with a sensory-smacking
smoked kipper on the side, these
days breakfast is normally a briefer
affair. In Scotland the breakfast of
choice for centuries was porridge,
traditionally eaten while walking in
order to prevent being stabbed by an
enemy whilst sleepy (or so the
tourist blurb reports).

How do the British shop for their food?

Large supermarkets continue to pull the public with long
opening hours and one-stop shopping, but a growing
concern for food provenance is slowly pushing Britons
back toward specialist shops and delis. Farmers'
markets are popular throughout towns and cities
(however urban), providing shoppers with the chance to
meet and support local producers. Farm shops are also
growing in number. The growth of organic produce is
pushed along by increased public awareness on issues
like health, food provenance and the environmental
impact of consumption choices – supermarkets are
increasingly questioned about ethics, animal welfare and

1. Identity: the
foundations
of British culture

2. Literature
and philosophy

3. Art, architecture
and design

4. Performing
arts

5. Cinema,
photography
and fashion

6. Media and
communications

7. Food and drink

8. Living culture:
the state of
modern Britain

quality when, for instance, they start selling whole chickens for £1.99; the goods aren't simply bought without conscience. Some supermarkets are amending their practices (albeit slowly) to mirror changing public attitudes.

Market forces: four London legends

Billingsgate. A medieval market that began concentrating solely on fish in 1699. It left a grand arcaded riverside Victorian home (now an exhibition space) on Lower Thames Street for the current residence on the Isle of Dogs in 1982.

Borough. Foodies have been visiting the market south of the River Thames for 250 years. Has a reputation built on fruit and veg, but sells much more.

Smithfield. The best-known meat market in Britain has been trading in one form or another just north of the City of London for at least 800 years. Its current accommodation, dating to the Victorian era, has undergone recent restoration. A good place to rub shoulders with restaurateurs, caterers, and butchers.

Covent Garden. For 350 years Covent Garden supported a fruit, veg and flower market (where the Eliza Doolittle character scratched a living in *Pygmalion*); in 1974 the neo-Classical piazza was turned over to shops, eateries and entertainers, and Britain's largest fresh produce market, New Covent Garden, opened just south of the river in Nine Elms.

What's with the fork you big girl? In 1608 'Grand Tourist' Thomas Coryate introduced the fork to England from Italy. Deemed too effeminate (surely the fingers were better for eating food?), they were ridiculed but did eventually catch on. Coryate also got Britain acquainted with the umbrella.

Ooh, what's she like?
The indispensable fork, unbelievably ridiculed in the 17th Century as a bit of an un-masculine eating iron.

7.2 Drink

The subtleties of artisanal ale, the gently impressive rise of native wine, an enduring tenderness for the dear old cup of tea – there's more to drinking in Britain than a rare talent for simply getting pie-eyed. Although that too has its own deep-seated role in national culture...

Builders' Tea

British drinking culture has always been led by beer.
Ale has been plentiful (on tap you might say) for
centuries, and the traditions of the pub have fostered
its enduring popularity. While wine has a similarly
venerable relationship with the nation, the masses
have really only been quaffing since the 1950s.
These days Britain imports more wine (by value) than
anywhere else in the world (partly because it still
struggles to produce its own) and you're almost as
likely to see it consumed in homes and pubs as beer.
Away from the demon drink, Britain cuddles the teapot
like a life support system, resorting to a cuppa at the
merest excuse.

Bittersweet: a love affair with beer
The Romans probably introduced brewing to Britain
but it was the Middle Age monks that monopolised
early beer production. They added hops to the mix,
developing the taste that diverges from the norm in
most beer-drinking countries. Brits brew bitter; they
haven't traditionally made much lager (even while
the effervescent amber stuff, brewed in Britain with
foreign recipes and names, is consumed with relish).
Bitter uses the same basic ingredients as lager, albeit
with darker malts, but is fermented at a higher
temperature using different yeasts. Varying quantities
of hops are added to modify the flavour. The common
bitter of today, usually served flat and at cellar
temperature, is a descendant of pale ale, a light
version of the old strong British beer, created in the
19th century to keep colonial types cool in the Raj.
Scottish bitter drinkers still sometimes ask for a pint
of 'heavy', a term of old used to distinguish from a pint
of 'light' (mild). In Northern Ireland, Guinness, as you
might expect, is more popular than elsewhere in the
UK; although the dry stout isn't brewed in the province
itself but to the south, in Dublin.

1. Identity: the
foundations
of British culture

2. Literature
and philosophy

3. Art, architecture
and design

4. Performing
arts

5. Cinema,
photography
and fashion

6. Media and
communications

7. Food and drink

8. Living culture:
the state of
modern Britain

Know your ales

Bitter. The most common ale type is highly hopped and of variable strength (from light 'session' beers below 4% abv to strong beers over 5% abv).

Mild. Less hoppy than bitter, mild is rarely poured in modern British pubs.

Porter. A dark, slightly sweet hoppy ale. Again, not much found in pubs today.

Stout. The dark strong version of the porter, with a thick creamy head and a grainy taste.

Small beer

Since 1971 CAMRA (the Campaign for Real Ale) has banged the drum for real ale – that's the sort kept in a cask and pumped by hand. With four-fifths of British beer brewing controlled by six companies they've had an uphill task, and yet the volunteer organisation has successfully pushed the cause of so-called microbreweries and traditional methods with beer festivals, books and newsletters. Real ale pubs around the country now serve up guest beers from the smallest of brewers. It means you can sup the likes of Cripple Dick, Dog's Bollocks and Bishops Finger till you fall off your stool.

A Quiet Pint
in the Snug

This one being
enjoyed at
The Radnor Arms,
Salisbury

A bloke down the pub said that...

In medieval Britain drinking beer was safer than drinking water. And so they drank it with breakfast, in the fields, at lunch...

Henry VIII apparently refused to drink beer with hops in it because the hop was a Protestant plant.

Ale used to be ordered in pints and quarts. An unruly drinker would be told to mind his Ps and Qs (pints and quarts), a phrase still in use.

Black times for beardies

A highly worthy study carried out by Guinness confirmed what beard wearers have always feared – that a significant amount of the black stuff is deflected by interfering facial hair. They even came up with a stat: Britain's 92,370 moustachioed Guinness drinkers are collectively losing up to 162,719 pints a year.

French bred: the Brits and their wine

Wine drinking has been part of British culture for centuries. Romans and monks maintained a home-grown industry but the good stuff was always imported from France. Henry II's marriage to Eleanor of Aquitaine in 1152 established a trade route from Bordeaux that saw Britain become the main beneficiary of claret for the next 300 years. When the Hundred Years War and high taxes severed relations, taste buds were retrained toward Iberian sherry, Madeira and port. The taste for European wines re-emerged in the 19th century but was confined predominantly to the middle or upper classes until the later 20th century when French, German, Italian and, in the 1990s, unpretentious New World wines found their way into bars, pubs and supermarkets. Britain's similarly long relationship with champagne is also in rude health; more is imported today (about 40 million bottles a year) than ever before. Only the French drink more.

On the home front, English and Welsh wine (Scotland and Northern Ireland don't get involved) was something of a joke 20 years ago. However, while the climate remains a shade too damp and cold to have a sizeable wine industry, the native talent for producing light, aromatic whites has improved significantly. Vineyards are scattered throughout southern England, with the highest concentration in Kent and Sussex. There are more than 350 making saleable wine: the largest, Denbies Wine Estate on the Surrey Downs, has over 250 acres under vine but most average a couple of acres at most. In common they tend to grow Müller-Thurgau, Seyval Blanc, Bacchus or Reichensteiner grapes. English Wine Week at the end of May celebrates the growing tradition.

Less than one per cent of all wine sold in Britain is made on home turf.

The largest exporter of wine to Britain is Australia, followed by France and the USA.

Around 15 per cent of all English and Welsh wine is sparkling.

Read before you quaff
If you're going to go native with the wine in Britain, make sure you study the label carefully. You need it to say English or Welsh wine (the Welsh have about 15 vineyards). Anything labelled 'British Wine' is fermented from imported grape juice, rather than made from home-grown vines.

Defining quality
In 1992 the Quality Wine Scheme, creating a strict criteria for cultivation, region, yield and taste, was set up as an English and Welsh equivalent to the AOC system in France. There are three labels: English (or Welsh) Vineyard Quality Wine, produced in a specific region, English (or Welsh) Regional Wine and UK Table Wine.

Still waters: whisky

Uisge beatha, the 'water of life' as the Gaels call it, has been made in the Scottish Highlands and Ulster since at least the 15th century. These days sales at home and abroad are huge, with Scotch whisky contributing some £100 million to the Exchequer each year. Of the two main varieties, single malts come from a specific distillery and are made solely with malted barley, while blended whisky is created from a mixture of single malt and grain whisky (produced using malted and unmalted cereals) and may come from more than one distillery. Various factors determine a whisky's character: the quality of the water, type of malted barley, amount of peat used in drying the grain, type of wooden barrel used for maturation, length of maturation – all will affect the taste and 'nose', which can range from deep, pungent and smoky to light, gentle and sweet. Scotland harbours over a hundred distilleries, almost half secreted in the Speyside whisky heartland of the north east. Elsewhere in Scotland Islay, Orkney and the Campbeltown peninsula also produce distinguished malts. Northern Ireland retains only one distillery, Bushmills, but it does claim to be the oldest in the world, having received its licence from King James I in 1608.

A taste for gin

British troops fell for a juniper-flavoured spirit while fighting in the Netherlands in the 1580s and brought 'Dutch courage' back to England where it was put on sale in chemists. By 1720 a quarter of households in London were distilling their own gin and drunkenness, particularly amongst the poor, had become a serious problem. 'Drunk for a penny, dead drunk for two pence' said the engraving above a gin

Give me a Welsh on the rocks
In 2000 Wales got its first whisky distillery in a hundred years. The Welsh Whisky Company produces two barrels of Penderyn single malt a day using water from a local natural spring. When the first 4,000 bottles went on sale on St David's Day in 2004 they sold out in less than four hours. England joined in the fun a couple of years later and opened its first whisky distillery in a century, in Norfolk, close to the source of much of Scotland's malt.

Honey, I drunk the mead
Meadhing, the process of fermenting honey, water and various spices, has been around since Celtic times, and the resultant drink, mead, has several variations. Metheglin, a Cornish version made with root ginger, is one of the few that anyone in Britain might have heard of. Most meads are of a similar strength to wine. An old Norse tradition prescribed mead for fertility in the first month of marriage; hence 'honeymoon'. Few actually imbibe it these days.

After the Queen Mother's death in 2002, her equerry revealed a daily drinking routine that began at noon with a gin and Dubonnet. Apparently she would hide bottles of gin in hatboxes when she travelled.

High times
on the high seas
For over 300 years the Royal Navy supplied its sailors with a daily tot of dark rum. Prior to 1740 the ration was a half pint a day (alternative choices included a pint of wine or a gallon of beer). The practice came to an end in 1970 when the Admiralty Board concluded that "in a highly sophisticated navy no risk or margin for error which might be attributable to rum could be allowed".

The original summer sup
Drinking in Britain can be a distinctly seasonal sport. Spiced ales and mulled wine both have their associations with the short, cold days of winter but in summer reach for the Pimm's and lemonade. It's the work of a Kentish farmer's son, James Pimm. In 1823 he served the dark reddish mix of gin, quinine and herbs (the full recipe remains closely guarded) at his oyster bar in London, hoping it would aid digestion.

store in Hogarth's print, *Gin Lane* (1751). Others called it 'mother's ruin'. One cattle drover reputedly sold his 11-year-old daughter for a gallon of the bad stuff, while 'gin palaces' amounted to furniture-less drinking factories. Gin's reputation climbed in the mid 1800s with the introduction of a less rough version, dry gin. It later became known as London Dry, named by association with the capital. British gin tends to be higher proof than European or American versions and has the distinction of dried lemon and citrus peel in its mix of botanicals.

Down the hat – hatch!

The Queen Mum enjoying
a lunchtime tipple

1. Identity: the
foundations
of British culture

2. Literature
and philosophy

3. Art, architecture
and design

4. Performing
arts

5. Cinema,
photography
and fashion

6. Media and
communications

7. Food and drink

8. Living culture:
the state of
modern Britain

Spirit levels

Beyond the native tipples of whisky and gin, Britons may also reach for foreign-made spirits. French brandy – Cognac, Armagnac or Calvados – sometimes appears after an evening meal, although you'll probably be in a high social setting if it does. Bar staff are more likely to field requests for bourbon, rum and vodka, each usually chosen with a soft drink mixer, probably Coca Cola.

Mellow fruitfulness: cider and perry

England, notably its southern, East Anglian and West Country patches, has been making cider since Roman times. Medieval monasteries kept their coffers stocked by selling spiced cider to a thirsty public and by the mid 17th century almost every farm had its own orchard and cider press. Farm labourers would even receive part of their wages in cider. In the later 20th century cider production became a more industrial affair, generating the gassy, clear, concentrate version sold in pubs around Britain. However, traditional cider – the flat, cloudy sort to which varying apple varieties and blends bring subtly different flavours – is enjoying a revival. Today, no one drinks more cider per head than the British. Perry is the pale gold coloured pear cousin of cider, made in the South West for centuries using a similar method to cider, albeit with the addition of a secondary fermentation.

In-cider information
Mix with the real cider aficionados in the West Country of England and you might hear them referring to the amber liquid as scrumpy, probably from 'scrump', slang for a withered apple.

Can I get a wassail at the back?
The pagan art of wassailing, pursued annually between Christmas Eve and Twelfth Night, was all about paying tribute to the humble apple tree. Farmers and labourers would carry jugs of mulled cider into the orchard and drink a toast to the trees in anticipation of next year's harvest. They still wassail down in Somerset, hub of English cider production.

Earl Grey tea, a black tea flavoured with bergamot oil, was apparently named after the Prime Minister for whom it was brewed in the 1830s. If the fable is to be believed, the PM had just saved a Chinaman's life; the grateful man duly put the kettle on and named his tea in Grey's honour.

Tea tattle

Some Brits call their tea 'char', from a Mandarin Chinese word for tea. 'Builder's tea' refers to a strong, long-brewed cup of tea with milk, usually fortified with a couple of sugars: as enjoyed by the construction worker on a tea break.

Stimulating stuff: tea and coffee

The common cup of tea (a basic black tea) is a British institution – a daily, often hourly, ritual for millions. Taken with a splash of milk, it's the nation's favourite drink. The Chinese have been knocking the stuff back for 5,000 years but tea didn't hit British shores until the mid 17th century, made fashionable by Catherine of Braganza, the tea-mad Portuguese wife of Charles II. The drink really took off when the East India Company began importing tea from China, before Britain introduced tea cultivation to India, Ceylon and Kenya in the 1830s. Coffee appeared in Britain at a similar time to tea but its fortunes have been less consistent. Like tea, coffee carries its own social and cultural weight, even while it is, perhaps, silently adjudged less 'British' than tea because of its popularity in the rest of Europe. The first coffee house opened in Oxford in 1650 and the coffee shop or bar has been an important social unifier ever since, somehow more bohemian than the humble tearoom. In recent years the unstoppable rise of international coffee house chains has – depending on your worldview – broadened or narrowed choice. Today Brits drink about twice as much tea (165 million cups a day) as they do coffee, although the gap narrows every year.

When and where do the British drink?

Most Brits come round to the smell of tea or coffee in the morning, a caffeine crutch that continues to provide support to millions throughout the day, although many office workers will reach as readily for the water bottle as for the mug these days. A glass of wine isn't unusual as an accompaniment to food in the evening but most Brits still save their alcohol consumption for dedicated drinking 'sessions' in the pub or, less often, at home. Friday and Saturday nights are still the main contenders for a pub visit.

I'm going down the pub…

When Brits socialise they often do so with an alcoholic drink in hand – chit-chat over an evening coffee is rarely the British way. Such habits begat the public house, integral to popular British culture for centuries. The nation's 60,000 pubs, declining in number each

Morning mouthful

Such is the attachment to the early morning cuppa that the Teasmade, a peculiarly British combination of automated tea-maker and alarm clock, was the height of sophistication in the mid 20th century. All concerned were no doubt relieved when the Apparatus Whereby a Cup of Tea or Coffee is Automatically Made, patented by Birmingham gunsmith Frank Clarke in 1902, was shortened in name.

Pub trivia

Around 15 million people go to British pubs at least once a week.

The most common pub name in Britain is The Red Lion, of which there are more than 750.

Around two-thirds of British pubs are owned by breweries. The rest, 'freehouses' (free to choose which beers they sell), are in private hands.

"I HAVE TAKEN MORE OUT OF ALCOHOL THAN ALCOHOL HAS TAKEN OUT OF ME."
Winston Churchill

A good old Pompey (Portsmouth) pub
The Country House in Commercial Road. Served its last pint in 1982.

year (by the rate of 36 a week at the last count),
provide a place to meet after work, to catch up with
friends or to enjoy a meal with the family. They still
account for two-thirds of all beer consumed in the UK,
although drinking at home is increasingly popular – the
number of pints pulled in pubs dropped nearly a fifth
between 2005 and 2008. Most pubs outside built-up
areas are now reliant on food sales to make ends
meet. Reputations are built on the quality of food
served, and the addition of beer gardens, live music
and pub quizzes all keep the punters coming – despite
an indoor smoking ban, in force since 2007. Licensing
hours were revamped in 2005 to accommodate 24-
hour drinking yet most pubs still open at 11am and
close not long after 11pm.

Still getting to grips
with wine
Despite enjoying a glass
or two, the British still
have a few hang-ups
about wine. Wine
snobbery, or the idea
that wine knowledge is
indicative of social
status or intellect, can
still rear its head.
A recent poll revealed
that over three-quarters
of diners feel awkward
when asked to taste the
wine in a restaurant.
A similar number are
dissuaded from ordering
a wine they can't
pronounce, and nearly
half admitted that the
price of a bottle was the
prime factor in choosing
wine.

"Would Monsieur like
to try?"

The five most unwelcome
words in the language

1. Identity: the
foundations
of British culture

2. Literature
and philosophy

3. Art, architecture
and design

4. Performing
arts

5. Cinema,
photography
and fashion

6. Media and
communications

7. Food and drink

8. Living culture:
the state of
modern Britain

Drinking for Britain: boozy culture

In the eighth century Saint Boniface wrote to Cuthbert, Archbishop of Canterbury, and mentioned "the vice of drunkenness" in English parishes. Not much has changed. Rarely does a week in modern Britain pass without the media crowing about the 'new' British disease, binge drinking. Press hysteria aside, it's a problem. British women aged 18 to 24 consume more alcohol than any of their European counterparts, getting through around 200 litres each a year (the European average is just over 100 litres), and young adult males are similarly fond of episodic heavy drinking. Promotions for cheap drinks by pubs, brewers and supermarkets are usually blamed for binge drinking, even while the roots of the problem are surely cultural. Ongoing Government initiatives to reduce consumption seem unlikely to reverse the age-old British taste for excess drinking and all its associated ills, from liver disease to lager louts and kebab shop brawls.

317

8 Living culture: the state of modern Britain

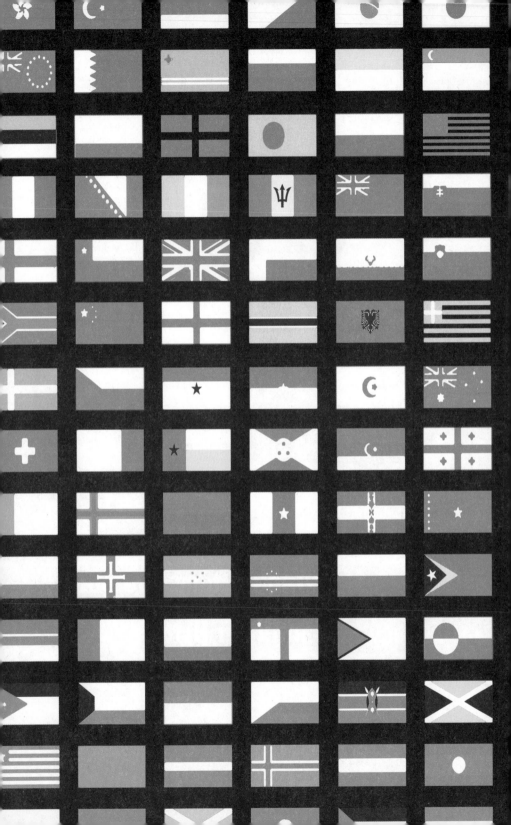

It's all about diversity.

Different classes, creeds, races, nationalities, languages, politics –

perhaps we should marvel that Britain doesn't tear itself apart on a daily basis. So how does it all work: how do so many varied lifestyles coexist and contribute to such a thoroughly modern nation?

321

8.1 Divided loyalties: class, race and family

"A CLASS-FREE SOCIETY...IN BRITAIN CAN BECOME A REALITY."
Gordon Brown, addressing the Labour party conference in 2007

Know your place: social mobility and the wealth gap
The gap between rich and poor in Britain is wider now than it has been in 50 years, and social mobility looks plodding compared to other developed nations. The richest ten per cent of the population earn nine times more than the poorest ten per cent. A recent poll found two-thirds of parents unhappy about the prime role their own wealth (or lack of it) would play in determining their children's chances of climbing the ladder.

Old habits die hard: the class structure

Half a century ago people knew their place. The working-class, a majority defined by its manual jobs, shoulder chips and lack of a car, were distinct from the 'professional' middle classes and from the top sliver of society, the upper class with its inherited wealth, status and sense of superiority. Movement between the stations was rare. Ostensibly it was all about economics, but social, political and behavioural factors, set over generations, were equally important. Today, if analysts are to be believed, the large majority of Brits are middle class; a claim usually based on level of income.

If we do take earnings as the foundation of the current class structure, one generalisation from the many seems vaguely apt: the upper classes will never need a mortgage, the lower classes will never get one and everyone in between is essentially middle class. This might be neat but it ignores the infinite nuances of social status in 21st century Britain. To be well educated is to belong to the middle class, even while your earnings might fit the working class model. Conversely, you can own a £300,000 house yet still be judged as inherently working class based on your taste in curtains. The anomalies are endless: the young family staying in a tent on an English campsite will invariably be middle class, while the middle-aged couple in the caravan on an adjoining (more expensive) plot, would probably call themselves working-class. Culture, ethics, politics, consumption, dress, accent – each has its associations with class (for more on accent and class see Section 1.3.1.). The British acknowledge these markers intuitively, often subconsciously, on a daily basis.

322

Keeping it in the family...or not

Like class, the family structure has changed significantly since the Second World War. Find a mate, get married, have children; she gives up work, he earns the bread: so went the pre-war blueprint for family life. It seemed to work, and the familial hub – typically of three tight-knit generations – was a cornerstone of British life, even while the timeless issues of adultery, domestic violence and sex before marriage weren't absent, simply gagged. Divorce, birth control and abortion all became considerably easier in the 1960s (apart from in Northern Ireland, where abortion is still illegal) and, by the end of the century, co-habitation was viewed by most as a legitimate living arrangement. So, fewer people are getting married today than ever before, and of those that do, 45 per cent are likely to divorce. The number of lone parent families (and that's overwhelmingly lone mothers) has risen steadily to comprise around a quarter of all families with children, 40 per cent of children are now born out of wedlock and the average couple now have 1.8 children, down from two in 1970. Perhaps the most telling statistic of all is the one that reveals a third of all people now live alone. Some blame the changing structure of the nuclear family for wider social problems, even though polls consistently show the British place as much value on the family unit as they ever did.

Abortion in Northern Ireland

The political factions in Northern Ireland, notably Sinn Fein and the Democratic Unionist Party, don't agree on much, but they do agree on the issue of abortion. Both sides are opposed to legalisation in Northern Ireland, even while the rest of the UK has allowed abortion for more than 40 years. Around 1,500 women travel from Northern Ireland to mainland Britain each year to have an abortion; others procure illegal terminations at home.

Two per cent of British marriages are interracial, on a par with the USA despite Britain's much higher proportion of white residents.

Almost a gay wedding... but not quite

Since 2005 Britain has allowed civil partnerships between same-sex couples. This affords most of the legal niceties of a mixed-sex marriage, but doesn't actually constitute a 'marriage' as such, something that gay and lesbian groups still campaign for. The Civil Partnership Act forbids any religious aspect to the attendant ceremony.

Could do better
The Race Relations Act of 1976 (amended in 2000) sought to engender tolerance toward Britain's ethnic minorities in employment, housing, training, education and so on. Huge progress has been made, but there's much still to achieve. For example, even in the early 21st century, members of the ethnic minorities in Britain are twice as likely to be unemployed and living in poverty as white people. Any progress in the realm of public acceptance is harder to quantify. Britain's long-term relationship with racial diversity has generated a widely tolerant society, yet prejudice is far from dead.

Mergers and margins: multicultural Britain

Ethnic minorities make up more than seven per cent of the British population. Around half of them were born in Britain. Afro-Caribbean, South Asian, Chinese, Turkish, Eastern European and other migrant groups are integral to modern Britain; each contributes key elements to the national culture. London is among the most multi-racial cities on Earth: around a third of inhabitants were born outside Britain, it resonates with the sound of 300 different languages and harbours 50 non-indigenous communities with populations of 10,000 or more. Traditionally, inner London has supported a large Afro-Caribbean population, while the suburbs are more likely to support Indian, Bangladeshi and Pakistani settlers. Towns and cities in the Midlands are home to a large British Indian population, and Pakistanis form the largest ethnic populations in the North West of England, Yorkshire and Scotland. Only Chinese settlers, it seems, are spread relatively evenly throughout Britain. Northern Ireland is the least ethnically diverse part of the UK, with only 14,000 'non-white' residents recorded in the last census (from a population of nearly 1.7 million). Perhaps correspondingly, the level of racially motivated attacks is far higher in Northern Ireland than elsewhere.

But does all the talk of multiculturalism, of ethnic identity, cause more problems than it solves? Does it marginalise rather than integrate? It's fair to say that most Britons' knowledge of migrant culture extends little beyond their favourite choice of takeaway food. In the arts, especially, there's still much to achieve;

only music seems to have pushed ethnic minority culture into the mainstream. Race riots in Bradford, Burnley and Oldham in the summer of 2001 revealed how some communities have become divided along lines of ethnicity. The spectre of Islamic extremism on British soil, rightly or wrongly, is regularly touted as a consequence of this segregation.

Migration to Britain: some key dates

3rd century: an African division of the Roman army was stationed at Hadrian's Wall.

1565: Oliver Cromwell allowed Jewish settlers to enter England; Edward I had expelled Jews in 1290. However, Jewish migrants didn't arrive in any great number until the late 19th century when they fled the Russian empire.

Late 17th century: Huguenots arrived in their thousands, fleeing religious persecution in France.

18th century: Lascars, Muslim sailors, serving on British merchant ships settled in port cities.

1948: the SS Empire Windrush docked in Tilbury, Essex, with 500 Jamaicans onboard, and a large Afro-Caribbean migration began, initiated to resolve a British post-war labour shortage.

1950s and 60s: Settlers from former colonies in South Asia arrive, eventually forming Britain's largest ethnic minority groups.

2004: Migrant workers arrive in Britain en masse as a clutch of Eastern European countries join the EU.

2031: A further seven million migrants are forecast to arrive in the UK by the third decade of the 21st century.

The UK Border Agency removes one 'immigration offender' from the country every eight minutes, according to a 2008 Home Office report.

They came from the East
In the four years after 2004, one million migrant workers arrived in Britain from the ten Eastern European countries newly signed up to the EU. Around half a million of these were Poles. Their contribution to the British economy was hotly debated – they were willing to work for less and for longer than the average Brit, but weren't they taking British jobs? By 2008 about half of the Eastern visitors had returned to their native countries and the number of migrant workers arriving in Britain had tailed off significantly.

Living on a prayer
The Church of England may still be tied to the apparatus of state but it doesn't receive public funding. Three quarters of the £1 billion required each year to finance 13,000 parishes and 43 cathedrals comes from worshippers; much of the rest is generated by the Church's £4.8 billion worth of assets.

A Protestant land

Britain has been a largely Christian land since the seventh century when St Augustine, on a mission from the Vatican, won out over Celtic modes of worship. The major flux of the intervening years came with the Reformation that pushed Britain away from Rome and toward the Protestant tradition that remains dominant today. In fact, but for Henry VIII's wife-swap strategy, Britain might still be a Catholic country today (see section 1.2 for more on all of this). While the monarch, the Supreme Governor, is still head of the Church of England, the true, spiritual leader is the Archbishop of Canterbury. He (or perhaps one day, she) also heads up the Anglican Communion, the collection of bodies and Churches around the world (such as the Episcopal Church in the USA) that calls the Church of England papa. The Church in Wales, established as an Anglican body in 1920, has its own archbishop and HQ in Cardiff although beliefs mirror the Church of England's. However, the dominant denominations in recent Welsh history have been nonconformist – still Protestant but independent from the Anglican Church. The nonconformist chapels that became a focus for life in every Welsh village and town from the mid 18th century were mostly Methodist.

The Church of Scotland isn't Anglican. Instead, it flourished on the Calvinist principles of the 16th century and, in particular, the Reformation led by Scottish clergyman John Knox. By 1690 the Church of Scotland had become Presbyterian, administered not by the monarch or by bishops but by ministers and elected elders. Scripture, sermons and singing take precedence over festivals and prayer for the Presbyterians. The smaller Scottish Episcopal Church is the Anglican Communion's church in Scotland.

It's also worth noting that Catholicism never really left Britain. Instead, it hid, finally resurfacing in the mid 19th century when the restrictions on Catholic worship were relaxed. Emancipation coincided with the sizeable migration of Irish Catholics to mainland Britain (fleeing the famine in Ireland), boosting the revival in England, Scotland and Wales.

A special case: religion in Northern Ireland

Northern Ireland has a story of its own. The province is split largely between Catholics and Protestants (the last census counted 53 per cent of Protestant background and 44 per cent of Catholic). Gradually, over the last 40 years, the proportion of Catholics has grown as the share of Protestants has shrunk. The state of Northern Ireland itself was created along religious lines, its attachment to the UK born of a Protestant leaning that dates back to the plantations of the 16th century (see section 1.2.2. for more), even while it always retained a sizeable Catholic minority. So, religion, politics and daily life have always been inseparable. Even today, after a rare period of prolonged peace, lives are dictated by sectarianism. It affects where people live (by neighbourhood in urban areas or by village or region in rural parts), where children go to school, who marries who, which football team they support – all remain governed to a significant degree by religious background. As for the denominations in Northern Ireland, the Roman Catholic Church shares the stage with two large Protestant bodies: the Presbyterian Church in Ireland, which took its lead from Scottish settlers in the 17th century, and the Church of Ireland, an Anglican body.

Fighting over the women
In 1994 the Church of England ordained female priests for the first time. By 2007 more women (244) were being ordained than men (234). Women now comprise a quarter of the Anglican clergy. The divisive issue of female bishops (as yet unsanctioned) rumbles on, but their eventual ordination seems inevitable.

The Church of Scotland has been ordaining female ministers and elders since 1968.

"AN IT HARM
NONE, DO WHAT
YE WILL"
From the *Wiccan Rede*,
the doctrinal verse by
which many of Britain's
neo-Pagans live

Ducking the insults
The name Baptist was
initially coined as an
insult by opponents of
the movement that
immerses new converts
fully in water. It only
became accepted by the
Baptists themselves in
the 19th century.

Christian names: know your denominations

Methodist. Initiated by John Wesley and his brother Charles in the mid 18th century. Popular with the new working class, Methodism emphasised the individual's relationship with God, social welfare and a pared down style of worship. Over 300,000 British faithful.

Salvation Army. Charity founded in 1865 by William Booth along quasi-military lines, intent on caring for the disadvantaged. The evangelical services are led by an 'officer', male or female. Sally Army brass bands never fail to impress. 60,000 regulars.

Baptist. Probably began life with the 17th century Puritans. Big emphasis on scripture, baptism for those capable of expressing their faith (i.e. not infants) and governance by congregation rather than hierarchy. Around 150,000 British members.

Pentecostal. Emphasising the role of the Holy Spirit and the power of God within the individual, sometimes realised by speaking in tongues, prophecy and the ability to heal. Fastest-growing Christian faith in Britain: currently a million strong.

1. Identity: the
foundations
of British culture

2. Literature
and philosophy

3. Art, architecture
and design

4. Performing
arts

5. Cinema,
photography
and fashion

6. Media and
communications

7. Food and drink

**8. Living culture:
the state of
modern Britain**

Where have all the followers gone?
Is modern British society as secularised as it seems?
A recent survey concluded that just over half of Britain
considers itself Christian. A further six per cent aligned
themselves with other faiths, while almost 40 per
cent claimed no religion. However, the same survey
confirmed what ministers have known for decades; that
congregations have shrunk alarmingly. Half the population
might be Christian but only one in ten people actually go
to church on a regular basis.

Two thirds of Brits have no physical connection with
the church at all, despite their belief (ingrained in
childhood for many). It seems that many who claim
some Christian belief are choosing a 'Christian' approach
to life rather than allegiance to a congregation. 'Believing
without belonging' is the glib media-friendly evaluation;
'Apathetic' is another. Middle-aged Brits are more
inclined to talk about 'spiritual' feelings than a direct
allegiance to any faith. Worryingly for organised religion,
youngsters are the least likely to express any belief at all.

Only Northern Ireland remains widely enthusiastic about
its Christianity: even while the numbers are slowly falling
here too, almost half the population still regularly attend
church. Catholics in Northern Ireland are more likely to
express their faith with a church visit than Protestants.

Non-Christian religions in Britain buck the trend for
decline. Ethnic minorities in Britain are far more likely to
attend a church than people of British descent. Islam has
become Britain's second religion with around 1.5 million
followers, the vast majority of them Sunnis. Around half
regularly practise their faith. In contrast with Christians,
their numbers grow consistently, as do British followers
of Hinduism and Sikhism.

"IF THERE IS ONE
THING I LONG FOR
ABOVE ALL ELSE, IT
IS THAT THE YEARS
TO COME MAY SEE
CHRISTIANITY IN
THIS COUNTRY ABLE
AGAIN TO CAPTURE
THE IMAGINATION
OF OUR CULTURE,
TO DRAW THE
STRONGEST ENERGIES
OF OUR THINKING
AND FEELING."
Dr Rowan Williams,
Archbishop of Canterbury

Faith and footie: Scotland's sectarian divide

Roman Catholicism in Britain made significant strides in the later 20th century. The Pope paid a historic visit in 1982 and in 1995 the Queen even set foot inside Westminster Cathedral, invited by the progressive Cardinal Basil Hume. Scotland, however, dragged its heels. In parts of western Scotland, Glasgow in particular, the Sectarian divide remains. Both elements have their allegiances with Northern Ireland, with Republican and Loyalist factions. 'Old Firm' football matches between Glasgow rivals Celtic (traditionally Catholic) and Rangers (Protestant) provide the greatest flashpoint for verbal and, sometimes, physical attack.

Taking tolerance for granted

Britain has had its shameful episodes of organised bigotry – Edward I expelled Jews in 1290; Queen Elizabeth tried the same with blacks in 1596 – but, comparatively, it enjoys a reputation for tolerance. The Protestant-Catholic divide never quite evoked the burning ire that afflicted the Continent, and the two sides peacefully coexist – interact even – today outside occasional sectarian outbursts in Scotland and the Troubles across the Irish Sea. Similarly, the relaxed, long-held attitudes to nonconformist religions reflect an admirable tolerance. In 2006 the Racial and Religious Hatred Act finally outlawed religious enmity. However, as non-Christian religions continue to grow in Britain, and with them the calls for the disestablishment of the Church of England, a sizeable minority might have to work harder at their liberalism. Dr Rowan Williams, Archbishop of Canterbury, caused uproar when he said the adoption of moderate, civil elements of Sharia Law would be 'unavoidable' in Britain as its Muslim population grew. Much of the bile that flew Dr Williams' way came from senior, conservative elements in the Anglican Church.

British political history is strewn with power struggles, the biggest being the transition of authority from monarchy and clergy to Parliament. Yet Britain has, in the main, avoided the bloodshed that characterised the emergence of other democracies. Instead, the processes of government derive from centuries of evolutionary adjustment. And so the constitution is uncodified: there is no single document to explain the balance of power, the roles of each branch of government or even the rights and liberties of a British citizen.

Proto parliament
The first English congress may have been the Model Parliament called by Edward I in 1295. Inclusive of bishops, abbots, earls, barons and the representatives of townspeople and shires alike, its primary function was raising taxes to fund war, although it did offer a forum for griping to the king.

How does government in Britain work?
Britain is a liberal democracy. The monarch remains as head of state but the Prime Minister (PM) and other members of government hold the reins of power. So we can talk about a 'parliamentary sovereignty', whereby Parliament has the power to make or curtail laws. The legislative role is fulfilled by the bicameral Parliament, comprising the House of Commons and the House of Lords:

The **House of Commons**' 646 Members of Parliament (MPs), nearly all of whom belong to a political party, are elected by their local constituents in a general election at least once every five years. The party with the most constituency seats is invited to form a government, with party leader as Prime Minister (PM). As per the adversarial nature of British politics, the second placed party forms the Opposition. The PM forms the Cabinet, an executive of ministers to head up the various governmental departments, which meets weekly at Number 10 Downing Street, the

Prime Minister's official residence. Periodically the Prime Minister 'reshuffles' the Cabinet, sacking, promoting or moving ministers. The Opposition, meanwhile, form a Shadow Cabinet.

The **House of Lords**, around 750 strong, checks and revises the laws proposed in the House of Commons. Usually deemed more independent than the Commons (peers (lords) are more inclined to ignore the party whip; many aren't even aligned to a political party), its members have a wider expertise. Although they can delay legislation – possibly long enough to get it withdrawn by the Government – peers don't have the power of veto on proposed laws and they can't approve Government taxation or spending. The House of Commons, its Labour contingent in particular, has pushed to modernise the House of Lords (and in some votes, abolish it entirely – because most peers are appointed rather than elected) throughout the last century.

The winner takes it all
To be elected to public office in Britain a candidate must simply secure more votes than their nearest rival – the so-called First Past The Post (FPTP) system. They don't need an overall majority of the total votes cast.

First amongst equals
The role of Prime Minister has evolved over time. Traditionally seen as *primus inter pares* or 'first amongst equals' – in other words, no more senior than other MPs – many would concede that the Prime Ministerial persona is becoming increasingly presidential.

Bully boys
Each party in the Commons appoints a **Chief Whip**, with the status of a senior minister, and assistant whips. They're charged with ensuring a Government majority in House votes. MPs are instructed by whips on when to attend; a 'three-line whip' means attendance is essential. Errant MPs may have the whip withdrawn – the equivalent of being expelled from the party. The **Speaker** chairs the House of Commons, deciding which MPs speak when and ensuring the rules are followed. The Speaker is chosen by fellow MPs at the start of each new Parliament or when a previous Speaker retires or dies.

1. Identity: the   2. Literature   3. Art, architecture   4. Performing   5. Cinema,   6. Media and   7. Food and drink   **8. Living culture:**
foundations   and philosophy   and design   arts   photography   communications   **the state of**
of British culture   and fashion   **modern Britain**

Prime Ministers you should have heard of

Robert Walpole (1721-42 Whig). Became Britain's first de facto Prime Minister, despite a brief spell in prison for corruption.

Benjamin Disraeli (1868 and 1874-80 Conservative). Britain's only Jewish PM was a close friend of Queen Victoria. Also wrote romantic novels.

William Ewart Gladstone (1868-74, 1880-85, 1886 and 1892-94 Liberal). Queen Victoria called Disraeli's bitter rival a "half-mad firebrand". He campaigned for social reform, Irish Home Rule and an ethical foreign policy.

David Lloyd George (1916-22 Liberal). The only Welsh PM thus far won his spurs as Chancellor, proposing a large tax hike for the landed classes to fund higher social spending.

Winston Churchill (1940-45 and 1951-5 Conservative). Voted 'Greatest Ever Briton' in a recent BBC poll, Churchill masterminded victory against Nazi Germany in the Second World War.

Margaret Thatcher (1979-90 Conservative). The 'Iron Lady', the first woman to lead Government, was the longest serving PM for 150 years. The grocer's daughter from Grantham privatised state industry, lowered taxes and reduced social spending.

"IF BRITAIN – ITS ECCENTRICITY, ITS BIG HEARTEDNESS, ITS STRENGTH OF CHARACTER – HAS TO BE SUMMED UP IN ONE PERSON, IT HAS TO BE WINSTON CHURCHILL."
Mo Mowlam MP

Bill hits the pavement
Even while serving as Prime Minister in the 1840s, William Gladstone would walk the streets of London trying to convince prostitutes to give up their work.

Margaret Thatcher
giving that handbag-swinging hand
a bit of a workout

Nothing but outlaws and rebels
The Tories (who evolved into the Conservative party in the 1830s) first appeared in the 17th century as a group supporting James II's succession claim on the English throne. The word Tory probably derives from an Irish term for 'outlaw' (*toraidhe*), re-hashed and fired pejoratively at James and his Catholic cronies. In contrast, the Whigs (became the Liberal party in the 19th century) first formed in support of the lords and merchants who argued for Parliament in the face of royal dominance. They too probably took their name from a derisive term: *whiggamore*, a Scots word for 'rebel'.

Political parties: the big three

Labour. Established to represent the newly enfranchised working class in 1900, Labour remained the third party until 1945 when it won its first overall majority. After winning power in 1997, led by Tony Blair, New Labour dragged the party increasingly from the left to the centre.

Conservatives. Right-of-centre party that evolved from the Tories in 1834 when Robert Peel became leader. Thatcherism gave the party a clear, modern ideology based on free enterprise and private ownership, but they were blighted by scandal in the 1990s. David Cameron finally brought some semblance of unity to the party in the early 21st century.

Liberal Democrats. Born by merger of the Social Democratic Party (SDP) and the Liberals (the old Whig party) in 1988. As the name suggests, a liberal party concerned with social justice and personal freedom. The only one of the big three to oppose war in Iraq, they're also the most pro-European. Consistently third in the political race.

Political parties: the other options

Scottish National Party (SNP). Founded in 1934 to press for an independent Scotland, and usually defined as moderately left of centre. They hold the biggest share of seats in the Scottish Parliament.

Plaid Cymru. Founded in 1925 to champion Welsh cultural and linguistic identity, not least by demanding independence. A historical link with the Green Party places the environment high on the Plaid Cymru agenda.

Green Party. First identifiable in 1973 and first known as the Green Party in 1985. Committed to environmental issues and the decentralisation of power but struggling to win seats in Parliament.

UK Independence Party (UKIP). Founded in 1993 on a campaign to withdraw Britain from the EU. Did well in the 2004 European elections but has since faltered, not least after a leadership debacle starring TV talkshow host Robert Kilroy-Silk.

British National Party. Far right, whites-only party. They took less than one per cent of the vote in the 2005 election, but usually fair better in local elections. Reviled by mainstream politicians, most of the press and a good proportion of the public.

Commons knowledge

The MP with the longest unbroken service in the House of Commons is referred to as 'Father of the House', or presumably 'Mother' should the situation ever arise.

The 2005 General Election placed 520 male and 126 female MPs in the House of Commons.

The average age of an MP after the last election was 50.6 years.

15 of the 646 MPs elected in the 2005 General Election came from ethnic minorities

Cornwall smells freedom
Some in Kernow
(Cornwall's Celtic name)
want autonomy. They've
got their own political
party, Mebyon Kernow
(Sons of Cornwall in
Cornish), pushing for
a Cornish assembly,
hoping to secure
recognition for their
region as a distinct
nation within the United
Kingdom. The flag of
Saint Piran, a white
cross on a black
background, plays a
highly visual role in the
push for independence.

Britain devolved

The Scottish Parliament

Almost 75 per cent of voters in Scotland said 'yes' to a national parliament in the 1997 referendum. The body, Scotland's first in 290 years, has significant law-making powers, controlling health, education and justice, although certain matters, notably foreign policy, are still governed by Westminster. The assembly features 129 members (MSPs), comprising 73 constituency members (all but two are also MPs in Westminster and therefore elected using the FPTP system) and 56 regional members (elected using the Additional Member System (AMS) of proportional representation). SNP members took most seats in the Parliament's formative years.

The Och Ayes have it.
The Scottish Parliament building

The Welsh Assembly

Wales voted for its own legislative body in 1997 with far less conviction than Scotland: only half the population turned out, and only 50.3 per cent of them voted 'yes'. It was deemed enough of a mandate to create the National Assembly for Wales. After a rather toothless start, in 2006 the Assembly gained legislative powers on devolved matters like health, education, social services and local government. The Assembly has 60 members, comprising 40 constituency representatives and 20 members of regional seats, the latter being elected like their Scottish equivalents through AMS. The first Welsh Assembly was dismissed after a vote of no confidence in February 2000, and its early years seem dogged by voter apathy.

The Northern Ireland Assembly

Northern Ireland gained a measure of autonomy much earlier on; the act of 1920 that established the province also made provision for a two-house legislature in Belfast. It stumbled to a final collapse in 1972 when the violence of the Troubles brought rule direct from Westminster under a Northern Ireland Secretary. All attempts to restore devolved government failed until 1998, when the Good Friday Agreement – endorsed by 70 per cent of the Northern Irish population via referendum – attempted to establish a power sharing assembly that would work for both Unionists and Nationalists. A false start or two later, the 108 member assembly now tentatively governs the province; the historic power sharing agreement between Sinn Féin (Nationalist) and the Democratic Unionist Party (Unionist) in 2007 (when previously they refused to even meet one another) has brought the chance of success.

The growth of green politics

After years in the shadows, environmental issues finally burn bright in British politics. The leaders of all three main parties now crow about their green credentials, while new policy is scrutinised for its environmental concern and legislation is adapted to the changing mood. So, 'gas guzzling' cars will be taxed more than small cars, while industry, commerce and the public sector are subject to the Climate Change levy, taxing their use of energy. Finding alternative energy sources has become a key issue; wind farms are being built and argued over (Britain still only produces two per cent of its total energy from renewable sources) but the biggest area of debate concerns nuclear power. In 2008 the Labour Government set the goal of an 80 per cent reduction in carbon dioxide emissions by 2050 (based on 1990 levels).

Do the British public actually care about politics? The British don't vote as much as they used to – election turnout has been sliding for decades. In 2005 only 61 per cent of the voting population visited the polls in the General Election. But while there is an undeniable apathy for politics among the public, there is also considerable criticism when politicians fail to deliver. Occasionally, the involvement goes beyond simply grumbling on the sofa. Over a million people marched peacefully through London in 2003, urging then PM Tony Blair not to lead Britain into a war against Iraq. The fact that he did anyway and was re-elected just two years later (albeit with a greatly reduced majority), even after the fabled weapons of mass destruction failed to materialise and post-war Iraq descended into bloody chaos, hints at the primacy of home over foreign policy for most Brits, and also perhaps the weakness of the then Opposition.

1. Identity: the
foundations
of British culture

2. Literature
and philosophy

3. Art, architecture
and design

4. Performing
arts

5. Cinema,
photography
and fashion

6. Media and
communications

7. Food and drink

**8. Living culture:
the state of
modern Britain**

Long since overtaken as the world's leading economy, and destined to be outpaced by the BRIMC countries (Brazil, Russia, India, Mexico and China) in the 21st century, the British economy, nevertheless, still punches well above its weight. Britain harbours less than one per cent of the world's population, yet remains sixth in the world rich list (measured by GDP at purchasing power parities) and accounts for over three per cent of world output. As individuals, the Brits are less well off. The heady days of the 1860s, when they had more money in their pockets than anyone else, are long gone; in 2007 the International Monetary Fund ranked Britain 28th for GDP per head.

How Britain grew wealthy

The Industrial Revolution made Britain rich, fed by the captive markets of a sprawling Empire and a large, new labour force at home. By the mid 19th century, Britain was by far the world's biggest producer of consumer goods and capital equipment. The major cities mushroomed around particular industries: Glasgow and Belfast had their shipbuilding; Newcastle its coal; Sheffield its steel; and, later, Birmingham and Coventry their automotive industries. The products were shipped around the globe from vast docks in London, Liverpool and Bristol. When manufacturing declined in the 20th century, the attendant industrial cities declined with it. Their reinvention in recent decades has enjoyed mixed success. Leeds and Manchester, former centres of the textile industry, have become a leading financial centre and mass provider of higher education respectively. Other cities, like Glasgow, Newcastle and Liverpool rely on heritage and culture for much of their modern verve.

Bully for Belfast
By the late 19th century Belfast was producing more linen than any other city in the world; people called it Linenopolis. It also had the largest shipyard anywhere, responsible for building giants like the Titanic. In addition, the city became the world's prime manufacturer of rope and oversaw the birth of air conditioning.

The key institutions of the British economy

HM Treasury. The economic and financial arm of the British Government, presided over by the Chancellor of the Exchequer.

The Bank of England (also referred to as the Old Lady of Threadneedle Street). Britain's central bank issues banknotes, sets the base interest rate and rescues troubled banks like Northern Rock.

The London Stock Exchange. Where shares are traded in Britain's largest companies. Dismissed by pre-eminent economist J.M. Keynes as a 'casino'.

Lloyd's of London. The major British insurance market, individual members of which are known as 'Names'.

Here to serve: the modern economy

It's well over a century since Britain was 'the workshop of the world'. A history of under investment and poor industrial relations (the 'British disease') has contributed to manufacturing's parlous long-term state. The slow decline of industry quickened in the Thatcherite 'service economy' revolution of the 1980s, establishing a distinctly post-industrial nation. Today, service industries employ 78 per cent of the British workforce and manufacturing 20 per cent; only two per cent now work in the primary sector. The modern powerhouses of the British economy are financial services, telecommunications, high-tech manufacturing, retail and a range of property-related services. Turn-of-the-21st century Britain enjoyed a sustained period of stability and growth, led by the property market where house prices tripled in a decade. However, the expansion began to falter in 2008 amid fall out from the US sub-prime market crisis and the subsequent global credit crunch. As Britain slumped into recession, commentators said the bust, after such a large, often reckless boom, was inevitable. As stock markets tumbled, confidence withered and lending fizzled out, the British banking system teetered on the edge of collapse: the Treasury responded with an unprecedented £500 billion rescue plan.

Filthy lucre

The British hold complex attitudes to wealth. Chasing money was deemed unwholesome until the 1980s, when entrepreneurship was encouraged and the nouveau riche grew; rich lists appeared in newspapers for the first time. But the line between admiration and scorn was, and still is, fine. Comedian Harry Enfield's Loadsamoney character successfully parodied the small businessman's lust for cash, while overt displays of wealth invoked hostility, however hard-earned the spoils. More recently, media glee as the dot.com bubble burst in 2000 reflected a rather British kind of envy. Public perception can be everything. If, like Richard Branson or Tom Hunter, you're adjudged a self-made success, most will admire your achievements, private jet and all. But if you're the director of a large, formerly nationalised company, you can expect be called a 'fat cat' and generally loathed, however hard you've grafted.

The great divide

"It's grim up north," the saying goes. And while Harrogate, Chester, Edinburgh and other smart northern towns and cities contradict the cliché, northern England, Scotland, Northern Ireland and Wales have, nonetheless, been hit hardest by the decline of manufacturing. There are noticeable disparities of income between the four nations. English household incomes hover around two per cent above the average for Britain as a whole; Scotland's are around 5 per cent below, while incomes in Wales and Northern Ireland are up to 12 per cent beneath the average. The north-south divide in England provides sharper contrasts. The average disposable household income in London is almost 50 per cent higher than its northern equivalent. An even greater gulf exists in property prices: in 2008 the average property price in

The mogul model

Britain and the USA are home to the 'Anglo-Saxon model', in which markets and individuals play a greater role in the economy than governments. The entrepreneur is central to the model. The British Government has worked hard to cultivate an 'enterprise culture' in recent years, while TV shows like *Dragons' Den* have tapped into the get-rich-quick mentality. In reality, an inventor who also possesses business skills – in the mould of James Dyson (see more on Dyson in section 3.1.6) – is something of a rarity. Britain has a comparatively poor record of profiting from invention, and Richard Branson remains the only entrepreneur most Britons could name who also heads up a large organisation (Virgin). Managers rather than entrepreneurs run the vast majority of companies.

Haves and have nots

Britain is apparently now home to some half a million 'dollar millionaires'. Meanwhile, around one in five Brits are thought to live below the poverty line (in households where earnings are 60 per cent or less of the national average).

London was two and a half times that in the north. However, London traditionally has the highest level of unemployment in Britain, much higher than in Scotland, Wales and Northern Ireland. But again, the greatest disparities are within England, where the proportion of jobless is twice as high in the North East as in the South East.

Pensions, dole and healthcare: the welfare state

Britain faces the conundrum of an aging population: as the number of pensioners grows, the working folk supporting them shrinks. In response, an older pensionable age of 68 will be phased in over the next three decades (up from 60 for women and 65 for men). Successive schemes, from personal equity plans to stakeholder pensions, have been introduced in a bid to wean Britons off their state pensions and onto private provision instead. However, deficits on many employers' pension funds and the mis-selling of endowment policies haven't convinced a sceptical public. Government attempts at reducing unemployment in recent years have been more successful, with the jobless halved from their mid 1980s high of three million. Redirecting unemployment benefit, or the Dole as it's commonly known, toward those genuinely looking for work has no doubt helped the figures. In 2008, Government plans to make the long-term unemployed work for their benefits were leaked.

Work and Pensions is the biggest spending Government department, but Health runs it a close second. The National Health Service (NHS), established in 1948, is a Soviet-style planned economy-within-an-economy, setting prices and rationing healthcare. It's vast, with over a million employees and an annual budget that exceeds £100 billion; a spend that matches the EU average of between nine and ten per cent of GDP. Some view the NHS as the crowning achievement of post-war Britain, others as an archaic monolith ripe for reform. 'Marketisation' has been attempted by contracting out support services and introducing consumer choice, self-governing trusts and 'foundation' super-hospitals. The NHS still accounts for over 90 per cent of healthcare provision, which is generally free at the point of use to everyone in the country. Both dental and optical care have largely opted out of the NHS.

Legal differences: systems of law

England and Wales have a different legal system to Scotland. They employ a form of common law (referred to as 'English law' despite the shared status with Wales), controlled by judges and based on case precedent, whereby a ruling on one initial case sets the standard for subsequent trials. In Scotland, swayed by the Auld Alliance with France, a civil system operates – the laws are defined first and then applied to each case as appropriate. Even while the processes vary, the bulk of the law in Scotland, England and Wales is the same. Both make the same distinction between criminal cases (where an individual is prosecuted by the Government) and civil cases (in which one individual or organisation prosecutes another). Northern Ireland law uses a common law system very much like England's, albeit with a few procedural differences born of the region's unique political situation.

ASBOlutely fabulous

The ASBO (Anti-social Behaviour Order) was introduced in 1998 to deal with anyone disrupting neighbourhood calm with noise, vandalism and the like. It's a civil court injunction, each one tailored to the individual offender with a series of rules and restrictions. Breaching these terms amounts to a criminal offence. Critics have suggested that youngsters collect ASBOs like trophies. The term itself, ASBO, has become an oft-used piece of popular language.

Court orders

England, Wales and Northern Ireland:

Magistrates' Court. The lowest criminal court; for small offences and the initial hearing of larger crimes.

County Court. For civil cases like debt and divorce.

Crown Court. Criminal cases are tried by a judge and a jury of 12.

The High Court. Used for bigger civil cases and for hearing appeals from lower courts.

Court of Appeal. For appeals on judgments passed down in Crown, County or High Courts.

The House of Lords. The highest court in the country; presided over by the Lord Chancellor.

The worst kind of tree London used to hang its crims from the Tyburn Tree (not actually a tree but a three-legged gallows that allowed for mass hangings) every Monday. Over the centuries (the last death was in 1783), between 40,000 and 60,000 people were executed, roughly on the spot where Marble Arch stands today.

Court orders

Scotland:

District Court. Handles minor criminal offences, such as drunkenness.

Sheriff Court. Covers civil and criminal cases, tried either by a lone Sheriff or with a jury of 15.

Court of Session. The top level of civil court.

High Court of Justiciary. The top level criminal court.

The House of Lords. The last say goes to the Lord Chancellor and the Law Lords once more.

Don't believe the hype

If the statisticians are to be believed, overall crime in Britain has been falling steadily for more than a decade. You're less likely to be a victim than ever before. And yet, two-thirds of Brits actually think crime is rising on a national level (even while they feel it's falling locally). Youth crime and anti-social behaviour are perceived as particular problems. Media attention on gang culture and knife crime in inner city hotspots – where the stats do buck the national trend – instils a general (many would say, ungrounded) sense of panic. Confusion from the top down over how crime is recorded and how the figures are presented does little to encourage public confidence. In 2008 it emerged that several police forces had been recording crimes in the wrong categories, most notably under-recording the most serious violent crime. Out on the streets, the police find their fiercest critics in those inner city areas where crime is worst; in broader terms they remain relatively well regarded by the public. However, concerns persist about the authorities' failure to cope with a minority of young repeat offenders.

Jail debate

The British prison system is full to bursting. Back in 1993, there were 42,000 inmates; in 2008 the number hit 82,068 – that's 96 prisoners over the Prison Service's 'operational capacity'. Various long and short-term measures have been announced to combat the problem, from the temporary use of police cells for prisoners to encouraging foreign inmates to leave the country. Campaigners blame the growing prison population on politicians and their clamour to appear tough on crime.

Top of the cops

Aside from the regular bobbies on the beat, Britain also has:

British Transport Police. Responsible for the rail network (not to be confused with the traffic division of the regular police).

CID (Criminal Investigation Department). Plain clothes detectives with a responsibility for major criminal investigations.

Special Branch. Responsible for issues of national security.

Special Constabulary. The volunteer section of the regular police force.

Off the straight and narrow: five antiquated laws (that everyone ignores)

A pregnant woman is allowed to relieve herself anywhere she wants.

All swans belong to the Queen.

All males over the age of 14 must undertake two hours of longbow practice each week (to be supervised by a member of the local clergy).

It is illegal to be drunk in a pub.

Black cabs in London have to carry a bale of hay and a shovel (a vestige from their days as horse drawn carriages).

Crime time

The Great Train Robbery (1963). A London to
Glasgow mail train was stopped and relieved of £2.6
million, much of which was never recovered. Gang
members like Ronnie Biggs became household names.

The Moors Murders (1963-65). Five young people
from the Manchester area, aged between ten and 17,
were abducted, tortured and murdered; four were
buried in shallow graves on Saddleworth Moor. The
culprits, Ian Brady (still alive) and Myra Hindley (died in
2002), remain vilified.

The Yorkshire Ripper (1975-80). After killing 13
women and horrifically injuring several others, Peter
Sutcliffe gave rise to the largest manhunt in British
history. Eventually caught after he was stopped for
displaying false car number plates, Sutcliffe claimed
that God ordered the murders.

The House of Horror (1967-87). In 1994, police found
a number of bodies buried in the garden and cellar of
25 Cromwell Street, Gloucester. Fred West was
convicted of 12 counts of murder and his wife, Rose,
of ten. The true death toll at the house is still unclear;
witnesses relayed a disturbing story of prostitution,
incest, rape and paedophilia.

Doctor Death (c.1974-98). Although Dr Harold
Shipman, a GP from Hyde, Greater Manchester, was
convicted of 15 murders, he may have killed as many
as 250 patients. His 'MO' was to give a patient a lethal
overdose, sign the death certificate and then edit
medical records to show ill health.

1. Identity: the
foundations
of British culture

2. Literature
and philosophy

3. Art, architecture
and design

4. Performing
arts

5. Cinema,
photography
and fashion

6. Media and
communications

7. Food and drink

**8. Living culture:
the state of
modern Britain**

The education pages of the British broadsheets make for depressing reading. Chronic teacher shortages, catchment lotteries, exam board blunders, strikes, interminable testing, league table rows – education appears to lurch from one crisis to the next. The stats seem to back up the editorial: Britain is slipping down the international league tables in the key areas of maths, science and literacy. But are things really that bad? The pass rates for GCSE and A-levels rise every year ('dumbing down' cry critics; 'better teaching' respond teachers), class sizes are shrinking, school standards appear to have slowly risen in the last decade and Britain retains an enviable reputation for higher education. Above all, perhaps, the right to a free and full education remains a positive cornerstone of British life.

How are British children schooled?

Every child in Britain must brave full-time education between the ages of five and 16. Nine out of ten do so in the state school system; the remainder are educated at fee-paying schools or at home. Their experiences differ based on location and on whether they pass through 'maintained' or private education. In England, Wales and Northern Ireland, state schools employ a broadly similar system based around the National Curriculum that aims for a balanced, consistent mode of learning across the board. A state school career is divided into four Key Stages (five if it runs into further education). Students are tested at the end of each Key Stage. The exams taken at seven and 11 are National Tests, or SATs (Standard Assessment Tasks) as they're commonly known (SATs tests for 14-year-olds were scrapped in 2008); at the end of the fourth Key Stage, usually aged 16, students sit GCSE exams (General Certificate of Secondary Education).

Are British children depressed?
In 2007 a United Nations Children's Fund report concluded that British school children were the unhappiest in the Western world. They cited a decline in social cohesion as the cause. Others pointed to the rigid system of targets and testing in British schools; they said it stressed kids out and contributed to anti-social behaviour.

Public perceptions
In England, Wales and Northern Ireland, public schools, private schools and independent schools amount to the same thing: they're all privately funded. Technically, the term 'public school' only refers to the group of schools named in the Public Schools Act of 1868, but most British people couldn't tell you that. The confusing name dates from a time when new public schools offered the first alternative to private tutoring. In Scotland, as in the rest of the world, the terminology is reversed: a public school is a state-funded institution.

Timetables
The British school year,
running from early
September to mid July,
is traditionally split into
three terms, although
some local authorities
now operate six terms
in order to achieve
equity of term lengths.
Students receive a two-
week break at Christmas
and at Easter, and a one-
week 'half term' break in
the middle of each term.
The average school day
runs from 8.30am to
3.30pm, although many
schools vary their
schedule to suit.

Then follows, at Key Stage Five, the option of A-levels
in three to five subjects (studied in the sixth form – an
extension of secondary school or a dedicated college),
or more vocational forms of further education such as
the GNVQ (General National Vocational Qualification).
In 2008 the Government introduced 15 diploma
courses to further education, intended as an equivalent
(and eventual replacement) to A-levels.

The National Curriculum doesn't apply in Scotland,
where the distinction from English education has been
maintained since the 1707 Act of Union. Instead, local
authorities and headteachers, furnished with certain
guidelines by the Scottish Executive's Education
Department, take responsibility for the syllabus. At 16,
pupils sit their Standard Grades, the equivalent of
English and Welsh GCSEs, and then have the option of
studying for Highers and Advanced Highers (equivalent
to A-levels) between 16 and 18.

Britain's 2,000 or so fee-paying independent schools
are free to set their own curriculum and their own
rules. They can admit whomever they like and turn
away whomever they don't. The Common Entrance
Examination (CEE), taken at preparatory school (junior
school) around the age of 13, decides who makes it
into senior school. In common with the state system,
most independent schools will test their 16-year-olds
using GCSEs in England and Standard Grades in
Scotland, although many are moving over to
International GCSEs, considered more academically
challenging. Some public schools, and even a few
state schools, are testing their 18-year-olds using the
International Baccalaureate (IB) system rather than
A-levels.

1. Identity: the   2. Literature   3. Art, architecture   4. Performing   5. Cinema,   6. Media and   7. Food and drink   8. Living culture:
foundations   and philosophy   and design   arts   photography   communications   the state of
of British culture   and fashion   modern Britain

How the schooling system breaks down

Nursery Freely available, non-compulsory pre-school education for three and four-year-olds.

Primary School The most common path through the state school system starts here, which takes pupils from four to 11.

Secondary School Secondary schools all teach children up to age 16. Some also provide further education.

Sixth Form College Teaching pupils between the ages of 16 and 18, but not found in Scotland.

Which school did you go to?

Education in Britain has an enduring duality. The gulf between the state and private sectors in terms of academic achievement (the latter routinely attains better grades), social makeup and cultural identity is wide. Chris Parry, chief executive of the Independent Schools Council, spoke recently in terms of a "sectarian divide". If you're British, the type of school you attended can carry a relevance throughout adulthood; prepare to be prejudged based on whether you attended the local comprehensive or boarded at Eton. The seven per cent of children attending an independent school are far more likely to attend university than their state school counterparts – Oxbridge still derives 40 per cent of its intake from private schools. Similarly, they'll find better paid jobs and achieve a higher standard of living. Although the 'old boys network' isn't as dominant in the upper echelons of British industry as it once was, there is still a sense that attending the right school can be very beneficial. On the downside, a certain cultural stigma – an inverted snobbery perhaps – can await the private school pupil out in the wider world.

The school inspectors
State schools have experienced an unprecedented level of Government intervention over the last 30 years. The initiative which has had the greatest impact is probably the Ofsted visit. Every school in England receives a periodic Ofsted (The Office for Standards in Education, Children's Services and Skills) inspection. The resultant report helps determine a school's popularity, offering parents a measure of standards. A failing school can end up in 'special measures', whereby the local authority focuses resources on improvement. If that doesn't work, the school may close. Wales (Estyn), Scotland (HMIe) and Northern Ireland (ETI) have their own inspection bodies carrying out similar work.

A 2008 opinion poll revealed that 57 per cent of parents would choose to send their children to an independent school if they could afford to. The prime motivation was, as it always has been, 'a better standard of education'. However, the expectation of 'better discipline' was also a key motivation.

Breaking down language barriers
After years of underachievement, the Government is trying to improve the approach to modern languages in schools. Traditionally, few children were taught a second language at primary school but the proportion had leapt to 70 per cent by 2007. Alas, modern languages remain optional from the age of 14, and with 50 per cent of students opting out, the system appears in disarray. In Wales, Welsh language lessons are compulsory throughout the school system at all ages. At primary level, a quarter of all Welsh schools use the native language as the sole or prime mode of instruction.

Doing the honours: university education

Britain has some of the most prestigious universities in the world. Oxford and Cambridge in England and St Andrew's in Scotland are, in that order, the three oldest in the English-speaking world. They fall among the elite clique of 'Ancient' universities. Another group, the 'Redbricks' were built in the Victorian era, with Manchester and Birmingham among their number; and a third, the 'Plateglass' universities, including York, Lancaster and East Anglia, date from the 1960s. In truth, such terms are rarely applied today. A fourth group were originally called polytechnics but gained university status in 1992 amid the late 20th century drive toward mass higher education. Gradually, the mild stigma attached to attending an old 'poly' rather than a traditional university is fading.

A little under half of A-level and Highers students go on to attend university. Initially they study for a Bachelor's degree (with the option of adding 'honours'), graded as first class, upper second class (2:1), lower second class (2:2), third class or fail. Debate has been rumbling for some time about whether or not to scrap this 220-year-old classification system, and a radical revamp looks inevitable. Scottish honours degrees usually run over four years, and those in England and Wales over three. Students at Scottish universities who attended a Scottish secondary school are exempt from the tuition fees which, at up to £3,000 per year, see students at English, Welsh and Northern Irish universities graduate (or drop out) laden with debt.

On holiday with the Brits

The cherished, annual week in the sun has become a birthright for most Brits. Today, the most popular destination is Spain: Britons made the trip 17 million times in 2007. France comes next. Alas, the great British seaside holiday isn't what it was. Or perhaps, more accurately, it's exactly what it was, which is why most tourists have moved on. The gushing migration to Southend-on-Sea, Blackpool, Bognor, Scarborough and the other historic seaside resorts each summer has slowed to a trickle. The practice lasted a century, initiated in the Victorian era by the growth of the railways offering factory workers an escape on their days off. Piers, pleasure beaches, donkey rides, Punch and Judy, fish and chips: it became a very formulaic cultural experience.

In 1936, entrepreneur Billy Butlin opened his first holiday camp in Skegness, cutting the template of prefab chalets, knobbly knee competitions and variety acts that would host so many post-war working-class summers. And so it went until the 1960s when holidaymakers swapped Britain for the Med, lured by cheap package deals. Air travel has pushed British holidaymakers around the globe and the recent budget flights boom has made the Continent as popular as ever. However, as fuel prices and environmental awareness grow, so do the optimistic calls for reviving the English seaside resort. In truth, Britons are more likely to venture into the native countryside – to the Lake District, the Mourne Mountains and the Scottish Highlands.

Away days

The statutory minimum leave in Britain is 24 days a year for full-timers, although many get more. An additional eight days (nine in Scotland and ten in Northern Ireland) are set aside for public holidays: six of them are 'bank holidays', two (Christmas Day and Good Friday) are known as

What goes on tour stays on tour...apart from the architecture

Back in the 17th and 18th centuries, any young aristocrat worth their stockings would take a year or two out for the Grand Tour. It was a cultural safari; a trip that took in the architecture and art treasures of Paris, Venice and Rome. Some made it as far as the Balkans and Germany. They drank, gambled and philandered, but essentially they were there for intellectual stimulation. Indeed, the knowledge acquired on the Tour circuit is often credited with improving British art and architecture, notably in its taste for classical design. The French Revolution and the arrival of the railways sounded the death knell.

'common law' holidays. Some employers insist on their faithful absorbing bank holidays into annual leave. It was a banker, Sir John Lubbock, also an MP, who successfully put the bill for bank holidays to Parliament in 1871. They were so called because bills of exchange due for payment on the days in question, when the banks closed, could be delayed till the following business day. Today, the banks are about the only things guaranteed to close – shops, restaurants, stately homes and so on usually work on through. British public holidays don't all – as they do elsewhere in the world – celebrate national heroes or crushing military victories. Instead, they're a somewhat haphazard mix:

New Year's Day (or in lieu of 1st Jan). Because everyone needs a day to recover from New Year's Eve.

2nd January (or in lieu of 2nd Jan). In Scotland only: they need two days to recover.

St Patrick's Day. Northern Ireland alone enjoys a day off on 17th March.

Good Friday. The Friday before Easter Sunday, marking the Crucifixion.

Easter Monday. The day after Easter Sunday, in Wales and England only.

May Day: Of confused Pagan and Labour Day origin, taken on the first Monday in May.

Spring bank holiday. The last Monday in May lost its Whit Monday label in 1971.

Orangemen's Day. On 12th July Northern Ireland gets another day off, this one marking a win for William of Orange at the Battle of the Boyne in 1690.

1. Identity: the   2. Literature   3. Art, architecture   4. Performing   5. Cinema,   6. Media and   7. Food and drink   **8. Living culture:**
foundations   and philosophy   and design   arts   photography   communications   **the state of**
of British culture   and fashion   **modern Britain**

Summer bank holiday. Falls on the first Monday in August in Scotland, and on the last in England.

St Andrew's Day. In Scotland only: their patron saint has only afforded the 30th November off work since 2007.

Christmas Day (or in lieu of 25th Dec). Pubs serve lunch and petrol station tills still ring, but nearly everyone else has the day off.

Boxing Day (or in lieu of 26th Dec). Named for the (now defunct) tradition of giving presents to the poor.

Banks cash in their holiday
The Bank of England used to close on around 40 saints' days and anniversaries each year. In 1830 the number was reduced to 18, and then, four years later, was slashed to just four: Good Friday, May Day, 1st November and Christmas Day.

For the love of David, just give us the day off
A 2006 poll revealed that two-thirds of Welsh people would sacrifice an established bank holiday if St David's Day were declared a national day off. A year later, Tony Blair rebuffed a petition demanding as much.

Organised fun: fetes and festivals

The likelihood of persistent drizzle doesn't stop Britain stuffing a raft of outdoor festivals into the calendar. At their heart lies the humble village fete, the colourful jamboree of cake stalls, tombolas (the mildest of gambling in which contestants vie for tinned carrots, alcopops and so on), coconut shies and morris dancers that pulls Britain back to the 1950s, to an allegedly simpler time. In truth, the multicultural madness of the Notting Hill Carnival or loud revelry of Edinburgh's New Year Hogmanay celebrations are more representative of modern British culture. Scotland, Wales and Northern Ireland all acknowledge their national saints: St Andrew (30th November – shared with Russia, Romania, Greece and Sicily), St David (1st March – shared with vegetarians and poets) and St Patrick (17th March – shared with Nigerians and engineers) respectively, with festivals. Scotland celebrates with music, dance and a wee dram or two; in Wales they hold parades, sing and wear a daffodil or leek (both national emblems) on the lapel; and in Northern Ireland the parades in honour of St Patrick reach their height in Downpatrick, where some think the saint was buried (clue's in the name). England's saint, St George (shared with Catalonia, Portugal, Georgia, Serbia, Lebanon and others), enjoys little in the way of an organised party on his national day, 23rd April, despite a vigorous campaign lobbying for some kind of recognition. These days the English are more likely to raise a glass to St Patrick.

353

I'm not desperate but… As the clock struck midnight on 29th November, heralding St Andrew's Day, lassies in Scotland traditionally began praying for a husband. Various practices were used to heighten their chances of bagging a bloke. Some would throw a shoe at a door; if the toe pointed toward the exit, she'd be married and out of the parent's home within a year. Others threw apple peel over the shoulder, looking to see if the peel formed a letter, hinting at the name of their future mate.

Victory for the village fete When Yvonne Cole fell in a hole left by a maypole after a village fete in East Sussex, she lodged a £150,000 damages claim against the charity that organised the event. But her claim was dismissed on appeal. One judge expressed concern that if claims like Ms Cole's were successful, "There would be no fetes, no maypole dancing and no activities that have come to be a part of the English village green for fear of what might go wrong."

Cheese Rolling Race. Brockworth (Gloucestershire); May.

Man versus Horse Marathon. Llanwrtyd Wells (Mid Wales); June.

World Snail Racing Championships. Congham (Norfolk); July.

Bognor Regis International Birdman Competition. Bognor (Sussex); July.

Biggest Liar in the World Competition. Stanton Bridge (Cumbria); November.

Killing time before the pub opens

The weird public and private habits of the average Brit, from trainspotting to taxidermy, are well documented. However, the truth about spare time is usually less offbeat. The most popular leisure activity in Britain is watching TV or listening to music, consuming around two and a half hours daily, double the 'quality time' spent with family and friends. But don't write the Brits off as sofa slobs; they're equally at home sabotaging domestic decor with bouts of DIY (do it yourself) or pottering around in the garden. Walking, cycling and trips to the gym get the British blood pumping, but the most popular leisure activity outside the home is a trip to the pub.

Common cause: days when British people will be doing the same things

Christmas. Celebrated on the 25th December, with a week's build up and fallout either side. The one time of the year pretty much guaranteed to generate a family gathering. Most swap presents in the morning, some go to church and nearly all enjoy an epic dinner.

New Year's Eve. Almost universally celebrated with a party leading to the countdown at midnight on 31st January, when the inebriated form a circle and sing *Auld Lang Syne*, the song whose Scots ancestry hints at the import of New Year (Hogmanay) north of the border.

St Valentine's Day. As elsewhere, a day of romance on 14th February, when cards are sent to woo, sometimes anonymously. With flowers, chocolates and fancy underwear involved, St Valentine's Day breaks free of the typical British reserve.

Shrove Tuesday. The final day before Lent allows for a blow out on pancakes, traditionally consumed to use up staple foodstuffs like egg, milk and sugar. Villagers run through the streets with frying pan in hand for pancake races. A few towns still play Shrove Tuesday Football, a fairly lawless, mob version of the beautiful game dating to the 12th century.

Easter. Perhaps the most enduringly reverent date in the British calendar. Children receive chocolate eggs on Easter Sunday – the origins of which probably lie in Pagan spring rites – and bakers cook up hot cross buns.

Halloween. Originally a Celtic rite marking the start of winter, the eve of All Saints' Day, 31st October, used to bring the dead back to life. These days it brings children in batman outfits to the door demanding sweets (derived from the British 'Mischief Night' not, as many suppose, from American traditions).

Bonfire Night. Fires are lit, fireworks let off and toffee chewed in celebration of the Catholic Guido Fawkes and his attempt to blow up Parliament on November 5th 1605. Alas, the tradition of making a straw-filled 'Guy' dressed in your dad's best cheesecloth shirt, and dragging it around the neighbourhood to the call of 'Penny for the Guy' seems to be fading. For obvious reasons, the Guy Fawkes tradition gets less attention in Northern Ireland.

Burning issues
Bonfire Night and Halloween have become clearly defined in modern Britain – one's about warding off evil spirits the other's about a Catholic plot to blow up Parliament. But both, it seems, share ancient Pagan origins tied to the Celtic festival of Samhain, an event that traditionally marked the start of winter. Evil spirits were sent packing with bonfires, ghoulish masks and the occasional human sacrifice.

"PING PONG IS
COMING HOME."
London Mayor Boris
Johnson looks forward
to the London 2012
Olympics

What role does sport play in British life?

Sport has been a key ingredient of British life for generations. It's enjoyed as a rare, undiscriminating mode of mass entertainment – a 'great leveller' in the words of any pundit worth their keep. Everyone from labourer to lord is likely to have an opinion on, for example, Chelsea's title hopes this year. For the British male, in particular, it's the default conversation starter, while sporting success – from a rare Ashes victory in the cricket to Andy Murray reaching the latter stages of Wimbledon – will knock 'real' news off the front page. The fact that many of the major global sports (football, rugby, rowing, baseball, tennis etc) were first played or codified on British soil no doubt helped establish the passion, even while the rest of the world now repeatedly beats the British at their own games. Wearing 'your' team colours has become important as an expression of allegiance and identity. In many sports, notably football and rugby, it brings the chance for English, Scots, Northern Irish and Welsh fans to assert their national pride; to recall the differences that once caused bloodshed. Any call for the national football teams to merge into a single British side – in the way that other sports do for the Olympics – always meets howls of protest.

As for participation, around half the British regularly undertake some form of exercise, from tennis to hang-gliding to fencing and jogging. The other half causes concern as obesity levels rise, particularly amongst children. As the average British lifestyle enjoys ever closer ties with the sofa, booze and bad food, and the NHS groans under the strain of the related health issues, exercise and sport are climbing up the political agenda after years of neglect. National Lottery funding is helping the drive toward better 'grass roots' facilities, although the 2012 London Olympics have commandeered sizeable chunks of the available cash.

1. Identity: the
foundations
of British culture

2. Literature
and philosophy

3. Art, architecture
and design

4. Performing
arts

5. Cinema,
photography
and fashion

6. Media and
communications

7. Food and drink

**8. Living culture:
the state of
modern Britain**

Compulsive viewing: the main British sports

Football. The rules of Association Football (always call it football, never 'soccer', if you want to be taken seriously), the national sport of England and Scotland, were invented in Cambridge. Today, England and Wales share four tiers of professional football. The top flight, the English Premier League, is the richest – and some claim the best – league in the world. The 'Big Four' clubs of the 20 involved – Arsenal, Chelsea, Liverpool and Manchester United – are global brands whose players can earn over £150,000 a week. The Championship, League One and League Two, comprise the other divisions (collectively called the Football League) between which promotion and relegation occurs at the end of each season. The gulf in form, money and crowd sizes between the top of the Premier League and the foot of League Two is huge and, to the consternation of many, grows annually. Scotland, with a similar four division set up, has an even greater cleft between top and bottom. The FA Cup is the top club competition in England; Scotland has its equivalent.

Rugby. Named after Rugby School, Warwickshire, where the original game was probably invented, rugby is split into two codes: league and union. The latter is Wales' national sport, and also widely popular in England, Scotland and Northern Ireland. At club level, England has its Premiership, while Scottish, Welsh and Irish clubs play each other in a Celtic league. Club rugby union has grown in strength since turning professional in 1995, but for many fans the season's focus lands on the Six Nations tournament, played out during February and March between the home nations (Ireland comprises players from both Northern Ireland and the Republic), France and Italy. England enjoyed a rare national sporting success with their victory in the 2003 Rugby Union World Cup. Rugby league, union's breakaway cousin,

An end to the English disease?
British football fans had a nasty reputation in the 1970s and 80s. Hooliganism (or the 'English disease' as pundits so often said) was endemic, and the big clubs each had their 'firm' of bad lads. Two events brought the situation to a head. When Liverpool hooligans charged opposing supporters in the 1985 European Cup final at Heysel Stadium in Brussels, a wall collapsed killing 39 Juventus fans. Four years later, 96 Liverpool fans died, crushed against a high fence built to combat crowd trouble. Their deaths sparked the Taylor Report that ultimately introduced all-seating stadia to English football and helped bring the bad times to an end. Today, in its top tiers at least, British football has become a family game with an inclusive, anti-racist ethos. Some, no doubt nostalgic for the terraces, complain that it's gone too far toward a sanitised, 'corporate' experience.

357

finds most of its clubs and supporters in northern England. League teams are comprised of 13 players, two less than union.

Cricket. Unfathomable to many, Brits included, cricket is a complex game played out over a brief, rain-affected summer season. The first-class domestic game features 18 county sides (17 English and one Welsh) split into two divisions. It has its diehard fans but most county cricket is poorly attended, eclipsed by the five-day Test matches that see England play throughout much of the summer against former British colonies including Australia, India and the West Indies. One day cricket and, more recently, Twenty20 cricket (in which each side bats for 20 overs) have brought new fans to the game.

The great events of British sport

The FA Cup Final. The finale of the most famous (and longest running) domestic cup in the footballing world takes place in May at Wembley Stadium, London.

The Grand National. The one day of the year when most Brits take an interest in horse racing. Aintree, near Liverpool, stages the richest National Hunt race in the world in early April.

The Boat Race. The rowing clubs of Oxford and Cambridge Universities have raced each other along the Thames each spring since 1829.

The Ashes. Biennial cricket test series between England and Australia, named after Australia won on English soil for the first time in 1882 and a newspaper announced the death of English cricket: "the body will be cremated and the ashes taken to Australia".

London Marathon. Held in the capital in April since 1981, the course starts in Blackheath and finishes on The Mall. Around 35,000 runners take the pain.

Wimbledon. The most prestigious fortnight in world tennis unfurls in early summer in south-west London at the All England Club. If only Britain could produce a winner…

The Open. Britain's premier golf tournament, held in July, moves around nine links courses in England and Scotland. St Andrews, home of golf, is the most regularly visited.

1. Identity: the   2. Literature   3. Art, architecture   4. Performing   5. Cinema,   6. Media and   7. Food and drink   **8. Living culture:**
foundations   and philosophy   and design   arts   photography   communications   **the state of**
of British culture   and fashion   **modern Britain**

Five sporting legends

Gareth Edwards. The greatest Welsh rugby union player, and among the best the sport has ever seen, played at scrum half for Cardiff during the 1960s and 70s and won 53 international caps. In 1973 he scored what many regard as the greatest try of all time in a Barbarians match against New Zealand.

Jim Clark. Not the best-known Brit to drive a Formula One car but surely the most talented. Clark, of Scottish farming stock, won a third of the 75 Grands Prix he contested in the 1960s and took the Driver's World Championship twice. Died on the Hockenheimring, aged 32.

Stephen Redgrave. Britain's greatest Olympian won a gold medal in rowing at five consecutive Olympic games (1984-2000), a feat only equalled by four other athletes and bettered by just one. Steve was knighted for his trouble.

Bobby Moore. Captained England to their first (and only) football World Cup win in 1966, and with 108 appearances still holds the record for most caps by an outfield player. Moore spent most of his career at West Ham United, playing in the centre of defence.

Ian Botham. The best all-rounder of modern English cricket beat the Aussies virtually single-handed in 1981 – duly dubbed 'Botham's Ashes' – and went on to become the nation's leading wicket taker. The Botham fable was fuelled by an off field irreverence; he was briefly banned from the game for smoking marijuana.

Logs, nuts and pants: the alternative Brit sports

Tossing the caber. The best-known event in the Highland Games, the regular festivals of sport, dance and bagpipery held in Scotland, involves throwing a slender pine tree trunk in the air. It's not about how far you toss but how close your pole lands to the 12 o'clock position.

Cumbrian wrestling. Practiced by burly men in saggy pants, stockings and a vest in England's north-western corner. You begin with your chin on the opponent's shoulder, hands clasped around their back, and try to finish by flinging them to the floor. Has its equivalents in Scotland, Lancashire and the West Country.

Conkers. A conker (horse chestnut) is pierced and threaded with a lace, and then swung at an opponent's similarly prepped nut with the intent of smashing it. The World Conker Championships are held in Ashton, a Northamptonshire village, each October. Soaking in vinegar or baking in the oven for added durability is simply bad form.

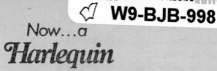

Now...a
Harlequin
romance
by Anne Mather
comes to life
on the movie screen

starring
KEIR DULLEA · SUSAN PENHALIGON

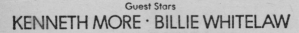

Guest Stars
KENNETH MORE · BILLIE WHITELAW

featuring GORDON THOMSON as MICHAEL
and JEREMY KEMP as BOLT

Produced by JOHN QUESTED and CHRIS HARROP
Screenplay by ANNE MATHER and JILL HYEM
Directed by GERRY O'HARA

An Anglo-Canadian Co-Production

CHAPTER ONE

IT was lucky for Nicky, while she was visiting Alice Springs with Guy Sonder, that Juliet rang her up at the motel to beg her, '*Please* come to Coochin Brim-brim with me, Nicky. I can't face it alone, and Jarry insists that I come.'

If that hadn't happened, she'd have been hurried back to Adelaide and she would never have found Cass and Howard again.

Guy had already told her, 'You'll never find them, Nichola. Don't you realise the Northern Territory is big—really big? There's more than half a million square miles of it.' Nicky knew that, but if you were looking for people you loved, and if you believed as Nicky did that fate meant you to find just one special person—like Howard Johnston— then the thought of half a million square miles didn't frighten you. It would happen somehow. It had to ...

In Alice, she had gone with Guy straight to the house that had been her home from when she was five till she was going on for fourteen. The cottage parents had been constantly changing even when she was there, so it was no surprise when it was a stranger and not 'Aunty' Pat who came to the door. Disappointingly, though, there was no record of the past, nothing at all to tell what had become of Cass and Howdie Johnston. She didn't suppose anyone would now know, either, that a girl called Nichola Iris Reay had once lived there and then, incredibly, been whisked away to boarding school in Adelaide, and a new life that bore absolutely no resemblance to the one she had led in Alice.

Guy had hated visiting the foster-home, seeing the little children chasing each other round the untidy yard, and seeing, too, the rather bare institutional look inside. Nicky knew it without his saying a word. He didn't like the idea

5

that she had spent years of her life in such a place, and he couldn't wait to get away from the reality of it. For her part, Nicky had never dreamed in those days that she would one day come back with a handsome opal buyer of thirty, or that she would be wearing a big shady picture hat, tiny gold earrings, and a fragile white broderie anglaise dress.

'Are you satisfied now?' he had asked as he helped her back into the hired car parked in hot sunshine by the kerb.

Of course she wasn't satisfied, and already her thoughts had run on ahead. The Johnstons' father had run a store and petrol station a hundred miles or so up the bitumen on the way to Darwin, and she smiled at Guy ruefully. 'I could ask at the Red Lily store up the track. Please—could we go there?'

'Okay, honey.' His acquiescence was resigned, half-hearted. He was prepared to humour her, but he wanted to get it over. She might be just nineteen and only out of school since the end of last year, but she was well aware how he felt. She was well aware, too, that he planned to leave Alice with her the following morning, feeling that his duty had been done. But he didn't know that she was steeling herself to resist.

They drove north through the heat of the day and found the store. It had an unexpectedly newish look about it, and a big sign announced to the traveller, 'Petrol—Accommodation—Meals—Refreshments.' It didn't take long to discover that the Johnstons had gone. The new proprietor was called Capper, and a small bright-looking blonde girl who looked about sixteen offered the information that the Johnstons had started a business in Darwin, and she could let Nicky have their address and telephone number.

'Now for God's sake, Nichola,' Guy said, irritable now, 'Darwin's almost a thousand miles on. You won't want to go *there*——'

'Not without checking,' she agreed with a sigh. She had tossed her picture hat on to the back seat, and she ran her fingers through her curling copper-brown hair as Guy turned the car. She was sure that Cass and Howard wouldn't be in Darwin. Their stepmother, Ruby, had never

6

wanted them, which was why they had been relegated to the foster home. But their father might know where they were.

He didn't, however. She rang through from the motel in Alice when they returned late that evening. It was a woman who answered. 'Ruby Johnston here.'

'I'm Nicky Reay,' Nicky said politely. 'I'm an old friend of Cass's, Mrs Johnston. Could you please tell me where she and Howard are now? I'm in Alice Springs——'

'I can't tell you a thing,' Cass's stepmother interrupted sharply, 'Why the hell do you think *we'd* know where those two are? We haven't heard from them in years.' Bang! She slammed the receiver down, and Nicky grimaced. Guy had heard that coarse, raucous voice, and he was not impressed.

'You're wasting your time,' he said shortly. 'I can't afford another day. You'll have to forget it and resign yourself to going home tomorrow. You're just chasing moonbeams, you know. As one grows up one has to accept the fact that one loses touch with many of one's childhood friends.'

'Are you telling me that?' she flashed back, her cheeks flushed, her pretty heart-shaped face turned to his. 'When you've spent eight or nine years of your childhood with cottage parents, and seen dozens of kids you've come to think of as your brothers and sisters just disappear overnight, you do rather get used to the fact that one loses touch.'

'Okay, okay.' Guy's shoulders in the expensively cut soft cotton shirt lifted in a shrug. 'Don't get uptight about it. I'm sorry. But it doesn't alter the fact that you can't go back to a past that doesn't exist any more. That's what you've got to face up to ... Now run off and take a shower and get ready for dinner. I'm going to phone through and confirm our flight bookings for tomorrow.'

'Not mine,' Nicky said stiffly. 'I'm not going.'

'I'm afraid you are,' he countered coolly. 'I'm not leaving you here on your own.' He turned his back and lifted the telephone receiver again—they were in his motel unit—and after a second she left, with a feeling of despair, and went to her own unit, a few doors along from his.

7

It didn't matter what Guy said, for her the past did exist. For her, Cass and Howard were family—the only family she had ever had. Jack, her guardian, had always kept his distance. Guy, Nicky thought broodingly, would like all her past, up to the time she was fourteen, to be obliterated. He didn't like any of it. He hated, and never mentioned, the fact that her father had been a crocodile shooter up at the Top End, and a mate of Jack's, who was—rough. It puzzled her, in these circumstances, that he seemed to have ideas of marrying her, once she had forgotten Alice Springs and acquired, as his sister Claudia had said, a little polish and sophistication. She had learned of his feelings only two weeks ago, when Jack Lane had died and she had wept in his arms and he had kissed her for the first time. He had groaned against her hair, 'Oh God, why does it have to be you, Nichola? You just—turn me on.'

Thinking about it later, when she was calmer, Nicky had wondered at her own lack of reaction, and reached the conclusion that she was safe from him because of the funny warm melting feeling she always experienced when she thought of Howdie Johnston. Anyhow, Guy hadn't said anything more, not specifically. She had been stupefied when she learned that Jack had named him as her guardian if he died while she was still young, and she was even more stupefied when he saw the size of the bank balance that Jack had been holding in trust for her and that Guy Sonder was now to administer until she was twenty-one, or until she married—with his consent and approval. Jack had left her some opals too, faced, polished, and ready to be set. He had been the sort of man people called a rough diamond, and thought he had been responsible for Nicky since she was three years old, she scarcely knew him. She hadn't even known that he wasn't her uncle until the one and only time she went to stay with him in Coober Pedy, where he was mining for opal.

She had been a quiet little girl with red-gold hair that had gradually darkened to deepest auburn. Lost, lonely, looking for brothers and sisters in the other children at the foster-home—children whose parents didn't want them, or

8

were having problems and for one reason or another couldn't cope with family life. She had vague memories, that grew vaguer still as the years went by, of another life lived away from the town—with Jack, but she didn't know who else. When Nicky was about nine, Jack turned up in Alice and gave her a little silver ring with a glinting milky stone in it—an opal. And then he disappeared from her life again till a year or two later, when he took her to Coober Pedy for a few days during the school vacations.

It had been exciting to find that he lived in an underground house cut out of the sandstone into a low hillside. Gypsum glinted from the rough walls, there were air funnels in the roof instead of windows, there was a stove and a fridge—and a bed for Nicky which was pretty nearly as comfortable as the one she slept in in Alice! Coober Pedy was a real frontier town—ugly and incredibly bare and dusty, and full of rough characters who drove beat-up old cars that often didn't even carry a number plate. There were stores, minute and cluttered, that sold everything, and made Nicky think of scenes from old Western movies she'd seen on television in Alice. Jack wouldn't let her go anywhere at all on her own, and once when she was with him she saw a sign outside a mine that said, 'Moonlighters will be shot at'.

Jack's own mine was several miles from the town, and he had taken her to see that and told her he'd struck a bit of opal.

'How would you like to go and live in Adelaide, Rainbow?' he'd asked. 'Go to a boarding school for young ladies and have lots of pretty dresses and all that? It could happen—I've got Lady Luck on my side now.'

She had stared at him round-eyed, unable to imagine such a thing, and she'd asked instead of answering, 'Why do you call me Rainbow?'

'Because your mother did.'

'Was she your sister, then?'

'No, your dad and I were mates, that's all.'

'Why don't—didn't they want me?'

'Now what gave you that idea, Rainbow? You bet they wanted you, but they died, see.'

'How?' she had asked quaveringly. 'What happened?'

'Nick—your dad—he was killed in an accident.' Jack stopped, and she looked at his leathery brown face anxiously until he continued reluctantly. 'Your mother died soon after, of grieving and a broken heart—though the doc gave it some fancy name. She left you in my care. She was one of the Wests from Kooriekirra cattle station, Iris was.'

'Was she?' It didn't mean anything to Nicky.

'Square dinkum she was. And don't you forget it. That's why one of these days I'm going to send you off to Adelaide like I said, and you can forget all about Alice Springs and Coober Pedy. And Jack Lane,' he had added, his blue eyes squinting at her.

'Never,' said Nicky aloud now, as she got under the shower in her motel room. 'I'll never forget any of it—I'll never want to.'

Guy wasn't going to stop her searching for Cass and Howdie. Somehow, she would find a way to stay in the Centre. Even if he was now her guardian, she wasn't going to let him tell her what she was to do and what she was not to do. She was too old for that, and quite definitely she wasn't going with him on the business trip he was making to the States in a few days' time. He wanted her to come—he had told her, 'Travel will do wonders for you—you'll acquire some poise——'

The telephone in the bedroom rang, and with a slight grimace she draped a towel around herself and went to answer it. It would be Guy to tell her what time the plane left tomorrow or something. As if she couldn't wait till dinner time to hear it! And there was going to be an argument then—an argument that she would have to win.

But after all, it wasn't Guy. It was a long-distance call from Adelaide, and it wasn't even Guy's sister Claudia, with whom she had stayed all the time Jack had been in hospital.

It was Juliet Buchan, who had been her best friend at school.

10

'Nicky! You're still there, thank goodness. I rang Claudia and she said she expected you back any time, so I was scared stiff I'd be too late.'

'Why? Whatever's happened, Juliet?'

'Oh, Jarry wants me at Coochin Brim-brim. I'm supposed to be flying to Alice Springs tomorrow.' Juliet sounded disgusted. 'Tracy had an accident and she's been evacuated to hospital in Alice, and *I'm* supposed to come and cook and cope with the children and all that. All sorts of threats if I refuse—no allowance and off to work in a jam factory or somewhere equally frightful. He *knows* I loathe the Never-never, yet the minute Mother and I come back from Europe *this* happens! Please come with me, Nicky, and give me some support. I just can't face it on my own——'

Nicky's thoughts raced. Of course she wanted to help Juliet, but as well, it was a godsend for her. She had no idea how far from Alice Juliet's half-brother's cattle station was, but at least it was in the Northern Territory, and it would give her some sort of a chance to continue her search for the Johnstons.

'Okay, Juliet,' she agreed quickly, 'of course I'll come. I'll have to explain to Guy——'

'Guy? Oh, this new guardian of yours. Well, he won't mind, will he?'

'He'd better not,' said Nicky gaily.

She told Guy over dinner in the motel restaurant, as they sat at a table for two that was softly lit by a tall pink lamp. Guy was definitely not pleased. He frowned as he listened to her putting her case, then, although she had said she wouldn't have any, he poured her a glass of wine from the bottle he had ordered, and looked across at her frustratedly.

'You do have a will of your own, don't you, Nichola?' He put a hand to his head, ruffling just slightly the well-groomed thickness of his dark corn-coloured hair. 'Well, I suppose I shall have to agree. You've made it very plain you don't want to come to the States with me. Frankly, I'd have thought a taste of world travel, or even a month or so in Adelaide getting yourself culturally clued up, would have

11

been more exciting than holidaying with a school friend. You haven't had time to appreciate your freedom yet, after all.'

Nicky winced slightly at this oblique reference to Jack's death. He had been a long time in hospital, and she had spent a great deal of time with him. Now she was free—that was how Guy saw it.

Both of them were silent while the chicken Guy had ordered was placed before them by the waitress. Glancing about, Nicky saw a big, broad-shouldered man with rather wild dark hair which definitely needed cutting walk in and take a table nearby. For a few seconds her concentration was riveted on him. He looked very much the he-man, despite the obviously top quality navy shirt and dark silk tie he wore with dark trousers. His jaw and upper lip had a blackish look as though he could do with a shave, and as she stared at him he turned his head slightly and looked back at her—openly, and somehow with a deadly accuracy, as if his almost black eyes went straight to the centre of some target. Bang on to her innermost being. She blinked and bit her lip and hastily disengaged her glance from his.

Guy, attacking his dinner, asked her, 'What's the name of this cattle station you say you've been invited to?'

'Coochin Brim-brim,' she said.

'Coochin Brim-brim,' he repeated. 'Then I suppose I must let you go—though you'll hardly learn anything about the civilised world there—or how to cope with your new role of social adult. When I come back from the States, however, I shall be right out to fetch you back where you belong.'

Nicky sighed and nodded automatically, aware that the man at the other table was watching her again from under his heavy straight black eyebrows. He had no manners at all, she decided, and with an effort she contrived to ignore him completely, and didn't even glance his way fleetingly. Deliberately, she kept her voice low while she talked to Guy, who was intent on discussing such practical considerations as whether she had sufficient funds, and whether her wardrobe was suitable for a holiday on a cattle station.

12

'I'll make you out a cheque,' he decided. 'You can open a bank account for yourself in town in the morning. As well, you'll need some extra cash to buy yourself jeans, I suppose—shirts—that kind of thing. Walking shoes. Only for God's sake don't become addicted to outback gear. You're feminine, and I like you to look that way ... When is your girl friend arriving?'

'Tomorrow afternoon,' Nicky said quickly, though actually Juliet had said before she hung up, 'I mightn't make it for another day—Jarry might just have to wait.'

Guy was looking relieved. 'Then you'll have the morning for shopping. I don't like leaving you alone, so see you don't lay yourself open to any trouble—there's plenty of that to be found by a pretty girl on her own even in a place like Alice Springs.'

Nicky wrinkled her nose, and protested mildly, 'Guy, I've been on my own a lot.'

'At boarding school?' he asked wryly.

'During holidays,' she corrected him. He didn't know how she had spent her holidays with no home, no family to go to. He knew nothing about the swimming schools, the riding schools, the educational coach trips Jack had sent her on. 'I got around quite a bit,' she said mildly. 'And I kept out of mischief, even with no one to tell me how to behave myself.'

He frowned. 'All right, so now someone's concerned for you. Me. It had to happen one day.' The look he sent her was disquieting, and she wished she had said nothing. She thought of Howdie and waited for that warm melting feeling, and knew instead a little cold chill of doubt. She might have to forget about Howard Johnston; she might never see him again. And even if she did, he might have another girl.

She couldn't finish her chicken. She was suddenly edgy and depressed and dead weary, and that man staring at her from his table was just the last straw.

She didn't go out to the aerodrome with Guy the following morning. She didn't tell him either that Juliet had rung at half-past seven to tell her she wouldn't be in Alice till next day. Guy said goodbye to her in the motel garden, kissed her on the lips, and put his arm around her shoulders while she walked out with him to the cab he'd ordered. The hired car had been returned—'You won't need it,' he'd said. He didn't much like her driving, though she had her driver's licence. She watched the taxi start off, gave a last wave and turned back to the motel, and almost collided with the dark man she had seen the evening before. She murmured an apology and walked past him quickly. He had looked as if he were going to speak to her—to pick her up, now she was on her own, she supposed, as she hurried back to the safety of her own unit. She didn't want to be picked up by a tough-looking man like that. He just didn't appeal to her.

She was wearing a simple yellow sleeveless dress this morning. It was of silk jersey, and with it she wore a macramé belt. Claudia Mallard had helped her shop for clothes in Adelaide when she left school to discover Jack was in hospital, and now in her room she put on a wide-brimmed hat of fine panama, trimmed with yellow ribbon. All very feminine—Guy would be pleased. She looked curiously at herself in the mirror. Nichola Iris Reay, a girl from the city of Adelaide. But her roots were somewhere here, in the Northern Territory, and now she was on her own she had a strange excited feeling that she was going to discover herself.

Not many minutes later she was in Todd Street, ready to begin her shopping. She was aware that Alice Springs had changed considerably during the six years since she had lived there. Yet it was still decidedly a frontier town, despite the many tourists busy at the travel agencies, booking trips to the Valley of the Eagles, to Kings Canyon and Ayers Rock, and to the Ross River Resort. Cattlemen, miners and all kinds of adventurers still found their way to Alice, and Nicky felt there could be nowhere like it in the whole world, with its tree-lined streets, its rich red backdrop formed by the MacDonnell Ranges, presently softened here and there by a haze of grey-green vegetation, the legacy of a run of extraordinarily good seasons. Yet despite

14

those good seasons, the River Todd was still no more than a wide dry sandy bed, and Nicky liked it that way. Adelaide was nearly a thousand miles to the south, and the only sealed road—the Bitumen, the Track, as it was called—went north to Darwin, even more distant. In between there was no town anything like the size of Alice with its thirteen or fourteen thousand inhabitants.

Nicky had barely been conscious of these things when she had lived here, but now she was very much aware of them and of the romance of this isolated settlement almost in the very centre of the driest continent in the world.

'Alice, I love you,' she whispered, as she crossed the street in search of jeans and shirts, a cotton hat, a couple of long cotton dresses that would do for evening wear, if ever there was an occasion for dressing up.

Necessities disposed of, her bank account opened, she lunched at Lizzie's Restaurant, then browsed around some of the aboriginal arts and crafts shops that had sprung up. She bought a long necklace of bush nuts, and a wooden coolamon that she planned to take back to Adelaide for Claudia. The aboriginals used coolamons for holding water or seeds, but they would make attractive fruit bowls.

Everywhere she went, she enquired about Cass and Howard Johnston, but no one had heard of them, and in her heart she knew they must have left Alice. It was deeply disappointing, and she found that the thought of going back to spend hours alone at the motel was not appealing. Instead, she made her way through the heat of the afternoon to the Guth Art Gallery, and it was while she was there that she saw the dark-haired man from the motel again.

She had never been to this art gallery before, and she climbed the spiral staircase to view the extraordinary painted panorama of Central Australian scenes in the octagonal tower. When she descended, she sat down in one of the solid-looking tropical armchairs to rest and to think, her parcels on the red-carpeted floor beside her. This room, from the centre of which the elegant and airy spiral stairway ascended to the tower above, was like a little world apart, quiet and peaceful and cool. Nicky's blue eyes made

15

a lazy dreamy tour of the paintings on the dark-timbered walls. There were Tiffany lamps on tall brass stands, and in the middle of the room near the base of the stairway was a small tiled pool, containing a small sculptured figure and a tiny fountain. She had already spent some time in the adjoining gallery with its aboriginal paintings and its glass cases containing aboriginal objects—kadaitcha shoes, tjuringa stones, rhythm sticks and bull-roarers, objects made of human hair, and so on. But in this particular small inner gallery where she now sat, she no longer had the feeling of being in the Red Centre—she could have been in some gallery in Adelaide, except that there, more people would have been thronging the gallery.

She had reached this point in her reflections when she was suddenly no longer alone. A tall man in an open-necked black shirt and tight-fitting dark pants had come through the doorway from the other gallery—and Nicky caught her breath. It was that tough, dark-jawed man with the disturbing eyes, and she felt colour flood her cheeks as she glanced quickly away from him and stooped to pick up her parcels, intent on escaping. She was on her feet and ready to beat a retreat when he turned from the painting he had apparently been assessing, and said casually, 'Don't let me drive you away.'

What a cheek! she thought, and she raised her small pointed chin, thankfully feeling her heightened colour subsiding. 'You're not driving me away. I—I have to go, that's all.'

One of his thick level brows rose slightly. He had folded his arms across his chest, and her eyes went to the dark hair springing from the long open V of his shirt, then quickly away again. She felt a curious kind of panic and was annoyed with herself. Surely she was perfectly safe in a public place like this! Yet once again she had the distinct though unreasonable feeling that the way she had stared at him last night had given him the idea that he could pick her up—even that she wanted it.

She took a deep breath and moved across the thick carpeting towards the door. He moved too, as if he were going

16

to block her way. She raised wide frightened hyacinth-blue eyes to his face, and found him looking straight down at her. She felt herself colour again, furiously, deeply, guiltily, simply because of the way he was looking at her.

She knew what it was that disconcerted her now. He looked at her—*sexily*. His eyes were too plainly the eyes of a man looking at a woman, and she was conscious as she had never been conscious before of the shape of her breasts revealed by the clinging silk jersey of her dress. She was conscious too of the pale scattering of freckles across her nose and cheek bones, of the shimmer of her darkly auburn hair washed under the shower last night. Of the vulnerability of her mouth that was warm and trembling. Guy Sonder regarded her as still emerging from the schoolgirl stage, but this man when he looked at her saw nothing of the schoolgirl, she was certain of it. Something in the line of his lips where they met—he had a wide mouth, curving sensuous lips—seemed to tell her that. It was strange how she read it, as clearly as if it had been writing, for she'd certainly never made a study of men, and their attitudes to women.

Her gaze had become fixed on his mouth and on the dark stubble around it that was an indication he was a man who needed to shave twice a day. His chin was deeply cleft——

The curiously mesmerised state into which she had passed was broken abruptly as two more people came into the room, and immediately Nicky moved—stepped quickly past him into that other brighter room from which she could see the dazzle of daylight in the world outside. The pick-up hadn't come off, she told herself.

She went back to the motel immediately, feeling utterly exhausted. In her room, she peeled off her dress, kicked off her sandals, and lay on her back on the bed. With one hand flung protectively across her closed eyes, she curiously experienced that encounter again. It was as if, walking in the jungle, she had seen some proud wild creature staring at her from thick gold-streaked darkness.

It was a mad and fanciful image and she banished it, yet still some words from Blake's poem drifted maddeningly through her mind—*Tyger, Tyger, burning bright, In the forests of the night*——

Presently she slept a little. After the release from Guy, she told herself, she needed it . . .

When she got up, she showered and got into a yellow and blue flowered white dress with long sleeves—another of Claudia's selections. It was young, yet subtly elegant, and very flattering to her small waist and rounded hips and bosom. Brushing her hair at the mirror, she thought unwillingly of that—that *savage*-looking man, and hoped with a slight quickening of her heartbeats that he would not be dining in the motel restaurant—where she had more or less promised Guy that she would dine tonight, with Juliet.

She saw him as soon as she reached the restaurant door. He sat alone at a table for two—the one she had shared with Guy last night—and she averted her face quickly as she walked forward. Out of the corner of her eye she saw him get to his feet and then to her alarm his hand was on her arm, detaining her. She gave him a cold look of annoyance, intended to make him abandon the idea that she was willing to be picked up, but it didn't get across.

'I'd like you to join me,' he said. His voice was deep yet unexpectedly low and cultured and somehow seductive, and she was momentarily disconcerted.

'I'm not in the least interested,' she managed then, and saw his lip curl a little.

'You might have to be interested—if you're visiting Coochin Brim-brim,' he told her. Her eyes widened and she swallowed nervously, not knowing what it was all about. 'I'm Jarratt Buchan. Does that mean anything to you?'

Nicky's mouth fell slightly open. She couldn't believe her ears. This—this savage-looking man, Juliet's brother? But memory reminded her, hadn't Juliet once confided at school, 'My half-brother is a brute—he's so uncivilised he scares me out of my wits——'

'Sit down,' said Jarratt Buchan softly, obviously amused at her reaction. Wordlessly, Nicky sank into the chair he pulled out for her and looked at him warily through her thick lashes, trying hard to see him as Juliet's brother and failing utterly to do so. Juliet was tallish too, but there the resemblance ended, for she was slim and fair with delicacy written all over her. In the soft light from the pink-shaded table lamp, Jarratt Buchan's dark eyes glowed like devilish coals, and his deeply tanned face was washed over with a red colour. He had shaved, no doubt, but his chin and upper lip and the line of his jaw were as dark as ever. His black hair was combed and shining, yet it didn't lie neatly down against the shape of his head but seemed to have a wild character of its own. He wore a roll-necked shirt of soft creamy cotton and dark pants. Nicky's eyes fell helplessly to his hands, and the gold gleam of a watch at his wrist, from which dark hair sprang.

'Now let's hear about this visit you're planning to my cattle run,' he said, sitting down opposite her and leaning across the small table. 'Or is it all just a story you made up to rid yourself of your—gentleman friend?'

Nicky stiffened, flushing at his tone. She wondered how much he had heard of her conversation with Guy, and was thankful to remember that she had lowered her voice. She had half a mind to tell him what she thought of him for listening to other people's private conversations, but obviously that would be a bad start to make when she was going to be a guest at Coochin Brim-brim, so she controlled her natural impulse and tried to hide her annoyance as she said, 'Of course it's not a story. I'm a friend of Juliet's. She must have—she must have forgotten to tell you she'd invited me to come home with her.'

'Home?' he repeated ironically, his eyebrows rising. 'You surprise me! I hardly think Juliet regards Coochin Brim-brim as *home*. But you're right, she certainly forgot to mention you. I had a telegram from her at the hospital this morning, telling me to expect her tomorrow. And that was all. However'—his dark eyes flicked over her in that disconcertingly frank way he had—'you're very welcome. All visitors are welcome at Coochin Brim-brim,' he added, in case, she supposed, she should mistakenly think he meant anything personal. He moved back in his chair and signalled negligently to the waitress, who hurried forward at

19

once. 'Will you have soup, followed by steak and a salad?'

Nicky nodded. It was the easiest thing to do, and while he gave the order, she watched him thoughtfully, trying to marshal her thoughts and accept him as her host-to-be. Somehow it was difficult. Despite what he had said about her being welcome, she didn't think he was at all eager for her to come along. Well, he would have to put up with her, that was all. She wasn't changing her plans now.

The waitress departed and he took a bread roll from the basket on the table and reached for the butter.

'You haven't told me your name.'

'It's Nicky—Nicky Reay.'

He closed one eye and repeated it slowly. 'Nicky Reay ... and where do you fit into my sister's life? You're a school friend?'

'Yes,' she said briefly.

'Hmm. And at a loose end like Juliet. Well, I hope you aren't misled enough to be expecting to have a riotous time outback.' He shifted his arm on the table to make room for the soup the waitress had brought. 'I suppose you've already heard about my cruelty in tearing my young half-sister from the arms of her would-be lover in France.'

'No,' she retorted, feeling shocked. She took up her soup spoon and added stiffly, 'And—and I don't think you should talk about Juliet's private affairs to—to anyone.'

He smiled lopsidedly. 'Don't worry, I'm not about to go into the details. You'll have the whole story in the next day or two in any case. You're not going to find all that much to entertain you at the homestead.'

Nicky lowered her lashes and began to eat her soup. She was beginning to feel very certain that she wasn't going to like Jarratt Buchan much at all.

He too concentrated on his meal for a few minutes, then pushed his plate aside and asked her abruptly—rudely, she thought—'What brought you to Alice?' He tilted back his dark head and viewed her appraisingly.

For a moment she considered telling him that that was her business, but common sense made her answer casually enough. 'I had some friends to look up.'

20

'The friend you farewelled this morning didn't look like he belonged in these parts. Who was he?' He asked it outright, bluntly, as if he had a perfect right to question her.

'Guy Sonder,' she said briefly, 'if that means anything to you.'

'Should it? Has he some special call to fame?'

'No.' She didn't know why she felt compelled to enlarge, but she added, 'He's an opal buyer.' One hand moved nervously to push back a strand of hair from her forehead, and his eyes followed the movement, and noted her little opal ring.

'Is that his ring you're wearing?'

She coloured and shook her head, then sat back as the waitress removed their plates and set the steaks and accompanying salads before them.

'He's interested in you, though,' Jarratt Buchan went on, as though there had been no interruption to their conversation. He took up the silver pepper-pot and paused, his eyes on her. 'I mean, as a man is interested in a woman. It's a sexual interest.'

Nicky felt a shock of distaste at his words and knew that her flush had deepened. Guy *was* interested in her, but that was outside the limits where she was going to allow Jarratt Buchan to probe, and to fox him, she told him with a slight smile, 'You're guessing, and you're wrong. Guy happens to be my guardian.'

He narrowed his eyes and subjected her to a long brooding look. 'I'm not guessing,' he said flatly. 'As for his being your guardian—it's a classic situation, isn't it? The beautiful young ward and the older man. Does he control your affairs?'

'Till I'm twenty-one,' she admitted. She felt angry with herself for answering his questions, and more angry with him for asking so many, and blinking her blue eyes hard as if to rid herself of the sight of him, she cut into her steak. It was tender and it smelt delicious, yet she had lost her appetite; she felt nervily on edge.

'Or till you marry,' he said musingly after a moment, revealing that he was still thinking about her and Guy. He

21

had guessed right again, but Nicky stayed silent, saying neither yea nor nay. 'How old are you now? Eighteen?'

'Nineteen.' He was wrong this time at least.

'Older than Juliet,' he commented, 'a year behind your age group. Illness? You look healthy enough. Too much social life, I suppose. There's plenty of entertainment to be had in Adelaide if you're not short of cash, isn't there?'

'Is there?' she countered coolly. 'I was a boarder, and I've only just left school.'

'Oh, you've had a few months,' he amended her statement. 'Long enough to make a few experiments. Juliet had no hesitation in France. I shall be interested to see if travel has matured my sister ... I warn you, however, that you'll find life rather different at Coochin Brim-brim—you won't catch up on social life there. We're way out in the Never-never, so far beyond the black stump you'll lose track of the miles.'

'That's not news to me,' Nicky said lightly. She found his conversation bewildering, even disturbing. She had no idea what he would say—or ask—next, or how she would react to it. Of course, she could have told him how she'd spent time since she'd left school—visiting at the hospital —but she didn't feel like offering information when he was so adept at asking questions and imagining he could guess all the answers. His big mistake was in taking for granted that she was just like any other girl at the ladies' college in Adelaide. She quite decidedly—oh, quite decidedly!—was not. As for his cynical warning about the Never-Never, if he only knew she was deeply stirred at the thought of going there. Deep down, she felt her roots begin to stir into new life, into a blossoming that had its beginnings a long way back in her life. Because during the long weeks Jack had been in hospital, he had told her things she had never known before about her own background, about the time before she had gone to the foster-home. She hadn't known till lately that her father had been a crocodile shooter, that her mother's people, the Wests, hadn't sanctioned the marriage, and even now she knew nothing about Nicholas Reay except that he had been a mate of Jack Lane's. So he must

22

have been tough—rough. Guy Sonder knew that too, and he didn't like it at all.

Nicky wished she had been able to ask Jack a lot more things about her past, but he had been a very sick man and most days he hadn't been able to talk at all, he had just been content to have her there with him. But who could tell? Out in the Never-Never, her own hidden memories might surface. Something might come back—she might learn to recognise in herself part of a continuing pattern of life. She might discover what made Nichola Iris Reay the girl she was ...

'I wonder,' said Jarratt Buchan into her thoughts, 'what made you decide to go into exile with my young sister?'

She didn't reply immediately. It would have required a multiple answer, part of which might well have been found in the thoughts she had been entertaining. As well, there was her determination not to let Guy drag her away—her need to continue her search for Cass and Howdie Johnston. But she told him none of those things. She merely said with a little shrug. 'As you remarked—I'm at a loose end. The thought of visiting the outback appeals to me.'

'It does, does it? Then you must have very different tastes from Juliet. It could be because you're more ignorant about this part of the world than she is. Let's hope your enthusiasm will prove robust enough to survive an encounter with reality—a not so brief encounter, if you intend seeing it through with Juliet. I may require her to stay for some considerable time.'

Regardless, she thought, glancing at him quickly and seeing the hardness of his face, of whether or not Juliet was happy.

She said with sudden daring, 'Why should Juliet stay longer than she wants? Suppose she decides she'd like to go home—surely you could find someone else to—to house-keep for you, or whatever it is she's supposed to do.'

He shrugged and shifted the salad bowl so that she could help herself. 'It's time Juliet was given a good long look at where the Buchan fortune comes from. It's not good to go through life doing only what one wants or likes to do. In my

23

opinion, a girl is vulnerable in a number of ways if she doesn't experience a taste of rough handling when she's reasonably young. You girls at your ladies' college—you were protected from all the knocks. Life's been too easy for Juliet, and the fact that her mother never lived at Coochin Brim-brim since before her birth hasn't helped one little bit. Juliet needs a lesson in hardship. Let's put it this way.' He moved the salad bowl slightly, then raised narrowed black eyes to her face. 'Juliet needs to be deprived of her protection—stripped down to her skin—flung into some cold, fast-moving water and forced to swim for her life. To think, in other words. To realise she can't take her comfort, her pampered life, for granted. If she survives, she won't ever again be all that exacting over what she uses to cover her nakedness—whether it's a Paris model or a bunch of gum leaves. Or even over who sees her skin.'

Nicky looked back at him, wary, puzzled, wondering if he were trying to shock her with his imagery. Yet in his eyes she read nothing but a kind of hard thoughtfulness, and she could have sworn he was not looking out for any kind of reaction on her part. It didn't even occur to him that she might find what he said embarrassing. Guy, now, would never talk to her that way—never! But the thing was that though he was talking specifically of Juliet, she suspected he was implying that she too needed a dose of hard experience.

Her suspicions were confirmed when he went on, 'The trouble is, of course, that someone always comes to the rescue of girls in a predicament, particularly pretty girls like you and Juliet—girls who are well heeled. The best I can do is to insist that Juliet spends a few weeks on my cattle station! Perhaps even you may learn a lesson or two from your visit. I'll guarantee you've rarely, if ever, had to do anything that really went against the grain. Have you?'

She didn't reply, and he ladled out a pile of greens for himself before answering his own question. 'You're in the same boat as my half-sister—pampered, secure, wanting for nothing.'

Secure! Pampered! Nicky thought of the foster-home

before Aunty Pat took it over—before Cass and Howdie came. She remembered her feeling of desolation when Jack simply disappeared from her life—she had been five years old, and unable to understand why she had been suddenly abandoned. She never told Jack how deep that wound had gone, or how lonely and unhappy she had been. 'I done it all for you, Rainbow,' he'd told her before he died. 'I quit shooting crocs and took a job as stockman in the centre. You was growing up needing a proper education—kids to play with other than little Abo kids—some sort of future ahead of you other than roughing it. I tried the opal diggings in Coober Pedy so I could give you the sort of life that should of been yours with a mother like you had.'

It had taken Jack years before he began to make enough money out of opal to take Nicky away from Alice and send her to boarding school in Adelaide. That had been another devastating break, because by then she had come to love Cass and Howdie. But Jack had simply come to Alice and taken her away on the Ghan. And during that long train journey south he had told her, 'Look, Rainbow—you don't have to tell the kids at school anything about Alice or me or where you've been living. See?' She could still see his bright blue eyes looking at her worriedly from his brown leathery face as they rocked down south through the dust and heat.

'What—what do you mean, Jack?' she had faltered. 'I don't *have* to tell them——'

'I jest mean *don't* tell them, Rainbow. Don't go and blab everything out—that's one of the first things an opal miner learns. You don't want to make yourself out to be different, you remember you'll be mixing in with the kind of people your mother was. You'll soon learn their ways.'

She had scarcely seen Jack after that—she had been alone again, starting all over.

Yes, she thought now, there had been many things she had had to do that went against the grain. She didn't know a great deal about being pampered—secure——

She finished her salad and refused dessert and told Jarratt Buchan moderately, 'Actually, I haven't had it all my own way. I've been an orphan since I was very small—about three years old——'

'But a privileged orphan—with a wealthy guardian,' he drawled, leaning his arms on the table and looking quite unimpressed. 'Will you have coffee? A liqueur?'

She didn't contradict what he had said. He thought he knew it all, so who was she to argue?

'Just coffee, thank you,' she told him politely. She hadn't yet developed a taste for liqueurs—though Jarratt Buchan probably thought she'd been brought up on them. It would have been nice, she thought irritably, if he'd expressed some sympathy when she'd told him she was an orphan, instead of simply qualifying her statement. Though on second thoughts, she supposed sympathy at this stage was a little late. And besides, he thought she'd immediately acquired a wealthy guardian.

If he only knew!

CHAPTER TWO

THE coffees came, plus one Drambuie, and Jarratt Buchan asked abruptly, 'Well, Nichola, who were your parents, anyhow?' His eyes, as he stirred sugar into his coffee, skimmed her face, her bosom, all that could be seen of her above the table edge, in fact, in a way that made her stiffen.

'Are you checking that I'm a suitable guest to come to Coochin Brim-brim?' she asked dryly. The name tripped easily off her tongue, like some strain of familiar music. Yet it had never sounded that way at school, when Juliet used to talk about the place—and her older half-brother—disparagingly, Nicky thought. She became aware that what she had said displeased him as he leaned forward and looked smoulderingly into her blue eyes.

'Look here, Nichola Reay—whether your father was a dustman or a doctor or a deep-sea diver, or a lord or a louse or a lunatic—it would make no difference to your coming as a guest to my cattle station. You would still be welcome . . . but knowing something about your parents, your background, just might make a little bit of difference to my understanding of you.'

She flinched at his tone, and bit her lip before she said shortly, 'I don't know much about my parents. But my mother—my mother was Iris West from Kooriekirra cattle station, if you've ever heard of it. Still, I don't see how it will help you to understand me better, because both my parents have been dead for about sixteen years and I don't remember them—not one single thing about them.'

He sat back in his chair and she blinked hard and sipped her coffee. Jarratt Buchan sipped his liqueur and continued to stare at her, but not angrily or smoulderingly any longer. Then he remarked conversationally, 'So you have connections with Kooriekirra. Do you know what the name means, by any chance?'

She shook her head, interested despite herself. 'No.'

'It's an aboriginal word meaning the rainbow. Iris—your mother's name—that's the rainbow too, as you probably know from Greek mythology. Iris was the goddess of the rainbow—the messenger of Juno, the queen of the gods.'

Nicky hadn't known, but wasn't going to admit to it. She was a little surprised that this tough-looking man knew anything about Greek mythology, however, and what he had said made her widen her eyes, because it was like a little bright revelation. It was like looking through a slit in a high wall and seeing for a fleeting instant into a secret and forgotten garden. A tantalising glimpse. Her maternal grandparents, of whom she knew nothing except that they had rejected her father, had called their cattle station after the rainbow, and they had linked their daughter's name to it too. And it was why her mother had called *her* Rainbow—— She felt a little ache in her heart for all that was past and lost, for all that she would never know.

She said on a faint sigh, 'My second name is Iris too. But I never went to Kooriekirra.'

Jarratt Buchan's dark eyes narrowed and he stared at the tiny amount of liquid still left in his glass.

'You'd scarcely have been old enough to remember it if you had,' he commented.

'What do you mean?' she asked quickly.

'Well, I've never been on Kooriekirra either—it's up towards the Top End. And I never knew the Wests, but I do know they went broke—they had to get out during the long drought that must have already been in progress when you were born.'

'Where are they—now?' She almost whispered it, her lips pale.

'Nobody told you?' he said curiously.

She shook her head.

'Both your grandparents were killed in a freak accident as they left the place. There was an electric storm and as they drove across the dry river bed, an old river red gum was split in two by lightning and fell on the car.'

Nicky reached for her coffee. Her hand was shaking. It

28

was weird to hear such things about your grandparents from someone who was a perfect stranger and yet knew more than you did. She wondered whether perhaps, if they had lived, her grandparents would have looked after her—and she would never have been left in Jack Lane's rough, if well-meaning, hands. But that was something she would never know.

He asked, looking at her hard, 'Your mother was an only child, wasn't she?'

She nodded. Jack had told her that.

'Still, it's a wonder no one told you about the Wests.' He frowned darkly. 'This—Guy Sonder—surely can't always have been your guardian? He's not all that old.'

'No,' she agreed. 'A—a friend of my parents looked after me before.'

She waited for him to ask who it was, who her father had been, because this whole conversation had started that way, and he had said quite specifically that knowing about her parents would help his understanding of her. But he didn't ask, and when he spoke it was to say dryly, 'Well, you haven't done too badly, have you? And these friends you were looking up in Alice—who were they?'

'Nobody you'd know,' she said quickly. And that was funny, because later she was proved quite wrong about that. She added, 'You ask a lot of questions, don't you, Mr Buchan?'

'If you want to know something, you ask,' he said dismissively. 'But if your friends are to remain a secret for some reason, then forget it. But tell me this—are you and Juliet cooking up something between you?'

She wrinkled her smooth forehead. 'Such as what?'

'I wouldn't know. But I do know Juliet was throwing tantrums over my request that she should come out to the Centre. If the two of you have worked out some scheme, you might as well tell me now.'

Nicky laughed. 'Do you really think if we did have a—a scheme, I'd tell you?'

He didn't answer immediately. He first explored her face anew with those disturbing, disconcerting black eyes. Then

29

he told her lazily, 'If you're waving the banner of schoolgirl loyalty in my face, you may as well forget it. Everything about you tells me you're not young enough—not naïve enough—for that kind of thinking. So yes, I do think you'd tell me—with a little pressing.'

'Don't bother with it, because I wouldn't,' she said, bright colour flaring in her cheeks. She pushed back her chair. 'Please excuse me now——'

'I'm ready to go too,' he said. She moved quickly from the table, but almost instantly felt his fingers under her elbow, and a strange tremor ran up her arm. They reached the foyer from which a door led to the motel garden, and it was towards this door he was guiding her.

'I'm going to bed now, Mr Jarratt,' she told him, resisting the pressure of his fingers.

'Unwise immediately after dinner,' he said, unmoved. 'A little exercise will help you sleep better.'

'I don't want a little exercise—I had plenty today.'

'Then you can breathe in some fresh air and look for shooting stars.'

She resisted a moment longer, remembering, perhaps ridiculously, Guy's warning, 'See you don't lay yourself open to any trouble.' Yet as Jarratt Buchan, still gripping her by the elbow, led her into the garden, she had the feeling she could be putting herself in a spot. She was uncomfortably aware that this man, although he certainly didn't have a high opinion of her, regarded her as a woman. No man before had ever given her that intense awareness of her own sex, and it was a sensation she had not yet learned to deal with.

There was no one else in the garden. The swimming pool glinted, the stars were just as bright as she always remembered them being in Alice, and, most disturbing of all, she realised she was going to spend the next week, two weeks, or who knew how long? as a guest on this man's cattle station. She didn't know quite what she thought of him, but she found him decidedly over-positive, and she knew Juliet was at least a little afraid of him. Right now she was frightened of him too. She had the feeling that he was going to kiss her, and she had no idea how to cope. Guy had kissed her several times, firmly yet gently, as if he were afraid to disturb her roots—as if she were a seed that had been planted and had only just begun to grow. She didn't think Jarratt Buchan would kiss that way...

But after all she was not to find out yet, as they stood together in the garden in the caressing warmth of the darkness, both of them staring upward.

'A falling star!' Nicky exclaimed.

'The eye of Thuwatha, the Rainbow Serpent,' he murmured. Then almost abruptly he released her. 'You'd better get in and have your sleep after all. We've a long drive ahead of us tomorrow.'

It was not till she was in her motel unit with the door safely locked that she thought, 'I should have asked about Tracy.' But she had forgotten.

Once she was in bed, she lay awake for a long time, her eyes fixed on the high window against which the shadows of the orange trees outside moved gently. Tomorrow, Juliet would arrive on the plane. Tomorrow the three of them, Juliet, Jarratt, herself, would be on their way to Coochin Brim-brim away out in the Never-Never. What hope would she have out there of ever finding Howdie Johnston? She didn't know, and yet she felt almost madly excited. It was as if something unknown were beckoning her on.

Jarratt Buchan didn't offer to take Nicky out to the airport with him the following morning, to meet Juliet.

'I can't give you the exact time we'll be leaving for Coochin Brim-brim,' he told her. He had come to her suite while she was still having breakfast. 'I shall take Juliet straight to the hospital to visit her sister, and I'll pick you up here later, some time before lunch. See that you're ready, won't you?' He glanced at her scattered belongings—jeans, shirts, yesterday's purchases, not yet packed—and the quizzical look on his face annoyed her intensely. At least she was dressed, and it wouldn't take her more than five minutes to pack up. 'Don't flit off to do more shopping—if you're short of country gear you can get some-

31

thing from the station store. Make sure you're wearing something suitable for driving through the dust, by the way—I don't have an air-conditioner in my car, and that pretty little thing you're wearing now won't look so fresh and nice after a few hours of dirt roads. We leave the bitumen just past the Red Lily petrol station—though of course that doesn't mean anything to you, does it?'

It did, but she didn't say so. She merely shrugged and buttered another piece of toast in a leisurely way. 'I'll be ready, Mr Buchan.'

He gave a quick frown. 'For God's sake—my name's Jarratt, and that's the name you'll use. Till later, then.' He turned abruptly and was gone.

Nicky finished her breakfast and did her packing. Deliberately, she kept on the 'pretty little thing' he had referred to so scathingly. It was a sleeveless ivory-coloured cotton with pale blue binding at the neck and armholes, and a short sleeved matching jacket. It was cool and comfortable, and it washed easily and dried in a flash, so ...

She left her luggage at the office, and decided to make one more effort to trace Cass and Howard. This time she went to the post office, and rather wondered why she hadn't thought of doing so before, particularly when, to her complete amazement, the man behind the counter told her promptly, 'Yeah, there's a Catherine Johnston out on one of the cattle stations.'

Nicky's heart beats quickened. 'Which cattle station is it, please? She's a friend of mine——'

'Coochin Brim-brim—that's four hundred, maybe four-fifty kilometres from Alice.'

Nicky could hardly believe her ears! It was fantastically impossible! What on earth could Cass be doing at Coochin Brim-brim?

'And Howard—Howard Johnston?' she asked.

The man shook his head. 'Sorry, miss. Can't recollect any mail going through for him.'

Nicky thanked him and stepped out into the sunny street feeling curious and elated and excited all at the same time. It seemed quite extraordinary that Cass should be at

Coochin Brim-brim. It was as if Fate had meant her to find the Johnstons. Walking back along Todd Street, she thought about Howdie; soon she would at least learn where he was and what he was doing, and whether there was a girl in his life. Suddenly she couldn't wait to be there, to see Cass again, to talk over all that had happened since last they met. Mixed in with her excitement was a little fear that they might have grown apart, be constrained with each other. Nicky had gone away from the foster-home to such a different life—the Johnstons might resent it. It was a disturbing thought.

She made her way slowly back to the motel, loitering on the way to look in shop windows, yet seeing nothing because she felt quite sick with apprehension. Even the sight of her reflection in a shop window bothered her. Did she look too different from the rather untidy child who had lived at Aunty Pat's and giggled with Cass, and made toffee in the kitchen or played french cricket with the children in the garden? Would Cass feel estranged? Would Howdie, if she should ever meet him again? Yet wasn't she the same girl—exactly the same girl—inside? Outwardly she *was* different. She had been playing a part ever since she had gone to Adelaide, and Jack had always provided money for suitable clothes when she went away on excursions during the school holidays. She always had the right things to wear for riding or swimming or skiing, or simply travelling. One of the teachers used to be deputised to take her shopping and no expense had been spared, though Claudia Mallard, supervising the purchase of a post-school wardrobe, had deplored the lack of flair. Actually Nicky was looking forward to wearing jeans and shirts—the clothes Guy had said he hoped she wouldn't become addicted to. And she rather wished she had changed into them before she packed. Perhaps it wasn't too late now—she didn't really want Cass to see her looking like a city girl.

But when she reached the motel Juliet was already there, waiting in the garden beyond the office.

The two girls greeted each other enthusiastically.

'It's great to see you, Nicky,' Juliet exclaimed, and

Nicky asked as they sat down in the shade, 'Where's Jarratt? I hope he's not looking for me—I didn't think you'd be here so early, and I don't want to be in trouble.'

Juliet grinned. 'It hasn't taken you long to catch on! Everyone's in trouble with Jarry unless they do exactly as he orders. But right now, he's gone to get the mail.'

Looking at her, Nicky thought she was thinner than she had been at school, and her grey-green eyes looked larger. Her long pale blonde hair floated down her back, giving her a fragile air. She wore a white hand-embroidered blouse with tiny sleeves, and a green skirt and sandals, apparel that was no more suited to an outback journey than was Nicky's dress. Nicky asked, 'How's your sister?'

'Oh, poor Tracy is really sick. That's why we didn't stay long at the hospital. The Sister said it was better to let her sleep. She was thrown by her horse, and she has broken ribs and pretty bad concussion and a lot of bruises. They had to get the ambulance out to Coochin to fly her in. I just can't think why she was riding at all—she doesn't like outback life any more than I do, with the hideous heat and dust and no one around except a lot of rough men.' She turned to smile at Nicky. 'Jarry said you and he met at the motel yesterday and had dinner together last night. You must know already how bossy he is. He just gets his own way about everything, no matter how—yet he talks about me being spoiled! He's like some atrocious he-man from the old pioneering days, isn't he? In looks, I mean.'

Nicky thought of Jarratt's dark brooding eyes, of the blackness of his jaw, of his dark-springy-looking hair, and she remembered with an inward tremor the feeling those eyes had given her of being a woman, a woman in danger——

'He's not a bit like you, Juliet,' she admitted. 'But we shan't see all that much of him, shall we? Won't he be out working most of the time?'

Juliet shrugged. 'I don't really know. Coochin Brim-brim is a place I avoid visiting all I can—a couple of weeks now and again during school vacations has been more than enough for me. I only ever came when I absolutely couldn't get out of it. All I know about Jarry is that he likes to order everyone around. I'm positive he could have managed without dragging me out here now, but he says I've been frittering away my time ever since I left school, and I can come to Coochin and learn what makes it all possible.' She tossed back her blonde hair frowningly. 'And wait till you hear how he interfered with my—my private life, in France! My mother's just so weak—she tells him everything that happens. She's afraid she'll be cut off without a penny or something if she doesn't—Jarry's been the head of the family ever since he was about twenty, when Father died, and left everything in his hands without reservation. Except the house in Adelaide—that's my mother's—and she does have a small personal income apart from what she gets from the cattle station.'

She jumped up suddenly. 'Here's Jarry now. We'd better go out to the car before he shouts for us.'

Nicky followed her towards the car that had pulled up outside the motel, then with a murmured explanation went into the office for her luggage. She reflected that for all her talk, Juliet evidently obeyed her brother, and probably held him in just as much awe as her mother did. She discovered that Jarratt had come to help her with her suitcase and handed it over to him.

'So you didn't change,' he remarked, his eyes flickering over her dress disparagingly. 'You're not going to impress anyone in that when you step out of the car at the end of the day.'

'I didn't think there was anyone to try to impress out in the Never-Never—except you,' Nicky retorted. 'And you wouldn't be impressed anyway.'

'I'm not going to take that up,' he said sardonically, 'not yet.' He gave her a half smile and a look from his dark eyes that made her wish she had held her tongue.

The two girls were relegated to the back seat in the station wagon—'That way, you can whisper to each other without dislocating your necks,' Jarratt said, 'and I shan't be bothered with your nattering.'

The arrangement suited Nicky very well, but actually

35

she and Juliet scarcely talked at all, and she rather suspected that Juliet's pose of apathy and boredom was intended to impress on her brother the sacrifice she was making in coming here at all. It was a bad situation when you had left school, Nicky reflected, to have to comply with disagreeable orders simply to make sure of being given your usual bread and butter. How would she herself react, she wondered, if Guy should try to push her into something against her will—if he should say, 'Right! Your allowance is withheld unless you do as I say.' She had nearly two years to wait before she turned twenty-one, though certainly she did have the little box of opals Jack had left her. Guy had said they were worth a packet, but he hadn't put a figure on the packet, and he hadn't offered to buy them from her.

'I wouldn't sell them,' Nicky thought, gazing out at the spinifex and the thick stands of mulga as they sped along the Stuart Highway. 'I'd get a job—take up nursing.' She might do that in any case, because she wasn't interested in living a useless social life, but while she was at school her main ambition had been, quite simply, to *belong* to someone. She had fully intended going to Coober Pedy to look after Jack in his dug-out home, although she knew he was dead set against it. It was 'no life for Iris West's daughter!' As well, she had wanted to find Howdie again; and perhaps marry him, she admitted to herself now.

And that brought her thoughts back to Cass.

She glanced at Juliet, whose eyes were closed and whose long lashes lay against the pallor of her skin. She did look washed out, and no wonder, for the heat was increasing as the day wore on and as they travelled north. At least on the bitumen they weren't bothered by dust, except occasionally when Jarratt had to pull the station wagon on to the red verge to let a cattle train pass, as he did now. He had tuned in the car radio to a programme of light music, and when the dust had subsided, Nicky looked out once more at the countryside. A few red termite mounds were dotted about among the desert oaks and mulgas, and low scrub, yellow-flowered, made a patch of colour against the rich red of the earth. To Nicky's eyes it looked utterly beautiful, and she was sorry that Juliet couldn't enjoy it as she was doing. There had been a succession of good seasons in the Centre, and the flamboyant reds and purples of the landscape were softened by unusually luxuriant plant life. When she had come this way with Guy two days ago she had been too preoccupied to feel thrilled, but now her blood pulsed with excitement and with a warm and deep love for this desert land in which soon she and Cass were to meet again.

By the time they reached the Red Lily Store, looking infinitely isolated at the side of the narrow highway, Nicky was feeling ravenous. Not so Juliet, who was really feeling the heat now, as the dew of perspiration on her forehead and upper lip showed. As Jarratt pulled up she opened her grey-green eyes, looked with dislike at the store and the petrol station, and said emphatically, 'Don't ask me if I'm hungry! I couldn't eat a thing—and decidedly not the stuff they'd serve up in that little dump. All I want is a cold, cold drink, but I don't suppose such a thing is available in this boiling hot place.'

Jarratt turned his back and walked off in the middle of her speech, and Nicky said sympathetically, 'Poor Juliet! But you'll get a cold drink—and there's a shady place to sit too, next to the store. Are you coming?'

Juliet didn't answer her smile. 'There'll be flies—besides which, I don't feel like putting up with my brother and his bloody-mindedness. I'll get out and stretch my legs presently, but I would appreciate it if you'd bring me a can of something cold.'

Nicky frowned. She wasn't all that keen on coping with Jarratt alone, and it wasn't really very fair of Juliet to be so sulky. She suggested reasonably, 'Can't you cheer up a bit and forget your grievances? After all, Tracy is in hospital, and someone has to take her place.'

'Someone doesn't,' Juliet retorted. 'There's a girl to mind the children, and there's Lena who's been practically running the homestead for years and years. Jarry's just throwing his weight around.'

Nicky shrugged resignedly. 'All right, I'm sorry. I'll see what I can get for you.'

Jarratt was already sitting in the outdoor eating place with its shady roof, but before joining him she went into the store where a woman, presumably Mrs Capper, served her and she was able to buy a carton of frozen orange juice which she took back to Juliet. She joined Jarratt at his table just as the little blonde she had spoken to the other day appeared with the lunch he had already ordered, the thonged sandals she was wearing flip-flopping as she crossed the beaten earth.

'I'm afraid it's not up to Adelaide fare,' Jarratt told Nicky dryly as she took the chair he pulled out for her.

'Now, fair go!' the little blonde girl protested cheerfully. 'If there's one thing I *can* make, it's a salad—and this is a super one.' She unloaded from her tray a large bowl of tropical salad and a platter of pink ham decorated with sprigs of crisp-looking parsley. Another bowl held bread rolls, and there was a small slab of butter.

'Did you get in touch with your friends?' she asked Nicky when everything had been set out on the table.

Nicky nodded. 'I'm right on their trail, thank you.'

'That's great.' The girl glanced at Jarratt. 'Tea?'

He nodded and she disappeared. He asked Nicky negligently, 'Whose trail are you on?'

More questions! This time she couldn't say, 'Nobody you'd know,' but she told him casually, 'Oh, just some people I knew in Alice.' She knew she had to resist or he would drag all her private life out of her. She helped herself to salad and buttered one of the rolls, then asked him a question.

'Don't you care whether Juliet has any lunch or not?'

'Why should I care? It's entirely up to her, isn't it? *I'm* hungry—and I can see you're hungry. But if Juliet isn't hungry, I'm not going to insist she should eat. I'm not quite such a bully as all that ... Where did you get to this morning, by the way? I told you to be ready.'

'I was ready when you were. I didn't keep you waiting. It

38

just happened I had some business to do in town, that's all.'

He didn't look as if he believed her. 'Did you get it done satisfactorily?'

'Yes, thank you.' She changed the subject. 'Juliet says her sister had a bad accident.'

'Bad—but not all that bad,' he conceded. 'It could have been a great deal worse.'

'I thought she didn't like riding——'

'You thought?' His brows rose. 'What would you know about it? You mean Juliet told you. I hope she didn't also suggest I might have cracked my whip and forced Tracy into the saddle.' Her eyes fell before his and she felt a fool—and disliked him for making her feel one. 'Tracy makes her own decisions,' he continued. 'Sometimes they're wrong ones, like thinking she could handle Smoke. And like marrying, at eighteen, a man she scarcely knew—against my advice. When her marriage fell to pieces, she came to seek refuge at Coochin Brim-brim. Did Juliet tell you that?'

'No,' Nicky said. She hadn't even known that Tracy's marriage had broken up. She asked lamely. 'How many children are there?'

'Two girls, Marcie-Ann and Medora. Bright as buttons and a lot noisier.'

'Who's looking after them?' The moment she asked, she knew the answer. Cass—of course! Cass had always liked children—she had wanted to be a teacher.

'A girl called Catherine Johnston,' Jarratt was saying. 'A very competent, very charming girl.'

Nicky wasn't sure why she didn't say at once, 'I know her,' but she didn't. And then she reasoned with herself it would mean too many explanations—confessions, even—on her part. Telling him things about herself that even Juliet didn't know. So she took another roll and said casually, 'She's young, of course.'

'About your age. A country girl, who's used to the outback.'

Nicky had a ridiculous and almost uncontrollable impulse to ask, 'Is she pretty?', because Cass had been pretty. A little bit plump, with long straight light brown hair, a wide mouth and a habit of smiling with a sort of expectant innocence in her shining hazel eyes. She didn't ask, of course, and Jarratt elaborated of his own accord, 'The kids are safe with her. She has a load of good honest common sense.'

She hadn't always had a lot of *that*. She had been a dreamer, a romantic. Nicky remembered her saying once, with a faraway look in her eyes, 'If I could have three wishes—you know what they'd be, Nicky? I'd wish to have blue eyes, like yours. And to fly—all by myself, you know, so everyone would look up and see me and stare, and marvel. And the third wish—I haven't quite finished making that up yet. Something about love and getting married, though.'

'Oh, heavens,' Nicky thought now, 'it will be good to see Cass again!'

She asked Jarratt, 'We'll be leaving the bitumen soon, won't we?'

'Very shortly,' he agreed, his dark eyes glinting. 'Are you looking forward to it?'

She was, as a matter of fact, dust and bumps and all, but he wouldn't believe her if she said so.

'Should I be?' she asked with raised eyebrows. He answered her with a crooked smile and she reflected that his teeth were excellent—and that he didn't smile often enough for the fact to be appreciated. Not at her, at any rate . . .

The little Capper girl reappeared with cups and a pot of tea and the query, 'Anything else you'd like?'

'I think we're right for nourishment, thanks, Shirley. How's your father today? Is his back still bad?'

'Yes, it's really crook. He's all twisted up.' She stood with her arms folded and her feet apart. She was wearing shorts and she had no qualms about showing her rather chunky, muscly legs. Her blonde hair was tied back at each side of her face, and she wore no make-up at all, and she was enjoying talking to Jarratt Buchan. Nicky reached for the teapot and poured two cups of tea.

40

'What we need at this place,' Shirley said, 'is another man. Able-bodied. But we can't run to it. I'm pretty competent and I can manage the petrol and all that, but we do need a man.'

Nicky was watching her as she spoke, and she suddenly saw that it was only her smallness that made her appear so young. She was probably eighteen or so. She glanced at Jarratt and he was looking at Shirley too—exactly the way he had looked at Nicky. He was looking at a woman, and Shirley was enjoying it.

'Oh, blow!' she exclaimed. 'There's someone wanting petrol. See you!' She raised her hand and flitted off.

'Bright girl, that,' said Jarratt. 'Not afraid of a bit of hard work, either.' He picked up his cup and drank his tea down without drawing breath. The thought entered Nicky's head, '*She* doesn't need to be thrown in the creek. That treatment's strictly for girl's like Juliet and me!'

'Something's amusing you,' the man opposite her remarked. 'I won't ask you what it is. That's a very private little smile you're wearing.'

'Is it?' Nicky felt colour come into her cheeks. 'I'm surprised you aren't asking. You generally do, don't you? Ask questions, I mean.'

He was pouring himself another cup of tea. 'When they're relevant. In this case they're not. And as I said, your thoughts looked very private.'

Her flush deepened. What on earth did he imagine went on in her head? She said carelessly, 'They weren't private, as a matter of fact. I was just thinking that Shirley Capper and Cass—Catherine Johnston are apparently two girls you wouldn't like to throw in the creek.'

'What the devil are you talking about?' he asked, pausing with his cup halfway to his lips.

'Juliet and me. Didn't you have ideas of grabbing our clothes and making us swim for it? There was some lesson girls like us have to learn——'

'Oh, I see.' He smiled very faintly, his dark eyes regarding her broodingly from over his cup, and she felt again that strange sensation spreading out from her being, down

41

her spine and along her limbs, and she stared back at him for a long moment before flicking down her lashes defensively.

'Well,' he said matter-of-factly, 'if you've finished you can go back to the car and I'll get hold of some ice creams. That way, Juliet won't starve to death.'

They were on their way again very soon after that and after about ten or fifteen minutes they turned off the bitumen on to a red road, and the uncomfortable part of the journey had begun. It was some time since the road had been graded and as well the dust was bad.

'This isn't my idea of fun,' Juliet muttered, then raising her voice asked her brother why he didn't have a plane. 'Then I wouldn't have to endure this specific form of torture.'

'When I marry will be time enough for an expense of that kind,' he told her, and Juliet said, 'I hope it will be soon.' After that, she relapsed into silence and Nicky became absorbed in the scenery and in her own thoughts. She noticed that the termite mounds here were bigger, and some of them, she thought fancifully, looked like sculptured figures of Buddha. The land was low and swelling, sometimes open and parklike, with mulga trees standing deep in the pale spiky spinifex grass that from the car had a deceptively plushy look. Galahs and green and yellow shell parrots flew up from the sides of the road in hundreds, and now and then there were cattle to be seen among the trees.

Juliet had closed her eyes to it all once more, but Nicky watched and dreamed, half stunned by the heat, and seeing everything through the dust that curled up and floated about them like red smoke as the car rolled on. In the front seat Jarratt Buchan concentrated on driving, or perhaps he was listening to the radio or thinking about his cattle. At all events, he didn't make any effort to converse. The road was a purplish red and sharp black shadows from low trees lay across it as stark as splashes of paint. The thought came to Nicky that she had lived in country like this before, perhaps in those two years when Jack had worked as a stockman after her parents had died. She didn't remember a thing about those years, except perhaps—perhaps little black children and red sand——

Nicky opened her eyes and discovered she had been asleep and dreaming, and the afternoon had nearly gone. Lovely desert grevilleas, golden-flowered, dark-branched, floated on the pale sea of the spinifex and all along the roadside there were wild hops in flower. She exclaimed impulsively, seeing Juliet had her eyes open at last, 'It's beaut-looking country, isn't it, Juliet? All those marvellous reds, and the yellow flowers.'

Juliet shrugged. 'It doesn't do a single thing for me.'

Jarratt switched the radio off and said distinctly, 'You have a closed mind, Juliet. It's a pity your mother decided to live in Adelaide. If you'd spent more of your childhood here you'd have had a sense of belonging.'

'It's too late for that,' said Juliet pettishly.

'Well, don't think your moaning and moping and mooning about are going to persuade me to send you back to Adelaide. You're unemployed and unemployable as far as the big world is concerned, but you can make yourself useful in Coochin Brim-brim, with Tracy in hospital. It's high time you learned something about the cattle station that pays for your comfort—and that was for many years your father's home.' He paused and Nicky saw his dark eyes glaring at Juliet in the rear-vision mirror.

'You should have lived in Victorian times, Jarry,' Juliet said. 'Then you could have pushed the womenfolk around all you liked without them uttering a sound. Though you do your best now, don't you? First Tracy, now me. You'll be starting on Nicky next.'

Jarratt ignored that and merely remarked, 'You can enjoy yourself at Coochin if you give your mind to it.'

'So could the pig enjoy the pepper,' Juliet retorted, and Nicky couldn't help laughing—which drew Jarratt's attention to her.

He asked suddenly as the car bounced through flying red dust on a particularly rough stretch of road, 'What have *you* been doing since you left school, Nichola?—while my

43

young sister's been in France falling violently in love with someone else's fiancé?'

'I've been watching my guardian die,' said Nicky, and as soon as she'd spoken wished she had kept quiet.

'Oh, my God——' she heard him mutter. Then, 'I apologise.'

'It's all right,' she said evenly. 'I didn't ever get to know him terribly well—it was something I'd hoped to do when school was over.'

'I'm sorry about that,' he said sombrely. 'You really could have told me about it before—you had the opportunity. It might help in future if you dispensed with at least a little of your reticence. We're going to be fairly closely associated with each other during the next few weeks, and communication's important when you live in the outback.'

Nicky edged into the corner of the seat so she wouldn't have to meet his eyes in the rear-vision mirror. Reticence was part of her nature, and she was by no means ready to confide in Jarratt Buchan. She felt, for some reason, more wary of him than she had ever felt of anyone in her life. It was on her conscience at this minute that she hadn't told him she knew Catherine Johnston, but she wasn't going to confess to that now. She would work it out with Cass later—after all, how did she know what Cass had chosen to tell her employer about her past? She and Cass had always understood each other anyhow. They had been united by their solitariness, their uncertainty as to whether or not the world wanted them.

She sighed a little and glanced at her watch.

'How long before we reach the homestead—Jarratt?' His name didn't come easily to her lips, but she forced herself to say it.

'We shan't arrive till dark. This road doesn't lend itself to high speeds, and I don't want to shake you girls out of your skins.'

'We're already covered in dust,' Juliet complained. 'I hope we can get a hot shower when we arrive. Or shall I have to put on Lena's apron and stoke up the stove and cook dinner? Because I warn you, I can't cook.'

44

'I'm aware of that, but at least you'll have a chance to learn while you're here. Lena will have cooked dinner to-night, and you can take your turn tomorrow. As well, you can start getting yourself clued up on a few of the things you should have learned to do at home.'

'When you're studying, you don't have a lot of time,' Juliet retorted.

'That would sound more convincing if you'd distin-guished yourself scholastically,' he answered dryly.

'Everyone can't be intellectual. I was good at Art and French, anyhow.'

'Oh, French, of course! And what were your pet sub-jects, Nichola?'

'I coped with most of them,' Nicky said, flushing, 'I was very mediocre. Why do you ask?' she said daringly.

'You rouse my curiosity,' he said sardonically.

It was practically dark when at last, after crossing several cattle grids, they came in sight of the station buildings. The homestead lay not far from the bank of a long waterhole, and away beyond it, across a plain where spinifex showed palely and isolated trees made dark shadows, there was a line of low flat-topped hills against the horizon. An empty world. The car headlights flashed over the white limbs of a beautiful ghost gum, then dipped as they crossed the wide sandy bed of a creek. River red gums lined the bank, but they were left behind as the car continued on towards the homestead, half hidden in its garden and sheltered by tall trees. Further ahead were cottages and a few lights, but there was not a soul to be seen as Jarratt pulled up at the end of the homestead drive.

Nicky, full of an inner excitement, looked expectantly towards the long low house with its grey roof as she climbed, somewhat stiff-limbed, from the car in Juliet's wake.

CHAPTER THREE

'WITH Tracy in hospital we have to do without a reception committee,' Jarratt remarked. He took some of the luggage and went ahead into the house while the girls followed.

It was an old house, Nicky noted, with a comfortable air of blending in with its surroundings. The floors were of polished wood, and there was a long carpet runner down the hall through which Jarratt escorted them.

'You can use these two rooms. Quite possibly there's only one bed made up, I couldn't be sure, but there are plenty of sheets in the linen closet.' He set down their suitcases and added, 'I'll get the rest of your gear after I've let Lena know we're three and not two. Don't take more than fifteen minutes, will you?'

Nicky and Juliet looked inside the bedrooms, switching on the lights to do so. Both rooms were airy and spacious, with doors opening on to the verandah. One room was predominantly green, the other blue, and while the furnishings were tasteful and adequate they were far from sumptuous.

Juliet grimaced. 'Which cell will you have, Nicky?'

'Oh, Juliet, they're hardly cells! With some flowers and a few pictures on the walls and—and one's personal possessions about, they'd be lovely rooms ... I'll have the blue one, if that's all right with you.'

'Perfectly.' Juliet slid her suitcase across the polished floor. 'If we only have fifteen minutes, we'll have to make do with a wash till after dinner, I suppose.' She looked at herself in the mirror. 'I look as big a mess as you—we're both dressed in pink!' She giggled a little and Nicky felt relieved that she was cheering up. 'I'll see you later in the dining room. The bathroom's just along the hall, by the way.'

In her blue room, Nicky stripped off her dusty dress and ran her fingers through her hair, reflecting that it could certainly do with a wash. She was standing in her bra and half-slip looking round for a bath towel when someone knocked on the half closed door, and Jarratt's dark-jawed face appeared.

'Here's the rest of your luggage,' he said, his eyes flicking over her half-clad body quite openly. She looked back at him feeling as if she were naked, then moved quickly away from the mirror, turning her back on him. He had no manners, she thought—he could have begged her pardon and disappeared instead of standing staring at her.

She stammered out, 'I—I don't think I have a towel. And do you make a habit of coming into guests' bedrooms while they're undressing?'

'I haven't thought about it,' he said, and she could imagine the mockery in his eyes. 'But you're pretty well covered. Besides which, I thought it was the city girls who had the broad minds and liberated ideas. Haven't you caught up with that set yet?'

'No, I haven't,' she said coldly. 'Could I please have a towel?'

'That's something Juliet should have seen to,' he commented.

He disappeared to her relief, and she had slipped into her dressing gown when a hand holding a large blue bath towel appeared round the door and Jarratt's voice said. 'Here we are, Miss Nichola Reay. Is this what you want?'

'Thank you.' Nicky moved across to take it. She pulled the door open and walked past him, and he said after her, 'The bathroom's on your left.'

It was a big disappointment not to find Cass in the dining room when, much refreshed, but still conscious of her dulled dusty hair, she went in to dinner. Juliet hadn't yet put in an appearance, but Jarratt, his jaw shaved, his hair damp, rose from the table until she was seated, and almost immediately Lena came in with a large casserole dish which she placed on a mat in front of Jarratt. She was a plump, cheerful-looking aboriginal woman with a round dark face and bright eyes, and she wore a short-sleeved blue cotton overall.

'This is Lena, Nicky,' Jarratt said. 'Lena—Nicky's a friend of Juliet's.'

'Hello, Nicky,' Lena said with a wide smile that showed her white teeth. Nicky smiled back at her. Sometimes, at the foster-home in Alice, there had been aboriginal children, and she felt she had been used to them all her life. Lena disappeared, and Jarratt took the lid off the casserole.

'If you'd come out earlier, I'd have offered you a gin or a sherry or whatever your favourite tipple is,' he told Nicky.

'That's all right, I don't have a favourite tipple.'

'No? I'm sure Juliet's become addicted to some exotic aperitif since her sojourn in France ... Are you going to have some beef and vegetables?'

'Yes, please.'

He proceeded to serve her a portion, remarking that they wouldn't wait for Juliet, who was quite likely to have no appetite anyhow. They were sitting before two steaming plates of food when Juliet joined them, saying predictably, 'Just give me a very small amount, Jarry. I'm not hungry—it's too hot.'

They ate in silence, all of them tired, Nicky supposed. It wasn't a very tasty meal—Lena was certainly no cook—but Nicky ate out of politeness and because she was hungry. 'Where are the children?' she asked presently. 'And—and Catherine?'

Juliet stared. 'Who on earth's Catherine? Is she the girl who looks after the children?'

'She is,' Jarratt said. 'But as from tomorrow you'll be doing your share of that. The children are sleeping in Catherine's bungalow tonight, Lena tells me, so she can keep an eye on them while she does her study.'

'What study?' Juliet asked the question that was on Nicky's lips too.

'Catherine's sitting for her final school examination at the end of the year. She didn't finish her schooling and she wants to train to be a teacher. So she studies. So you will help with the children,' he finished.

Juliet didn't look at all pleased. 'That's the weirdest thing I ever heard! You mean I've been summoned all this way just so the—the nursemaid or governess or whatever she is can *study*, instead of doing what she's paid to do?'

Jarratt's frown was forbidding. 'That's quite enough, Juliet. You're here for your own good.'

'I'm here for *Catherine's* good,' Juliet cried with hostility in her grey-green eyes. 'Now I know why you insisted I should come back from France with Mother——'

'Now calm down, Juliet. You know that's not true. Tracy hadn't fallen off her horse at that stage, so just don't get carried away by your sense of injustice.'

'It *is* unjust,' Juliet insisted unrepentantly. 'You've got Lena to cook for you'—she made a face, showing plainly her opinion of Lena's cooking—'there's someone here whose special job it is to look after the children—and now, as well as me, poor Nicky's been dragged into it.'

Jarratt looked both exasperated and amused. He turned his dark eyes on Nicky. Very much aware of it, she tried not to look back, but to go on eating her dinner. But for some reason or other she finally had to meet his gaze, and they exchanged a long and searching glance, during which her cheeks flushed slowly to a deep crimson. She hoped Juliet didn't notice, and was pretty sure she didn't because she was now angrily buttering a slice of home-baked bread.

Finally Jarratt said softly, 'If you feel you've been dragged into something, you're quite free to go—Nicky.' She flinched at the soft drawling way he said her name, giving it an entirely new sound. 'Actually, I had the idea it suited you to come here, though it didn't appear to suit your—guardian, in Alice Springs.'

'It—it suited us both,' she stammered, not knowing what he was getting at. 'And I don't feel I've been dragged into anything, Juliet.'

'Well, you have,' Juliet insisted. 'We're obviously going to have a couple of little kids on our hands all the time.'

'You're exaggerating,' Jarratt said with restraint. 'Why don't you try, for a change, to think of this as your home—a home where you naturally share in the activities and the duties? Catherine won't thrust her charges on you unduly, I assure you. She's a most conscientious and agreeable girl.'

And a charming one too, Nicky remembered, while Juliet muttered rebelliously, 'She'd better be!'

None of them lingered at the table once Lena had brought in the tea. Jarratt rose, excused himself and disappeared, and Juliet said she would have a shower and go to bed.

'I know I should offer you first go, Nicky, but I'm so dead tired! Arguing with Jarry just wears me down—as well as the heat. I shan't be long, I promise.'

'Don't hurry on my account,' Nicky said with a smile. She reflected that all the arguing had made her tired too, and she hadn't even seen Cass! She wondered if she should go to the kitchen and help Lena with the dishes, but she thought she could hear Jarratt's voice coming from that direction. After a moment she went to her room, where she discovered on turning back the quilt that her bed was made up. She took her pyjamas from her suitcase, switched on the reading light and stood in the middle of the room feeling restless and uncertain. Across the verandah and beyond the garden, she could see lights shining. Cass's bungalow must be over there, and suddenly she knew she couldn't wait any longer.

She went through to the verandah, ran down the steps and across the dark garden. There was no moon yet, but the stars were bright, and for a few seconds she stood staring upwards. Outside the garden she moved along the track and into the trees amid shadows that were suddenly dark and confusing. She no longer felt sure that she would find Cass here—these bungalows might belong to the men. A dog began to bark, and her heart thudded. The sensible thing to have done would have been to ask Jarratt where Cass's bungalow was—to tell him they knew each other, and now it was too late.

Ahead of her, she saw a man come on to the verandah of one of the bungalows. He wore nothing but a pair of trousers, and she stood stock still, feeling herself an intruder. When he called out in a pleasant educated voice,

'Who's there?' she didn't answer, She waited till he had gone inside again and then, feeling defeated, she turned back towards the homestead.

She had almost reached the verandah, and her nostrils were filled with the sweet and indefinable scents of the night, when she saw Jarratt Buchan at the top of the steps. 'Damn,' she thought. 'More questions!'

'Don't tell me we have a night owl on our hands,' he remarked as she came up the steps.

'What do you mean?' She paused and looked up at him, her breath a little uneven, though she felt relieved he hadn't shot out the question she had been expecting—'Where have you been?'

'Do you only begin to come alive around nine o'clock at night?' he elucidated.

'No. But you told me last night one should take a walk after dinner. You can't have it both ways.'

'You have me there,' he said with a grin. 'Who did you see?'

'No one,' she said promptly. 'Not even the man in the moon.'

'Heaven help me! Am I going to have two defiant creatures on my hands? I mistakenly imagined that you at least were a little mature.'

'I'm sorry,' Nicky said with a sigh, 'it's just that your questions bother me. I'm just not used to anyone taking such an—interest, in what I do—what I think.'

'Pity,' he said.

She began to move past him, murmuring, 'Goodnight.'

'Sleep well,' he said. 'Do you want to come out with me in the morning?'

The question came as a surprise, and she answered quickly, thinking of Cass, 'I'd rather just poke around, thank you.'

He shrugged and smiled wryly, and she saw that she had fallen into a trap. 'Go ahead then. It's more or less what I expected of a friend of Juliet's.'

She sighed inwardly and didn't protest that she wouldn't want to 'poke round' every day—that, in fact, she would like to go out with him some time and see what went on on a big cattle station. He probably wouldn't ask her again.

Looking up at him, she felt him uncomfortably close. In imagination she could see the expression in his eyes very clearly—and she reminded herself that it had been there, too, when he had looked at Shirley Capper.

'Goodnight,' she said again, and this time she got past him.

Cass was there in the morning. 'The boss' had gone out in the utility, Lena told Nicky cheerfully, and Juliet was still in bed—'having her brekfus on a tray'. But on the end of one of the side verandahs, two small girls and Cass sat at breakfast at a table covered by a bright green and white checked cloth.

'*Nicky!*'

Cass got up from her place at the table unsteadily, staring as if she couldn't believe her eyes.

'Lena said someone called Nicky had come with Juliet— but I didn't imagine even for an instant that it would be you. Oh—I can't believe it! How did it happen? Did you know I was here? Sit down and tell me everything.'

Nicky took a chair and laughed and sipped her glass of orange juice, and then the two of them looked at each other for half a minute without saying a word.

Cass, Nicky thought, was reassuringly the same—yet different. Still a tiny bit plump, still with long straight brown hair, still with the same clear honest hazel eyes, and wide wistful mouth. But she looked older than Nicky had expected, and there was a sort of maturity about her, even dressed as she was in blue jeans and orange and blue checked shirt. Nicky's shirt and jeans were brand new and looked it, and she felt self-conscious about them and wondered what impression Cass was gaining. She glanced at the two little girls who were staring at her, their faces sticky with toast and jam.

'You haven't met the children,' Cass said. 'This is Marcie-Ann, who is six and is a pupil at the School of the Air. And this is Medora, with the curly hair. Tell Nicky how old you are, pet.'

'Free! And I can count! One, two, three——'

'Later, darling,' Cass interrupted with a loving smile—exactly the smile she used to give the small children in the fosterhome—and how they had adored her, Nicky remembered! 'If you've had enough to eat, you can both go and play in the yard while Nicky and I drink our coffee.' They scrambled off their chairs and made for the steps, and she called after them, 'Now mind—don't go out of the garden!'

When they had gone, Nicky asked, 'Cass, where's Howdie?'

'Out at the muster. Oh, won't he be excited when he finds you're here! You're going to stay awhile, aren't you?' Cass asked anxiously.

Nicky could hardly answer. Howard was out at the muster!—here on Coochin Brim-brim!

'Cass, you can't mean Howdie's here—right here—on this very cattle station! It's like a dream—I just can't believe it.'

'Neither can I,' Cass agreed. 'To think we've met up again after all these years! I never thought I'd see you again after that rich old relative of yours came and spirited you away.'

'He wasn't a rich old relative. He was my guardian,' Nicky started to explain.

Cass interrupted, 'Your hair's gone dark—it's darker than mine.'

'That's since I had it cut short.'

Cass's hazel eyes were on her, curious yet loving. 'I always wanted blue eyes like yours. Do you remember?'

Nicky nodded. 'And you wanted to fly——'

'I've become reconciled to having neither of those wishes come true. And Nicky, do you remember the fairytale Aunty Pat used to tell us about the two vain princesses whose plaits were braided together by a wicked fairy, so neither of them could get free to go to the king's feast and meet the handsome prince? You always said you'd let someone cut off your hair so I could go, if it were you and I——'

'And you said the same,' laughed Nicky. 'And do you

remember the little glass Cinderella slipper you got out of a Christmas cracker——'

'I still wear it round my neck.' Cass fished down the neck of her shirt and produced it.

'Oh, all the things there are to remember!' Nicky exclaimed. 'When will Howdie be back? I just can't wait to see him!'

'I've no idea. They only went out three days ago. It will be weeks—this is a huge place. You'd have to ask Jarry, though.'

'Jarry? Do you call him that?'

'Why not? He expects me to.' Cass coloured faintly. 'Isn't he the most generous, friendly man you ever met, Nicky? He's been absolutely wonderful to me and Howdie—and we looked such tramps when we turned up here, asking for work.'

Nicky didn't answer directly. She certainly hadn't seen Jarratt Buchan in that particular light, she saw him more through Juliet's eyes, perhaps, and she was inclined to think Cass must be just as romantic as ever she had been.

Cass got up and began to stack up the dishes. 'I have about half an hour before the School of the Air session. Shall we go into the garden and talk? Or do you want to wait around for Juliet?'

Nicky pushed back her chair. She hadn't yet told the Buchans that she already knew Cass, but she brushed that thought aside as something to be dealt with later, and soon she and Cass were sitting under the pepper trees while the children built castles out of a heap of river sand.

'You've probably had an exciting time since last we met,' Cass said, 'different from us. And you look kind of—elegant.'

Nicky frowned, not sure that she liked this. 'I haven't had an exciting time really. It was mostly school. And Jack—my guardian—died last month in hospital.'

'Oh, Nicky, I *am* sorry. Then you're all on your own again.'

'In a way. Except I have a new guardian now, mostly to—to administer the money Jack left me.'

Cass listened wide-eyed. 'I suppose you're quite rich and could do anything you liked—go to Europe, see all those old castles and cathedrals and historic places.'

'I'd have to get Guy's permission first—and he probably wouldn't give it,' said Nicky lightly, feeling embarrassed. 'Anyhow, I'd far sooner be here with you and Howard.'

'You were sort of in love with Howdie, weren't you?' Cass said. 'I know he thought you were wonderful—he's hardly looked at another girl since you went, either. I used to make up stories with happy endings—you and Howdie would be married and I'd find someone too—and now it's all beginning to come true.'

Nicky laughed a little. Cass's imagination had always been inclined to run away with her strangely enough, for in many ways she was a very practical girl, perhaps because she had had to be. At least she never let circumstances get her down—she had always made the best of things.

'Anyhow,' Cass went on, laughing too, 'go on about school and all that. Was it fun? Did you have marvellous holidays with—with Jack?'

'I hardly saw him at all. I used to be sent away to riding school, things like that. I was lonely, Cass. I missed you and Howdie. I used to cry myself to sleep some nights, the girls at boarding school were—well, so different from me. I wrote to you, but you didn't answer.'

'I never got your letter,' said Cass, appalled. 'We were shifted about a lot after you went. Aunty Pat left and there were new cottage parents, real mean ones. We weren't allowed in the sitting room to watch TV—and we couldn't make pikelets or toffee in the kitchen like you and I used to do. After a while we were moved to another home and—well, it wasn't bad, but Howdie got fed up and decided we'd clear out, and so we did.'

'You didn't finish school?'

'I couldn't! I'd have had to stay on by myself, and I wanted to stick to Howdie. He bought an old motor-bike with the money he'd earned doing odd jobs around the town after school, and we went bush. We got jobs all over the place—mostly on cattle stations. Howdie did fencing or tank building or digging dams or serving petrol—anything at all.'

'And what did you do, Cass?' Nicky asked, aware of how different from theirs her life had been. No wonder Jarratt thought she and Juliet were soft!

'Oh, I cooked—minded kids—did sewing or mending. It was hard sometimes, but we got along. Now it's different. We've been really lucky. Jarry Buchan said he'd give us both a chance when we turned up here early in the year. He was so *kind*. He asked a lot of questions——'

'He's certainly good at that,' Nicky agreed, and Cass gave her a puzzled look.

'Oh well, he had a right to ask questions. I mean, you don't take two strangers practically into your home without finding out something about them. Not that we told him everything, Howdie said we didn't want to make it sound like a sob story. Anyhow, Jarry gave him a job as a stockman, and he said I could help Tracy with the children. I don't think she's terribly strong,' she explained naïvely, 'and she feels the heat. As well, he said it would be a good idea for me to do correspondence lessons and sit for exams at the end of the year. I've been really happy here. The only thing I wish is that Howdie could work up to being independent. That's what he wants most of all, and we've been saving every cent we can. So that's us,' she said with a smile, then leaned over and picked up Nicky's left hand. 'You're not engaged, are you, Nicky?'

'No.'

Cass frowned thoughtfully. 'You liked Howard a lot, didn't you? But I suppose things are different now. I mean, we still have nothing, and you're friends with people like the Buchans.'

'It doesn't make any difference,' Nicky protested. 'How can you imagine it would, Cass—ever?'

Cass shrugged and glanced back at the house. 'I haven't met Juliet yet. I thought it best to keep out of the way last night, though if I'd known you were coming, I'd have been waiting on the verandah!'

'I looked for you,' Nicky confessed. 'I went to some

56

buildings along the track, where there were lights, and a man with no shirt on came on to the verandah and called out, and I was scared.'

'Oh, Nicky, that was only Lewis Trent. He teaches the aboriginal children on the property, and he helped me with my lessons while Jarry was away. You'll like him.'

There was a slight pause, then Nicky said, 'I didn't tell the Buchans I knew you, Cass. You probably won't understand, but—I've never said anything to Juliet about living in Alice or the foster-home and all that part of my life. Jack told me I wasn't to talk, that I had to make a new start and forget the past. I couldn't do that, of course, but I didn't talk, and now explanations are going to be pretty complicated.'

'Why make them, then?' Cass asked sensibly. 'Don't think you have to do so on my account. It's nobody's business but our own whether we met here or somewhere else. Not that it would matter if the whole story came out, if Juliet's anything like Jarry. He'd take it all for granted. He judges people on what they are themselves.'

And what he doesn't know he guesses, and often guesses wrongly, thought Nicky wryly. 'If it comes up,' she decided aloud, 'I'll talk about it. But not otherwise.'

'Agreed,' said Cass with a smile.

Cass and Juliet met later in the morning. To Nicky's discomfiture, Juliet was offhand and not very friendly, probably because she considered Catherine was partly to blame for the fact that she had been 'dragged' out to Coochin Brim-brim. Cass devoted herself to the children all the morning, and after lunch—for which Jarry did not come home—they were sent to have a rest. Usually Cass then got on with her study, but today she introduced Nicky and Juliet to Lewis Trent, the schoolteacher. He was a brown-faced, brown-eyed young man in his late twenties, good-looking, mature and quiet. He was going off somewhere in a rather battered-looking car, and he didn't invite anyone to come with him.

As the three girls went back to the house in the hot sun, Juliet remarked caustically, 'He's not exactly sociable, is

57

he? You'd think he'd have asked me and Nicky if we'd like to go for a drive. Where's he off to, anyhow?'

'Probably to talk to some of the aboriginals,' Cass said. 'Or he might be going down to the cool of the creek bank to work. He only has school in the mornings, and he's writing a thesis for his doctorate. It's about the aborigines. He's made a study of them, in the Kimberleys and in Darwin, and now here, on a cattle station.'

'He sounds as if he'd be an intellectual bore,' Juliet said unkindly. 'It's just as well he didn't ask us to go along with him. I don't want to talk to the blacks.'

Cass said nothing and neither did Nicky.

That afternoon, while Cass studied—'The place is a hive of industry, isn't it?' Juliet commented sarcastically— the other two girls decided to take a swim in the waterhole. They were about to set out when Lena appeared to tell them with a cheerful smile that showed her big white teeth, 'Jarry says you going to cook tonight, Juliet. He doesn't go much on my cooking and Tracy—sometimes she's not much better. Those girls, Noreen and Daisy—they'll peel the veg'ables. Catherine and Lewis, they'll have dinner here too.'

'I see,' said Juliet faintly. It was all she did say until she and Nicky were out of earshot, and then she burst out explosively, 'Did you ever hear anything like that? What on earth are we going to do? I haven't the remotest idea how to cook dinner for—five people. Jarry's mad! He knows perfectly well I've never done any cooking in my life.' She flipped at the flies with her towel, her fair face flushed with annoyance.

'Don't worry, Juliet,' Nicky soothed. 'We'll manage. I can cook a bit. Claudia Mallard taught me when I stayed with her in Adelaide this year. All we need do is get back from our swim in time to see what there is in the fridge.'

'If there is a fridge,' said Juliet—though she knew very well there was.

They had their swim. The waterhole was pleasant and shady, with river red gums ranked along its sides, but all the same Juliet's nose got sunburned and Nicky's freckles multiplied.

When they got back, Lena had already lit the oven, and Nicky prepared the roast of beef, seasoning it with mustard and brown sugar in the way Claudia had taught her, before putting it in the oven. Cass was already giving the children their meal on the verandah, and Daisy and Noreen were peeling potatoes and cutting up pumpkin. There were fresh beans that didn't need stringing, too, from the vegetable garden. Dessert? Nicky found some cream that had gone sour, and a tin of cherries. She soaked the cherries in a little brandy, then later added the cream, and that was it.

Juliet lounged around the kitchen helplessly, protesting, 'I'm not sure I should let you do this, Nicky. It might teach Jarry a lesson if there just wasn't any dinner. Only,' she added thoughtfully, 'I don't want to start a row and be made to look a fool in front of the nursemaid and the schoolteacher, whatever his name is.'

'Lewis Trent,' Nicky supplied, putting the dessert in the huge refrigerator and reflecting that she was acting as if this were *her* home rather than Juliet's. 'Didn't you think he looked rather nice? He must be clever too, from what Catherine said.'

'Then Catherine's welcome to him,' Juliet said indifferently. 'Anyone who *chooses* to work out here is past my comprehension.'

When Jarry came home, Nicky was alone on the verandah. Cass was putting the children to bed and Juliet had gone to her room to change for dinner. 'Not for anyone's benefit but my own, and because I like to change for dinner,' she assured Nicky. Nicky had carried a jug of fresh orange and lemon juice through to the verandah and was sitting in one of the big armchairs of fine split rattan, sipping her drink and cooling down after the heat of the kitchen. Tomorrow morning, she decided, she was going to take a look at the garden, and maybe do a spot of weeding and watering. Daisy and Noreen did sweeping and dusting and washing, but she didn't think anyone attended to the garden. Probably when Tracy was here she did that. She

59

wondered, as she gazed out across the garden that was softly hazed with the light of sunset, how long it would be before the muster was over, and whether there was any chance of her getting out to it to see Howard. If she had known earlier that he was working here, she would have given Jarry a different answer last night when he had asked her if she wanted to come out with him.

The wire screen door banged, and Jarry came on to the verandah. He saw her immediately and came towards her, looking the complete husky outback male in dark shirt and narrow-legged drill trousers that emphasised his lean hips.

'Well, how did the poking round work out, Nicky?' The cultured voice was at such odds with his roughness, his unshavenness, that she was almost shocked. His dark eyes roved over her sardonically, as she sat sipping her drink, and she had no doubt he saw her as the spoiled and protected girl keeping well clear of all the harsher aspects of a remote cattle station.

'It worked out very well, thank you,' she said coolly, though she felt far from cool under his scrutiny. She moved nervously, reaching out to put her glass on the cane table. 'Juliet and I got around to meeting Lewis Trent—and of course Catherine. And this afternoon we went for a swim.'

'I guessed as much,' he said with a grin. He had poured himself a drink, and he lounged, big and masculine, on the tropical couch, his legs stretched out in front of him, his dusty boots in evidence. 'How are you enjoying the birds and the bush and the quiet?'

'They're fine,' she said.

'And the sun? You appear to have acquired a few more freckles.'

'Do I?' She wished she could control the quick colour that came into her cheeks. 'Well, that doesn't matter, and anyhow, the sun doesn't bother me.'

'Take care you respect it, all the same. It has a power that's not to be taken lightly.'

'Oh, I know—dehydrated travellers and all that,' she said flippantly.

He frowned at her tone and asked abruptly, 'Where's

Juliet? Because I'm damned sure she's not in the kitchen.'

'Not now. But she has been.' Nicky assured him, her eyes glinting with malicious triumph.

'She has? Then God help us all.' He got up. 'I suppose I must make myself civilised, seeing I'm to dine with three beautiful girls.'

The quality of the dinner surprised him. He complimented Juliet, but asked no awkward questions, and Juliet accepted his praise blandly, with an offhand, 'Oh well, Nicky and I got together——'

Afterwards, when Lewis had gone to his bungalow and Cass had gone to fetch her books so that Jarratt could explain some mathematical problem that had been bothering her, Jarrett asked his sister, 'Did you manage that dinner all with the aid of a cookbook? There must be more power than I thought in the written word—or else I've been underestimating your abilities. You'll make some man a good wife after all.'

'Not if you have your way,' said Juliet smartly. 'Making me come home from France.'

'You're only eighteen yet,' he pointed out. 'And if your French boy-friend is seriously interested in you—and manages to disentangle himself from his other engagement—he'll come out to Australia for you.'

Cass came in then, and he transferred his attention to her.

It was the first of several similar evenings, except that soon, although Jarratt didn't know it, Juliet scarcely came into the kitchen at all. She had discovered a box containing all sorts of scraps of dress and furnishing material, and had decided she'd like to make a fabric collage. Art had been one of her good subjects at school, and as she had made paper collages, why not experiment with fabric? It could be quite intriguing!

'You don't mind if I don't help, do you?' she asked Nicky apologetically. 'I know I do nothing but get in the way and fuss you, and I'm not in the mood to apply myself to learning to cook when it's all for the benefit of Jarry and the nursemaid and Lewis Trent. The incentive just isn't there. Jarry needs a wife, and I'm going to tell him so. He can't expect Tracy to stay here for ever, it wouldn't be fair, and he needn't think I'm going to run to the rescue if he doesn't like Lena's cooking. We'll have to watch out he doesn't discover *you're* the cook, Nicky, or he'll try to strongarm you into staying. Would you?'

She laughed as she said it, but Nicky was disconcerted.

'Would I—what?' she asked, tasting the cucumber soup she had concocted in the morning, and that had been chilling in the refrigerator all day. She hardly thought the time would ever come when Jarratt Buchan would try to strongarm her into staying on his cattle station, whether she could cook or not.

'Stay—marry him,' Juliet said.

'You must be joking,' Nicky retorted.

'I am,' said Juliet with a giggle.

A few nights later Jarratt, coming home earlier than usual, caught Nicky red-handed in the kitchen, busily preparing a special sauce to go with the roast chicken they were having as a change from beef.

She looked up for no particular reason to see him leaning against the doorway, his dark brows tilted quizzically.

'Well, well—it looks like the end of the fiction, doesn't it? Where did you learn to cook?'

'Me?' she said flusteredly. 'What do you mean? We—Juliet and I—work things out together—she's——'

'Liar,' he said. 'Juliet's so wrapped up in sticking bits of velvet and lace on to a sugar bag she doesn't even know it's getting on for dinner time—or that I'm home. So where and when did you acquire your skill? Because you're not bad, you know.'

Praise, she thought wryly, for the one and only thing she had been discovered able to do. She said resignedly, 'Oh well, my guardian's sister taught me a few tricks.' She wasn't going to tell him she had discovered she had quite a flair for cooking when she had been given a free hand now and again at the foster-home, when she was about twelve years old.

'Which guardian was that?' he asked. 'The one you were with in Alice?'

Her colour rose. She knew what he was thinking. He had decided that Guy was 'interested' in her—and had seen to it that she learned to cook. And the fact was, there was more than a grain of truth in that.

'Yes, that one,' she said after a moment.

'Hmm. You keep a lot of secrets, don't you, Nicky Reay?' he said enigmatically. She had no idea if he was referring to the fact that Juliet didn't do the cooking, or if he meant she kept secrets about herself—and she certainly did that.

'I try to,' she said wryly, 'and one of them's the way to make this sauce. So would you please go away and let me get on with it?'

'Certainly,' he agreed. 'I'll see you later. We'll have to drink a toast to the cook, I think.'

There was wine on the table for the first time that night—a delectable white from the Barossa Valley, to complement the chicken, and though there was no formal toast drunk, Jarratt lifted his glass and smiled at Nicky before he drank. Her eyes fell before his, yet she felt a little warm glow that was certainly not due to the wine. The glow made her think of Howard. Jarratt had never asked her to come out with him since that first night, and now she supposed he never would. If she wanted to see Howard, she would have to suggest it herself, and somehow she shrank from doing so. The alternative was to wait till the end of the muster, and that, according to Cass, could be weeks off.

Perhaps, she thought, as he was in a good mood tonight, she might ask him after dinner—provided she could get him to herself for a moment. But that proved not to be easy. When she came in from the kitchen with the coffee, Cass had fetched her books and was perched on the arm of Jarratt's chair, leaning over his shoulder while he read some essay she had written.

Juliet took her coffee out to the verandah, and Nicky followed her.

'That *girl*,' Juliet said impatiently. 'She does hang

63

around Jarry, doesn't she? Every night it's the same. As if he'd be interested in a nursemaid! It's painfully plain she has her eye on him—all this study business is just a scheme to monopolise his attention.'

Only a moment ago, Nicky had been impatient with Cass for taking up Jarry's time, but now she was up in arms on her behalf and retorted without thinking, 'Of course it's not a scheme! She has to pass her exams—she wants to be a teacher.'

'So she says.' Juliet was cynical. 'But I don't believe it. If that was all she was interested in, then I'm sure Lewis Trent would be more help to her than Jarry.'

'Lewis has work of his own to get through.' Nicky had a brief battle with herself and decided the time had come to be honest. She had suffered on and off from a feeling of guilt for days now, and finally she said firmly, 'I happen to know Cass does want to be a schoolteacher, Juliet, be-cause—because I knew her years ago in Alice Springs—and it was her ambition then.'

Juliet was staring at her in utter amazement.

'You knew Catherine Johnston! But how—extraordin-ary! Why on earth didn't you say so before? Or didn't you remember her at first? I didn't know you'd even been to Alice Springs before this year.'

'I used to live there,' Nicky explained with a sigh. She leaned on the verandah rail and looked out into the starry night. 'Cass and I went to school together.'

'Good—heavens!' Juliet seemed unable to get over it. Then she said, 'Well, I suppose there aren't any private schools in Alice ... And I haven't changed my ideas, no matter what you say. She's got her sights fixed on my brother. Wouldn't you say it promised a brighter future to marry him than to launch herself into a dreary teaching career? Not that she has a chance, if she had the sense to realise it. Despite his tough all-men-are-equal act, Jarry just wouldn't marry beneath him. Not ever.'

Nicky's mouth opened on a soundless exclamation. 'Marry beneath him!' What a thing to say in this day and age! And there was nothing wrong with Cass, she would fit in anywhere with a little practice. For all Juliet knew, Cass's father could have been a cattleman who'd been ruined by drought—her background could be brilliant. It was absurd how shallow her judgments were. Nicky, for instance, was okay because they'd gone to the school and because her guardian had been cashed up. But just suppose she had ever met Jack, who had been a mate of Nicky's father when they were both shooting crocodiles up in the Top End. Jarratt had nothing on Jack when it came to being tough. And Jack had had no finesse, no social manners, no soft cultured voice. He'd had ambitions and a heart of gold where Nicky was concerned, even if he hadn't understood the emotional needs of a growing girl. Heavens, if Juliet had met Jack, she'd think Nicky was beneath her.

Nicky felt quite sick. She was a fraud. She had deliberately told Jarratt that her mother had been a West from Kooriekirra—that had sounded great, and she had let it sound that way by withholding the rest of her background from him. The strange thing was that he hadn't followed up and persisted in having her tell him something about her father. He had said earlier, 'Whether your father's a lord or a louse or a lunatic you will still be welcome as a guest on my cattle station'.

As a guest—or as a nursemaid, she thought now. But when it came to marriage, that would be a different kettle of fish. Juliet had said so. Not that that aspect of it interested her—or Cass.

She turned abruptly from the verandah rail. 'I'm going to bed.'

'Oh, not yet,' Juliet protested. 'Let's go in and break up the party. Jarry should put himself out to entertain us sometimes. He has a whole pile of records in there, and I'd like to hear some music, anyhow. If it disturbs the nursemaid's homework, she can jolly well bundle up her books and take them over to her bungalow. Though I bet she'll hang around and listen too. You just see.'

Nicky followed her inside unwillingly. She was still in a false position, yet she couldn't see that it would do any good to come out with the whole truth. It would, in fact, merely create an awkward situation. Rather naïvely, she had never suspected this streak of snobbishness in Juliet. She was aware of it in Guy and Claudia, but it was disconcerting to find a school friend with similar narrow views. Jack had known what he was talking about after all when he had advised her to keep her mouth shut at school. She'd probably have found herself without friends. He'd probably have told her not to blab it all out here, too . . .

But she wasn't going to desert Cass, who had been her friend once and always would be so.

All the same, she was relieved to discover Cass already in the process of packing up her books.

'I'll go and work on that idea,' she was telling Jarry. 'Thanks for putting it into my head.' She gave him one of her wide trustful smiles, said goodnight to Nicky and Juliet and was gone.

So Juliet had her music, but Nicky, though she sat and pretended to listen, found herself thinking constantly instead about her own doubtful position. What on earth was Juliet going to think when she discovered that Nicky was in love with the 'nursemaid's' brother—a stockman?

In some ways, it was perhaps as well that Howdie wasn't around . . .

CHAPTER FOUR

NEXT afternoon, while Juliet was 'sticking velvet and lace on a sugarbag', as Jarratt had put it, though he knew very well she was creating a fabric picture, and Cass was poring over her books, Nicky took a ride. There were plenty of horses available, and the cowboy, Billy, suggested she should take Sandover Lily, a rather handsome grey.

It was great to get away from the homestead and the thoughts that had begun to oppress her, and she relaxed completely as her horse cantered over the gently undulating land, through the scattered mulga scrub with its undercover of rose and straw-coloured grasses. Galahs and black cocka-toos flew out of the trees, the sky was hazed with heat, the shadows were indigo, and the low flat-topped distant ranges were pale violet shadows floating on a horizon that wavered and shimmered like water.

Nicky loved it, and yet she didn't know why. This country seemed to stir memories that she couldn't yet grasp, memories that spoke of happiness. It was as if long ago she had crossed just this creek bed, so wide and sandy and dry, and, moving into the feathery shade of the desert oaks on the far side, had seen the bright flowers of the yellowtops spread their gold across the vermilion earth. Had seen, too, this little witchetty bush standing tiptoe in the red sand, its roots exposed, its leaves soft blue grey, its golden flowers dancing, a confident little Port Lincoln par-rot strutting about underneath.

She rode for a long time and when she took Sandover Lily back to the horse paddock, she didn't go back to the homestead. Feeling a need to be alone a little while longer, she wandered down past the white-painted schoolhouse, the machinery shed and the garages, and there under some trees, she saw three little aboriginal children playing in the red sand. They were very young—they wouldn't qualify yet for school with Lewis Trent—and she stood where she was, motionless in the tree shade, watching them.

Afterwards, she had no idea at all what game they had been playing, of whether or not she heard their voices, because there grew in her mind a kind of vision, or memory, that became inextricably confused with what she saw. Shadows flickered on her face and in her eyes, the hot sun warmed her as she stood dreaming...

Long ago *she* had squatted on the ground like this, chattering and sifting the clean red sand through her small fingers. She and those little dark children had dug out fat, creamy grubs from the roots of witchetty bushes, and she could see the small round black faces tilted up, small fingers holding a plump witchetty grub by the head. She had a strong sensation of, herself, biting off the body—the nutty taste, the texture—she remembered it all. And she could picture herself, her little freckled face, her red-gold hair, her childish blue eyes wide as she looked at the tasty morsel and opened her mouth to bite. And then, as she savoured the delicious mouthful, a man looked down at her from an immense height, his eyes fixed on her.

She frowned slightly, turning her head. Had it been Jack watching her? Were they his eyes that had scrutinised her?

Nicky blinked. Right now, she was looking into a man's eyes, but they weren't blue, like Jack's, they were black and—oh God!—they had the most devastating effect on her. They pulled her right out of her dream and smash-bang back into her own adult body. They belonged of course, to Jarratt Buchan, and just now there was something very sexy about them. She drew a deep and almost painful breath, glanced guiltily at the children still absorbed in their game, and moved away from the tree against which she was leaning. Wishing she could as easily move away from those watchful eyes.

'What's taken your fancy?' His voice was very soft. 'Are you having sentimental thoughts about little black children?'

She shook her head. 'I was—half asleep. I've been out riding all afternoon.'

68

'So you ride, do you?'

'With a short stirrup,' she agreed, deriding herself. 'I learned at riding school.'

'Where else?' he murmured.

Without either of them having said anything further, they began to move under the trees away from the children, until they were quite alone. Nicky felt dizzy. She didn't know why—whether she had ridden too far in the sun or whether it was something to do with the thoughts she'd been having. She had a very strong feeling that she'd been reliving an experience, and perhaps she had, because once she had lived on a cattle station somewhere in the Northern Territory with Jack. But the thing that was troubling her most of all was the memory of those eyes. Black watchful eyes. Could that have happened before? But if it had, they couldn't possibly have been Jarratt Buchan's eyes. She did a quick calculation. Fourteen—fifteen years ago, he would have been how old? Maybe twenty-one or two——

'What's the matter?' he asked her suddenly. 'Are you all right? You've gone slightly green.'

She felt a dew on her forehead and on the back of her neck, and she thought, 'I'm going off my head. Of course it wasn't Jarratt. Of course it wasn't here.' She longed to tell him what was in her mind, and yet she couldn't. Not possibly. He would think her distinctly odd.

She said quickly, defensively, 'I've had too much sun. And I'm hungry.'

'No lunch?' he enquired.

'Yes, I had lunch.' They had left the shade of the trees and were walking across a wide stretch of red earth towards the homestead. The westering sun cast purple shadows, and the heat was almost tangible. Light in the inland, Nicky reflected, had a special quality. You were deeply aware of its luminosity, its dramatisation of every little thing, so that a blade of grass, an insect, a flower, stood out not just three-dimensionally, but as something seen in a hallucination. She watched her own feet in the thick-soled sneakers, each one as it moved raising a little cloud of dust—a little red sandstorm. *That* was something she had contemplated as a child too.

She put a hand to her brow to push back the fall of hair that made the low slanting rays of the sun a glitter of burnished red in her eyes, and once again she was aware of that man looking at her—that man who Juliet had said wouldn't marry beneath him.

She thought of Howard and she felt a physical ache in her heart. She had been forgetting Howard. It would have been different if he'd been there at the bungalow with Cass; she'd have known by now.

Known what? she asked herself, taken by surprise by the involuntary thought. She walked on beside Jarratt Buchan, but she didn't look at him. Instead, she tried to visualise Howard, and found she couldn't. Yet all the time she had been at school in Adelaide, his face had been as clear to her as though she had seen him yesterday. She had dreamed of him often—not always happy dreams, for there was a recurring one in which he and Cass always ran away from her. But sad or gay, whatever the dream, his face was always clear and familiar—a face she knew like the back of her hand. Now it had vanished.

Light brown hair, she reminded herself in desperation, hazel eyes like Cass's, but with shorter darker lashes. His mouth—young and soft and—he had kissed her once, and his skin had been smooth, young——

She glanced up and saw Jarratt's jaw, dark with stubble, his dark hair, dark brows. His dark eyes. She bit her lip.

'When will the muster be over?'

He looked surprised at the question. 'Not for some time. Coochin Brim-brim is a big property. We have a lot of ground to cover, a lot of cattle to round up—calves and cleanskins to brand, castrating to be done—weaners to be separated from the cows, beasts cut out for sale. Our paddocks are bigger than you could imagine. Why do you ask?'

Nicky's heart had been sinking. She might easily have gone before Howdie came back. Once Tracy was better, Juliet wouldn't want to stay, and she would have to go too.

Guy would be at her as well, insisting that she return to Adelaide. So she would have to ask now.

She took a deep breath. 'I just wondered.' She raised her eyes and sent him a guileless glance. 'I'd like to see part of the muster.'

'You would? Tired of poking about?' There was cynical speculation on his face. 'Well, we should be able to arrange it. You can come out with me some time.' She'd barely murmured 'Thank you,' when he shot out unexpectedly, 'Juliet mentioned you've met Catherine before.'

'Yes.' She told herself she was glad he knew that at least, but it didn't stop her from feeling guilty, or from colouring to show it.

'Why didn't you say so?'

'I hardly thought you'd be interested in—in such a trivial detail.' Oh, what a lie—when he was always asking questions!

'And her brother,' he pursued relentlessly, 'Howard. Have you met him too?'

'Y-yes,' she repeated minimally. Head down, she determinedly watched her feet in the dust.

'Am I right in guessing they're the people whose trail you were on? You said something to that effect to Shirley Capper the day we came up.'

Another guess, and a good one. Nicky sighed, feeling foolishly caught out, more guilty than ever, and hating the feeling. She said pertly, 'Yes, you've guessed right. Imagine your remembering what I said to Shirley Capper!'

Her attitude didn't divert him for a second. 'So who was it you wanted to chase up? Catherine? Or her brother?'

She raised her head, regardless of her flushed face. 'Oh, honestly, do we have to make such a thing of my private business? You ask questions—questions—all the time.'

'Is it bothering you? Surely you have nothing to hide. Catherine's a nice girl, Howard's got good stuff in him, though he suffers from a few hang-ups.'

'What do you mean?'

'Those kids have had to battle. They're still battling. They haven't had it easy like you.'

71

What did *he* know? As for the Johnstons, she knew a heap more about them than he did. She wanted to say, 'I know all that and a lot more. And I haven't always had it easy—my guardian had to battle for opals in the dust of Coober Pedy before he could take me away from the foster-home I was in.' But she wasn't going to say it. She'd had all that out with herself already. It wouldn't do anyone any good, and moreover she was sick and tired of his relentless probing. Thank goodness the girls at school hadn't been so inquisitive! But Jarratt Buchan—he was determined that she would open her heart to him, tell him everything. So he was not getting his way.

'Well, so what about it?' she asked maddeningly, and widened her blue eyes at him.

His wide mouth straightened. 'All right, we won't talk about it. But you can come out with me in a day or two. I'll be going out to the muster camp with fresh supplies for the cook. See if you can talk Juliet into joining the party, will you? It's something she ought to do, as a Buchan. We'll have a night camping out. Does that appeal to you?' There was mockery in his voice, and she wondered if he expected her to renege when he mentioned camping. It was far more likely that he would be the one to pull out of the arrangement if Juliet refused to come—which she was quite likely to do.

She said coolly, 'It sounds great fun. I can hardly wait.'

His smile was enigmatic.

Sure enough, Juliet wasn't in the least interested in the tentative arrangement when Nicky mentioned it to her. She said a definite 'No,' and that was that. 'He'll call it off,' Nicky thought, 'he won't take me on my own.'

A couple of nights later, Jarratt announced over coffee, 'Tomorrow I'm driving out to the camp. Have you two girls talked about coming along?'

Juliet, who had been contemplating the collage that she had laid out on the sitting room floor, raised her head. 'You must be joking! Go bush—sleep out? Not in a million years!'

Her brother frowned. 'You just don't want to see beyond

72

your own little circle of light, do you?' He looked at Nicky. 'What about you? Have you had second thoughts?'

'No. I'd like to come,' she said firmly.

'You'll be a lone female in a strictly male world,' he warned.

Nicky shrugged. 'I'm not worried.'

They stared at each other and she had no idea what he was thinking. For her part, Nicky was determined to see Howard, and if Jarratt Buchan was going to find it a bore having a lone female on his hands, then that was too bad.

'All right,' he said finally. 'That's settled, then.'

That night she woke with thumping heart to the sound of a child's sobbing, and for a fleeting instant she thought she was away back in the past at the foster-home, where it was not unusual for the little ones to cry in the night when they first came. She tumbled out of bed, switching on the reading lamp as she did so, and groped for the slinky silk jersey housegown she had bought on Claudia's advice in Adelaide —because the 'garment' she had used at boarding school had been too hopelessly unattractive, according to Guy's sister. Juliet's room was still in darkness as she went quietly past, which was not surprising because Juliet's ear wasn't attuned to the distress of small children.

It was Medora, she discovered when she reached the children's room. She had fallen out of bed and given herself a fright. Nicky turned on the night light and discovered Marcie-Ann angelically asleep, and stooping, she lifted the little one and took her in her arms.

'It's all right, darling, Nicky's here. You just tumbled out of bed, that's all. Wasn't it a silly old thing to do?'

The child clung to her, whimpering a little, but half asleep again already, and as Nicky cuddled her and murmured soft comforting words, her amazingly long lashes fluttered down against her sleep-flushed cheeks, and presently Nicky was able to put her back under the sheet. For a few moments she stroked the curly head and then when she was sure the child was sound asleep, she straightened up with a little sigh.

To discover Jarratt standing in the doorway, watching

73

her with a quizzical expression in his smouldering dark eyes.

Nicky caught her breath, and wondered how long he had been there. He wore pyjama trousers but was naked from the waist up, and his chest hair showed dark and curling on the broad bronzed expanse of his torso.

'Everything okay?' His eyebrows rose interrogatively and his voice was so low that Nicky was suddenly conscious of the quiet of the house and of the huge empty endless dark outside. She nodded, and moved, feeling the cool smoothness of the silky jersey swishing against her calves and her bare ankles, aware at the same time that those lazy eyes had travelled slowly down from her face to the curve of her bosom, revealed by the clinging garments she wore. She didn't know what she expected as she drew nearer to him, but her heart was beating quickly.

She made herself say, in a whisper, 'Medora had fallen out of bed, that's all.'

'You must sleep lightly,' he commented. He let her pass him, then murmured, 'Or were you awake thinking about tomorrow?'

'Of course not,' she said quickly. 'I wake easily, that's all.'

'I see ... Would you like a glass of milk before you go back to bed?'

She had no idea why she said yes instead of no—because she wasn't hungry, or thirsty either. Yet she said yes, and moved ahead of him towards the kitchen. There she stood awkwardly leaning against the wall while he took glasses from the dresser, and the milk jug from the fridge.

'Quiet, isn't it?' he commented as he handed her a glass. 'No cars or buses whizzing by, no next door neighbours holding a party. No city glow on the horizon even. We're in an empty world, just you and I.'

His words were disquieting and she sipped her milk, swallowing audibly in her nervousness.

'So you're coming with me tomorrow despite Juliet's lack of interest,' he stated rather than asked. 'I'd hoped you

74

wouldn't wriggle out of it. It will be something new for you, won't it?'

'Yes,' she agreed reluctantly.

'But as far as you're concerned, that's not the draw, is it?'

'What—what do you mean?'

He perched himself on the edge of the table, and she blinked and looked away from the male nakedness of his chest, and his hair, tousled from sleep.

'I'm not altogether sure what I mean,' he murmured after a minute, 'but I know you had something in mind when you angled for an invitation to come out with me.'

Nicky crimsoned slowly as his eyes held hers once more. He didn't know about Howdie and how she felt about him, so—did he imagine she was coming because of *him*? Quite definitely she wasn't, but she wasn't going to make a full confession about Howdie—that was private and personal business, that was part of a dream, and she closed her eyes for a fleeting instant trying to conjure up Howdie's face and managing instead, infuriatingly, to see Jarratt Buchan's. She opened her eyes with a grimace.

'What would I have in mind?' she demanded. 'It's all very simple, as you'd realise if you put yourself in my position. I haven't seen much of your cattle station since I've been here. It's not much fun to go out riding on one's own, and Juliet doesn't like horses——'

'Oh, Juliet!' he exclaimed impatiently. 'It's a pity she can't put herself out for other people now and again.'

'She does.' Nicky sprang instantly to Juliet's defence. 'She came out here, didn't she?'

'And so she should, seeing her sister's laid up in hospital.'

'But Catherine's looking after the children,' Nicky persisted. 'And—and you're not really her concern, are you? Anyhow, Juliet says you don't need a sister, you need——'

She stopped and bit her lip, and drank down the rest of her milk.

'I need a wife,' he finished for her, his dark eyes glinting. 'Well, that's a topic I don't intend discussing with you, though I know marriage is a subject dear to a woman's heart.'

'Not—not to mine,' she interrupted, confused. 'Girl's don't spend all their time dreaming about getting married these days—there are lots of other things to do.'

'I'm sure there are. However, I thought it was the desirability of *my* marriage that was under the microscope—not yours.' She coloured furiously and he laughed. 'I haven't had much of a chance to talk to you so far, have I, Nicky?'

'To ask me questions, you mean,' she said defensively.

'If you like to put it that way. What with helping Catherine with her lessons and catching up on problems connected with my way of earning a living, I've been a poor host. We'll have to start remedying that tomorrow.' He moved towards her and she felt herself shrink back a little, but he only reached for her glass and put it on the sink, then told her casually, 'Don't bring that slinky seductive-looking garment you're wearing along with you to the muster, will you? Not that I don't like it, but——' He paused and his eyes had that warm look in them that she found so disturbing she had to lower her lashes to escape it. 'I'll take along a tent for you to sleep in, and you can please yourself whether you bring pyjamas or not—but you won't need anything like that to drift around in.'

'You must think I'm off my head if I don't know that,' she said stiffly, and covered her mouth with her hand to stifle a yawn that was not quite genuine. 'I'm going to bed. Goodnight, and thanks for the drink.'

'I hope it gives you pleasant dreams,' he said.

Nicky felt vaguely uneasy next morning about leaving Juliet on her own, and it was little consolation to think that Cass would be there. There didn't seem to be much rapport between them, and she was well aware that Juliet thought Cass was given too many privileges for someone who was working for her living. As well there was her conviction, which Nicky didn't share, that Cass had her eye on Jarratt. However, all that was left behind once she was on her way in the utility with Jarratt. The back of the vehicle was loaded up with fresh provisions for the musterers, and Nicky's own gear—a change of socks and underwear, a pair of short pyjamas and her toilet bag, a fresh blouse—were packed in a small soft bag that Cass had loaned her. Cass would have liked to be coming today too. Nicky had been aware of that when she had slipped out to the schoolroom to say goodbye, but of course it was out of the question.

'Give my love to Howdie,' Cass instructed. 'Oh, I wish I could see the look on his face when you turn up! He'll be just knocked out.'

Now, Nicky felt slightly sick with apprehension as Jarratt drove the ute along the rough red track through the never-ending spinifex grass and scattered mulga. She tried to imagine her meeting with Howard, and she didn't know why she should feel slightly afraid. What if he didn't even recognise her? And what did he look like now? The thing was, he was a man now, and she was a woman. They had been so young when last they met. She had been not quite fourteen—but as much in love as a girl of that age is capable of being. And she had hung on to that feeling—that dream—for years. Now she felt full of nerves and uncertainties. Her hands were clasped tightly together in her lap and she stared ahead of her, seeing nothing that actually existed—seeing instead a blurred image of a disconcerting faceless Howard, and of herself running to meet him. She started when Jarry's voice said, 'Relax! What's worrying you, Nicky?'

'Nothing. I was just—thinking.'

'Of what? Or should I say, of whom? Your handsome guardian?'

She shrugged, drew a deep breath and leaning back in the seat she forced herself to give her attention to what was outside the car—the ring of low, flat-topped red hills they were driving towards, the river red gums that lined the dry watercourse that wound through the spinifex, the vermilion of the double track they were following. Red dust clouded out behind the utility like smoke, and against the blue of the sky the powdery white trunks and limbs of ghost gums were spread. There was a strange familiarity about it all so piercing that it hurt, and she knew she must have seen country like this long ago, before she was five years old, when she had lived in the bush with Jack.

Soon they were driving between the walls of the red gorge, deep purple shadows lay across the track, pools of soft blue water reflected rock and sky and flower and flying bird, as a hawk appeared from nowhere and wheeled high above. The rose red of the vertical cliffs on either side glowed incandescent and beautiful and remote. This land—this hunting ground—had once belonged to some aboriginal tribe, long since dispersed, yet it seemed still to be haunted by the shadows of tall dark, almost naked men, moving gracefully through the sunlight, spears upraised ...

The track had petered out now, and Jarratt steered the utility skilfully along the pale sandy bed of the river, dodging boulders and pools of water. Nicky, looking about her alertly and with a kind of inner excitement, caught a glimpse of a couple of small rock wallabies hopping away into the shadows.

'You're all eyes,' Jarratt commented. 'It might interest you to know that this is a track we can't always use. When there's been a good fall of rain further upstream, this river bed swirls with water that reaches ten or fifteen feet—maybe more—up the gorge walls.'

'Then how do you get out to the other side of the run?'

'We do an extra fifteen miles.'

They talked on and off after that, but impersonally, about the land, the birds and animals, the cattle, and then at last they reached the muster camp, where Jarratt pulled up in tree shade. The men had lunched, and were in the process of resaddling their horses for the afternoon's work. Nicky, her heart bumping, sought among them for Howdie. They all wore checked shirts, narrow-legged trousers, wide-brimmed stockmen's hats, and she felt hopelessly frustrated. Surely—surely—she would know if she saw Howard, but she felt no leap of recognition as, sitting in the utility, she searched and searched. The cook had come across from his truck, and he and Jarratt were unloading the supplies from the back of the ute. Nicky turned in her seat so she could see the mob of cattle that had been rounded up, and now she saw there were three stockmen slowly circling the mob to hold it. Howard must be one of those three men. He *must* be. She thrust open the door and slid out, pulling on the cotton hat she had bought in Alice, and putting on the sunglasses she had discarded a few minutes previously.

Jarratt turned sharply. 'Where are you off to?'

'To—to see the cattle,' she stammered.

'Well, just hold on,' he said. It was such a definite command she stopped dead in her tracks despite herself. 'We'll have some tucker first, then you can see as much of the cattle as you want. The men are taking them over to the yards now, and it will be more interesting for you to see them cutting out and branding than to go careering off in the heat now just to gawp. Besides, you must be hungry, and I certainly am.'

Nicky gritted her teeth and bowed to fate in the form of Jarratt Buchan, and fifteen minutes later, when the cattle had disappeared in a slow cloud of red dust, she was eating a delectable barbecued steak and a hunk of bread—made by the cook in his gas oven, she guessed—and drinking billy tea that won, hands down, over anything ever brewed in a pot.

As she ate, she thought of Howdie riding out under the burning sun with the cattle, and wondered how he would feel if he knew she was here. How would he react when he saw her? Would he recognise her instantly? Ridiculously, she longed to look like the almost-fourteen-year-old girl she had been when last they met—perhaps not so much age-wise as clothes-wise, character-wise. She was wearing tough blue jeans, but the shirts she had bought in Alice were lightweight and cool rather than utilitarian. The one she was wearing now was pale blue and she wished it was checked, like the ones Cass wore. Holding out her mug for more tea, she worried over her image. Did it shout 'Ladies' College'? Would Howard feel alienated? And would she look better in the other shirt she had put in her pack—the red one? Yet suppose she wanted to change—— Quite suddenly she was very much aware of the all-male environment into which she had been projected.

The cook and his assistant had finished packing up their gear, the campfire had been put out, the truck was on the move. There were only herself and Jarratt left now. The string of horses led by the horse-tailor was on its way through the spinifex grass of the endless paddock, and Nicky was suddenly far more aware of being alone with Jarratt than she had been in the utility. Her thoughts raced ahead to the night, when she would be sleeping out, though he had said she would have a tent. She felt vulnerable, alone, doubtful about coming—suspicious that in bringing her along Jarratt had been issuing a challenge of some sort, or testing out a theory.

She looked at him wearily. He was packing up the utensils they had used for their meal, but now his dark eyes glanced over at her amusedly as she sat in the red sand, her back against a tree.

'You're looking pale. Are you wishing you hadn't come?'

'Of course not.' She asked a question of her own. 'Why did you bring me along?'

He looked surprised. 'You wanted to come.'

'Yes, but you didn't have to let me. Why did you?'

He shrugged his broad shoulders. 'It will do you good. Besides, I guess you're curious. Women are like cats that way—curious. And sometimes it gets them into trouble. Nevertheless, I'd sooner a woman was adventurous than not—even if she has to take a beating now and again. Do you want to go down to the waterhole and have a wash? Take your time, and when you're ready we'll be on our way.'

'Thank you.' She needed a little time alone, and down by the waterhole it was quite secluded, with trees around and a few birds fluttering, and the peculiar silence of the outback that was not really silence at all, but full of minute singing sounds. She sluiced her face in the cool water, reflecting how clear it was. She could see green weed growing at the bottom, see her own reflection—her face slightly flushed from the heat, her hair, now she had removed the cotton hat, a bit of a mess. She could feel it clinging stickily to the back of her neck where she was perspiring.

She took her time, but when she emerged into the open again, Jarratt wasn't there. She walked leisurely across to the utility and climbed in. Jarratt's cigarettes and matches were there and she took a smoke from the packet and lit up, leaned back against the seat and inhaled. At school the older girls had been allowed to smoke if they had their parents' written permission, but it was not approved of. Jack had never given his permission, so if Nicky smoked, as she had now and again, it was guiltily. She felt guilty now, partly because of that, partly because Guy didn't like her smoking either.

When Jarratt reappeared, strolling across to the ute with his rather swaggeringly lordly air, she looked him straight in the eye and blew smoke. But all he said was, 'Ready?' Then he climbed in beside her and started up the motor.

Quite suddenly he switched it off again and sat, eyes narrowed, staring ahead of him. Somehow disturbed, she finished her cigarette and looked around for somewhere to crush it out.

He turned his head.

'Don't toss that butt out of the car—we don't want to start a fire. It may not look much, but this is some of my best grazing land.' He handed her a tin lid from the top of the dashboard, and, a little put out because she certainly hadn't intended being so careless with her cigarette, Nicky mashed the butt out in the improvised ashtray. Her hand was shaking and she was very conscious that he was watching her. She had the feeling anything might happen—though what could happen she had no idea. It was sheer nervousness that made her ask for another cigarette, a request that he ignored completely. She was about to repeat it when she found her eyes locked with his.

'What's behind that veneer of maturity of yours, Nicky?' he asked suddenly, his voice oddly tense. 'I haven't got the strength of you yet—not by any means. I can't get near to you—questions make you curl up. Are you scared of me for some reason? Or do you want——' He stopped, and there

81

was that expression in his eyes again that made her pulse rate quicken, made the colour rise in her cheeks, made her lashes flutter. Then abruptly he moved and pulled her against him, twisting her body round so sharply and decisively that his mouth had found hers before she had the least idea what was happening. She had been kissed before, of course—there had been boys, young men about, even on her carefully planned vacations. And there had been Guy. But this was different. Completely. And whether or not Jarratt queried her 'veneer of maturity', he kissed her as though she were a woman—with no concessions. She felt his lips, his teeth, his tongue. Her whole body burned and a tiny river of perspiration ran down between her breasts. His body was hot too, but rock hard, well under control.

'The right man,' he said when he had finished with her—and as he spoke he was reaching for his cigarettes—'could make what he liked of you.'

Nicky didn't know what he meant, and she had no idea what to say. Her head was spinning. She didn't know why he had kissed her, or why she had submitted—as she had submitted. It had been her instinctive reaction, for heaven knew what reasons. But now she was all uncertainty. What on earth must he think?

'Why did you do that?' she asked shakily, not looking at him—not daring to. Her breathing was fast and there was something unnerving in the fact that he could now so casually light up a cigarette with fingers that were, when she glanced at them from the shelter of her lashes, completely steady.

'Why? I guess I've been hovering on the brink of it ever since first I met you. And from your—co-operation—I'd guess you've been expecting it too. Do you want to talk about it?'

Her cheeks were hot. 'I *haven't* been expecting it! And I—I don't want to talk about it, whatever you mean. There's—there's nothing to talk about.'

'There's not?' His mouth curved in a crooked smile. 'Okay. If you see it that way——' He stuck the cigarette in the corner of his mouth and started up the car again and this time got it moving. 'I'm going to look around here first, make sure there aren't any stray beasts lurking in the scrub. You might keep your eyes skinned too.'

It was gently rolling country, its open woodland consisting mostly of mulga trees and a few corkwoods, and he drove slowly, ignoring her and ignoring, too, the fact that she wasn't having a particularly comfortable ride as he swung the utility over the spinifex clumps and dodged among the trees and the giant termite mounds. When she glanced at him, he looked quite absorbed—lynx-eyed—seeing to it that his ringers had done a thorough job.

She didn't know how long they drove, but not a beast moved in the shadows of the scrub, not a creature was to be seen lying in the grasses.

It was mid-afternoon when they caught up with the musterers again, and Nicky discovered the yards to consist of no more than an open-ended horseshoe shape of wire and posts. She had expected the usual cattle yards, but before she could ask Jarratt a single question, he had pulled up in the shade and got out of the truck without a word, jerking his wide-brimmed hat forward over his forehead, and she watched him stride away from her.

She leaned back exhaustedly and, keeping her sunglasses on, looked over at the yards where the work was going on. It wasn't long before she picked out Howard from the lean dark-skinned stockmen. He was riding at the open end of the yard, and his job was evidently to keep the jostling cattle from breaking away. The head stockman, a wiry weatherbeaten-looking character, rode along the outside of the fence, selected the beast to be cut out and worked it with his stockwhip to the open end and drafted it out. The business of branding and castrating was tough work for tough men, and Nicky watched the beasts being leg-roped and thrown, and she was part fascinated, part repelled by the swiftness of the operations.

She watched till the scene began to swim and waver and her eyes closed ...

When she opened them again, she was instantly wide awake. A man was striding towards the utility, and with a shock that made her heart beat fast, she saw that it was Howard. He no longer wore his stockman's hat, and his thick brown hair was dulled with dust. Nicky stayed where she was, watching him come, thinking that it was happening at last, yet curiously reluctant to move and unable to analyse her reaction. Unmounted, he didn't seem as tall as she remembered him, but he looked older than his twenty-one or -two years, and a lot harder. And he was *thin*. But very, very good-looking, and very suntanned.

So this was it.

CHAPTER FIVE

NICKY moved at last.

With fingers that trembled a little, she manipulated the door handle and got out of the utility. The sun was in her eyes and she had a smile ready, but it was wavering. Quite suddenly she was aware of nervousness, of uncertainty, of a number of nameless doubts. Then Howard had reached her, and his darkly lashed eyes were looking down into her own. They were hazel eyes like Cass's, but lacking totally in dreaminess. In fact, the impression she got from Howard's eyes was that he'd been around, and she wondered if Cass had played down the hardness of the times they'd been through since they'd left Alice.

He said, after a long moment during which they both stood motionless staring at each other, 'It *is* Nicky, isn't it?' and he put out his hands to her.

'Oh—Howdie!' she said chokingly, laughingly. Then her arms were around him tightly and he was holding her hard, and she smelt dust and sweat and felt the heat of his hard, sinewy body. She said, her face turned in to his shoulder, 'I couldn't believe you and Cass were here—I looked for you in Alice. Isn't it——'

'It's great,' said Howard. 'Let's have a look at you.' He held her away from him and looked at her, half-smiling. 'I thought it was some crazy joke when Jarratt Buchan told me you were in that ute. You've changed, Nicky—you've had your hair cut and you've lost your—orphan look. In fact—well, you're some looker, and too classy for me!' He raised his eyebrows and glanced down at his dusty boots, his far from clean shirt and his crumpled trousers. 'I'm hardly fit for unexpected female company, am I? How long are you staying?'

'At the camp? Just overnight——'

'At Coochin Brim-brim, I meant. What are you doing

here, anyway? Did he'—with a movement of his head that she took to indicate Jarratt Buchan—'invite you?'

There was a hard look in his eyes and she felt herself colour. 'Jarratt? Of course not,' she said quickly. 'I never even met him till it was all arranged. I came out with Juliet, his sister—well, his half-sister, really. We were at school together.' She stopped, feeling she was babbling.

'I get it.' The smile was back in her eyes, and she wondered if he'd imagined Jarratt might be in love with her—which was a laugh. Her thoughts skidded quickly away from that topic. 'So you're here for how long?'

'Till Tracy comes home from hospital, whenever that will be.'

'Let's hope we'll manage to see something of each other, then.'

'Oh, we must,' she agreed.

'I might, just possibly, work it so that I can get in to the homestead on Saturday night. It wouldn't have been hard if I'd had my motor-bike out here. I'll have a word with the boss, anyhow.'

'Jarratt?' she faltered.

'Wally Barker, the head stockman. He's not a bad sort of bloke. The trouble is, we're a bit light on when it comes to transport and this is such a damned big place. Still, we'll see ... How have you and Cass been getting on together? You're one friend she's never forgotten—she gets quite maudlin over you at times.'

Nicky smiled. 'I never forgot her either. Or—or you,' she added, and as she said it it sounded not quite real, more like a line from a play. Things just didn't happen in real life the way you dreamed them. But then she'd never dreamed of meeting up with Howard in the red dust in the middle of nowhere, with a mob of stockmen knocking off from the day's work and—when she glanced around—watching her and Howard curiously.

'I'd have thought you'd have forgotten us pretty quickly, once you went off to your classy boarding school.'

'I wrote,' she said, 'but you didn't answer.'

'We never heard.'

'Cass told me.'

'We were shifted around after you went. Things were really crook. They were cows of people at the new place—if your letter was sent on, they wouldn't have bothered seeing we got it. Cass and I weren't any too popular. It was my fault, I suppose, and Cass was always so loyal about sticking up for me. But I was too old to be shoved around, and so we finally cleared out. Meanwhile, you were in clover, weren't you?'

'In a way,' she said, flushing. Howard had changed more than Cass had, or at any rate, she was finding it harder to rediscover him. He was blunt, too, and he seemed to be emphasising the difference between them—unless she was imagining it. As if she must have become a completely different person because she had gone away to boarding school. But she hadn't—inside she was exactly the same. Or almost, she amended.

She raised her head. 'I didn't like boarding school all that much. It wasn't easy to make friends, and—and I missed you and Cass dreadfully.'

He listened, but his darkly lashed eyes looked her over in a way that was totally unfamiliar, curiously, as though she belonged to a different breed.

'What's it like having money? Doing what you like—tripping round the countryside with girls like what's-her-name Buchan?'

He paused and Nicky shook her head helplessly, aware of tears deep inside her. Her life wasn't in the least the way he saw it.

'I suppose you live with your guardian now in some big house in the city,' he went on.

'No, Jack died just recently. He was in hospital in Adelaide for months—ever since I left school.'

'Oh. I didn't know,' he said uncomfortably. 'I'm sorry about that. I suppose you're feeling pretty cut up.' He ran his fingers through his hair. 'I'd better get cleaned up. We can talk some more later on.'

'Yes, of course.' She felt faintly relieved as they smiled at each other, and then, when he had walked away, she drew a deep and trembling breath. She felt disturbed and frustrated—cheated, perhaps. She had wanted everything to be the same, and obviously it wasn't. So much of what had been seemed to have vanished. They had hugged each other, yet essentially Howdie was—a stranger. She'd thought he'd be warm and welcoming and talkative like Cass, which was stupid, because men were different—they didn't babble on like girls. But she was convinced that if only they had been able to meet normally at the homestead, instead of out here, it would all have been a lot easier. She felt more than a little weepy, but it would never do to give way to it. Not here, with the stockmen moving about the camp, and in the shade of some trees, Jarratt Buchan erecting a small tent—for her.

Nicky pulled herself together and went over to stand watching him, and he turned to ask her, 'Conversation concluded? Where did you say you'd met Howard Johnston?'

Her cheeks flushed. 'In—in Alice. Why do you ask?'

'Well,' he drawled, 'that reunion—it was certainly dramatic. Tears and hugs and kisses. I'm sure every man in the camp who witnessed it is now convinced that you and that stockman mean something special to each other.'

She wanted to retort, 'Perhaps we do,' but she couldn't quite manage it. She merely said offhandedly, 'I can't be worried what they think. It's my business, anyhow.' She peered inside the tent. It had a central pole, and no guy ropes, but was simply anchored to the ground by metal pegs hammered through eyelets at each corner. Jarratt had tossed a sleeping bag inside and now he said dryly, 'I get the message—no questions. I'm going to ask you one, however. Would you like a softer mattress than the ground? If so, I'll get you a few clumps of spinifex grass.'

'Don't bother,' she said stiffly, and he grinned at her maddeningly.

'It's no bother.'

She followed him and watched while with his booted foot he kicked out a few big tussocks of spinifex that grew among the Mitchell grasses. The leaves were long and spiky, and she wondered how on earth they could make a

88

mattress, but she understood when he arranged them under-side up on the floor of her tent. She spread her sleeping bag on top and looked at it with satisfaction. In a way, she regretted that she wasn't to sleep in the open, but since Jarratt had organised the tent then she knew better than to argue. At least she would be able to keep the flap rolled up, so she could see the stars.

'Romantic, isn't it?' he commented as she emerged again. 'But don't let it give you ideas.'

'I don't know what you mean,' she said coldly, refusing to look at him.

'Don't you? ... Now I'll show you where you can have a wash and a tidy up.' He touched her arm, but she moved swiftly away from him, though she followed him through the trees to a place by the water.

'You'll be able to wash here without any difficulty. But just make it a wash—no skinny-dipping. If you have a swimsuit, all right.'

She nodded and refrained from telling him that she wouldn't in a fit strip down to her skin with a camp full of stockmen in the vicinity. 'I'll get my towel and soap now before the light goes,' she told him.

'Just a moment,' he said sharply as she turned away, and she found herself obeying him automatically.

'What?'

'Listen to me, Nicky,' he said after a moment. 'I'm be-ginning to catch on to why you were so eager to come out here with me today—and, something that's puzzled me all along, why you were so intent on shaking off that handsome guardian of yours back in Alice. An affair with a stockman would definitely not be encouraged, would it?'

Nicky listened in some bewilderment. In a curious way what he said was right, yet the way he said it made it completely wrong. He made her sound like a scheming little adventuress—which she was not. There was no 'affair'. The fact was, he didn't know a thing about her and Howard—unless Howard had talked to him this afternoon. She had opened her mouth to utter some kind of a protest when he said quizzically, 'Am I right in guessing that your friendship with the Johnstons isn't all that old? That you met them in Alice when they went in to the Rodeo three or four weeks ago?'

Her eyes widened in surprise. 'Of course you're not right! I knew Cass and Howdie years ago—when I lived in Alice.'

Now he was surprised, and she felt a small sense of triumph.

'Good God!' he exclaimed, his eyes narrowing. 'I had no idea you'd ever lived in Alice Springs.'

'Well, I did, so you don't know everything, do you? I went to school there, and——' She stopped suddenly, regaining her caution right on the brink of telling him far more than she wanted to. 'Don't blab out everything,' she could hear Jack telling her, and she bit back the words that would have come.

He studied her thoughtfully, then when she didn't say any more, he told her, 'Nonetheless, I'm going to do what I intended and give you a word of warning. I'll admit that I don't know a great deal about young Howard Johnston, but the facts relevant to this particular situation are that he's an adult male, and that out in these parts, a stockman probably doesn't see a pretty girl in months. And when he does, he can be pretty eager. So—watch it.'

Nicky would have liked to slap his face. In fact, she very nearly did. Her cheeks slowly crimsoned and she found she was clenching her fists. That was great, coming from him, wasn't it, considering the way he'd kissed her only a few hours ago? Her voice was shaking with indignation when she told him, 'You shouldn't judge everyone by yourself. Howard isn't like that—not in the least.'

He gave a low and derisive laugh. 'Come off it, Nicky— you don't really believe that.'

'I do believe it, because it's true and I know. Howard *isn't* like that. He—I—when we were young, we——' She stopped. It was hopeless to try to explain to this cynical man, and anyhow she didn't want to. He could just mind his own business.

But she had said enough to give Jarratt a lead, and with

his propensity for guessing, he worked out the rest for himself.

'What did you do? Swap friendship rings? And one day he kissed you and you've treasured the memory ever since? I'm a little surprised, because quite frankly I wouldn't have classed you as the mawkish hearts and flowers type.'

She turned away angrily. 'Wouldn't you? I'd rather be that way than—than cynical and materialistic.'

'That's what I am, is it? Well, you're part way right. But for you—you're nineteen, aren't you?—there should be a happy medium. You're intelligent enough. And I had the impression in the utility this afternoon—remember?—that you were somewhere near attaining it. You handled that situation quite well.'

'Is that meant to be a compliment? Because I don't feel complimented. And don't think I—I enjoyed the—the situation,' she flared.

He completely ignored her outburst. 'To return to my words of advice—I *am* just a little bit responsible for you while you're here, whether you admit to it or not. So please remember what I've said and watch you don't titillate Howard Johnston's senses unduly. Times have changed. You're no longer a child.'

Nicky pressed her lips together, seething with the indignity of it all, longing to turn and run away but knowing quite certainly that if she did so he would haul her back. And against those powerful muscular arms she wouldn't have a chance.

'When you've had your tucker tonight,' he pursued, 'see you stick around the campfire with the rest of us, will you? Don't be persuaded to go wandering off into the dark. The advances of a love-starved stockman, even if he's spent the day in the saddle, aren't always too easy to fend off.'

'Is that all?' she asked tightly when he stopped.

'I think so. As long as you've got the message.'

She turned and went quickly back towards her tent. What a colossal cheek he had! He was positively insulting. She knew volumes more about Howdie than he did. Howard would never behave as Jarratt implied—particularly not with her. So she would do as she pleased, and Jarratt Buchan couldn't stop her.

She fetched her soap and towel, but she barely had time to wash before it was dark. As she came back from the waterhole, the apricot of the sky flared briefly to crimson. There was a torch on her sleeping bag—she supposed she had Jarratt to thank for that—but she didn't need it yet. She changed into her other blouse, the red one, and brushed her hair, hoping to get some of the dust out of it. Then, on the point of emerging from her tent, she hesitated. It wasn't easy being the only female around. It would have been nicer if Juliet—or Cass—had been here.

The campfire was sending showers of sparks heavenwards, the sky was darkening to purple, and the stars had begun to burst open like silver-gilt flowers. She heard the cook call, 'Come and get it!' and she saw the men line up with their plates, then move off to squat in the light of the fire and eat and yarn. She wished Howdie would come and fetch her, it was difficult to make the move herself, to stroll over into that company of rough, good hearted males.

It was Jarratt, not Howard, who came for her finally.

'What's up? Aren't you hungry? Or aren't we civilised enough for you?' he asked with kindly mockery. He took her arm and she let him. 'Come along.'

There was a small canvas stool for her to sit on, and Jarratt brought her a plate piled with vegetables and a sizzling tender steak. Howdie strolled over and settled on the ground beside her, and Jarratt took the other side, but luckily he was occupied in talking to Wally Barker, the head stockman, most of the time, so she could forget him—or try to.

She talked to Howard, though she was very very careful over what she said, because she knew Jarratt Buchan wasn't above listening to other people's conversations. She let the burden fall on Howdie by asking him questions about the stockwork, and she solved the mystery of that open-ended holding yard.

'The stock don't get so bruised or knocked about shoving

92

against each other,' Howard explained. 'That open end gives them room to spread.'

Howard had his share of boiled fruit pudding and custard, but Nicky passed it up, and then, when they had both drunk a mugful of steaming tea, he said, 'Let's take a walk, Nicky.'

'I'd like that,' she agreed, getting up from her stool.

Immediately, as she might have guessed, she had Jarratt's attention.

'Remember what I was saying to you earlier, Nicky,' he said laconically, his black eyes glinting in the firelight.

Nicky didn't answer. She walked away with Howard.

'What did he say to you earlier?'

She shrugged. 'Oh, I don't know. He's always talking at me.'

'You don't sound as though you go much on him.'

'No.'

'He's all right. He's a bit wrapped up in Cass, I reckon. She took his eye the minute we landed here looking for work.' Howard had his arm around her waist now, and they strolled along slowly. Nicky was very conscious of the big sky overhead, the brightness of the stars, the fading voices, the diminished glow from the campfire, but most of all she was disturbed by what Howard said. Was Jarratt wrapped up in Cass? And if so, why should it disturb her?

They reached some trees in the midst of which was a stretch of relatively smooth sandy ground and they sat down there, Howard with his legs stretched out, Nicky with knees bent, her arms resting on them.

'Cass has had the hell of a life tagging along with me, you know,' Howard said. 'In a way, we hamper one another. This is the biggest break she's had, this job at Coochin Brim-brim.'

'It's good that she can study for her exams too,' said Nicky. 'She always wanted to be a teacher.'

'Yeah, she used to talk about that sort of thing a lot. When she mentioned it to Jarry Buchan, he had this idea she should do correspondence lessons. But maybe old Cass'll do even better for herself than teaching. She's handy in a lot of ways—she can cook and sew, and she's good with kids and she doesn't talk too much. As well as that, she's pretty. But not near as pretty as you, Nicky.' He paused and reaching out pulled her over against his shoulder, and she leaned against him thinking of what he had said. Did he mean Cass might marry Jarratt? Or was he thinking in terms of housekeeping? Nicky wasn't really in any doubt as to the answer, but she didn't ask Howard to elucidate.

'Anyhow,' he said against her ear, 'what about you, Nicky Reay? Are you in love or engaged or anything? I suppose these days, you know all the right people—the guys with the money——'

'I don't know anyone much,' Nicky protested. 'And I'm not engaged to be married or—or in love,' she faltered, thinking of the romantic dreams she had dreamed of Howard.

'Tell us about this guardian of yours—Jack. Did he leave you provided for?'

'Oh yes. He left me quite a lot of money—and some opals.'

'Opals?'

'Yes. He made his money digging for opals. Didn't you know? He lived in Coober Pedy. He was—well, kind of rough and simple. I'd have gone to live with him this year,' she added earnestly. 'It's no fun not having anyone of your own, Howdie. You and Cass have always had each other.'

'Yes, it does help. Still, you've got friends—you've got the Buchans, for instance.' He paused. 'Funny that we should meet again here, isn't it, seeing we've travelled such different roads. You a guest, me and Cass on the working side of the deal. I tell you, it was a very pleasant surprise seeing you today.' As he spoke, he altered his position slightly so that now her face, instead of being against his shoulder, was turned towards his, and she could feel the warmth of his breath.

'I'm glad you're here, Nicky,' he said huskily. 'You're a sweet kid—you always were.'

His lips found hers and she didn't resist, but after a moment she tensed. His kiss was becoming more passionate

94

than was comfortable—or even allowable—and he was slowly but inexorably pulling her down on the sand beside him. She began to struggle and try to free herself, and when she managed to tear her lips away from his she whispered agitatedly, 'Howdie, don't—*don't*——'

He didn't free her, and she was frightened by his strength. He muttered, 'I won't hurt you, Nicky. Just let yourself go——'

At that moment she heard the crackling of twigs, and so did he, for instantly she was free.

'Nicky?' It was Jarratt Buchan's voice, and biting her lip in mortification, she struggled up. Howard got up too, and they were both on their feet when Jarratt appeared. Nicky's breath was erratic, and she wondered how much he had heard--how much he had seen--and she hated him for tailing her, for contriving to make her feel—cheap, for that was how she did feel, even though the man was Howard whom she had known so long ago.

She could see Jarratt's eyes glittering as he said curtly, 'There's some tea made. You two might as well refresh yourselves before you turn in for the night. It's an early start in the morning,' he concluded, his voice abrupt, unfriendly.

Howard put his arm around Nicky, sighed audibly and said with perfect sangfroid, 'I might have known I wouldn't be allowed to have the only girl around the place to myself for long.'

'That's right,' Jarratt agreed, 'you're not allowed.'

They began to walk back towards the campfire. Nicky wished Howard hadn't been so insistent just now as he had pulled her down on the ground beside him. It was something she hadn't expected of him—not so soon, not so—inconsiderately. Though even if Jarry hadn't come along, she was sure--she was *sure*—everything would have been all right. Howard wouldn't have done anything she didn't want—and they would have talked again. She was conscious of an odd feeling of despair all the same, and she knew it was not due to having Jarratt take over. She suddenly didn't feel like having Howard's arm around her, and she slipped away from his touch and stumbled a little on the uneven ground. Jarratt caught her arm to steady her and she thrust him away too.

The two men began to talk unconcernedly about the work that was to be done tomorrow, and Nicky, walking between them, feeling isolated, alone, wondered how they could. She felt both angry and mortified at the way they ignored her. It was as if she didn't matter—as if she were an object merely, and fleetingly she hated them both. But mainly, she hated Jarratt. She supposed he was feeling pleased with himself for catching her out in something that she had been so certain wouldn't happen, and she felt sick, nauseated. She wanted to go away and be by herself.

Meanwhile, Jarratt was telling Howard, 'You're not doing too badly. Wally says you've got the makings of a good stockman in you.'

'Stockwork's not my ultimate ambition,' said Howard, 'I've got plenty of other ideas.'

Back at the camp, the men were still sitting yarning in the firelight, and red and gold sparks flew upward against the impenetrable dark of the outback sky. It was all so beautiful, yet it was all spoiled, and Nicky's heart was aching.

She took her mug of tea and went to stand by herself and steady her nerves. Howard was talking to the cook and to Wally Barker, smiling, self-assured, and she watched him for a while and found his face in the firelight totally unfamiliar. She wondered how he could ignore her now, how he could laugh and talk and act so unconcernedly when she was in an agony of hurt pride inside. Didn't he have even an inkling of that? And what must the cook and the head stockman—oh, and all the other men—think they had been doing in the shadows of the trees? Of course, she reflected bitterly, they must all take it for granted that Howard had been making love to her. Oh God! She wished futilely now that she hadn't wandered off with Howard.

But it had been *Howdie*—her Howdie. It hadn't been just any stockman.

Yes, times have changed, she thought cynically. As Jarratt had said, she was no longer a child. And Howard was a man, a man whom she didn't know very well. But not for the life of her would she admit that Jarratt had been right. Not to him. Only—just a little—to herself. Because Howard *wasn't* like that...

She raised her head and looked cautiously at Jarratt. At least he was leaving her alone. She couldn't have borne it if he'd come to say 'I told you so'. As it was, he wasn't even looking at her. He too was standing apart from the others, and his face looked sombre, remote, absorbed. She thought unexpectedly, 'He looks like a man who lives with the elements.' There were purpose and intensity in his face, his chin was aggressive, he wore his masculinity like an armour. Strength, muscle, purpose, power—there was no place in his life for tenderness and romantic love. She felt a shiver run through her right to the very marrow of her bones.

Suddenly his gaze was lifted and came straight to her, and she remembered the expression in his eyes, and the way she had felt earlier on, in the heat of the afternoon, before he had kissed her.

Why had he kissed her? Because he was an adult male and he didn't see many pretty girls? But there was Cass, wasn't there? She was pretty, and Howdie had said he was a bit wrapped up in Cass...

She glanced quickly away from him, not knowing what strange emotion had shaken her.

Nicky found it hard to sleep that night. The spinifex mattress was uneven, but it was springy and comfortable enough, and the silence of the night, once the men had all rolled themselves up in their swags, was profound.

Through the open flap of her tent she could see the sky and the stars—the Milky Way streaming across the heavens —and down below, the red glow of the dying campfire.

For a long time she lay on her back, her hands behind her head, thinking about Howdie and wondering if he had wanted to make love to her because she was Nicky Reay or simply because he was a love-starved stockman. She hadn't yet come to terms with the fact that Howard at twenty-two was—and had to be—very different from the Howard of six years ago; that the dreams you start dreaming in your early teens have to catch up with reality somewhere along the line, that physical passion is, after all, a part of love.

Her mind flipped disconcertingly to Jarratt, and the way he had kissed her, no holds barred, for no reason at all—except that he had been hovering on the brink of it ever since he met her. She didn't know how true that was, but she thought he'd had a hide to suggest that her compliance persuaded him she'd been expecting it. She hadn't. Not ever.

'You handled it rather well,' he'd told her later on. How had she handled it? She hadn't attempted to evade him, she hadn't pushed him away. Was that handling it well? She only wished she'd had the chance to handle the situation with Howard in her own way, instead of having Jarratt come in and break it up.

Suddenly she felt agonised. Everything had gone wrong– everything. And now, as she began to drift into sleep and her control of her mind and emotions slipped, it was that other man's embrace she re-experienced. She felt again Jarratt's hard mouth against her own, knew the subtle demands of his hard, male, experienced body that had deliberately attempted to arouse her in some way. And had succeeded, because just thinking of him now made her breath uneven, sent tremors through her body.

She heard herself groan out softly as if asking for help, for reassurance, 'Oh, Howdie– *Howdie*——'

She closed her eyes tightly in a kind of agony, then startled by some faint sound, opened them to see the dark shadow of a man against the sky. She struggled to sit up.

'Howdie, is that you?'

'No, it's Jarratt,' came the drawled reply. 'Did you want anything? I thought I heard you muttering.'

'I must have been dreaming,' Nicky murmured, feeling ashamed. She tried to see him through the darkness, but he was no more than a silhouette. 'I'm perfectly comfortable, thank you. I wish—I wish you'd just leave me alone.'

'Don't worry, it's what I had in mind,' he said dryly. 'So long as you haven't developed a raging fever—your stockman is snoring in his swag, by the way. You'll be able to talk to him tomorrow before I take you back home, I give you my solemn promise.'

She lay back in her sleeping bag again. She didn't—couldn't—answer him, she found his whole attitude totally aggravating. He said goodnight and waited, obviously, for her to answer him, but she bit hard on her lower lip and obstinately said nothing. Her body was tense as she waited for him to go...

When she woke in the morning, the world was red and birds were screeching in the trees. She sat up quickly and scrambled to the opening of the tent to stare out. Unbelievably, the musterers had gone, the cook and the horse tailer were packing up. The campfire was smoking, and Jarratt Buchan, riding a magnificent-looking stallion, was coming towards her over the Mitchell grass, straight out of the rising sun.

Nicky pulled down the flap of her tent. He hadn't wakened her, despite his promise. Howdie had gone and—oh God! she wanted to see him again. She wanted him to reassure her somehow, to be—to be the Howard she knew. If only he could come back to the homestead instead of being stuck out here—that way, everything would come right. She knew it would.

When she joined Jarratt for breakfast—steak and eggs that he cooked himself over the fire, toast made on the end of a long battered wire fork, billy tea—she taxed him with breaking his promise.

'Why didn't you wake me? You promised——'

His dark eyes looked at her inscrutably, slightly amused.

'You are in a fever, aren't you? But don't get in a flap, Rainbow. You'll see Howard Johnston soon enough, when we follow up the muster later in the day.'

She barely heard the last part of what he said. She was in a state of shock. He had called her Rainbow. He had, she was certain. And yet he couldn't have. She must be imagining things.

He said, 'What's making your eyes as big as saucers?'

She stammered, 'What—what did you call me?'

He looked at her consideringly. 'Well, what *did* I call you?'

'Rainbow,' she said faintly.

'So maybe I did call you that,' he agreed laconically. 'It's a pretty feminine name for a pretty feminine girl—much more to my taste than Nicky. Your second name's Iris, didn't you tell me—after your mother, who came from Kooriekirra.'

Nicky swallowed and nodded, not understanding why she was so put out, because his explanation was logical enough. But she was confused by those black eyes, and that day at Coochin Brim-brim when she had watched the children in the red sand. And now he was calling her Rainbow, the name Jack had always used. It was—crazy. She wanted to ask him if she—and Jack—had once lived in the stockmen's quarters here.

So why not?

She raised her eyes to his and he looked back at her, and something—something in the tilt of his head, the slight curl upwards at the corners of his decidedly sensual mouth—some expression deep in the warm, unnerving blackness of his eyes, warned her to beware. To ask such a question would be to open wide the book of her life at its most secret pages, and she didn't want him to see. She didn't want him to ask his calculated, analytical questions—'So you lived with the dark children? So your guardian was a rough stockrider? So how the hell did you come to be attending the same school as my sister, and to be here as my guest?'

Of course she was fooling herself to think that way, and she knew it. He would accept her as she was, just as he accepted Cass and Howard, and Shirley Capper—everyone—for what they were. So what was wrong with asking him? Except, instinctively, she knew that confession brought you close to your confessor—and she was frightened of getting too close to Jarry Buchan. Definitely frightened.

'Well, let's get moving,' he said casually into her

thoughts. 'Do you want any more tea? No?' He stooped to pick up the billy, and slung the remainder of its contents over what was left of the fire, and then, as he efficiently cleaned up, she got up to help him.

Not much later they were on their way, but by the time they'd inspected various bores where windmills pumped water into tanks, from which it gushed into long troughs for the cattle, it was close on lunchtime before they reached the new camp. Nicky was feeling exhausted both emotionally and physically. The heat was overpowering, and she and Jarratt had talked very little. Everything seemed somehow to have gone flat. Everything that had seemed so simple had now become vastly complicated—her meeting with Howard, her dreams of happy ever after——

'Damn the muster camp!' she thought quite violently. 'And damn Jarratt Buchan too'—who, in her mind, seemed to be responsible for everything that had gone wrong.

Midday dinner was not yet in progress when they reached the camp, though the cook was busy with preparations. Nicky was parched and longed for a cup of tea, but none was forthcoming and she didn't ask for it. There was a mob of cattle on the flat, the stockmen were coming in with more beasts, the dust was rising and it was hideously hot. Jarry parked the utility in the shade and without either explanations or instructions, got out and left her. She saw him cast a practised eye over the horses, select one, saddle it and ride away without sending her a single glance.

For a few minutes she relaxed, leaning back against the hot leather of the seat, then with a sigh she left the utility and wandered down to where big coolabahs marked the line of a waterhole. She thought with longing of the feathery shade, of glinting water reflecting back the blue of the sky, and she began to feel a little more at peace with herself as she walked. This wildness, this isolation, were food for the spirit if you were receptive. They—regenerated. The word flipped into her mind as effortless and as visionary as a silver fish leaping from water, yet if she expressed such a thought aloud, everyone—Guy, Juliet, Jarratt Buchan—would probably think she was off her head.

Down in the coolabahs, she heard the white corellas screeching, and she saw a hawk high up in the heavens, wide wings outspread as it glided on the invisible currents of the air. Nicky wandered slowly on in the shade, no more than half aware of her surroundings. She stooped once to pick a couple of small yellow daisies with spiky leaves, and twirled them mindlessly between finger and thumb. Then presently she began to think of Howard and to wonder if the magic of their relationship would ever come back. She knew, of course, that Guy wouldn't approve of Howard, for a number of reasons. And on consideration, she didn't think Jack would have approved of him either—not for her. Jack had had ambitions for Rainbow Reay. He wouldn't have wanted her to marry a stockman, not even a stockman who had plenty of other ideas.

Jack, Nicky mused, would have wished her to marry someone like Guy Sonder, or even, her thoughts led her on absurdly, Jarratt Buchan.

Now *that* was a mad thing to have thought up!

She began to walk quickly as though to escape from something, letting the daisies fall from her hand. She reached the edge of the tree cover, and from there she saw a little mob of cattle coming in, moving quite briskly over the spinifex. They were great hump-backed Brahmin-based cattle, and though they looked ugly and cumbersome, Nicky knew they had been specially bred to withstand the hard conditions of this land. Shading her eyes with her hand, she discovered that the stockman riding behind was Howdie, and her heart gave an odd little jump that was not entirely of pleasure. She watched him flick his whip, and saw it curl slow and graceful to touch the rump of a beast about to make a break. The creature, head down, lumbered back to the mob, and Nicky felt a flicker of admiration for Howard. He was a good stockman, whether he wanted to pursue a career of that particular type or not.

Red dust rose in a lazy hazy cloud as the mob moved on, then just as the leaders drew about level with where she stood, one of the animals suddenly broke away, and Howdie's horse was at once in pursuit, flying after it through the

102

rough tussocky grass. Howard's hat was on the back of his head, he brought his stockwhip into play, the runaway turned and then, unexpectedly—it was unbelievable!—the horse stumbled, its knees buckled——

For a moment the whole scene was like a still from a movie as Howard rose into the air and seemed suspended there. Then Nicky heard the thud right in her heart as he fell sickeningly to the ground.

After a moment during which she seemed completely paralysed, she began to run.

'Howdie—*Howdie*! Are you all right?'

To her relief, she saw that he was struggling to sit up, and then someone else reached him before she did—Jarratt Buchan. He had swung down from his horse and was stooping over Howard as Nicky arrived white-faced, just in time to hear Howard swearing shockingly, his face contorted. Then he caught sight of her and managed a grin.

'Sorry, Nicky. You should've covered your ears. Don't cry, I'm okay.' He was holding his left elbow in the palm of his right hand and his face was twisted with pain. There was nothing for Nicky to do but stand back and wait while Jarratt made a swift examination, then pronounced, 'You've broken your collarbone. Look, I've got bandages in the utility, but before you start walking, we'll get that bone back into position. Now hold on——' His hands were on Howard's shoulders, his knee was on his back between the shoulderblades.

Nicky closed her eyes and heard Howard's grunt of pain. When she looked again, Jarratt was taking off his shirt, and he used it as a rough clumsy-looking bandage to strap Howard's arm across his chest, the hand high up near his right shoulder.

The three of them walked back to the camp, Jarratt leading his horse, Nicky at Howard's side, silently sympathetic, though he assured her he wasn't in agony.

'Do you know much about first aid, Nicky?' Jarry asked pleasantly, and she shook her head. She did know a little, but it was so elementary it wasn't worth mentioning. She could deal with the little everyday accidents that happened

103

to children, but when it came to a fractured collarbone she was totally ignorant.

'Well, you might learn something today,' Jarratt commented. 'We're going to put a good-sized pad under Howard's armpit, and fix him up with a figure eight bandage. Then we'll see how you feel, Howard. One thing's for sure, though, you're not going to be much use at the muster. Or anywhere else, with one arm strapped across your chest,' he added with a grin.

Nicky was not amused.

CHAPTER SIX

HOWARD came back to the homestead with them in the utility after lunch. Oddly enough. Nicky no longer knew whether she felt pleased that Howard would be around or whether she felt embarrassed about it. She sat between the two men, with Howard on her left and his uninjured arm against hers. She endeavoured not to have any physical contact with Jarratt, but it was difficult, squeezed in as they were, and she had to consider Howard who, even if he wasn't in any real pain, must at least be uncomfortable. Jarratt had given him some tablets he carried in the first aid box that apparently went with him everywhere about the property.

When they reached the homestead, Jarratt pulled up to let Nicky out, remarking absentmindedly, 'Go and find Catherine, Nicky, will you? Tell her what's happened and that I want her to come straight over to the bungalow.'

'All right,' she agreed. Howard was trying to get the door open and she leaned across and managed it for herself, then slid out after Howard who, before he got back into the car, gave her a brief smile and told her, 'I'll see you later, Nicky.'

'I'll be over,' she agreed. She asked Jarratt, 'Shall I leave my gear?'

'Yes, yes—I'll deal with that. You won't be wanting any of the stuff you've got in the utility tonight.'

That was true. She was feeling very much in need of a shower just now, and she was certainly looking forward to getting out of her dusty jeans into something clean and a bit more feminine.

Inside, Cass had already put away her books and was giving the children an early tea on the side verandah. She looked up with a bright smile of welcome on her placid face when Nicky appeared, and exclaimed, 'Oh, Nicky, you're back! How did it go? Did you see Howard?'

'Yes. But look, Cass—he had to come back with us. He's broken his collarbone.'

'Oh no!' Cass gasped. 'Oh, Nicky, is he all right?'

'Perfectly,' Nicky reassured her. 'Jarratt's got his arm all strapped up and comfortable, but he wants you to go over to the bungalow straight away. I expect he'll tell you all about it and explain what's to be done and all that. I'll take over here for you. Where's Juliet?'

'She's started another collage. It looks rather good. Well, I'd better go, but I'll be back as soon as I can. You must want to freshen up.'

'It can wait,' said Nicky agreeably. 'Don't hurry.'

As it happened, she didn't see Cass again that night, or Howard either.

She supervised the children as they ate their meal, had them brush their teeth, and listened to them say their prayers before they got into bed—Cass had taught them that. Then having kissed them goodnight, she switched off the bedroom light and with a sigh of weariness went to look for Juliet. Juliet, she was sure, wouldn't even have thought of dinner, though she must be expecting them back, and though she herself felt too tired and unsettled to be hungry, what with Howdie's accident and one thing and another, she was sure Jarratt would be needing a good meal.

Juliet was in the spare bedroom that Tracy had used as a sewing room. It contained a large cutting-out table as well as a sewing machine, and she had her new collage—a very large one—spread out on the table, and a variety of scraps of different shapes and sizes scattered about. She put her hand to her mouth and stared in dismay as Nicky switched on the light, which she had neglected to do in her absorption.

'Nicky! You're back already? Whatever time can it be? Did you have a good time?' She tossed back her long blonde hair and got to her feet. 'You're *covered* in dust! Where's Jarry?'

Patiently Nicky answered her questions and explained

106

about Howard's accident, though it was plain that Juliet wasn't particularly interested in what had happened to Catherine's brother.

'I didn't even know she had a brother working here,' she said with a frown as she followed Nicky through the house in the direction of the kitchen. 'It's quite a family affair, isn't it? What's he like? I hope we're not going to have him hanging about all day expecting to be fed or something. Catherine will have to look after him—she's not as busy as all that. He's her brother. And they can eat in their own place.'

Nicky took a deep breath. Pretty soon Juliet was going to discover that she and Howard Johnston knew each other rather well. She said, 'Look, Juliet, I told you I knew Catherine long ago, and of course I knew Howard too. They were both my friends, and they always will be.'

They had reached the kitchen, and discovered Daisy and Noreen busy peeling vegetables, and grilling steak ready on the table. Nicky sighed with relief and presumed she had Cass to thank for this.

Juliet said with a little smile, 'You're sweet, Nicky, so terribly loyal—to me too. You're a far better person than I am. I agree Catherine's quite a nice girl, but all the same——' She spread her hands and gave a little shrug, implying, Nicky supposed, that 'nursemaids' and stockmen weren't the sort of people one mixed with socially. Nothing more was said, and she busied herself in the kitchen feeling more than slightly troubled. It looked like being a rather tricky situation. She wondered as she put on the vegetables to cook and seasoned the steaks, and Juliet laid the table, exactly what was going on over at the Johnstons' bungalow, and if all her own past was coming out. And if it did, what of it? Except that Juliet, if it was passed on to her, would probably be a bit cool to her.

At that moment Juliet came into the kitchen to ask, 'Where's Jarry? I'd like to know if I'm expected to lay a place at the table for the stockman. I shouldn't be surprised. Sometimes it seems my brother does have some rather unorthodox ideas. I mean, Lewis Trent is definitely superior, and a governess is—acceptable, but a stock-man—! Oh, sorry—they're your friends, I forgot.'

Nicky bit her lip and said nothing. She somehow didn't think Howard would be sitting at the dinner table with them.

And neither he was. In fact neither Cass nor Howard joined them, and over dinner Jarratt, quite deliberately she was sure, said very little about the injured stockman. It seemed he didn't want to pander to her interest in Howdie. Well, never mind, she thought, she would go over to the bungalow after dinner and find out for herself how Howard was feeling. She intended to have an early night, but she would certainly do that first, and then before she went to bed she would have the shower she was longing for—and wash her hair too. She had found time only for a quick wash and a brush up, and a change of clothing, before dinner.

Juliet had gone into the sitting room to play some records and Nicky was about to leave the dining room when Jarratt put a hand on her arm.

'By the way, Nicky, if you're thinking of going over to the Johnstons' bungalow, you'd better forget it. Howard was feeling a bit of a reaction and I've sedated him, and Catherine is trying to catch up on an essay she's been having trouble with. So leave it.'

She raised her head and saw the little mocking smile that lifted just slightly the corners of his mouth, and suddenly she was sure he had seen her struggling with Howard—heard her plead, 'Don't!' It was a hateful feeling, and she turned away without saying anything.

She didn't go to the bungalow. She went to her room.

It was not until morning that she knew he had fooled her. Because when she rose early, anxious to see Howard and learn how he was feeling, he had gone.

Cass was making breakfast for the little girls, and when Nicky enquired after Howard, she said, 'He went out like a light. I could hardly wake him this morning to be ready for Jarry.'

Nicky stared at her. 'What on earth are you talking

about, Cass? Surely Jarry hasn't taken Howdie back to the muster camp——'

'Of course not!' Cass widened her eyes. 'I thought Jarry would have told you. He decided to take him to Alice. We agreed it would be a good idea for Howdie to see the doctor.'

'Oh.' Nicky fought back the anger that was rising in her. Jarratt had deliberately not told her that, as though it were none of her business. She said controlledly, 'You should have gone along too, Cass. Juliet and I could have minded the children.'

'I can't take time off like that,' said Cass cheerfully.

The two little girls came in, their faces shining, Medora tugging a comb through her fair curls. Cass reached down as though it were second nature to help her. 'I thought you might have liked to go, but Jarry didn't seem to want to take anyone along, and I didn't like to suggest it. I mean, after all, I'm only employed here, and you're Juliet's guest. Besides, I didn't know if you'd said anything about—well, about you and Howdie.'

Nicky bit her lip. 'Jarry knows we were friends when we were children. But, Cass, there's nothing else to say yet, is there? What- what did Howdie say about me last night?'

'Oh,' Cass said with a smile, 'he said how pretty you are and that money hasn't made you big-headed. And Nicky,' she added apologetically, 'I know you'll be disappointed, but Howdie decided this morning that he'd stay in Alice for a while.'

'What?' Nicky stared at her. Just like that—the moment they met again! But Howard hadn't made that decision, she was positive. Jarratt Buchan had made it for him. It was just the kind of thing he would do.

'He'll be back,' Cass said reassuringly. 'Actually he wants to look around for another job—and I can guess why. Being the wife of a stockman out here isn't very attract-ive—not to the sort of girl he's interested in,' she added significantly.

Nicky scarcely listened, she was so furiously angry. And in fact she was thinking more about Jarratt than about the fact that she wasn't after all going to see much of Howard. She remembered what Jarratt had said about being responsible for her—how he had come after her the night she had walked away with Howard. As well, he had been hanging around near her tent close enough to hear her when she moaned a little. He certainly had a suspicious mind, she reflected bitterly, and she refrained from reminding herself that Howard had proved more difficult to handle than she had expected.

So now he was making sure he wasn't bothered by his responsibility, and she wondered how long he intended leaving Howard cooling his heels in Alice Springs, with no means of coming back to Coochin Brim-brim. A few days would be ample time to look around for work in a town of that size.

It was insufferably interfering on Jarratt's part, particularly when she and Howard had been childhood friends, and she felt an urge to tell him exactly what she thought of him. She would do exactly that, she decided, the moment he came home.

He wasn't back till after midnight.

Nicky was in bed, but she wasn't asleep. She had been lying in bed trying to fool herself that she was reading, but all the time she was thinking of Jarratt and how high-handedly he had acted—and how meanly. How officious he was, interfering in her private life! She burned to defeat him somehow, and certainly she would tell him what she thought of him, even if he was her host.

She had discarded her book and switched off her light when she heard his car, and then a few minutes later his footsteps, not loud but very decisive on the floorboards of the verandah. She reached for the light switch and slipped out of bed. In a few short moments she had pulled on a blue shirt and dragged a pair of jeans on over her pyjama pants. She looked quickly in the mirror, ran a comb through her hair and saw the flash of her own angry blue eyes as she departed to run Jarratt Buchan to earth.

He was in the kitchen. He had pulled off his tie and unbuttoned his shirt, and he was standing in the middle of the room, his head well back as he drank down a glass of beer. Nicky paused in the doorway momentarily, strangely arrested by the sight of this tall broad-shouldered man with the dark hairy chest. Drinking beer.

He emptied the glass and reached for the bottle on the table, stopping with his hand in mid-air as he caught sight of her. She was shocked, now she could see his face, at how tired he looked tired and haggard, and very much in need of a shave. The absurd thought entered her mind that she must have been mad to think Jack would have liked her to marry a man like Jarratt Buchan. He was rough—impossible——

'Haven't you got yourself to bed yet?'

As on other occasions, the moment she heard that cultured, almost murmurous voice, she was confounded. She blinked and swallowed hard before she could answer him. Why did he have to be so disconcerting?

'I couldn't sleep.' She added accusingly, 'Did you bring Howard back with you?'

He poured the rest of the beer into his glass while she was speaking then raised it to his lips, drank half of it down, and wiped his mouth on the back of his hand. His eyes looked black and there were dark shadows round them, almost as dark as the stubble of hair on his upper lip and along his jawline.

'No, I did not. Haven't you talked to Catherine?' He looked at her starkly, unreadably. 'Howard slept on it and decided he might as well stay in Alice a while.'

'Slept on *what*?' she flared. 'The— the slating you gave him last evening after I got out of the car?'

'My dear Nichola,' he drawled, 'I'm not in the habit of giving my stockmen a slating over personal matters. I suppose that's what's in your mind. Howard Johnston has human instincts that it's only natural for him to follow. If anyone deserves a slating, it's you.'

She gritted her teeth. 'How long is he going to be away?'

He looked at her with an intensity that made her shrivel up. 'That's his business, isn't it? He'll be useless to me as a

111

stockman for several weeks, so for the present I'm not greatly concerned.'

'You only think of yourself, don't you?' she accused. 'Juliet has to give up everything and come and stay here just for *your* benefit——'

He drank the rest of his beer in an unconcerned way, and now his eyes glinted with a hard amusement. 'That's right,' he agreed. 'And if it's of any interest to you, I visited Tracy in hospital today, and it seems likely that Juliet will have to stay here for quite some little while yet.'

'Why should she?' Nicky argued, 'if she doesn't want to. You could manage perfectly well with Lena if you wanted to.'

The glint in his eyes grew harder. 'Are you trying to run my life?' She didn't answer and he moved to the sink to rinse his glass. 'If I say Juliet's to stay, then she's to stay. At least it will prevent her from getting round her mother and racing off to land herself in some impossible predicament in France. That's how I see it, and I don't want an argument. As for you——'

'You can't order *me* about,' she said quickly.

'You took the words right out of my mouth,' he agreed dryly. 'So when would you like to go home? You have only to say the word. I dare say I'll adapt to life without your cooking, pleasant though I've found it.'

Her throat was dry as she stared back at him, her heart pounding. She knew she didn't want to leave. Of course she could go to Alice, to Howard. Yet she discarded that thought without even looking at it properly, and told him shakily, 'I—I don't have a home. I'd have to check I could stay with—friends——'

He looked amused. 'Don't worry, I won't push you out. You're welcome to stay here as long as you like.' A little smile lifted the corners of his wide mouth and he put out his hand and touched her hair briefly. She felt a little shock go through her and stepped quickly away, and his smile vanished.

'Was there anything else you wanted, now you know I've left your childhood love in Alice?'

112

'No.' She met his eyes and after a second her glance fell. She asked indistinctly, 'Why are you so set on keeping me and Howard apart?'

He looked surprised. 'I'm not set on it. Howard made his own decision—the right one, to my mind. He'd be wasting his time hanging round here with his arm bandaged up. He has ideas of finding himself a new job, I understand. He doesn't intend to spend the rest of his life rounding up cattle that don't belong to him. He's ambitious—like his sister—but a little slow in finding his direction. So don't pile all the blame on me, Rainbow,' he concluded. His voice unsettled her with its change to gentleness, and his use of that name did strange things to her heart. 'You can't go back in time, you know. All that's past is past—yet it's part of the sum that totals up to the person you are, and even the person you will become. It's better left unspoiled, intact, in its rightful place. You're young—your discoveries, your real discoveries, are ahead of you. You won't find them in your childhood.'

She listened and a number of things went through her mind—those days when she had played with the aboriginal children in the red sand; the years in Alice with Cass and Howdie. Boarding school and her dreams of love—of Howard. The last few months when Jack had been dying and had told her things she'd never known. It all added up mysteriously to her—to Nichola Iris Reay. To—to Rainbow. And now she was here at Coochin Brim-brim, alone with Jarratt Buchan in the small hours of the morning, in a sleeping house in the middle of the Never-Never.

She shivered slightly. Perhaps he was right, perhaps her real discoveries were still ahead of her. She felt terribly aware of him. He was so positive, so self-assured. The crazy thing was that she had left her bed to accuse him, and now—— She sighed. He had defeated her. She didn't have a hope of asserting herself against a man like Jarratt Buchan. Not when he called her Rainbow in that fraught-with-meaning way. Not when he looked at her the way he was doing——

Suddenly she turned her back on him and fled through

the dark house to her bedroom, without even wishing him goodnight.

For several days after that everything—outwardly—went on just as it had before she had gone to the muster with Jarratt. Yet for Nicky, something shattering had happened —her longed-for meeting with Howard. And it had been shattering because it had been so different from anything she had ever imagined. *Howard* was so different. Something fragile had vanished as though it had never been.

She and Cass and Juliet continued to co-exist amiably enough, each of them for the greater part of the time going their separate ways, occupying themselves with their individual tasks and activities For Nicky, there was the garden to be watered and weeded, flowers to be picked and arranged And there was the evening meal to prepare. Sometimes during the afternoons while Cass was doing her lessons, she took over the children for a short while, sometimes she swam or went for a ride. Jarratt, it seemed to her was even less in evidence than he had ever been, and though she had made up her mind to ask him when he would be going to Alice to fetch Howdie back, she never did it.

One searingly hot day when the sun stood out in the burnished sky like a vermilion moon, the three girls with the children walked over to the waterhole for a swim.

'Jarry should have given me the use of a car,' Juliet complained, 'but he's got it into his head that I'm not to be trusted behind a steering wheel. As if anything could happen in this vacuum!'

They walked slowly, the brims of their cotton hats flapping in the heat. They wore shirts over their swimwear and all of them gasped with relief when they reached the waterhole. Marcie-Ann and Medora raced down the bank, eager to plunge into the clear pale green water, so coolly shaded by the coolabahs and ghost gums.

When Nicky had been in the water so long that the skin on her fingers was beginning to crinkle, she decided it was time to come out. She stood on the bank to dry, tossing back her hair that was clinging to her neck and cheeks in curling tendrils, and literally watching the water evaporate from her pale coral-coloured bikini. The others were still in the water. Juliet, her long blonde hair pinned up on top of her head, her eyes protected by big sunglasses, sat on a rock in the water near the bank. She was submerged almost to chin level, and she was reading a magazine which was beginning to look rather bedraggled, and she was not in the slightest bit interested in what anyone else was doing. Cass, on the other hand, gave all her attention to the children, despite the fact that both of them were expert swimmers. Just now she stood waist-deep in water watching them build an underwater city out of stones, in the clear shallows near a little sandy beach in the curve of the bank. She wore a decorous one-piece swimsuit of faded green that didn't even pretend to glamorise her slightly plump figure, and her long brown hair hung down in rats' tails as she watched the two little girls busily building.

Nicky had fallen into a dream and was startled almost out of her skin when a deep blue shadow moved on the ground beside her, and Jarratt was there.

'I thought I'd find you all here,' he remarked, and she turned her head swiftly, feeling the colour creep up under her skin. His dark eyes travelled briefly over her figure in the revealing bikini, then came to rest quizzically on her face. 'What sort of a swimmer are you?'

'Average,' she said, aware that her heart was beating fast.

He pulled off his shirt and tossed it on the ground. He wore navy and white striped swim trunks that made his hips look lean and narrow in comparison with the breadth of his tanned shoulders, and there were dark hairs on his legs that matched those on his chest.

'Are you coming in again?' he asked her. She hesitated and a shower of water glittered in the air between them. Marcie-Ann had discovered Jarratt's presence and was throwing water to attract his attention. Immediately he forgot Nicky and strode down the bank, and in a few seconds he was with Cass, and sharing her interest in the underwater city. Juliet had done no more than raise a hand to acknowledge her brother's presence, though she had by now abandoned her magazine. Nicky stayed exactly where she was, and she stared down at the water as she had been doing, but everything was different. Her body, her mind, were in a fever, and she couldn't keep her eyes off Jarratt, whose white teeth were now flashing as he laughed at something Medora said to him.

Presently, he and Cass took the children into the deeper water, Cass towing Marcie-Ann along, and Jarry with little Medora riding on his back, her small brown arms wound around his neck, her childish voice raised as she uttered excited squeals. Nicky was forgotten, and she watched half-smiling yet with a feeling of edgy tension that was disquieting. Jarratt had asked her if she was coming in again, but now, quite obviously, he didn't care one way or the other. He could have waited for her, she thought, but he hadn't, and now she found it literally impossible to go and join him and Cass. She saw Jarratt say something to Cass, and Cass raised her head and smiled at him, and something inside Nicky was suddenly still.

Cass was plumpish, placid, kind. There had never been anything remarkable or dazzling about her, yet in that moment it struck home to Nicky that there was a very womanly dignity and even beauty in her smooth, sun-tanned face. Loving, romantic, warm-hearted Cass. Suddenly Nicky saw her as Jarratt must see her, and she knew that Howdie could easily be right in believing he was attracted to Cass. It would be a wonder if he wasn't, seeing her every day as he did ...

Nicky moved away rather slowly and found her shirt. She had pulled it on when the children came splashing up the bank and ran to join her. In the waterhole, Cass and Jarratt were wading along by the bank, their heads bent, deep in conversation. What were they talking about? Cass's lessons? Howard? Or was it something far more intimate and personal that absorbed them?

'What business is it of mine?' Nicky asked herself in annoyance. All the same, it would be great for Cass. 'If Jarratt loves her,' she added mentally.

So what was love?

What *was* love?

She stopped to help Medora with her sandals, making a pretence of listening to the child's chatter, but she felt cold inside. She thought in a kind of panic of Howdie, and of that old familiar warm glow that used to come over her when he was in her mind. It didn't come now. It hadn't come for quite a while. She was beginning to suspect that when it came to the point, she didn't know what love was. She didn't know the first thing about it. Her discoveries in that direction were certainly all ahead of her. Was that what Jarratt had been talking about? Love?

'Catherine says we can go home and ask Lena for a glass of milk,' Marcie-Ann said. 'Are you coming, Nicky?'

'Yes—yes, I think I'll come too,' said Nicky. 'I've had enough swimming for one day.' She was pulling on her cotton hat when Juliet called out, 'Hang on, Nicky, I'm coming too!'

A few minutes later the children were skipping, hand in hand, ahead of her and Juliet through the dried-out-looking grasses. It was still hot, but the sun was low in the sky now and the fierceness had gone out of the day. Juliet, her shirt slung round her shoulders, asked Nicky in a low voice, 'What do you think Jarry and Catherine are talking about, back there in the waterhole? I wish I'd had the hide to go and make it a threesome, but I suppose it wouldn't have been worth the effort. If Jarry didn't want me around he'd have told me, and I loathe being bossed around in front of—well, in front of other people.'

Nicky laughed carelessly. 'I don't think he'd have minded your being there. They're probably discussing Cass's lessons or something.'

'*Something*,' said Juliet emphatically. 'It might start with lessons, but that girl is definitely out to win my brother. It was she who sent the children out of the water— I heard her distinctly. Goodness knows, I wish he would get married—that would let me out, and poor old Tracy too. But I certainly wouldn't choose Catherine Johnston as a sister-in-law. That would be just a little bit hard to take. Next thing, we'd have her brother coming to stay with us in Adelaide, and from what I've seen of stockmen, I hardly

117

think that would go down well with any of our friends. Oh, I know Catherine was a friend of yours, but that was when you were children, and children don't discriminate. It's later on you learn you simply must have some standards.'

With difficulty Nicky held her tongue– mainly because she was afraid of what she would say if she did speak. She could destroy for ever her friendship with Juliet if she told her she was a snob, and that if she faced up to facts, she would know that Catherine Johnston was worth ten of her—and ten of Nicky too—in every possible way. Telling someone that was something you just didn't do when you were a guest.

She walked on breathing deeply and evenly, reminding herself that Juliet couldn't help having these attitudes. They had obviously been taught to her by her mother. Juliet had been born to comfort, to riches, to a sense of superiority over those less fortunate. As for Nicky herself, she was a fraud, and becoming increasingly and uncomfortably aware of it. And that was because she had obeyed Jack's injunctions to keep quiet when she went to school in Adelaide. She wished now that she hadn't kept quiet, that she had been honest and open. Children don't discriminate, Juliet had just said that herself. She'd have been accepted. All the same, she rather thought she wouldn't have been here now, a guest at Coochin Brim-brim—a girl whose guardian had lived in a dugout under the ground, whose father had been a mate of that rough man.

She was certainly, when she came to think of it, here under false pretences. And she had to say something on Cass's behalf.

She said slowly into the silence that had fallen between them, 'I think if two people love each other, then that's all that really matters. And—and I don't think Howard would turn up and expect to stay with you in Adelaide. He's just not the type to push in where he's not wanted, or to—to bludge on anyone. Even if he *is* only a stockman,' she concluded a little hotly.

'Loyal old Nicky,' Juliet said good-naturedly. 'You're a lot more tolerant than I am. But I don't think for a moment that Jarry is in love with that girl. If he ever did rush off and marry someone like that—someone beneath him—it would be because Tracy had jacked up or something, and he was pushed into a corner and just had to get married to the most likely person around. And that's one of the big disadvantages of living in the Never-Never—the choice is so limited, there are pitifully few people one could possibly marry. So let's hope he never is pushed into a corner. Tracy will come back, she likes the money as much as I do, and Jarry never hesitates when it comes to twisting our arms. Frankly, I should hate to be Tracy. I couldn't bear to live here, could you?'

'I like the outback,' said Nicky, knowing she sounded perverse, but meaning it. 'Probably because I lived in the Centre as a child,' she added.

'All the same, you'll be as pleased as I shall be to get back to Adelaide and civilisation,' Juliet said knowingly, and rather weakly Nicky didn't pursue the subject.

Cass and Jarratt didn't get home for quite some time. By then, Nicky was in the kitchen preparing the accompaniments to the peppered steaks she was going to serve for dinner. She was decorating a salad platter with sprigs of fresh mint when Jarratt, just showered and wearing bamboo coloured cotton pants and a vandyke brown voile shirt, put in an appearance.

'Mail day,' he informed her. 'Two letters for you, Nicky. I'm afraid I've made you wait for them—I didn't take them over to the waterhole.'

For some reason Nicky thought instantly of Howard, and dried her hands quickly on the kitchen towel so that she could take the letters he handed her. But when she looked at the envelopes, she saw one letter was from San Francisco—from Guy—and the other one was from Claudia Mallard, in Adelaide.

'Let me know when your guardian's coming for you, won't you?' Jarratt said.

'Yes, of course,' she said, colouring, 'I suppose you'll be glad to be relieved of your responsibility.'

He smiled slightly, but neither confirmed nor denied, and

stood watching her as she slipped the two letters into the pocket of the apron she was wearing, and returned to the salad.

His lips twisted wryly. 'First things first, is that it? I'm flattered. You must know how hungry I am ... That looks pretty, but I hope there are steaks too.'

'Yes,' she said briefly, 'pepper steaks.'

'Fine Do you like cooking Rainbow?' She felt her nerves jump at his use of that name. but he went on leaning indolently against the wall, and looked at her sleepily and maddeningly from half-closed eyes. 'Or do you do it all for love of me?' he asked.

'What do you think?' she retorted. "I do it to help Juliet out.'

'Thus defeating my foul purpose in bringing my sister here. Ah well, the man who marries her will have to suffer while she learns to cook.'

'I don't think he'll suffer all that much,' said Nicky practically 'And now if you don't mind, I'd like to get on with the dinner.'

She didn't read her letters till after they had eaten. Coffee had been made. and Cass had brought in a rough copy of some essay she'd written for Jarratt's criticism. The children. who found it too hot to sleep. were on the verandah in their pyjamas, drinking lemon squash as they lay on their stomachs on the cool wooden floor, and Juliet was determinedly playing records despite Cass.

Nicky sat a litle apart and read her letters, starting with Guy's. His main news was that he was prolonging his visit to the States, and she was conscious of a feeling of relief. With no date set for his return to Australia, it looked as if she could count on staying here for a little while yet at least.

Claudia's letter upset her—or at least, it made her blood boil. It assumed Guy's intentions towards Nicky to be far more specific than she had ever taken them to be, but Claudia didn't attempt to conceal the fact that she considered Nicky a nonentity. 'It's time Guy married, of course,' she wrote. 'I suggest, since he is prolonging his absence, that you come back to Adelaide immediately. We shall then be able to concentrate on making you more presentable, despite your youth and your rather dubious background. You may not be aware of it, but you're sadly lacking in that subtle aura a girl of breeding acquires at home. It's a blessing at least that Jack Lane has gone, and we shan't have that embarrassment to explain away when we begin making wedding plans.'

Wedding plans! Did Claudia take it for granted Nicky would say yes if Guy asked her to marry him? Because she wouldn't—she was not even the slightest bit in love with him. She felt so incensed by Claudia's lack of consideration, her tactlessness, that she didn't want to read any more. Moreover, she felt deeply hurt. It appeared that all Claudia's kindnesses to her in Adelaide—helping her to choose clothes, introducing her to 'nice' people, advising her about the 'right' thing to do—they had all been designed to remedy the—the deficiencies of a girl who lacked breeding. As for her remark about Jack, that was in the worst possible taste.

'Not pleased with your letters?' Jarratt's voice enquired dryly, and Nicky swiftly wiped the frown from her face. Jarratt stood looking down at her as she thrust the pages of the letter back into their envelope. Then he reached out and pulled up one of the rattan chairs for himself, and sat down, stretching his long legs out in front of him Nicky looked around her uneasily. Juliet had disappeared, and so had Cass. And the children. She and Jarratt were alone. From the darkness outside she heard the sad call of a mopoke, a sound she remembered from her earliest years, a sound she loved—evocative, nostalgic, oddly comforting. It belonged way back in the pre-Alice Springs days, to a time that was so vague she couldn't really remember it at all. And that smell of dust in the air—that was almost as evocative. Her nostrils dilated slightly.

'Dust,' said Jarratt briefly. 'We're going to have rain to lay it. Tonight ... Well, are you going to tell me what's new?'

In her letters, he meant, and she shrugged indifferently.

121

'My letters aren't all that interesting—to you.' She added deliberately, 'I thought I might have heard from Howard.'

'Ah yes.' His expression changed subtly, hardened. 'I've been hearing about your youthful amourette from Catherine. She gave it a really big wrap up—but I guess she's a romantic.' His eyes were intent on her, and she felt her spine prickle. 'Are you still interested in updating it? I wouldn't blame Howard for giving it a go, of course—you've got more than good looks going for you.'

Nicky bit her lip. He meant money, she realised, and it was a hateful thing to say, because Howard would never lean on a woman, and she'd said as much already to Juliet. But there was no point in getting into an argument with Jarratt about it—he'd have her tied up in knots in a moment, and what he thought didn't really matter one iota to her.

She said chillingly, 'I gather you and Cass were talking about me down at the waterhole.'

'Yes. Weren't your ears burning?' he countered maddeningly. His attention returned to her mail. 'Who was your other letter from?'

'My other letter?'

'One was from Guy Sonder,' he said reasonably. 'Who's Mrs Claudia Mallard? That's what I'm wondering.'

The cheek of the man—examining her letters!

'I thought you already knew,' she said icily. 'She's Guy's sister.'

She added nothing to that, though he waited. If he wanted to know why Claudia had written, what she had said, he was right out of luck. And later on she was going to tear that letter into tiny bits.

He said, 'You don't give much away, do you? One would think you have some guilty secret.'

She looked up and met his eyes. He was smiling in a speculative way that was more impersonal than unfriendly, and she thought how he had looked in the water this afternoon when he and Cass had been fooling about. He didn't look at her the way he had looked at Cass. Yet even so, as she met his glance, something happened to her—the same sort of thing that was always happening. She had always found the expression deep in his eyes disturbing. It affected her oddly- did something to her metabolism. Those almost black eyes seemed to say, 'You are a woman and I am aware of it.' Worse still, they made *her* aware of it. That was why this afternoon beside the clear green water under the coolabah trees she had been- shaken Her heart had thumped the way it was doing now. She didn't like being looked at that way. *Tyger, tyger, burning bright*——

'Well?' he drawled out. 'You're not going to deny it?'

'Deny what?' she stammered.

'That you have a guilty secret—something to hide.'

Something to hide—could he read her thoughts? She was aware of slight panic, but—of course, he was talking about her refusal to tell him what was in her letters. She moved quickly and stood up Her feet were bare because she had slipped off her sandals in the heat. 'I don't have any guilty secrets. I'm just not the sort of person who—who blabs out everything to anybody.'

He was on his feet too, and he seemed immensely taller than she.

'Am I—*anybody*, Rainbow?' He put his hand on her arm and her heart began to thud. Her letters slipped on to the floor. Now, as they stood facing each other, above the soft light from the table lamp, her glance settled for some reason on his mouth. His lips were parted slightly as though he were going to say something more, but he didn't. He simply pulled her close, so that her cheek was against the warmth of his chest. She could feel the beat of his blood, feel his body's heat through the soft cotton voile of his shirt. One of his hands slid up under her shirt and rested against her bare back, and his lips were on her hair. She felt herself tremble. Her mind had completely emptied- -she was like the cup of a flower waiting to receive the dew——

Then she heard someone coming, and he released her and was stooping to pick up the letters she had dropped when Cass appeared. Cass, she thought shaken. He wouldn't want Cass to see him with Nicky in his arms.

'Oh, Jarry,' said Cass blithely, 'I've made that alteration

123

you suggested. Is it too late for you to check it over? I want to be done with it.'

'Right! Let's have it—I'll take a look at it now,' he said, not briskly, not as if he minded the interruption in the least.

Cass had a sort of inky look about her. She looked like a student, Nicky thought. Her hair was ruffled as though she had been running her fingers through it, and there was a wistful, half-dreaming smile on her lips and in her wide eyes. Nicky felt jolted. Cass was so vulnerable, somehow. Jarratt sat down on the cane couch and she sat down with him, very close, looking over his shoulder trustfully as he read what she had written.

Quietly, unobtrusively, Nicky picked up the sandals she had discarded and went to her room. She felt full of nerves, she felt guilty that she had let Jarratt hold her like that, guilty that her heart had pounded. She had no idea what would have happened if Cass hadn't come with her school-books—with her request that Jarratt check over her work. Nicky had forgotten Howard, and the start of the conversation. She could only think of Jarratt, and the way he had called her Rainbow. That had been her undoing, that had led her on naturally into an elusive pleasure, half physical, half emotional, intensified by his holding her so close to him.

As she stood barefoot in her room, the rain that Jarratt had forecast began to fall, hard and heavy on the iron roof. She stared across at the mirror, but instead of herself she saw Jarratt's face. She envied Cass. Yes, she knew she would give anything to live here, to come to Jarratt as Cass did with her lessons, to lean over his shoulder, to listen to his voice——

When had it happened?

Nicky turned away from the mirror and got ready for bed, and when she had switched off the light she lay in the dark for a long time, kept awake by the sound of the rain. Yet if she were honest, she knew it was not the rain that made her wakeful, it was her own thoughts.

If Cass had not come...

CHAPTER SEVEN

NICKY slept at last, and had one of her recurring dreams.

She was on a train, and through the window she saw Cass and Howard, as they used to be, on the platform. She waved to them and they waved back, then, as the train began to move, she ran to the door in a sudden panic and jumped out, almost falling. When she regained her balance, Cass and Howdie were running away from her. Nicky ran too, but however fast she ran, they ran faster, and she knew with despair that she would never catch up with them. She sobbed out, 'Wait for me—please wait for me!' but they didn't hear—they never did. She was barefooted and wearing the checked cotton dress that she used to wear to school in Alice Springs, and she could see clearly the three-cornered tear in the skirt that she had mended herself, rather clumsily.

Then suddenly, as she was crying out 'Howdie—Cass!' it wasn't those two she was pursuing after all. They had vanished, and it was Jarratt Buchan who suddenly turned to face her and block her way. 'So this is what you've been hiding from me,' he accused 'How dare you come here with my sister, pretending to be what you aren't?' As he spoke, he began to shake her hard, until she gasped out, 'Don't—please don't——'

But the shaking went on until she woke, sobbing, her cheeks wet with tears. To find the bedside lamp was on and Jarratt, in a pair of dark blue shorts, was leaning over the bed and shaking her.

'Wake up—wake up, Rainbow. You're having a nightmare.'

To her horror, she went on weeping, and he reached out and pulled her hard against his muscular midriff.

'Now shut *up*. You've been dreaming, that's all. Tell me

about it—that's the way to exorcise it. Come on, tell me——'

'They wouldn't wait—they ran away—I was all by myself—and then——'

She stopped and he said, 'You're not by yourself any more. I'm here, see? I'm with you—you're safe with me, so wipe your eyes and stop crying all over my diaphragm.' He used an edge of the sheet to wipe her wet cheeks, and she knew her tears were ridiculous because they were over a dream. She struggled away from him, embarrassed at what she had dreamed and embarrassed still more at the way she had been clinging to him.

'I'm sorry. I'm all right now. It was just a stupid dream. I didn't mean to wake you.'

'Well, I know that,' he said dryly, and added, 'Who was it who wouldn't wait?'

'Cass—Howard——' she murmured.

'Good God! So you're crying over Howard Johnston.' He had put her right away from him, and she stared at him helplessly, intensely aware of the savage, almost ugly look that had come over his face. He moved to the end of the bed and looked at her through narrowed eyes. 'What do you want? For me to bring him back?'

Nicky hugged her knees to her and shivered, conscious now of her mussed-up hair and her tear-stained face, and the fact that half the buttons on her pyjama top were undone. Lashes lowered, she fastened them with shaking hands. She was utterly shocked, yet excited too, at the dark male look of him as he sat bare-chested on the end of her bed, eyeing her inimically.

She said unsteadily, 'I don't want you to do anything. You've interfered enough——'

'How am I expected to take that? I've interfered once and once only, and if you ask me, it was a kindness I did you. Unless you intended to allow yourself to be seduced that night just for old times' sake.' He got up abruptly, staring at her scarlet face mercilessly. 'I'm not interfering. Get that out of your mind. Make your discoveries your own way—do what you like. I don't want to be *in loco parentis*

126

to you—God forbid. I take some comfort, however, from the fact that Howard's been winged, and when he comes back he won't be such a menace. Well, I'll leave you to your dreams, Rainbow.'

'Don't call me that,' she said fiercely, upset by his attitude.

'Why not?' His eyes were dark and diabolical. 'Is it Howard's name for you? Does he call you that?'

She was somehow shocked. 'No one does,' she said, and added under her breath, 'now.'

'Well then, I do. It's a name that suits you.' He moved abruptly to the head of the bed, and she stiffened. But it was only to flick off the light. 'Goodnight,' he said into the darkness, and through the rain Nicky heard the sound of his bare feet as he left the room.

She lay quivering, her mind obsessed by his image, by his voice. No matter how he derided her, it had happened. When? she asked herself, though when didn't matter. Howard belonged well and truly in the past now. Even her dream—her nightmare—had become updated, because Jarratt Buchan had intruded into it. Catching her out—discovering her guilty secrets.

She woke in the morning nervy and on edge, remembering immediately what had happened during the night. The rain had gone, the garden was steaming drifts of white vapour moved across the red earth as the sun burned down, fiercely hot already As she dressed, she hoped no one had seen the light in her room or the man sitting on the side of her bed holding her against his half-naked body. What would Cass think? And—oh God!—the thought of Cass made her wonder if Jarratt had ever gone to comfort *her* in the night, held *her* in his arms.

She was thankful when she went out to breakfast to find he had gone.

The children had eaten, and she could hear Cass talking to them in the garden where she was probably giving them a nature study talk after the rain. Not to have to face Cass yet was somehow a relief too. All Nicky wanted was a strong cup of coffee and a piece of toast, and when she went to the kitchen for it, Lena was there singing happily. She took her breakfast on to the verandah, and her nerves had settled somewhat when Juliet appeared, wearing the pale green silk jumpsuit she sometimes wore first thing in the mornings. She too had settled for coffee, and she too had something on her mind, so if Nicky was looking pale and distraught she wasn't aware of it. She settled in one of the big rattan armchairs, her legs curled up under her, a brooding look on her face. Nicky supposed she was preoccupied with thoughts of her collage, until she suddenly turned to her and spoke.

'Nicky, I had a letter from Marc yesterday. He's broken off with that girl his parents were pressuring him into marrying. It's over—finished. He's asked me to come back to France.'

Nicky forced herself to give Juliet her full attention. The other girl's eyes were bright with determination now, and it flashed through her mind, 'We'll be leaving here—Juliet's going to refuse to stay on.' She asked, 'Will you go to France?'

Juliet hunched her shoulders. 'How can I? Trouble is, I don't have the money for my fare, and Jarratt's refused point blank to have any part in it. I talked to him last night when I finally managed to get rid of Catherine and her damned books—you'd gone off to bed. He says if Marc's serious about me, then he can come out to Australia. Full stop. The old sexist idea that the woman should be passive. Even the fact that Marc's actually asked me to go doesn't interest him one little bit.'

'Does Marc want you to marry him?'

'Of course!' Juliet widened her grey-green eyes. 'We're madly in love with each other. It happened the moment we met. We'd probably have been married by now if Jarry hadn't interfered and made my mother bring me home. Marc wanted me to stay, he said he was going to ask Marie-Laure to release him from a promise that was really his parents', not his. But my mother got in a tizz and wrote and told Jarry all about it. Threats flew up from the southern hemisphere and she was having such hysterics I was too

128

embarrassed to do anything but let myself be dragged off. Next thing, as you know, I was summoned here, to be kept under observation. Jarry's behaved like a pig. But he's not going to order my life for ever.'

Nicky listened with mixed feelings. She had had no idea that the French affair was so serious, and was a little inclined to wonder if Marc's charms hadn't faded somewhat—until this letter came. She agreed with Juliet that Jarry was interfering, she had personal experience of that—but he was looking after his sister's interests, she supposed, and she even thought it was reasonable to expect Marc to come to Australia if he was serious about Juliet.

'What will you do?' she asked Juliet.

'I'll lie low,' Juliet said promptly. 'Let Jarry think I'm bowing to the inevitable. But when I get back to Adelaide, I'm going to try to talk my mother into lending me some money, on the strength of Marc's letter. If she won't, I'll get it somewhere else.' She looked at Nicky speculatively. 'Would you lend me the money for my fare, Nicky? You'd get it back, I promise.'

'I'd have to ask Guy,' Nicky said a little uncomfortably. 'My finances are all in his hands.'

'Yes, I remember you told me that before. What are the chances, then? What's he like? Old? Middle-aged? Married? Stuffy?'

'None of those,' Nicky admitted, 'and he's somewhere around Jarry's age.'

'Good looking?'

'Very.'

'Is he in love with you? You could persuade him—'

Nicky shrugged, ignoring the question, and admitted, 'I might be able to. But he's in the States at present.'

'I suppose you'll have to live with him when he comes back,' said Juliet meditatively, but with a little giggle. 'Do you suppose you'll finish up marrying him, Nicky? For girls like us, let's face it, marriage is about the only thing, isn't it? It would be different if we were clever or career-minded—like Patricia James, remember, who always wanted to be a doctor, or Marilyn Scobie doing social work? Or even Jenny Birdsall who was going to be a cooking demonstrator.'

Nicky supposed Juliet was right—it would be different. But she wouldn't end up marrying Guy, and as for living with him in his bachelor flat, she never would, and he certainly wouldn't want her to. Nor could she live with Claudia again, after that letter she had written her. Nicky's whole future, in fact, seemed terribly uncertain.

Now that Juliet's French love affair had taken a new lease of life, she completely lost interest in her collages. Pieces of coarse linen lay about the place, there seemed to be coloured scraps of material everywhere, wherever she had left them. Daisy and Noreen, who had been scolded before this for daring to interfere with them, were now told to put the whole lot on the scrap heap. Juliet was as restless as Nicky, though for a different reason. Nicky found the day interminable, and she knew it was because she was waiting—though why, she didn't know—for Jarratt to come home. She was watering the garden when Juliet suggested they should go over to the schoolhouse and see what Lewis was doing over there.

Nicky didn't think they would be welcome, but Lewis didn't mind at all, and let them sit at the back of the room while he carried on with his lessons. Nicky found it interesting to see him handle a group of such different ages, but it wasn't long before Juliet decided it was too hot in the schoolroom, despite the big fan that whirred monotonously in the ceiling. So they went back to the garden.

After lunch, while the children were resting, Juliet suggested to Nicky that they should go for a swim.

'When the children wake up,' said Nicky. 'Then Cass can come too.'

'Oh, we don't have to wait for Catherine,' Juliet said offhandedly, and Cass flushed but merely said in her quiet way, 'No, of course you don't. I can come over later.'

'Will you, Cass?' Nicky asked, before she and Juliet set off. She didn't want Cass to have the feeling she was an outsider, that she was pairing off with Juliet and forgetting her.

130

Cass said with a smile, 'We'll be there—if the children feel like a swim.'

But they didn't come. Nicky and Juliet swam and lazed, and swam again, and then both of them fell asleep in the shade.

When they went back to the homestead, Nicky's heart gave a leap as she saw the utility there. Jarratt was home. Without being aware of it, she began to hurry.

'What's the rush?' Juliet protested. 'Let Jarratt wait for his dinner. You're not employed here, you know, Nicky.'

However, in the side garden, Jarratt and Cass were already setting up a barbecue meal, while Marcie-Ann bustled round with plates and table napkins, and Medora hung around Jarratt, watching him prepare the fire. It was a pretty domestic scene, and Nicky was shocked at her own reaction. Sheer green ugly jealousy. Of Cass. As if she had any right——

'It's Cook's night off,' called Cass gaily, catching sight of them. 'Jarry and I have taken over tonight.'

Jarratt lifted Medora and turned from the barbecue to greet his sister and Nicky. His eyes lingered on Nicky and she knew this was what she had been waiting for all day—to have him look at her, give her this feeling of excitement that was in no way related to the warm feeling she used to have when she thought of Howdie. 'You two shoot off and get yourselves showered or dressed up or whatever,' Jarratt said.

'I'm going to make orange drink,' Marcie-Ann said importantly.

Medora rolled her eyes at Jarry. 'What kin I do, Uncle Jarry?'

'You can help me burn the steaks, Medora,' he told her solemnly.

Nicky and Juliet went into the house.

'So that's why she didn't turn up,' said Juliet, meaning Cass of course. 'She's making progress, isn't she? I don't think Tracy will encourage her, but all the same, let's hope she gets to teachers' college next year.'

Nicky said nothing. Her feelings were terribly confused.

131

She wanted to defend Cass, but she was burning with intolerable jealousy.

After she had showered, she dressed with care in a long blue skirt and a sleeveless top of green and blue sea island cotton. Cass, she remembered, was in jeans and checked shirt, with her hair straggling over her shoulders. 'She's not out to win him,' she thought. 'No matter what Juliet says. She's grateful to him and she admires him. That's why she looks so happy.'

But Jarratt—was he in love with Cass? Nicky would have given anything to know. She felt sick thinking about it. Because if he was, then how could he behave as he sometimes did to her, Nicky? Why did he look at her the way he did—take her in his arms—call her Rainbow in that intimate way? Why did he wake and come to her if she was having a nightmare, comfort her—even if it did end up as a scrap of sorts? She couldn't understand any of it.

The barbecue, despite everything, was fun. Lewis, who shared it with them, talked to Nicky as the light faded about aboriginal education, about the problems of teaching the children white man's knowledge without alienating them from families in whose lives the old ideas and traditions still had the most meaning.

'Their education has to be useful, relevant, yet one has to realise that so many of our values still seem quite arbitrary or even totally incomprehensible to them and their parents.'

Nicky was interested, yet she found it an effort to keep her mind on what he was saying. The darkness had come—suddenly, as it did here—and Jarry went on to the verandah to switch on lights. Nicky watched him go, handsome and narrow-hipped in his light-coloured pants and open-necked navy and white striped shirt. Handsome? Yes—she found him devastatingly handsome. His attraction for her was even increased by that suggestion of the brute that had often in the past jarred on her. He was rugged rather than rough, masculine rather than uncivilised, and there were tenderness and humour in his make-up too, she had learned.

Suddenly she became aware that Cass was watching him too, with that wistful, gentle smile on her lips.

Lewis said softly, 'That kid certainly adores the boss, doesn't she?'

Nicky glanced at him. She said faintly, 'You mean—Cass?'

'Who else? Excuse me——' He went over to Juliet, who was standing near the table, looking around for a corkscrew to open a new bottle of wine.

'Cass adores the boss,' thought Nicky, baffled. She had decided that Cass admired him—was grateful. But exactly what had Lewis meant? He had called Cass 'that kid', so surely all that implied was that she was like—well, like Marcie-Ann or Medora, the way she looked up to Jarratt. And anyhow, Cass was studying—Cass's whole heart was set on becoming a teacher. 'Yet if I were Cass,' Nicky admitted to herself, 'wouldn't I adore the boss?'

It wasn't till Cass had taken the children in to put them to bed that Nicky received any attention from Jarratt. Lewis was pointing out some constellation to Juliet, and Nicky was clearing up the mess they had made with the barbecue and being determinedly practical. Jarratt came to help her and commented, 'You're very quiet tonight, Rainbow. What's the trouble? Not enough sleep last night?'

She merely smiled slightly, and after a few moments he remarked, 'I'm driving out to the muster camp tomorrow with some supplies for the cook. Do you want to come?'

Her heart leapt. Of course she wanted to come, to have him to herself; yet something made her hesitate, a feeling that she should say no. She hadn't answered when Juliet joined them.

'What are you two talking about?'

'I've just been inviting Nicky to come out on the run with me tomorrow.'

'Oh, have you? I'd like to come too,' said Juliet surprisingly.

Nicky thought Jarratt frowned slightly, but he said agreeably enough, 'Come by all means, Juliet. I'd have asked you if I'd known you'd be interested. What's happened? Is it a change of heart? Or is boredom catching up with you?'

133

'I'm getting acclimatised,' said Juliet, not meaning it, as Nicky at least knew.

Nicky went on packing up the dishes. She felt shamefully disappointed. It wouldn't be the same with Juliet there too, yet she had felt she shouldn't go, so now she would be quite safe. From herself, from Jarratt. Lewis went back to his bungalow, and presently when Juliet and Jarratt and Nicky were on the verandah, Cass came out to ask, 'Jarry—about Howard——'

She didn't have to say any more. Jarratt said so shortly that Cass looked quite crestfallen, 'Howard can come back with me when I go to Alice for Tracy. I'm not going to make a special trip.' He added with a significant glance at Nicky, 'If he's in a particular hurry, he'll find some means of getting here without my help, you can be sure of that.'

Next day, as they drove out with Jarratt, Juliet was full of chatter and questions. Nicky thought she was rather overplaying her hand if this was her idea of giving an impression of bowing to the inevitable. It was enough to make anyone suspicious, and Jarratt asked, 'What's making you so cheerful? The thought that Tracy will soon be back?'

Juliet shrugged her slim shoulders and tossed back her long blonde hair. 'Can't I take an interest? I thought that's what you were always wanting me to do—you ought to be pleased.'

'Oh, I am,' he assured her dryly.

They had left the homestead late in the morning and they stopped for a picnic lunch in the red gorge that Nicky had driven through with Jarratt once before. There the shadows were cool, and the pools of water that lay here and there on the wide rocky bed of the river were so clear they looked to be no more than an inch deep. Yet if you plunged your hand in, you were surprised. Juliet's simulated enthusiasm didn't extend to physical energy, and after they had eaten, she stayed sprawling exhaustedly in the shade while the other two, at Jarratt's suggestion, took a leisurely stroll.

The rock over which they walked looked as ancient as time itself. It was a conglomerate, with smooth shining waterworn stones of varying sizes set in the contrasting texture of a coarse red matrix. Nicky saw yellow and purple flowers blooming in shady damp spots, and paused to admire the pale silky-tasselled flowers of a native orange, that Jarratt told her were so fragile they lasted only a day. As they moved on, a dragon lizard rippled across their path, then stopped stone still, its colour changing from rock red to an unobtrusive greenish grey that made it almost invisible against the muted ground cover.

Nicky looked up at Jarratt, her eyes laughing her delight, and as she met his glance she felt a little shock in her heart that sobered her.

'You love it here, don't you?' he said, holding her gaze with a challenge in his own. 'Have you been here—in the outback—before?'

'I—I told you, I lived in Alice once.'

'And before that?' he persisted, and when she didn't answer at once he said with an odd look in his dark eyes, 'You don't talk about yourself much, do you, Rainbow? It's not shameful being an orphan, you know ... Who did you say your guardian was?'

'Guy Sonder.'

He frowned. 'You know I don't mean Guy Sonder. The other man, the one who was a friend of your parents, I recall you said, the one who died recently.'

'Jack Lane.' She said it softly, seeing Jack's face, hearing Jack's voice. The whole story was there hovering on her lips, waiting to be poured out. Jarratt was leaning back against a great red boulder, his eyes fixed compellingly on her face, and Nicky looked back at him, uncertain. She longed to talk to him about Jack, about the parents she didn't remember, about Alice Springs and the foster-home —to tell him everything. Yet as she hesitated, coherent thought vanished, she couldn't have talked if she had tried. She became a captive of those warm dark eyes, her body grew weak, she was filled with one overpowering desire— the desire to have him take her in his arms, smother her lips with his own—

She was shaken when he moved abruptly, looked at his

135

watch and said briefly, 'It's time we were on our way.'

She didn't have another moment alone with him after that, not until they reached home. They had shared the evening meal with the ringers round the campfire, and it was very late when they got back. Everyone had gone to bed, and no doubt the two little girls were sleeping over at Cass's bungalow. Juliet staggered exhausted up the steps and went straight through to her room with a murmured, 'Goodnight'. But when Nicky would have followed her across the verandah, Jarratt reached out and pulled her back.

'Don't go yet,' he muttered against her hair. 'I have to talk to you.'

'What about?' she breathed.

He put his hands on her waist and turned her slowly round to face him. There was no light except that of the moon coming in through the vines that wreathed the verandah posts. His face looked dark above hers, and she could feel the roughness of his chin as it brushed against her forehead.

'What do you think about?' he asked huskily. 'Us—all the things we've been saying to each other without words. The things your eyes have been telling me all day—in the gorge at noon—over the campfire when we were eating——'

She drew in her breath sharply, incredulously. 'Oh, Jarratt——' she whispered, and his lips found hers.

They didn't talk after all. They stood on the moonlit verandah kissing until she was breathless, their bodies close against each other. He murmured against her ear, his hands caressed her, his lips were on her eyelids, on the corner of her mouth, on her throat, and she felt sick with desire for him. He could have done anything he liked with her, her senses were reeling as if she were intoxicated—as in a way she was. Then as she clung to him, his hands gripped her arms hard and he said hoarsely, 'I think we'd better break it up, Rainbow. This is a dangerous hour to be making love, and we're both of us too tired to think straight.'

Nicky closed her eyes, her heart thudding. She had to

136

struggle with herself not to beg him to make love to her. He was right about the danger, but she didn't care, and as for their being too tired to think straight, she knew only too well what she thought—felt—about Jarratt Buchan now. And surely the words he had whispered in her ear, straight from his roused senses, were an admission that for him she had become—special. She lifted her face to his imploringly, her eyes seeking his, and with a groan, he once more crushed his mouth against her own. She felt an ache all through her body as she responded unresistingly to the urgency of his lips, suddenly to find herself thrust away from him, and to hear him mutter, 'Rainbow, don't do this to me——'

The very intensity of his voice brought her to her senses as they stood, breathing unevenly and audibly, and looking at each other through the darkness. Nicky's emotions gradually calmed, and she knew she had to co-operate with him in not letting things get out of control. She reached out and touched his hand.

'Goodnight, Jarratt,' she whispered tremulously, and immediately she went quietly into the house, leaving him on the dark verandah. She wondered how she would feel when she saw him next morning, but though he hadn't left the homestead, she didn't encounter him until well after breakfast. The three girls were on the side verandah, and Cass was on the point of departing with Marcie-Ann and Medora to give them their morning lessons when Jarratt came round from the office, where, it emerged, he had been in contact with Alice Springs over the two-way radio.

'I'm going in to Alice today,' he said without preamble, and they all stared at him. Nicky felt her heart drop. Tracy must be coming home. She and Juliet would be leaving. It was the end of the world. She stared at him, her eyes wide and tragic, and was shocked at the remote look he gave her, as if she were the last person on his mind.

Juliet asked hopefully, 'Is Tracy coming home?' and Cass followed up with, 'Oh, Jarry, can Howard come back with you?'

Howard! Nicky felt ashamed of her own reaction to the

137

sound of his name. She felt a deep reluctance at the thought of having to deal with him again. All that childhood thing was completely finished, and it would be simply awkward. But then, she reminded herself, if Tracy came back, she wouldn't be here much longer. She could have wept.

Jarratt answered Cass first. 'Sure, Howard can come back if that's what he wants. He's going to be no use to me for a while, so it will be entirely up to him.'

'Oh, he'll want to come,' Cass insisted, and looked at Nicky, her hazel eyes smiling dreamily. Nicky looked away from her, feeling sick.

Marcie-Ann piped up, 'Is Mummy coming home, Uncle Jarry?'

'Not yet, sweetheart,' said Jarratt—and hope sprang back into Nicky's heart. 'I'll talk to you later, Catherine.'

Cass, taking this as a hint that it was time to take the children away, departed, and Juliet asked impatiently, 'What's the great hurry about going to Alice if Tracy's not coming home? You'd think she was well enough by now, at any rate.'

'She wants to see me, that's all I know,' said Jarry briefly. 'I got the message over the air this morning.' He looked at Nicky, and now his eyes were warm and meaningful. 'Will you come to Alice, Nicky?'

Nicky flushed. He didn't mean because of Howdie, she was certain. His eyes told her that. It was because of last night. Last night they had both been too tired to think straight, but today was new, and it was all beginning.

She nodded, and Juliet complained, 'What about me? Don't I get asked?'

Jarry's eyebrows rose. 'I'd have thought the notion of driving all the way to Alice in the heat and the dust would have been too much for you to contemplate.'

Juliet shrugged. 'If you live in the bush, you have to do something. A trip to Alice seems pretty exciting, all things considered. Why do you suppose Tracy wants to see you, anyhow?'

'I wouldn't know,' he said guardedly.

138

'Perhaps she's homesick, and missing the children. You could engage a nurse to look after her here.'

'You're speculating. But in any case, it wouldn't mean that you and Nicky were no longer needed around the place, if that's what's in your mind.'

'Oh, it wasn't,' said Juliet with a falsely bright smile. 'I realise that I've become invaluable ... Anyhow, to get down to basics, when do we leave?'

'About noon,' he said with a frown. 'I can't get away this morning, I have several things to see to. We'll have a snack before we go. We'll have to spend the night in Alice.'

'Marvellous!' exclaimed Juliet. 'We'd better look over our clothes, Nicky. Who knows, Jarry might give us the thrill of taking us out dining somewhere tonight.'

Now that the threat of having to leave Coochin Brimbrim in the very near future had been removed, Nicky was happy again and full of excitement. It would be fun to dine out in Alice—even if it were in a threesome. The only thing that spoilt her pleasure was the thought of Howard's coming back. The fact was, she had let him kiss her, make love to her—she had let him see how she felt about seeing him again. He would hardly expect her feelings to have changed so drastically, and he would undoubtedly want to kiss her again. Even if he had been winged, as Jarratt had put it, he was not totally incapacitated. It was absurd, when she came to think of it, that she was here in the Never-Never with two men to handle, when one was all she wanted. But of course, girls were scarce. Not so scarce in Alice Springs, however, so perhaps after all Howard wouldn't be eager to come back to the cattle station.

Cass, she discovered, had no doubts at all as to what Howdie would choose to do.

Nicky packed a small bag with the things she would need for a night away, and included a long skirt and a cool evening blouse. Then she went into the garden to water a few plants she had been bringing along. Presently Cass appeared with the children, and Nicky went to join them in the side garden where two swings had been rigged up under the trees. The little girls had already climbed on to the seats, and Nicky and Cass gave them a few pushes then went to sit in the shade.

'Is Jarry still going to Alice today, or has he put it off?' Cass wanted to know.

'He's going today.' Evidently Jarratt had not yet talked to Cass about the situation. 'Tracy wants to see him for some reason or other. Juliet and I are going too, and we'll stay away for the night.'

'And tomorrow you'll be back with Howdie,' Cass said with satisfaction. 'That will be really beaut—the three of us together again at last. I can't wait, can you? Howdie's probably champing at the bit too—wanting to be back. It's funny how it's all working out, isn't it, even if he did break his collarbone. You two will still see a whole lot more of each other than if he had to stay out at the camp working the stock.'

She moved away for a moment to give Medora a few more pushes, then came back to the seat and pushed back her hair from her plump face. Nicky had been trying to think how she could explain that Cass must accept that she and Howard weren't, after all, going to fall in love and marry and live happily ever after, but before she could even begin, Cass said with a rush, 'Nicky, I have to confess something. I was so scared when you came here that you'd fall in love with Jarratt. I mean, he's so—so terrific. Or at least, I think so.'

She paused and Nicky's heart stood still. Cass's hazel eyes—that she had wanted so much to be blue eyes—were watching her trustfully, and Nicky knew intuitively exactly what she was going to say just an instant before she said it.

'I'm terribly—*terribly*—in love with him. Had you guessed?'

Nicky swallowed. Her throat was dry, and somehow she managed a smile. 'No, I—I didn't quite guess, Cass.'

'Well—it's a quiet sort of love,' Cass murmured. 'When he's helping me with my homework and he looks up at me—I have this feeling inside, all warm and happy and melting. He has the most wonderful eyes—looking at them's like heaven. Oh, I can't tell you! And sometimes we have long talks, Jarry and I. Not so much since you and Juliet came, there isn't so much time. But when Tracy was here—I can tell him anything, ask him anything—and I know he wants to hear it all, and that he understands. It's the most wonderful feeling. And I wouldn't care if he didn't have a penny, I truly wouldn't. It just doesn't count when you really love someone, does it?'

'No,' Nicky agreed, 'no.' She felt stunned, shaken. While Cass had been pouring out her love, for Nicky the world had turned upside down. She was sickeningly aware of just how much she had been expecting of Jarratt, and now Cass was practically confessing to a belief that Jarratt was in love with *her*. How could a man love a girl like Cass—so wholesome, so thoroughly nice—and behind her back make love to her best friend, who just happened to have turned up out of the blue for a short while?

For a short while. That was the crucial thing. Nicky was here just while Juliet was here. Cass had been here for months. They must know each other really well, she and Jarratt. What was between them wasn't a flickering elusive mirage, like this thing that had sprung up between Nicky and Jarratt. She remembered how Jarratt had said last night they must break it up because they were too tired to think straight. Was that the only reason he had made love to her—because he had been too tired to think straight, and remember Cass? Or had he meant that it was a toss-up between her and Cass, as far as he was concerned? Was his heart as little involved as that?

It was ironic that Cass read in his eyes the same thing that she read in them—that Cass too had that warm melting feeling. Nicky felt sick. She wished—oh, how she wished!—that she had never come here chasing Howard. She could see the utter absurdity of that now. She had been as silly as Cass with her dreams of flying. Now there was nothing for it but for her to step aside—to go away, to leave the field to Cass, who had been here first. You don't—you just *don't*—steal your best friend's man. She thought of the story Aunty Pat used to tell about the two girls in love with

141

the prince, and how the wicked fairy had braided their hair together so that neither was free unless one of them agreed to sacrifice her beautiful hair. She and Cass had said the same thing—'If it were you and me, I'd have *my* hair cut off.'

Nicky thought she could hate Jarratt Buchan for his heartlessness—really hate him. Briefly, she thanked heaven that nothing had happened between him and her—yet. And she prayed that the ending might be quick—that Tracy would come home after all, that she and Juliet could go. *Soon.*

'Your exams,' she asked Cass with an effort, 'teachers' college. You don't care about that? You won't go?'

Cass gave her wistful smile. 'I don't know. You see, love isn't to be rushed. If Jarry wants me to go, then I'll go. But I'd rather just stay here any day, even if it's only to look after Marcie-Ann and Medora ... What I would like most,' she resumed after a brief pause, 'would be for you and Howdie and Jarry and me to be here together—for ever.'

Nicky tried to smile. 'Is that your third wish, Cass?' she asked wryly, knowing it was just as impossible as the others. 'You remember—blue eyes——'

'And flying——'

'And something about love,' Nicky finished, with a twist in her heart.

'The only one that could come true,' said Cass. 'And the only one that matters.'

Nicky bit her lip. 'Make your third wish a simple one, Cass. Just about you and—and Jarry. I don't think I shall ever live here.'

'I suppose not,' said Cass regretfully. 'Howdie's probably trying to line up something super in the way of jobs in Alice. You'll know what's happened by tonight, won't you? And tomorrow when you come back, the three of us will have a tremendous get-together——'

Nicky struggled inwardly with herself for several seconds. It was wrong to let Cass hope like this, yet she couldn't admit just now that she didn't care a fig for How-

142

die Johnston. Cass would want to know why, what had happened.

She got from the seat. 'We're to have an early lunch—we'll be leaving soon. I'd better see what's happening in the kitchen.'

As she walked away, her legs were shaking. The whole world had changed in a matter of minutes, and all she wanted to do was to run away and hide. Instead, she went into the house to see about lunch.

CHAPTER EIGHT

In the kitchen, Lena was throwing a salad together. It looked exactly like that, and today Nicky didn't go to the rescue and try to make something elegant of it. It would have to do as it was.

Instead, she went to her bedroom and shut the door.

There, she kicked off her shoes and sat on the edge of her bed and stared at her bare feet. She thought of Jarratt Buchan who last night had kissed her and kissed her, and whispered in her ear, and generally stirred her up so that she had been certain he had fallen in love with her. He hadn't played fair—not with her, certainly not with Cass—and she had been gullible—oh, terribly, terribly gullible, to think he had meant those things he had murmured to her. She didn't, when she came to consider it, imagine for a moment that he was even in the process of deciding who would make the better wife for a cattleman—Catherine Johnston or Rainbow Reay. He had simply been amusing himself with her because she was available.

She frowned as a new thought struck her. The choice when it comes to marriage was very limited in the outback. Juliet had remarked on that. She had also said that he'd never marry anyone like Catherine—anyone *beneath him*—unless he were pushed into a corner. At the time she said that, it hadn't entered Nicky's head that Jarratt would think that way or consider Cass beneath him. Yet could he possibly be having second thoughts, now there were two girls to choose from? It was an unpalatable thought, and yet it persisted. Cass's brother was a stockman—an employee. Nicky wondered how much Jarratt knew about the rest of the Johnston family. She didn't know much herself except that Cass's stepmother was a disagreeable person with an ugly voice, who allowed her stepchildren to live in a foster-home rather than be bothered with them.

Jarry, with his propensity for asking questions when he wanted to know something, had possibly wormed some information out of Cass. With Nicky, he had not been very successful. He had drawn several blanks when she had clammed up on him. But when it came to the point—Nicky smiled bitterly—Rainbow Reay didn't have much of a background even if she had attended the same school as Juliet. So the choice, if he only knew it, was not all that wide when it came to marrying beneath him. If by Juliet's standards it was undesirable to sit down to dinner with a stockman, then how about a rough type like a crocodile shooter, Nicky's father? Someone probably quite like Jack Lane, with a leathery face, hands like sandpaper, few refinements when it came to society manners, and a vocabulary as rough as his voice? The fact that he had been gentle with Nicky and worked like a demon so she could become a lady didn't count.

Quite decidedly it was time for Nicky Reay to backpedal. Time for her to—to have her hair lopped off.

Nicky got up and went to the mirror and stared sadly at herself. Blue eyes, curly auburn hair, freckles, a heart-shaped face. She thought of Cass's pleasant face and hazel eyes and that dignified kind of beauty that had so surprised her that day at the waterhole. Rainbow Reay had no advantages at all over a girl like Cass. Blue eyes didn't matter...

'It's all over,' she told herself silently. What sort of a fool do you have to be to come as a short-term guest to a cattle station and fall in love with the boss?

Yet it had just happened. As simply as that, without her ever knowing it was going to. But that, she supposed, was how it was when it came to falling in love. Hearts ruled over heads any day, providing you had a heart. If you didn't, then you worked it all out in your head and it didn't hurt at all. Was Jarratt doing that?

If so, then she wasn't going along with his game any further. In fact, she didn't think she'd even go to Alice Springs with him today. She couldn't. It would make her sick.

She had actually opened her suitcase and started to un-

145

pack when she realised that not going would mean a day practically alone with Cass; questions about Howard; and even if she successfully parried those, inevitably, talk about Jarratt.

She put her clothes back in the case. It would be painful, but she would have to go to Alice. But if Jarratt thought she was in love with him, he was going to be disillusioned. She would make sure he knew that last night she *had* been too tired to think straight. If she had been in full possession of her senses, she would never have slumped into his arms as she had done, or so avidly returned his kisses. For Rainbow Reay—no, for *Nichola* Reay—it was all just an interlude before she went back to Adelaide where she belonged. It was great to have a holiday in the Never-Never, but it was great too to go back to the city. True, she'd grown out of Howdie Johnston, but her future was ahead of her and there were momentous discoveries to be made.

Goodbye, Jarratt Buchan, she thought, and the smile she forced to her lips turned into a sob.

The first thing they did when they reached Alice late that afternoon was to book into a motel, where Juliet and Nicky were to share a unit and Jarry would occupy an adjacent one. The girls washed their dusty faces and changed their clothes. Jarry was going to the hospital to see Tracy, and Juliet was going with him.

'You'll want to go and look up Howard Johnston, Nicky,' Jarratt remarked, and Juliet stared at him in amazement.

'Why on earth would Nicky want to do that? Just because she knew Catherine years ago?'

'Well, it's up to Nicky,' snapped Jarratt, who was not in the best of moods. Nicky had been very very cool to him during the long drive, withdrawn and uncommunicative, and she knew he had been baffled—after her behaviour of last night. But then he didn't know what Cass had been telling her. 'There's no point in her trailing along with us,' he said now. 'She doesn't know Tracy from Adam—or from Eve, I should say.' He returned his attention to Nicky.

146

'You might as well ask Howard to have dinner with us tonight.'

'Jarry! Is that necessary?' Juliet was outraged. 'I mean —one of your stockmen——'

'He's also Catherine's brother,' Jarry retorted, his black eyes glittering dangerously. Obviously he didn't think Cass Johnston was beneath him, and while Nicky was glad, she was also sick with jealousy. She was thankful when a little later he let her out of the car at the guest house where Howard was staying, and as he drove off she went up the steps to the front door and rang the bell, feeling decidedly nervous, especially when she remembered those kisses under the trees at the muster camp.

But she need not have felt nervous, for Howard wasn't there.

'Howard Johnston? No, love, he's not here now,' she was told by a pleasant-faced woman with her hair in curlers who came to the door.

'Do you know when he'll be in, please? I'm a friend of his.'

'He won't be in, love. When I said he's not here, I meant he's left. He went off yesterday.'

'Oh.' Nicky was taken aback. 'Do you know where he went?'

'Not exactly. Down south with a young couple who're driving round Australia. Heading for Adelaide they were, but I don't know how far he was going. With that broken collarbone, I said to him he should stay put. But of course it was none of my business, and I dare say he'll be all right. Sorry I can't help you further, love. Where have you come from?'

'The cattle station where he was working,' Nicky said briefly. She smiled and thanked the woman and went thoughtfully away. Howard appeared to be making the most of his free time, and, what was more, he didn't seem over-anxious to get back to Coochin Brim-brim and Nicky Reay. Cass would be sadly disappointed, but Nicky was relieved. The whole situation would have been impossible, with Cass so romantically and unrealistically determined on

147

a happy ending to a very youthful and very insubstantial love affair.

She glanced at her watch. She had almost an hour to fill in before it was time to meet Jarratt and Juliet at the motel. She decided to go back to her room and have a rest, it was something she could really do with after such a day.

She had actually slept and was just out of the shower and in panties and bra when Juliet came in. One look at her face was enough to tell Nicky that something was not pleasing her. Her grey-green eyes were smouldering as she slung her handbag on to her bed, kicked off her shoes and glared at herself in the mirror.

'What's wrong?' asked Nicky tentatively. The skirt and top she was going to wear were spread out on her bed, and she picked up her brush and started brushing her hair.

'Everything,' said Juliet sweepingly. 'Every rotten thing. Tracy's not coming back to Coochin Brim-brim. I'm in a *trap*. Jarry's going to expect me to stay there for ever. I've got a good mind to—to——' She stopped and grabbed a tissue from the box on the dressing table and blew her nose hard, and Nicky realised she was close to tears. When she had composed herself, she told Nicky more coherently what had happened. Tracy had met a man called Max Bonney. She had fallen in love with him and had every intention of marrying him and going to Adelaide to live.

Nicky was mystified. 'How can she possibly have met any men as she's been in hospital all this time?'

'Oh, Tracy's in a two-bed room, and his aunt or someone was in the other bed. He used to come to visit her, and when she was discharged, he kept coming—to see Tracy. She's been seeing him every day, but now he has to go back to Adelaide, and that was why she wanted to see Jarry.'

'Whatever does Jarratt think about it?'

'He's reserving his opinion till he's met the man—which will be tonight, because he's asked him to join us for dinner.' Juliet didn't ask about Howard. Apparently she had completely forgotten about him, which was not strange as she'd never met him and had never been interested in him. 'I hope he's *horrible*,' Juliet decided, beginning to make preparations for her shower. 'I hope Jarry will tell Tracy it's no go.'

'Oh, Juliet, that's mean,' Nicky protested. 'After all, wouldn't it be a good thing for Tracy to marry again? She has those two little children to bring up—they need a father——'

'Well then, she shouldn't have got herself married to the wrong man in the first place,' said Juliet unsympathetically. 'It's her own fault she's in a mess.' She blinked her eyes rapidly. 'Oh, I don't know—of course I'd like to see poor old Tracy married again and really happy, but'—her mouth twisted—'I don't want to be left holding the baby. Looking after Jarry, in other words. It would solve all our problems if he'd only find himself a wife, but I guess he's too bossy for most women. And who'd want to live in the middle of nowhere? What do you think?' she asked, turning back from the door of the shower room.

Nicky flushed deeply. 'Me?'

'Yes. Would you want to marry him?'

Nicky forced a laugh. 'What a question to ask! I—I scarcely know him, and——'

'I know. You don't have to be polite because he's my half-brother. He's too old, and you wouldn't like to live out in the bush, and you don't fancy being told what to do for the rest of your life.' Juliet sighed and closed the shower door behind her.

'Wrong,' thought Nicky, 'on three counts.'

Mindlessly, she began to get into her skirt, her top, her sandals. Her hair was newly washed and shining, and her freckles were minimised by the light tan she had acquired. She applied a little lipstick and eye-shadow, and looked at the time. Jarratt had said they would meet at seven-forty-five in the motel restaurant. It was now seven-forty-seven, and Juliet was still under the shower. She knocked on the door and called out, 'Will you be long, Juliet? We're going to be late.'

'Well, I'm not going to hurry,' Juliet answered unco-operatively. 'You go ahead. You can have a drink with Jarry while you're waiting for me.'

149

Nicky hesitated. She didn't relish the idea of a tête-à-tête with Jarratt, as things stood. But Max Bonney would be there. Reluctantly, she left the motel unit, pulling the door shut behind her. It was incredible to realise that only this morning she had been longing to be alone with Jarratt, and that now she had to be cool to him, because he was out of bounds.

When she reached the restaurant she saw him sitting at the small cocktail bar at the far end of the room, frowning rather moodily over a glass of Scotch. As she stood there uncertainly, he looked up and saw her and got to his feet. She was sure he was alone, and she wished she had waited for Juliet after all, but now it was too late. His eyes were on her as she made her way towards him, and she knew with a feeling of dread that he was bound to ask her why she had been so withdrawn this afternoon.

As she drew nearer and her glance met his fully, her heart seemed to miss a beat. That warm sexy look was still there for her, no matter what she had done, or how she had behaved. Or was it there not specifically for her, but merely because she happened to be a female? Cass too, she reminded herself, melted under that black smouldering gaze.

She glanced away from him with an effort and looked around the restaurant. 'I hope you haven't been waiting long,' she heard herself say aloofly.

He consulted his watch. 'Eight and a half minutes,' he said accurately. 'Where's Howard Johnston?'

Howard! Nicky had completely forgotten him. She coloured deeply. 'He—he's gone. He left Alice a day or two ago with some people he met.' She dared a glance at him through her lashes and saw his frown deepen.

'You had him on your mind today, all the way from Coochin Brim-brim to Alice Springs, hadn't you?' he accused.

'No—yes,' she altered it wildly, calculating it might be best for him to believe she had. He put his hand under her elbow and at his touch she felt a sort of helplessness overcome her.

He murmured, 'Look, we'll find a quiet table where we

150

can have an aperitif together. We can't talk here at the bar. What's become of Juliet, by the way?'

'She was still in the shower,' she said huskily, despising herself for going along with him so meekly.

'Then we shouldn't be disturbed for a little while. Max won't be here for twenty minutes or so yet.'

Listening, Nicky was filled with alarm. She didn't want twenty minutes undisturbed with Jarratt Buchan, it was far too dangerous. She didn't know if she could keep herself under control that long. The mere touch of his fingers on her arm made her quiver, and she was already aware of sensations she ought not to be experiencing—not now she knew how badly he had behaved, not now she knew about Cass.

The waitress found them a table quickly. Service in Alice Springs was inclined to be casual, but where Jarratt Buchan was concerned it was different. Their table was secluded, discreetly lit, and in no time at all Nicky was nervously sipping a pink gin and Jarratt had another Scotch, and across the table he was staring at her. No matter how hard she fought against it, eventually she had to raise her eyes to his.

He said softly in that murmurous, deep-toned voice that did drastic things to her metabolism, 'So what's bothering you, Rainbow? Are you going to tell me?'

She shook her head. 'Nothing's bothering me.' She felt terribly vulnerable. She was convinced her eyes were telling him all the things she was determined were no longer true.

'That's a lie,' he said after a moment. 'You're cut up because Howard's moved off. Is that it? I thought you'd put that little affair sensibly back in the past where it belongs.'

She played with the long glass swizzle-stick in her pink gin, lowering her lashes defensively. 'Did you?' was all she said.

There was a long tense pause, then he said tightly, 'You say that to me, in that cool little voice, after letting me make love to you as I did last night?'

'You didn't—make love to me,' she said indistinctly,

though her cheeks flushed to crimson, then paled. 'You—you kissed me, that was all.'

'It wasn't all, and you know it. If we hadn't done something about it, we'd have been making love in earnest. Look, Rainbow, have you somehow got it into your head that you owe it to Howard—to Catherine—to whip into life a love affair that's now fizzled out completely, if it ever got started? If you have, then you're being totally unrealistic. You're confusing sentiment with sincerity—sentimentality with love. Okay, you're only nineteen, but you have a basic maturity about you for all that. I've remarked on it before, and I'll admit I'm always surprised at your lapses.' He stopped, and she could feel the penetrating regard of his black eyes. 'Has Catherine been talking to you?' he asked abruptly.

Nicky's lids flew up and her pulses jumped guiltily.

'What about?' she asked huskily.

'About you and Howard, of course. Yes? I suspected as much ... Well, I advise you not to take too much notice of Catherine. She's a dyed-in-the-wool romantic, despite her agreeable ability to deal with practical everyday matters so competently.'

Nicky listened, her heart hammering madly. Of course Cass had been talking to her about Howard—but she had also been talking about Jarratt, though he didn't know *that*.

'Just don't think you have to arrange your life to fit in with her long-cherished dreams, that's all,' he continued, and through her lashes she could see his mouth curve in a faint and somehow disturbing smile. 'I can see I'll have to redouble my efforts to captivate you, if I'm to convince you of the sense in what I'm saying.'

Nicky bit her lip. She was well aware of the effect any further efforts from Jarratt were likely to have on her. But there weren't going to be any more kisses, there wasn't going to be any more lovemaking. He could save it all for Cass, not divide it up.

'You and I haven't seen a great deal of each other alone, have we?' he pursued. 'We have an extension of time, at all events. I suppose Juliet told you that Tracy wants to go to

152

Adelaide when she comes out of hospital?'

'Yes, but——' Nicky took a deep breath. 'I don't want you to—redouble your efforts to—captivate me. There's just no point.' She looked at him helplessly. How could she tell him that she had no intention of competing for him against her best friend? It would be easier all round if she could simply persuade him she wasn't seriously interested —despite the fact that she had been rather carried away last night.

'No point?' He frowned, then raised his glass and drank down the contents. 'Why not? Howard? Or have you decided you don't like the outback?' His eyes narrowed. 'Or is it something to do with that guardian of yours?'

Nicky too was giving her attention to her drink, but in a more prolonged way. It was a pretty drink in a tall frosted glass. There was a bright cherry in it and a twist of lemon. The taste was slightly bitter, slightly astringent, and she took a long drink—then had the feeling that the gin had gone straight to her head because she had a strong compulsion to say, 'I love the outback—I don't care if I never see Howard or Guy again. All I want is to stay at Coochin Brim-brim—with you—for ever.' Somehow she controlled herself, and told him aloofly, 'I don't really know what you're talking about. I came here with Juliet for a visit. I've—I've enjoyed myself, and I suppose I'll stay as long as she does. Unless it's *too* long. That was the arrangement— she asked me so she'd have company.'

'So you'd do the hard yakka, more like,' he corrected her, and now his voice had an icy edge to it. 'You're a cool little customer, aren't you? You say whatever suits you best. I know damned well you came here because of Catherine and Howard Johnston—'

'I didn't,' she retorted swiftly. 'I didn't know they worked for you when Juliet asked me to come. It was just— luck.'

'Or fate,' he suggested ironically.

Well, Nicky had believed in fate once. Maybe she still believed in it. But it wasn't a kind fate—not when it put you in the position she was in . . .

153

'All right, fate,' she agreed wearily. He was leaning towards her across the table, his dark eyes smouldering so that she dared not look into them. She said defensively, 'Anyhow, when Juliet and I go you'll still have—have Cass.'

'*Now* what the hell are you getting at?' he exclaimed explosively, and she flinched at his tone.

'I'm not getting at anything. I'm just stating a fact. Cass will be there. And I—I shan't be sorry to go back to Adelaide.' Her voice was steady, and she hated herself for her lies, her air of indifference. And the way Jarratt was looking at her was deadly—it was killing her——

It was at that precarious moment that Max Bonney arrived, and directly behind him, looking pretty in a sparkling black and white evening dress, was Juliet, all smiles instead of scowls, all apologies over being late. Jarratt, with a muttered, 'We'll have this out later,' got to his feet.

Max Bonney was thirtyish, mature, presentable, and he was full of open-minded goodwill towards Tracy's family. He wasn't being vetted, and he wasn't doing any vetting himself. This for him was a purely social occasion. After introductions had been made, dinner was ordered and the wines selected, and conversation proceeded to flow easily, mainly between the two men. Max was an Adelaide architect, he said, and this led to a discussion on Australian house styles and on pioneer homes in the outback. Politics were touched on, primary industry, cattle raising. The two men obviously approved of one another and the atmosphere was relaxed and friendly. For her part, Nicky thought Max Bonney a very likeable man, and even Juliet made no attempt to knock him, but was all charm and friendliness.

'Tracy and I realise we must experience each other in a more normal environment before we make any vital decisions,' Max said over coffee, accepting a cigarette from Jarratt, and holding his lighter for Juliet who was smoking too, though Nicky had declined. 'So far, I've rarely seen her out of bed, and never in anything more formal than a dressing gown.'

Jarry laughed and Nicky and Juliet exchanged smiles,

and Max continued, 'I'd very much like her to come and stay with my parents in Adelaide when she's discharged from hospital. I'm afraid they're too elderly to cope with a couple of little girls, and Tracy seems doubtful that Mrs Buchan will be able to take them, so I'm hoping it will be possible for them to stay at Coochin Brim-brim for the time being.' He glanced at Juliet and then at Nicky, and settled for her. 'Are you the one who's in charge of them at present? Tracy was telling me about you.'

'Nicky is my guest,' Jarry broke in pleasantly. 'Their governess is with them at the homestead. You'll want to make their acquaintance if you and Tracy are considering teaming up.'

'Yes, of course. I like children—I have several young nephews and nieces, and the thought of an instant family doesn't appal me. On the contrary, in fact.'

Later, when they left the restaurant, the two men walked on still talking. Then Max turned to say goodnight to Juliet and Nicky, and Jarratt elected to walk with Max to his hotel, 'To ask him all the nosey questions he wouldn't put while we were listening,' Juliet said, as she and Nicky went to their motel suite.

'He's nice, isn't he?' said Nicky, as they unlocked the door and went in. She was feeling both relieved and disappointed that the evening had broken up already.

'I suppose so,' Juliet said gloomily, sitting on the edge of her bed. 'I told you I was in a trap, didn't I? Tracy won't come back. I'll be expected to devote myself to Jarry and Coochin Brim-brim for the rest of my life. Nobody cares that Marc wants me to marry him, or that I want to go back to France. It's just not fair.'

Nicky looked at her helplessly, torn between sympathy and impatience, for she couldn't imagine Jarratt holding his sister a prisoner. 'You're exaggerating, Juliet. You can't be made to do what you don't want to do—Jarratt wouldn't try to dominate your life like that.'

'Wouldn't he? You just don't know my brother. All the female members of the family are afraid of putting one foot in front of the other without getting his seal of approval

155

first. Tracy's a married woman, but look how she's waited for him to come and meet this Max Thingummy before she makes a decision about him! And my mother—she wouldn't go against his wishes for anything. Andrew was sensible in selling out his share of the property and making a life of his own in France, but I suppose it suits Jarry perfectly to be the only male on the property. I just wish he'd hurry up and get himself married, that's all. Pretty soon he'll be too old.'

Nicky was sitting in one of the easy chairs, and she said with only a faint tremor in her voice, 'There is Catherine, Juliet. I think Jarry likes her a lot.'

'Oh, rubbish!' exclaimed Juliet angrily. 'He's not going to make a fool of himself by marrying a girl he's employed as a governess. He just wouldn't be in it. What happened to Catherine's brother, anyhow? I'd forgotten all about him. Didn't he want to have dinner with us?'

Nicky shrugged. 'He's left Alice. I expect he'll come back to Coochin Brim-brim when he's fit for work again.'

'I expect he will,' Juliet agreed. 'I suppose he imagines his sister is going to marry the boss, and he'll be on to a really good thing. They're a couple of go-getters, in my opinion.'

Nicky's colour rose. 'Don't be so silly,' she snapped. 'They're nice people. They're honest and they work hard. If you were fair instead of being so—biased, you'd admit that Catherine would make an ideal wife for Jarratt.'

Juliet glared at her. 'Never!' she said, then, muttering something unintelligible, she got up and switched on the television set, and both of them sat there without speaking.

Nicky wondered if Juliet was merely pretending, as she was, to watch the programme that was showing. For her part, she was very much on edge, upset at having quarrelled with Juliet, and wondering as well if at any minute Jarratt might knock on their door and insist she go out with him to continue the talk they had been having in the restaurant before the others arrived. She would simply refuse, she decided, and it occurred to her that the smartest thing to do would be to go to bed and pretend to be asleep if he should turn up.

She did this, and lay with her face turned to the wall, her eyes wide open, and conscious of the sound from the television set. It wasn't going to be possible to avoid Jarratt indefinitely, and once they returned to Coochin Brim-brim, it wouldn't be at all easy to escape him. Suddenly she wondered why she didn't get on the plane tomorrow and fly back to Adelaide. But she didn't have her luggage, and she knew it wouldn't be fair to Juliet. As well as that, Cass would be deeply hurt.

'No, I'll stick it out somehow,' she thought, gritting her teeth. 'But I'll make it plain to Jarratt that he can't continue to play me and Cass off against each other, if that's what he's been doing.'

After what seemed an interminable time, Juliet switched off the television set and came over to Nicky's bed.

'Are you asleep, Nicky?'

Nicky turned to face her with a sigh. 'No.'

'I'm sorry I was rude about your friends,' Juliet apologised. 'I was just feeling cranky, I suppose. But I'll get over it ... Did Jarry tell you we're not making an early start tomorrow? He promised Tracy he'd let her know what he thinks of her boy-friend. If I were Tracy, I wouldn't care what he thought.'

'All the same,' Nicky said thoughtfully, 'it's nice to be on good terms with your family, isn't it?'

'Nice old Nicky,' Juliet teased.

Nicky was wakened in the morning by a knock at the door indicating that their breakfast tray was about to be brought in. She sat up quickly, running her fingers through her hair. To her surprise Juliet, who answered the door, was fully dressed already, and she noticed she had been writing a letter at the table. To Marc, no doubt, Nicky thought with a pang of sympathy, telling him all the latest developments. However, Juliet appeared cheerful enough as they drank their grapefruit juice and started on the scrambled eggs and toast they had ordered the night before, and Nicky

157

concluded she had resigned herself to circumstances for the time being at any rate.

Jarratt came to their door while they were still drinking their coffee.

'We'll leave here around eleven o'clock,' he informed them, after enquiring how they had slept. Nicky's pulses leapt at the mere sound of his voice, but she concentrated on pouring herself another cup of coffee and managed to ignore him. 'Do either of you want to come to the hospital with me, or have you more pressing things to do before we leave Alice?'

Juliet raised her eyebrows comically. 'Pressing things—in a town like Alice? You can't mean it! I suppose we can look around the shops, if you call that pressing. I won't come and see Tracy anyhow. But tell her from me I think her boy-friend's beaut.'

'I'll do that,' he said quizzically. 'How about you, Nicky? You haven't met my other sister yet.'

Nicky sought frantically for an excuse for not going and said the first thing that came into her head. 'No, thank you. I—I want to have my hair cut.' And that, she thought when she had said it, was very apt—because wasn't the cutting of hair, in this case, symbolic?

His black eyes roved over her hair and then lingered on her lips.

'Well, it's your decision. But you look good to me just as you are.'

She felt agonised. She wanted to say, 'Don't say things like that to me,' but she turned away and said nothing.

After he had gone, she and Juliet finished their breakfast, Nicky dressed, and they both completed their packing.

'I checked at the office we can leave our bags there,' said Juliet. 'We have to vacate this room by ten.'

Jarry had gone with the car, when they took their bags through to the office, and putting on their sunglasses they both went out into the heat of the sun. Nicky fortunately found a hairdresser's where she could have her hair cut straight away, and she arranged to meet Juliet in half an hour's time at Lizzie's Restaurant. Everything went accord-

158

ing to plan, and after they had had a drink, they strolled into a shop that sold aboriginal arts and crafts. Nicky was looking through a pile of cards designed and drawn by children at one of the missions when Juliet said with an odd kind of nerviness, 'I'm going to that boutique across the street, Nicky. I think I'll buy a scarf for my mother. I'll— I'll come back and meet you here.'

'Right,' said Nicky agreeably. 'But don't be too long— we don't want to keee Jarratt waiting.'

Soon after Juliet had gone, she selected a couple of cards, paid for them and went into the street, intending to join Juliet in the boutique, but to her amazement, as she looked along the street before crossing over, she saw Juliet getting into a taxi some distance away. Puzzled, she began to run, and as the driver pulled out from the kerb, she signalled to him wildly. By the merest chance, he saw her and pulled up, and she hurried breathlessly towards the cab and looking in the back window at Juliet exclaimed, 'Juliet, what's happened? Were you going without me? We don't need a taxi—we have time to walk.'

'Oh, get in,' Juliet said rather shortly. 'Of course I wasn't going without you. It's getting too hot to be walking around, so when I saw this cab I grabbed it. I was going to pick you up at the shop.'

The taxi was moving again, and somehow Nicky was not entirely convinced by what Juliet said, particularly when, only a few seconds later, she saw they had taken the wrong turning.

'This isn't the way to the motel,' she said slowly.

'Don't *fuss*,' Juliet said irritably. 'The driver knows Alice Springs better than we do.'

Nicky said nothing. The fact was, she knew Alice Springs very well, and in no time she realised with something of a shock that they were heading for Heavitree Gap and the airport!

'We're going to the airport, aren't we?' she asked quietly.

Juliet let out her breath on a deep sigh. 'All right—yes, we are. But don't try to stop me, Nicky, that's all. I'm not going back to Coochin Brim-brim and letting Jarratt order

159

my life. No one can fight him and win, so I'm going while I have the chance. I'm sick of the outback, and Marc won't wait for ever. You do see, don't you?'

Yes, Nicky supposed she saw, but she protested, 'You could have told me instead of just trying to disappear. That wasn't fair. Besides, I could—I could come too.'

Juliet gave her a wry look. 'It just doesn't seem so bad if *someone* stays. I don't care what you say, I don't like leaving Jarratt alone with Catherine. If you were there I'd feel a lot happier.'

Nicky felt appalled. Just herself and Cass! It was going to be impossible. They were nearly at the airport and she wondered wildly what she was going to do. Without Juliet, she had no legitimate reason for staying. She had even told Jarratt she would go when Juliet did. Leaving him alone with Cass didn't worry her one little bit. In fact it could help things along for Cass, and maybe one of her wishes would come true. No, she couldn't possibly go back to Coochin Brim-brim...

The taxi pulled up. Juliet opened her handbag to pay the fare, and Nicky asked, 'What about your things—your clothes?'

Juliet shrugged. 'I couldn't care less. I've got plenty more clothes in Adelaide. Freedom's the important thing.' She climbed out of the taxi and turned to Nicky. 'Are you coming in with me? Or shall we say goodbye here? But don't rush back to Jarry and tell on me, will you? He'd quite likely pull a few strings and race out here and drag me off the plane.'

Nicky made a wry face. 'I don't really want to stay without you, Juliet. I think—I think I should go back to Adelaide too.'

'You know, Nicky, this is funny,' said Juliet. 'I had a sort of feeling you were beginning to like Jarry rather specially.'

Nicky said nothing, but inside the airport building she tried to get a seat on the plane, but there were none available. She didn't know what to do. She was completely disorientated. How could she possibly go back to Coochin Brim-brim without Juliet? It would sound a pretty weak excuse—'I couldn't get a seat on the plane.'

She made one more appeal.

'Don't go yet, Juliet. Wait just a few more days. You can't do this to Jarratt.'

'To Jarry? He doesn't need me. This will prove it. And a few days could turn into a few weeks—or even months. *Years,*' said Juliet. 'Jarry can jolly well get married if he needs a woman in the house to keep him happy.' Her grey-green eyes were determined. 'Don't try to persuade me, Nicky, and don't think I've left you to do all the explaining either. I wrote a note to Jarry this morning, telling him what I was going to do. I left it at the office at the motel. As a matter of fact, it's addressed to you—just to make sure he doesn't get it too soon. You'll be given it when you go in for your luggage. By that time it will be too late to stop me. Anyhow, cheer up—I'm sure you'll enjoy yourself. You're always saying you like the outback, and Catherine is a friend of yours.'

Nicky only half listened. She was wondering if she would be able to get a seat on the plane for tomorrow. It was cowardly in a way. Cass would be upset when she didn't come back, but if Juliet had gone too, she would perhaps understand. She looked at Juliet who had put her in this spot, and bit her lip. Juliet looked so unconcerned—so trim and pretty and determined, in her blue and white skirt, her tailored white blouse with the hand-embroidered collar, her long fair hair caught back from her face.

But now Juliet was beginning to look around her anxiously, almost as if she expectted Jarratt to materialise and snatch her away from the very doors of the plane.

'Don't wait, Nicky. Thanks for coming anyhow, and for being so understanding. You were wonderful at Coochin Brim-brim—a natural. I don't know what I'd have done without you. I'll be in touch. If I can't get my mother to let me have enough money for France, I might have to throw myself on your mercy. I'm sure you wouldn't have any trouble persuading your guardian to shell out a few hundred dollars.'

Nicky smiled palely. She could sell some of her opals; it

occurred to her she might be needing some money herself. Juliet squeezed her hand. 'Jarry can send my luggage down on the Ghan—or not, as he chooses. I hope you don't regret having come, Nicky—even if I'm sort of walking out on you.'

'No—oh, no.' The words came automatically.

After they had said a final goodbye, Nicky hurried back to see about making a booking for tomorrow. She wondered if she did regret having come. She had found Cass, and she had found Howard too, and her dreams about him had somehow crumbled into dust. It was probably falling in love with Jarratt Buchan that had done the damage. But to discover that he was playing both Cass and her along—that was the end. It wasn't fair to either of them, particularly as they were friends. If Cass had been a stranger—if Nicky, like Juliet, could have seen her as no more than the children's governess—things might have been different. Then she would have put up a fight—stayed.

Or would she?

No, the idea didn't really appeal to Nicky. If a man were to love her, she wanted it to be a wholehearted passionate love for her alone. Jarratt was looking for a wife. Romantic, passionate love didn't come into it. But by a stroke of luck, two personable and susceptible girls had turned up at his cattle station—and he thought he had the right to make a considered choice. *That* had been the meaning of their dialogue the other night.

Ah well, she thought dolefully as she waited at the counter for attention, she would be gone tomorrow. She was running away. And Jarratt, driven into a corner—a thing that Juliet had said would never happen—would marry 'a girl like Cass'.

She switched off her thoughts abruptly.

She made her booking—she was lucky this time—and managed to get a taxi back to town. She was late already, but she asked the driver to put her out somewhere in Todd Street some distance from the motel, and then she began to walk slowly, taking her time, so that Juliet would be safely on her way before Jarratt knew what had happened. She was dreading this meeting with Jarratt—being completely alone with him. It was all very well to plan to stay in Alice another night and leave for Adelaide tomorrow, but Jarrat wouldn't let her get away with it that easily, and she knew she was going to have trouble standing up to him. He could be quite terrifyingly forceful, and in a way she didn't blame Juliet for sneaking off as she had.

As she turned the corner into the street where the motel was, she saw that Jarratt's car was already there, and in another few seconds, she saw him come out of the motel carrying the luggage she and Juliet had left at the office. She felt herself begin to tense. He hadn't seen her, and had opened the car door to put the luggage in. 'I'll tell him straight away,' she decided. 'I'll simply say, You can take my bag out of the car, Jarratt. I'm not going to Coochin Brim-brim.'

The words were waiting on her lips as unconsciously she began to hurry to get it over, and then she saw that there was someone else in the car—and that it was Max Bonney.

She knew a sense of relief. Jarratt would hardly be likely to have a row with her in front of Tracy's boy-friend. There would be nothing for him to do but allow her to do as she wished.

CHAPTER NINE

'OH, there you are Nicky,' Jarratt said pleasantly.

He had turned to face her, and she felt herself weaken as she looked back at him. He had become so familiar with his broad shoulders and narrow hips, and that wild-looking dark hair that could do with a good trim, and she couldn't take her eyes off him. Everything she had planned to say seemed to have gone clean out of her head, and she simply stood staring.

'I was wondering what had happened to you two girls,' he resumed, 'particularly as I was handed a letter for you at the office which I suspect is from my young sister.' He fished it out of the pocket of his black and white striped shirt as he spoke and handed it to her, and she took it with a feeling of helplessness. Max Bonney had got out of the car and was smiling a greeting at her, and Jarratt explained, 'Max is coming to stay with us for a couple of nights. He's anxious to meet Marcie-Ann and Medora before he leaves for Adelaide.'

'Oh.' Nicky looked at Max rather wildly. She had no idea what to say. Everything seemed so ordinary.

Jarratt narrowed his eyes in the bright sunlight. "Is Juliet far behind you? Or did you girls split up?'

'We—we split up,' she stammered. 'Is there—have we left anything in the motel?'

'I don't think so. Two pieces of luggage—that's right, isn't it? The only thing missing appears to be my young sister.' He grinned wryly at Max. 'Maybe you already know, but neither of my sisters is particularly keen on the outback, Max. Tracy makes the best of it and accedes to my demands, but I'm afraid Juliet would disappear at the drop of a hat.' He gave Nicky a sharp look. 'You'd better open that letter. Do you know where Juliet is?'

'Yes,' said Nicky resignedly, realising he was beginning

to suspect the truth now. 'She decided to—to go home.' She looked at Max Bonney apologetically. 'She didn't want to stay indefinitely, and after all she has her own life to lead, she——'

'Oh, don't start pleading her case,' Jarratt interrupted, his mouth grim. 'She's gone on the plane, I gather. Without a word to me.'

'Not—not really,' said Nicky. She tore open the envelope she was holding and extracted the folded sheet of paper enclosed. It had Jarratt's name scrawled across it in Juliet's rather immature hand. 'She wrote you this letter.'

Max, aware that a family crisis was in the air, had discreetly moved away and was standing in the shade of a white cedar, lighting a cigarette.

Jarratt said, 'I'm surprised after our discussion last night that you're still here, Nicky. You told me you'd leave when Juliet did, remember? I'm glad you've changed your mind about that.' He smiled slightly, and she closed her eyes.

'I didn't change my mind.' She had to force herself to say it, and she hated the whole situation. How different it all would have been if Cass hadn't been so much in love with him—if he hadn't stirred both of them up—if he had contented himself with one girl! 'I would have gone,' Nicky told him, 'but the plane was full up. I'm—I'm going tomorrow.'

His head was bent as he read Juliet's note, and she saw a variety of expressions cross his face—annoyance, amusement—and finally anger. But the anger, she discovered, was for her, for now he looked up and his black eyes blazed at her.

'You're going tomorrow. Just like that.'

'Yes,' she quavered. 'I'll—I'll stay another night at the motel——'

'Will you!' he exclaimed savagely. He stuffed the sheet of notepaper into his trouser pocket. 'I'll tell you the contents of that letter later on, but right now'—he took her violently by the arm in a grip that hurt—'right now, you're getting into that car and you're coming out to Coochin Brim-brim. I'm prepared to use physical force if necessary,

Rainbow,' he threatened as she tried to pull away from him. 'I'd act civilised and stay in town another night myself if I could—we have unfinished business, remember?—but I'm obliged to take Max Bonney home and introduce him to Tracy's children. So you'll come along too.'

Nicky was white and shaken. She didn't doubt that he would carry out his threat if she tried to escape him, and she didn't fancy being picked up bodily and forced into his car in front of Max Bonney and anyone else who happened to be passing. Already his fingers were bruising her arm and he was urging her across the footpath. She stammered out angrily, 'I've booked my seat on the plane, Mr Buchan— you'll have to bring me back to town tomorrow.'

'Don't *Mr Buchan* me,' he snapped. 'And don't tell me what I'll *have* to do either. You can come into the motel with me now and we'll ring through and cancel your booking.'

Tight-lipped, she let him propel her towards the hotel. Juliet had been right when she had said he was a brute— and that he never hesitated to twist an arm. He was twisting hers right now—literally.

She said under her breath, 'You have a hide—treating me like this!' She glanced uneasily at Max Bonney, some yards off, smoking his cigarette and pretending that nothing was happening though she was sure he must be curious.

'Yes, I do have a hide, don't I?' he returned, also under his breath. 'I'm afraid you're going to learn I'm not the type of male to be got rid of so easily. I live too far away from civilisation to get my priorities mixed.' He called out to Max, 'We shan't be a moment, Max. Nicky has to make a phone call.'

'I don't have to make a phone call at all,' said Nicky— but she said it to Jarratt, not to Max. 'Why should I do what you say? I—I don't want to go back to Coochin Brim-brim.'

'You're coming all the same. I need someone to cook dinner for my guest,' he added with an unkind smile.

'Cass can do that.'

166

'Catherine is a camp cook. You have the Cordon Bleu touch.'

It wasn't Nicky who made the phone call eventually, it was Jarratt. And he didn't alter her booking. he quite simply cancelled it. Nicky had never felt so helpless. and she was almost speechless with rage. Yet she was frightened too. Why was he acting this way? She knew very well it wasn't because he wanted someone to cook the dinner. Cass wasn't a camp cook, and she wouldn't be surprised if Jarratt himself could cook. He was the sort of man who could turn his hand to anything. So why was he insisting on taking her back to Coochin Brim-brim?

There was only one answer to that question, and she was afraid to voice it even to herself. The fact that it was there lurking at the back of her mind was enough to make her feel sick. She—she *couldn't* do this to Cass.

As they went back to the car she said pathetically, 'Jarratt—please, *please* let me go.'

He ignored her.

On the way out of town he stopped at the post office. 'I'll pick up the mail before we go home. Will you come in with me, Nicky?'

It wasn't really a question. She knew it was an order. He thought she might run away if he left her for a moment. Wearily, she climbed out and followed him. Among the letters he collected, there was one for her, from Guy, and a letter for Cass from Howard.

'Howard hasn't written to you, I'm afraid, Rainbow.'

'Don't call me that,' she said, quivering, then turned away because he was aware of it and a smile lurked on his lips.

'Let's hear what your guardian has to say before we go back to the car.'

'I don't want to read my letter yet,' said Nicky obstinately.

'Well, I want to know what he has to say.' Jarratt was equally obstinate. 'Come on now—open it and let's have the gist of it. Or shall I do it for you?'

167

Nicky twisted away from his grip. 'I—I hate you, Jarratt Buchan!'

'No, you don't,' he retorted.

Nicky scanned the letter rapidly.

'Guy will be back next week. And he's coming to fetch me if I'm not back in Adelaide,' she finished triumphantly.

He didn't comment, and in another minute they were back in the car.

Nicky had a lot of time for thinking during the drive. Max sat in front with Jarry and she sat in the back. Max, she gathered from snippets of conversation she heard, had never been north of Alice Springs, but he was interested in the country, and interested to see where his beloved came from. He was, as well, a little anxious about the children. It was important that he should make contact with them and that they should like him. He talked a great deal about Tracy, and Nicky ceased to listen, and looking out at the passing scenery, she felt against all reason that she was coming home.

Later they stopped at Red Lily for petrol. Mr Capper was still not better, but Shirley was in attendance, though a little of her bounce seemed to have gone.

'We're going to have to get a man in to manage the place,' she told Jarry, and when they were on their way again he remarked for Nicky's benefit, 'That's a job Howard Johnston could take on. There'd be some future for him there, if he wants a place where he'd be boss.'

Nicky said involuntarily, 'His father used to run Red Lily.'

'I'm aware of that—Catherine told me not so long ago. I remember the Johnstons, as a matter of fact.'

Nicky, thinking of that coarse, impatient woman who had answered the telephone when she had rung Darwin, said quickly, 'Mrs Johnston was only their stepmother. Their own mother was—was a very nice woman.'

'You've met her, have you?' he asked, his voice courteous. But from the mockery in the black eyes she encountered in the rear-vision mirror, she knew he realised she had

168

never met Cass's mother—who had died before her husband came to Red Lily.

'Nicky used to live out this way,' Jarry told Max Bonney conversationally. 'She went to school with Juliet, but she's an outback girl at heart as well as by birth.'

'Oh no,' Nicky exclaimed, 'Jarratt's joking, Mr Bonney! I've lived in Adelaide so long now I—I belong there.'

'Never,' said Jarratt emphatically.

When they left the Bitumen, it was burning hot and out on the horizon mirages of trees floated on non-existent lakes that shimmered silver and blue. The spinifex looked like velvet, the red rocks glowed with colour and the shadows were purple. Dark groves of mulgas appeared and here and there cattle sheltered in the shade of the beautiful desert oaks with their drooping feathery branches. To Nicky, it was all so superb that it amazed her to hear Max Bonney remark thoughtfully, 'You've a cruel-looking country here in the Centre.'

'But it's beautiful!' Nicky exclaimed without thinking, then stopped, embarrassed.

'It is indeed,' Jarratt agreed. 'The more so as we've had a succession of good seasons. The aboriginals prefer dust and red earth, but I'll settle very happily for this mantle of vegetation we've been blessed with. I'm particularly happy it's been so attractive while Nicky and Juliet were here. I warn you, Max—Tracy will want to come back. She doesn't know it herself yet, but it will happen. You'll have to bring her and the children here for a holiday now and again. Once you've learned to love this land, you're faithful to it for ever. Nicky protests she belongs in Adelaide, but don't you believe it! Utter one word of criticism—as you did—and she'll spring to its defence as if she were a tiger defending her young. That's a sure sign she's lost her heart.'

Nicky didn't protest any more. She caught the glitter of Jarratt's black eyes in the mirror as he moved his head deliberately so that he could see her, and she shifted along the seat and refused to look at him.

Red dust rose around the car presently as they went

through a particularly bad patch of bull dust, and Jarratt said apologetically, 'I'm sorry about that. This side road will never be sealed—not in my lifetime—and the dust is something we just have to put up with. But by the way, Nicky, I'm having an air-conditioner fitted to the car shortly. That will make for much more pleasant travelling.'

Nicky wanted to ask, 'What's that to do with me? I'm leaving,' but before she had quite made up her mind whether or not to speak Max remarked, wiping the dust and perspiration from his face, 'I'm surprised you haven't done that before.'

'Oh, I'm used to roughing it, but women deserve a little pampering when they live outback.'

'Sounds as if you're thinking of getting married,' said Max.

'With Tracy deserting me, I shall have to,' agreed Jarratt blandly.

Nicky tossed up whether or not she'd say something about Cass, because she had an uneasy suspicion that Max thought *she* was to be the lucky girl. She decided on silence, but held her breath. Surely Jarratt wouldn't say anything that would put her on the spot?

He didn't, but he started talking about Catherine. So what did *that* indicate?

'You'll like the girl who's looking after Marcie-Ann and Medora. She's a natural with children, and charming as well. If she had the qualifications, she'd be all set for a happy career as a teacher. As a matter of fact, she's study-ing now with that in mind.'

Nicky stopped listening.

When at last they reached the homestead, Catherine was in the garden with the children, who looked cute and cool in cotton shorts and matching T-shirts, Marcie-Ann's blue, Medora's red, and Nicky could see at once that Max was charmed with them. As Jarratt, Max and Nicky came into the garden and Cass saw them, a lovely colour stained her round face, and she flipped her hair behind her ears and sent Jarratt her gentle wide-eyed smile. Nicky felt a strange pain in her heart. Poor darling Cass, who had always

170

wanted the impossible. But this time, what she wanted wasn't impossible, Nicky was convinced of it.

Jarratt introduced her to Max—as a friend of Tracy's—the children were presented, and they all went inside in a leisurely way. Jarratt had said nothing to Cass about Juliet, and she hadn't asked about Howard, taking it for granted, Nicky presumed, that he had got out of the car and gone straight over to the bungalow.

Inside, Nicky excused herself and went straight to her room. She had no intention of playing the hostess now that Juliet had gone. Jarratt would have to make his own arrangements about dinner and a room for Max, it was nothing to do with her.

She was in the process of changing out of her dust-stained clothes when there was a knock at the door and Cass asked, 'Nicky, may I come in?'

'Of course.'

Cass came in and flopped down in one of the armchairs and looked at Nicky ruefully. 'Did you get a letter from Howdie too? Isn't he awful?'

Nicky shook her head. 'I haven't heard a thing, except that I know he's not in Alice. What's happened?'

'Oh, he's gone to Coober Pedy! He reckons he's going to shift there and mine for opals as soon as he's fit again. It's just too bad of him to go away like that. Oh, Nicky, I feel so awful! What about you? And whatever put such an idea into his head?'

'Don't worry about me, Cass,' Nicky said wryly. She slipped into the silky slinky gown she had bought under Claudia's guidance, and heard Jarratt's voice telling her not to bring that along to the muster camp. It seemed an eternity had passed since that night! 'I suppose Howdie had been thinking what I told him about Jack. There's a fortune to be made at Coober Pedy—if you're lucky. I guess Howdie feels it's worth while giving it a go, while he has no responsibilities.'

'He could have waited,' said Cass. 'He could have come back here first. He can't start anything with a broken collarbone. He should have talked it over with us—with *you*——'

Nicky sighed. 'Cass, Howdie has to make his own decisions. He knows you're—you're in good hands. And he doesn't have to talk anything over with me, you know.'

Cass's face fell. 'I think he should,' she persisted. 'Oh, doesn't everything seem to have gone wrong all of a sudden? Will you still be here when he comes back for his things? He's asked me to tell Jarry he's not coming back to work here again.'

'No, I won't be here,' said Nicky positively. 'Juliet's gone to Adelaide. Did Jarratt tell you?'

'No,' Cass looked puzzled.

'She doesn't really like it here,' Nicky said uncomfortably.

'But you came back,' Cass said thoughtfully, and Nicky turned away from the look in her eyes.

'Yes, because—well, Juliet just made up her mind to go all of a sudden. I'd left all my things here, and I wanted to see you again before I went.'

'And Howard?' asked Cass warily.

Nicky sighed. She couldn't pretend to a feeling for Howard that she no longer had. 'If Howard really wants to, he can look me up in Adelaide, can't he? You just can't arrange other people's lives for them, Cass, no matter how fond of them you are.'

Cass said slowly, 'I don't think you care terribly about Howdie after all, do you, Nicky? And I was so sure you two would fall in love—I thought you *had*. I was so looking forward to him coming back and the three of us being together again, like old times. And then there was only that man, Max Bonney . . . Who exactly is he? Jarry seemed to want the children to go along with them just now.'

Nicky, relieved that her relationship with Howard was no longer the main topic of conversation, explained, 'He's a very special friend of Tracy's. She's going to Adelaide to stay with his parents for a while when she leaves hospital. The children will stay here, so she wanted him to meet them while he had the opportunity.'

172

Cass turned that over in her mind. 'You mean that Tracy's going to marry again, don't you?'

'It seems like it,' agreed Nicky.

'So she'll go—and the children. I won't be needed. Jarry will be on his own. Oh, Nicky, I hate to think of him here with just Lena to look after him! Even Lewis is going at the end of the year. There'll only be the stockmen. It will be such a lonely life for him—so stark! He needs a wife—a family——'

'Well then,' said Nicky, forcing a smile, 'what are you worrying about? If he needs a wife——' She paused and Cass looked back at her tearfully.

'It's no good looking at me like that, Nicky. He's never said anything to me—never! Oh, I wish I hadn't said I wanted to be a teacher when Howdie and I first came here! I wish I'd had the sense to keep quiet. But he did ask a lot of questions and—I just talked, I guess. Sometimes I have the feeling he doesn't say anything because of that. He thinks I should have the chance of a career. It was important to me once—but not now.'

'Then tell him so, Cass,' said Nicky firmly. 'It shouldn't be all that difficult. Look, I'd better have my shower and change. Will you do something about dinner, or are you going to leave it to Lena?'

Cass smiled reluctantly. 'I couldn't do that! I'll see you later, Nicky.' She went off to the kitchen and Nicky, relieved to have that ordeal over, breathed a sigh of relief. She was quite sure that Cass would produce a dinner that would prove she was no camp cook!

The children ate with the adults that night, and behaved themselves very creditably. Max had brought small gifts for them, he casually mentioned their mother now and again, and though he didn't force it, he certainly won their confidence, because Marcie-Ann asked him if he would tell them a story when they were in bed. While he was doing that, the others sat on the verandah, the girls with coffee, Jarratt with a glass of port.

'What did Howard have to say for himself?' he asked Cass.

173

'He's gone to Coober Pedy,' said Cass wryly. 'He thought he'd investigate what the chances are there for making some money.'

'Good lord!' Jarratt was evidently surprised. 'What gave him that idea? Is he coming back here to work?'

'No,' admitted Cass. 'I'm sorry, Jarry. He asked me to let you know. I hope it won't put you out.'

'I guess I'll get by,' Jarratt said ironically. 'It certainly looks as if everyone's making surprise decisions, doesn't it? Nicky will have told you about Juliet—and about Tracy's plans.'

'Yes.' Cass sounded subdued.

'The children will be gone before Christmas, if Max has his way. How's the study going, by the way?'

'I've been—battling on.' Cass glanced at Nicky, then said hurriedly, 'I don't know if I'll pass my exams, though. I—I might never get to teachers' college.' She added with an obvious effort, 'I won't really mind if I don't.'

Jarratt raised his dark eyebrows. 'Now that's nonsense, of course you'll get there. You've got plenty of brains.'

Listening, Nicky writhed. He is callous, she thought. He'd led Cass on—he must have—and now he sounded as if all he wanted was to see her go off to teachers' college. Worse still, he now told her, 'Don't feel you have to stay around socialising any longer now, Catherine. Nicky can kiss the girls goodnight. You're quite free to run off and do your study—your exams aren't all that far off. And by the way,' he added as she rose, her face turned away from him, away from Nicky, 'if you need any help, ask Lewis, will you? I have a guest to entertain.'

Cass went straight away, even though she hadn't finished her coffee, and Nicky felt herself boiling with anger. She got to her feet too and would have followed Cass except that Jarratt caught hold of her arm quite savagely and told her, 'Wait on, Nicky. You and I have several things to talk about.'

'I don't think so,' she said angrily.

'Oh yes, we have.' His eyes glittered with a sudden devilishness. 'There was something in Juliet's letter that concerned you. She suggested I should find myself a wife and she named you as the most likely contender. So how about it, Rainbow? Will you marry me?'

Nicky stared at him. She couldn't believe her ears. She felt the colour leave her face, and she felt both infuriated and utterly knocked out. What a colossal impudence he had! 'How about it, Rainbow?' She didn't even know if he meant it. The awful thing was that she *would* marry him—but for Cass. Yes, no matter how casual, how unprincipled his proposal, she would have said Yes in a flash—and granted him all the rights. But for Cass.

She looked into the dark mystery of his eyes and felt herself shiver right through to her very soul as she said coolly—oh, so coolly!—'Of course I won't. You must be mad. Guy Sonder is coming to fetch me home in a few days—if I'm still here.'

He stared back at her for a long moment, and then he said, as cool as herself, 'You're certainly a girl with a man for all seasons, aren't you? Guy Sonder—young Johnston—me. That's quite a list for a girl of nineteen, isn't it? Three men. Though I'm none too sure that Howard's amorous intentions towards you would be quite as clear-cut as mine —or Sonder's.'

To her infinite relief, Max came out to join them then, and she was quick to take the opportunity to excuse herself and go to her room. She said goodnight to both men, and as she turned away Jarratt said, coolly pleasant, 'Don't tuck yourself down yet, Nicky. Get your stuff unpacked if that's what's on your mind, and I'll see you about that matter we were discussing later on.'

Nicky didn't answer. If he thought she was going to stay up half the night waiting to be outwitted by him, he was wrong! She would go to bed and she would be asleep when he came to her door. Or if she wasn't asleep then she would pretend to be. There were going to be no more talks, no more discussions, between Jarratt Buchan and Rainbow Reay.

All the same, she didn't go to bed immediately. She put on the reading light, then went to stand and look out at the darkness of the night, filled with unrest and a terrible longing. She would give anything—anything—to be able to stay here. To be Jarratt's wife—to lie in his arms at night—to have the right to call him her husband and Coochin Brimbrim home. To bring up her children—hers and Jarratt's—here. Yes, she would give anything. But she wouldn't betray Cass.

The only sane thing to do take his absurd proposal at its face value—a mere piece of expediency—and to point him to Cass. The crazy thing was that, if Cass knew how she felt, she would step back and leave the field to Nicky. So Cass mustn't know. What was unforgivable was Jarratt's behaviour in creating the situation. He was utterly unscrupulous—he didn't care if he broke Cass's heart. And Cass, as Nicky had reminded herself more than once, had been here first. She, Nicky, was the intruder. It was for her to go.

It was terrible to have to reason and reason with herself as she was doing, and she didn't know how long she stood staring into the darkness. But finally she turned back into the room, dashing away the tears she discovered had wet her cheeks. She had stripped off her clothes and was groping blindly for her pyjamas when the door was suddenly flung open and Jarratt stepped inside. He shut the door behind him and stood with his back against it.

After an instant during which she stood petrified, her face first scarlet, then dead white. Nicky dragged the sheet from her bed and draped it around her. She stood quivering, outraged, unable to speak. She wanted to ask, 'How *dare* you?' but the funny thing was she had the feeling he hadn't even noticed she was naked. There was nothing but a sort of deadly determination in his eyes as he looked at her. He stood with his hands on his narrow hips. The three top buttons of the black and white shirt he still wore were unfastened, and he looked utterly tough, utterly wild—a hard, brutal, uncivilised man of the Never-Never. Yet as she stood clutching the sheet around her naked body, she felt strangely small-minded. Conventions seemed no longer to be of any importance. The only thing that mattered was truth. Or was it love? She saw it in his eyes, but she hadn't yet learned to read it.

He said with a tight-lipped smile, 'The end of the world hasn't come. I have other things on my mind besides seduction. You're well covered up now, if it's a comfort to you, but I warned you, didn't I, not to go to bed—that I was coming to talk to you.'

She swallowed down her shock, but when she spoke her voice shook. 'You don't have the right to tell me what to do. What—what do you want?'

Now the fire, the warmth, the hot disturbing element came back into his eyes and he moved indolently forward.

'You might be shocked if I told you.'

She was shocked already, and distinctly disconcerted to see a spark of amusement in the blackness of his eyes.

'But quite apart from that,' he said, 'I'd like to know if you asked Guy Sonder to come and get you.'

'No—yes,' she stammered, taken off her guard. She drew the sheet around her where it was slipping from one shoulder. 'He—he said in his letter——'

'I know what he said in his letter. You've already told me that. I want to know if it was in answer to what you wrote to him. Did you ask him to come and take you away? Am I making myself clear?'

She shook her head wildly, feeling her heart leap in fright. 'I don't see that it matters to you.'

'Don't you?' He sounded almost threatening. 'Have you forgotten already what I asked you tonight before we were interrupted?'

She turned away from him abruptly. 'Oh, that! You were being—ridiculous. I—I didn't take any notice of that. I'd rather forget it.'

'Do you mean that?' His voice was close behind her and she could feel the heat of his breath on her neck.

'Yes,' she said in a whisper.

'If I took you in my arms now you wouldn't want to forget it.'

Nicky stiffened. 'Don't—don't touch me!' Her heart was pounding and her voice was husky. He cupped his hands

177

over her bare shoulders. 'Please——' she said shakily.

'Then tell me why,' he said quietly.

'Because—because I didn't come here to stay. I came while Juliet was here, that's all.'

'So what's that to do with it?' To her relief, Jarratt's hands fell from her shoulders, but she stayed with her back to him. Her breathing was disturbed and her mouth was trembling. These things she didn't want him to see. 'It wouldn't be the first love affair to start that way,' he said reasonably.

Love affair? She shook her head almost imperceptibly. 'There's no—love affair,' she got out. 'I'm not interested, I told you. You have—you have Cass.'

'I don't "have" Cass,' he retorted, 'whatever you mean by that. Catherine is my nieces' governess. Do you imagine she's my mistress as well?'

'No, of course not! Cass wouldn't——'

'And neither would I. Catherine and I haven't been here alone—I've never wanted it that way. Do you think I asked Juliet here solely to attend to my creature comforts? Especially when I know very well she's neither interested in, nor capable of doing, that?'

'How should I know?' Nicky was beginning to feel weak and very much afraid that if he didn't go soon, something drastic would happen. She badly wanted time to herself— time to think. He had been telling her, she supposed, that marriage with Cass had never entered his mind. But she couldn't quite believe that. He *had* encouraged Cass. He had stirred her up—doubtless in the same way that he had stirred her, Nicky, up with his kisses, his lovemaking, with his particular way of looking at a woman. She was convinced that if she had never come here, then Cass would have been the obvious choice when he needed a wife.

She said again, 'Please—leave me alone, Jarratt. I'm— I'm tired. I can't—think.'

'Then tomorrow,' he said after a moment, and the very sound of his voice stirred her senses.

She nodded, and stayed where she was, and then he moved and she heard the soft click of the door as it shut

178

behind him. She knew from the sudden weakness of her
limbs how much she had wanted him to take her in his
arms—how much she had wanted to feel the wild thrill of
his lips on hers, the rising excitement as her soft body
yielded to the hardness of his—the delight of surrendering
to him completely—the right to say, 'I love you, Jarratt'.

The temptation to confess to Cass was almost intolerable. Because Cass would say, 'Go ahead—it was just
another impossible wish on my part'. And inside, Cass
would feel as she was feeling now ...

The following day, they all went to the gorge for a
picnic. Jarratt drove the station wagon, and Max and
Medora, who had taken a fancy to the man she didn't know
yet was going to marry her mother, sat in front, while Cass
and Nicky and Marcie-Ann sat in the back. As he drove,
Jarratt talked to Max about his two-and-a-half-thousand-
square-mile property, about the problems of beef raising
here, about his Shorthorns and the herd of Droughtmaster
cattle he was breeding—hump-backed, Brahmin-based,
more suited to the climate of the Centre than the British
breeds.

'My God, it's a hungry-looking country,' Max remarked,
and this time Nicky didn't utter her protests aloud. To her
it was so beautiful it brought tears to her eyes, and she had
to turn her head to hide them from Cass. Soon she would be
leaving—tomorrow, when Max went—never to see any of it
again. She stared through a blur of tears at the dark
mulgas that dotted the gently undulating plain and massed
into groves in the contours. Beneath them the earth was
rose-red, splashed over with the golden fire of the yellow
tops and the rich purple flowers of the wild tomato. Beyond
the mulgas was witchetty bush country, where the trees still
carried chrome yellow flower spikes, and Jarratt told Max
that these were the trees in which the aboriginals found the
delectable witchetty grubs.

'Delectable?' asked Max on a laugh.

Nicky caught Jarry's eyes in the mirror. He turned his
head slightly. 'What would you girls say to that?'

Cass gave a shudder. 'I've never tried them and I don't want to, thank you.'

'What about you, Nicky?' Jarratt asked quizzically.

Nicky's cheeks burned. She said, evading a direct answer, 'I believe these days they're offered as a delicacy to tourists who're interested in ethnic food. Grilled over coals or fried in butter——'

'And very nice too,' said Jarry with a grin.

In the cool shadows of the gorge against whose high red walls the white powdery trunks of ghost gums showed fantastic and unreal, they stopped. The children left the station wagon and scampered eagerly across the wide flat bed of the river to the pools that lay reflecting the cloudless blue of the sky, and there they paddled until they were called to lunch. While Cass and Nicky unpacked the food, Jarratt built a small fire to boil the billy—'It's not a picnic without billy tea,' he told Max, who grinned and wandered off to accompany the children on their tour of discovery. It wasn't often they came as far from the homestead, and they found everything wonderful and exciting.

Lunch was simple—cold roast beef with plenty of salad vegetables and fruit, and fresh orange juice for the children while the adults drank their slightly smoky, scalding tea. Nicky was quiet and dreamy, filled with a painful delight, thinking that she would remember this day—this last day—for ever more. She would always see Jarratt, in her mind's eye, against this background that was so much a part of him.

The steep rock walls towered against a sky whose colours ranged from deep cobalt to palest cerulean. Water glinted, birds alighted high up on the rocks where trees clung, their roots half exposed, holding on so precariously yet so fearlessly, it seemed. Nicky caught Jarry's eyes on her occasionally and wondered uneasily what he was planning, for she knew he wouldn't be content to leave her alone all day.

When lunch was over, the litter cleared away, the campfire extinguished, they all took a leisurely walk through the gorge. Deliberately, Nicky kept with the children, and by doing so found herself in Max's company, while Cass and

180

Jarratt lingered a little way behind. Nicky didn't look back once to see what Jarratt and Cass were doing. She pointed out to the children the wild orange flowers with their long silky stamens, the green pussy tails that grew in the river sand, their honey scent sweet on the still air, and when Marcie-Ann found a patch of pale pink spidery flowers, it was she who told her they were Sandover lilies.

'You know your outback flowers,' Max commented, and Nicky reflected that this was knowledge that had surfaced from back in her Alice Springs days—some of it possibly from even before that. Max asked her various questions about herself, and though she answered them she heard them only with the top of her mind. More than anything, she was aware of Cass and Jarratt walking so slowly behind, talking to each other—of what?

When they returned from their walk to get into their swimming gear and cool off in one of the bigger pools, the grouping arrangement was altered. When Nicky, taking hold of a child by each hand, would have gone across the sand to the water with them, but Jarratt intervened.

'You've had your turn with the children, Nicky. Catherine, Max will give you a hand.'

Max, in trunks, had gone ahead and Cass, her head slightly lowered, her cheeks flushed, went away with the children who had dropped Nicky's hands and run to her the moment Jarry issued his order—for order it had been.

Jarratt was lounging against a flat rock, his torso bare above the swimming trunks he wore, his dark eyes disconcerting. Nicky stood uncertainly, then with sudden decision she told him, 'I'm going to take a swim too—it's so hot.'

'In a moment,' he said sharply. His eyes were on her and she was suddenly aware of her figure in the revealing bikini. She almost wished there were a sheet handy to snatch up as she had done last night, and cover her nakedness. Because now Jarry *was* conscious of her nearly naked body. There was none of that harsh determination in his expression that showed he was concentrating on a single thing. Instead, she saw that warm sexy look in his eyes that frightened her so

181

much, and so excitingly, and with a little groan that she hoped he didn't hear, she dropped down on to the towel she had left lying on the ground, her face averted from him. Her heart was hammering madly. Oh God, why did he have to look at her that way? She shrank within herself, yet at the same time a fire ran through her veins.

He left his rock and came to sit near her on the ground, sprawling back on one hand, his face far too close to hers. She hugged her knees and knew from the curling of his lip that he read all sorts of things into her defensive posture.

He said, coming straight to the point, 'Well, what about it, Rainbow? That proposition I put to you last night. Are you going to marry me?'

She caught her breath and glanced towards the pool where the others were swimming, but of course they could not possibly have heard him.

'I told you—no,' she said indistinctly.

He reached out and put a finger on her lips. 'You don't mean that,' he murmured. His finger moved, tracing the outline of her mouth, then feathered over her chin and down her throat, and before she was aware of it he had leaned towards her and his lips had touched hers. She drew away from him swiftly, a long shiver going through her body. Her guilty eyes flew to the small group in the water, and she knew Cass had seen. She was shading her eyes, looking towards them. Nicky could have died.

'Don't touch me,' she gasped. She scrambled to her feet and stood for a moment feeling dizzy. Then before she could speed away as she had meant to do, Jarratt was on his feet too and his fingers had circled her wrist, making her a prisoner, and his eyes were looking compellingly into hers.

'Let me go,' she whispered. 'It's no use. I'm—I'm leaving tomorrow with Max. You can't stop me. And—and if you try, Guy will come for me.' She turned her head resolutely away from that look in his eyes and asked brokenly, 'Why don't you marry Cass?'

CHAPTER TEN

JARRATT said nothing for a long moment, then—'Get some clothes on, Rainbow. We're going to talk. After that, if you still want to go—as you say, I can't stop you.'

Nicky was shivering, but certainly not with cold. She felt very naked in her bikini and she would be only too glad to get her clothes on, and the minute he released her she went to the little group of twisted corkwood trees where she had changed, and pulled on her jeans and her shirt and her sandals. When she emerged, Jarratt, though still shirtless, was in dark cotton trousers and sandals. In the water the children were splashing and squealing, and Cass was standing a little apart, her head bent. Nicky's heart ached for her.

Jarratt took a firm grip on her arm. 'We'll find a quiet place and say all the things that should have been said long before this,' he told her.

'We can talk here,' she said pathetically. 'If we go away, Cass will—will——'

'For God's sake,' he exclaimed with controlled violence, 'what has Catherine Johnston to do with this thing between you and me?'

She blinked, her nerves shattered. 'I've told you—Cass is my friend.'

'So what? And you've told me nothing. Now come along, I have no intention of standing here in full view of the company where we're liable to be interrupted at any moment—though I don't mean by Catherine, I credit *her* with having some tact.'

Nicky, her feet planted firmly apart on the ground, didn't move. 'We can talk here,' she said stubbornly.

'If you continue to take that attitude, Rainbow,' he said, his mouth twisting in a sardonic smile, 'then one of two things is likely to happen.'

'What?' she asked involuntarily.

'Either I shall ravish you here in full sight of anyone who happens to look, or I shall pick you up bodily and carry you off into the bush.'

'All right, I'll—I'll come,' she said hurriedly, her cheeks paling.

He put his hand under her elbow and they walked on into the gorge in the shadow of the high red rock walls. They walked slowly, but in no time at all they were out of sight of others, and quite alone, moving through the long pink and silver grasses and the tangle of yellowtop daisies, through the wild figs and bloodwoods until at last, in a cleared space where a yellow-flowered tree had spread a carpet of long narrow leaves on the ground, Jarratt decided they had gone far enough.

'This is—silly,' Nicky began to protest, but anything more she might have said was stifled as his arms went around her and she was crushed against him, and he was kissing and kissing her. The world spun. It was a kaleidoscope of blue sky and red rock and yellow flowers, and with a feeling of complete helplessness, Nicky gave way to her senses. She let him kiss her throat, her shoulders, her eyelids, and then he held her palm against his lips and told her hoarsely, 'Oh God, I want you—I need you, Ranbow——'

'I—I can't,' she said brokenly.

'You can,' he said. Somehow or other they had both slipped to the ground and she was half lying on the thick carpet of leaves and leaning against his naked chest, feeling the steady thumping of his heart.

'But—*Cass*. I shouldn't,' she whispered.

She felt his chest move in a long sigh.

'You're intent on talking about Catherine, aren't you? Well, look—I've just been talking to Cass, as you call her. Cass knows what's happening. I've known all along she fancied herself in love with me. She's a romantic girl, and it's a common enough reaction when you're often in the company of one man. If I were already married, or considerably older, she'd most likely have looked another way and possibly have fallen in love with Lewis Trent.' Nicky

184

listened, silent but doubtful, her cheek against the warmth of his bare skin—where she still thought it had no right to be.

'Catherine's propensity to lose her heart was one reason why I asked Juliet to come here,' he continued. 'At least it lessened the danger of Catherine's becoming too—proprietorial, even in her mind. And you came along too, didn't you? The surprise package.' He took Nicky's chin in his hand and turned her face up to his. 'Rainbow, I give you my soelmn word that I have never given Catherine one word of encouragement—never once touched her, taken her in my arms, kissed her. Never deliberately played on her senses in any way, not even by making the slightest suggestion of verbal love. If she's built up a romance, it's on a foundation of daydreams, and she'll soon get over it. That will be natural too. The children will be gone soon—Tracy will want them with her in Adelaide. And Lewis is leaving in less than a month. He's a guy with a big and generous heart, and he's already offered to keep an eye on Catherine if she goes to the city. She'll be all right.'

Poor Cass, thought Nicky. Blue eyes, flying, and love—not one of her wishes granted, not yet. As if she had said it aloud, Jarratt reminded her, 'Catherine is not yet twenty. Remember I told you once that your discoveries were still ahead of you? Well, so are Cass's.' Once more his lips touched hers and he murmured against them, 'But I like to think your big discoveries are under way right now. Are you going to admit it?'

'Yes,' breathed Nicky. There seemed nothing else to say, and in the light of what he had said about his relationship with Cass, then denying her own heart was not going to do anyone any good . . .

She let him kiss her, hold her, make love to her, but finally she drew away to ask him something that was troubling her.

'Jarratt, is it because of Cass's background—because her family are ordinary people—that you weren't interested in her? Because I——'

His dark eyes, still smouldering with a desire he had

185

managed to keep in check, sharpened slightly. 'You—what, Rainbow? Don't tell me you want to talk about yourself at last, after all the questions you've parried—refused to answer.'

She bit her lip. 'I'll have to, because—— But is it because of that that you didn't fall in love with Cass? Juliet said you'd never—never marry beneath you.'

'My God! Did she? What a thing to say!' She had never seen him look so furious. 'What was all this sort of talk about, anyhow?'

'It doesn't matter,' she said hurriedly. 'It was just—we were talking about—people——'

'If I were in love with Catherine Johnston,' Jarratt said slowly, 'then make no mistake about it—I would marry her no matter what her background was. But as it happens, there's nothing in the least shady or suspect or anything else in Catherine's past. Her father used to run the Red Lily Store, as you know. Her mother—her real mother—quite obviously must have been the nicest of women, because Catherine is sensitive, charming, well-mannered, generous——' He stopped with a wry smile. 'If I go on much longer you'll be getting the wrong impression, won't you? Now what were you going to tell me about yourself, Rainbow?'

She paused for an instant, then said carefully, 'I told you my mother was Iris West from Kooriekirra cattle station, but I didn't ever tell you about my father.'

'No, you didn't, did you?' He smiled and touched the corner of her mouth with a gentle finger.

She thought of Guy and hesitated. Guy had hated the idea that her father had not been a—a gentleman. Would Jarratt care? She took a deep breath and said in a rush, 'He was a crocodile shooter. He was a—rough sort of man. My mother's parents wouldn't even accept him as their son-in-law.'

There was amusement in his eyes, and as well a kind of gentleness she had never seen there before. 'How do you know he was a rough man, Rainbow? I thought you didn't remember him.'

'No, but the man who looked after me till just lately—Jack Lane—he was a friend of my father's. He was a crocodile shooter once too, and he was—well, *he* was rough—but he was kind too,' she added loyally.

Jarry nodded. 'I know that,' he said casually. 'I knew Jack Lane. He was a fine type. He worked here once—maybe fifteen years ago. I often wondered what became of Jack's little girl Rainbow, and not so long ago I found out.'

Nicky's eyes widened and colour spread slowly into her cheeks. Her glance was locked with his, and once again she was a little girl sitting in the dust with aboriginal children. And a man was looking down at her as she bit into a fat creamy witchetty grub. A man with dark eyes. Jarratt Buchan——

'It was—you,' she said faintly.

'What are you remembering?' he asked.

'The—the witchetty grub,' she whispered.

He laughed a low laugh and pulled her into his arms. 'I'm glad you remember that. But what a woman you've grown into! I might have guessed—but never that I'd be asking you to marry me.' When he had finished kissing her again, he asked, 'What happened to Nick Reay, Rainbow?'

She looked at him, puzzled. 'My father? He was killed in a shooting accident. How did you know his name?'

'Because I met him once. When I was eighteen or nineteen, I took a holiday up at the Top End and joined a croc-shooting party. He was the man in charge.'

'Oh.' Nicky's face had gone white, and she stared at him without speaking.

'Your father was an Englishman, Rainbow—an adventurer. Young, daring—pioneer stuff. Pretty obviously he'd had a good education, but I don't know why he left home and came out to Australia. He must have been killed shortly after I met him, but I never heard about it. I have some photographs at home of that holiday—I'll show them to you later.'

'Thank you,' she said shakily. She wanted just a little to cry. Not because her father hadn't been as rough as Jack, but just because—everything was fitting together. Because she had two parents. Because Jarratt loved her. And as well, because of Cass—for Cass, real tears. She murmured, 'Poor Cass—she's the one who'll have her hair cut off after all.'

'What are you crying about?' Jarry kissed her eyes and smoothed back her curling hair. 'And what sort of nonsense are you talking now? Do you know I love you? And are you going to admit that you're wild about me—and that the sooner we get married the better?'

Nicky nodded, her face raised to his, and he put his arm protectively around her.

'Then shall we go and tell the others?' She held back a little, and he assured her gently, 'Catherine will have guessed. You're not afraid she won't wish you well?'

'No, of course not.' Cass would wish her well. And Nicky had a wish for Cass too. She spoke it aloud to Jarratt.

'I hope one day she'll be as happy—and as lucky in love—as we are.'

'I'll join you in that,' he agreed.

Did you miss any of these exciting Harlequin Omnibus 3-in-1 volumes?

Anne Hampson #3
Heaven Is High (#1570)
Gold Is the Sunrise (#1595)
There Came a Tyrant (#1622)

Essie Summers #6
The House on Gregor's Brae (#1535)
South Island Stowaway (#1564)
A Touch of Magic (#1702)

Margaret Way

Margaret Way #2
Summer Magic (#1571)
Ring of Jade (#1603)
Noonfire (#1687)

Margaret Malcolm

Margaret Malcolm #2
Marriage by Agreement (#1635)
The Faithful Rebel (#1664)
Sunshine on the Mountains (#1699)

Eleanor Farnes

Eleanor Farnes #2
A Castle in Spain (#1584)
The Valley of the Eagles (#1639)
A Serpent in Eden (#1662)

Kay Thorpe
Curtain Call (#1504)
Sawdust Season (#1583)
Olive Island (#1661)

18 magnificent Omnibus volumes to choose from:

Betty Neels

Betty Neels #3
Tangled Autumn (#1569)
Wish with the Candles (#1593)
Victory for Victoria (#1625)

Violet Winspear

Violet Winspear #5
Raintree Valley (#1555)
Black Douglas (#1580)
The Pagan Island (#1616)

Anne Hampson

Anne Hampson #4
Isle of the Rainbows (#1646)
The Rebel Bride (#1672)
The Plantation Boss (#1678)

Margery Hilton

Margery Hilton
The Whispering Grove (#1501)
Dear Conquistador (#1610)
Frail Sanctuary (#1670)

Rachel Lindsay

Rachel Lindsay
Love and Lucy Granger (#1614)
Moonlight and Magic (#1648)
A Question of Marriage (#1667)

Jane Arbor

Jane Arbor #2
The Feathered Shaft (#1443)
Wildfire Quest (#1582)
The Flower on the Rock (#1665)

Great value in reading at $2.25 per volume

Joyce Dingwell #3
Red Ginger Blossom (#1633)
Wife to Sim (#1657)
The Pool of Pink Lilies (#1688)

Hilary Wilde
The Golden Maze (#1624)
The Fire of Life (#1642)
The Impossible Dream (#1685)

Flora Kidd
If Love Be Love (#1640)
The Cave of the White Rose (#1663)
The Taming of Lisa (#1684)

Lucy Gillen #2
Sweet Kate (#1649)
A Time Remembered (#1669)
Dangerous Stranger (#1683)

Gloria Bevan
Beyond the Ranges (#1459)
Vineyard in a Valley (#1608)
The Frost and the Fire (#1682)

Jane Donnelly
The Mill in the Meadow (#1592)
A Stranger Came (#1660)
The Long Shadow (#1681)

Complete and mail this coupon today!